# The History of Communication

*Robert W. McChesney and*
*John C. Nerone, editors*

D1227500

# Selling Free Enterprise

# Selling Free Enterprise

*The Business Assault
on Labor and Liberalism,
1945–60*

*Elizabeth A. Fones-Wolf*

**University of Illinois Press**  Urbana and Chicago

Publication of this book was supported by a grant from the
Eberly College of Arts and Sciences, West Virginia University.

P 9 8 7 6

*This book is printed on acid-free paper.*

Library of Congress Cataloging-in-Publication Data
Fones-Wolf, Elizabeth A., 1954–
    Selling free enterprise: the business assault on labor and
liberalism, 1945–60 / Elizabeth A. Fones-Wolf.
       p.  cm.
    Includes bibliographical references (p.   ) and index.
    ISBN 0-252-06439-9 (paper: acid-free paper)
    ISBN 978-0-252-06439-5
    1. Free enterprise—United States—Public opinion. 2. Public
opinion—United States. 3. Political culture—United States.
    4. Corporate image—United States. 5. Trade-unions—United States.
    6. Industrial relations—United States. I. Title.
HB95.F66    1994
330.12'2'0973—dc20                                           94-10785
                                                                CIP

# Contents

*Illustrations follow pages 80 and 206.*

# Abbreviations

| | |
|---|---|
| *AB* | *American Business* |
| ACWA | Amalgamated Clothing Workers of America Records, Labor Management Documentation Center, Cornell University, Ithaca, N.Y. |
| AFL | American Federation of Labor |
| AISI | American Iron and Steel Institute Papers, Hagley Museum and Library, Wilmington, Delaware |
| ALUA | Archives of Labor and Urban Affairs, Wayne State University, Detroit, Mich. |
| *AM* | *Advanced Management* |
| AMA | American Management Association |
| *BW* | *Business Week* |
| *CC* | *Christian Century* |
| CIO | Congress of Industrial Organizations |
| *FF* | *Ford Facts* |
| *FMM* | *Factory Management and Maintenance* |
| GMA | George Meany Memorial Archives, Silver Spring, Md. |
| *HBR* | *Harvard Business Review* |
| HCLA | Historical Collections and Labor Archives, Pennsylvania State University, University Park, Pa. |
| HML | Hagley Museum and Library, Wilmington, Del. |
| HST | Harry S. Truman Library, Independence, Missouri |
| *ILRR* | *Industrial and Labor Relations Review* |
| *ISJ* | *Industrial Sports Journal* |
| *ISR* | *Industrial Sports and Recreation* |
| *L&N* | *Labor and Nation* |

| | |
|---|---|
| LC | Library of Congress, Washington, D.C. |
| LMDC | Labor Management Documentation Center, Cornell University, Ithaca, N.Y. |
| *M&F* | *Mill and Factory* |
| *MI* | *Modern Industry* |
| *MRec* | *Management Record* |
| *MRev* | *Management Review* |
| NAM | National Association of Manufacturers Records, Hagley Museum and Library, Wilmington, Del. |
| *NB* | *Nation's Business* |
| NCC | National Council of Churches Records, Presbyterian Historical Society, Philadelphia, Pa. |
| *NYT* | *New York Times* |
| OSH | Ohio Historical Society, Columbus, Ohio |
| *PJ* | *Personnel Journal* |
| *PLN* | *Pennsylvania Labor News* |
| *POII* | *Public Opinion Index for Industry* |
| *PRJ* | *Public Relations Journal* |
| *PRN* | *Public Relations News* |
| SHSW | State Historical Society of Wisconsin, Madison, Wis. |
| SLA | Southern Labor Archives, Georgia State University, Atlanta, Ga. |
| *SS* | *Steelworkers Sentinel* |
| *Stet* | *Stet: The House Magazine for House Magazine Editors* |
| *Trends* | *Trends in Education-Industry Cooperation* |
| UA | Urban Archives Center, Temple University, Philadelphia, Pa. |
| *UAW* | *United Automobile Worker* |
| UERMWA | United Electrical, Radio and Machine Workers of America |
| USA | United Steelworkers of America |
| USA/A | United Steelworkers of America Archives, Historical Collections and Labor Archives, Pennsylvania State University, University Park, Pa. |
| *WSC* | *Wisconsin CIO News* |
| *WSJ* | *Wall Street Journal* |

# Acknowledgments

Many people assisted me in the process of researching and writing this book. It began as a dissertation at the University of Massachusetts at Amherst where Robert Griffith and Bruce Laurie helped me think broadly about the role of business and labor in shaping America's political culture. Since then, Charles McGovern, K. Austin Kerr, David Farber, and Gary Gerstle have read the manuscript at various stages and offered criticisms and suggestions that I hope have strengthened the work.

I am also indebted to the assistance provided by archivists and librarians at the Presbyterian Historical Society in Philadelphia, the Bentley Library at the University of Michigan, the Wisconsin Historical Society, Labor-Management Documentation Center at Cornell University, Walter P. Reuther Library for Labor and Urban Affairs, Southern Labor Archives at Georgia State University, George Meany Memorial Archives, Historical Collections and Labor Archives at Pennsylvania State University, the Library of Congress, the Ohio Historical Society, and the Urban Archives Center at Temple University. I especially want to thank Michael Nash and Marjorie McNinch of the Hagley Museum and Library, Richard Strassberg of the Labor-Management Documentation Center, Warner Pflug of the Reuther Library, Les Hough, formerly of the Southern Labor Archives and Peter Gottlieb, formerly of the Historical Collections and Labor Archives at Penn State.

Financial aid from the Wayne State University Henry Kaiser Research Fellowship program, Radiological Consultants of West Virginia, West Virginia University Eberly College of Arts and Sciences Subvention Support program and West Virginia University Faculty Senate Research Grant program supported the work at various stages.

Friends, colleagues, and relatives who provided interest, encouragement, and help in a variety of ways are Elliott Shore, Peter Albert, Stuart Kaufman, Ron Story, Jack Tager, Pat Greenfield, Beth Michael, Ron Lewis, Robert Blobaum, Jack McKivigan, Julie and Elliott Maizels, Greg Field, Tom Zeiler, Mark Leff, Robert McChesney, Dan Clawson and finally Sheri and Jerry Stahler who made doing research in Philadelphia and Wilmington lots of fun.

Most of all I want to thank Ken Fones-Wolf. Ken patiently listened, prodded when necessary, and offered praise and encouragement that carried me through the whole process of writing a book. Moreover, he carefully read, critiqued, and improved each chapter more times than he cares to remember. It is to him that this book is dedicated.

# Introduction

During December 1951, half of the adult population of the industrial town of Latrobe, Pennsylvania, took regular breaks from work to study economics on company time. Employees from nineteen firms gathered in small groups to watch a series of films and to participate in discussions that focused on the values and symbols associated with the American way of life, including patriotism, freedom, individualism, competition, and abundance through increasing productivity.[1] That these firms halted production and pulled workers off the shop floor and out of offices for such a purpose was not an anomaly; in the years after World War II, millions of workers participated in similar corporate-sponsored economic education programs. Moreover, they and their families were exposed to these values and symbols in a myriad of other ways: through the mass media in articles, posters and billboards, newspaper and magazine advertisements, and radio and television programs; through the pageantry of business-orchestrated Americanism Weeks; through corporate industrial and community relations programs; and through business-sponsored educational programs aimed at schools and churches. All this activity was part of a systematic campaign launched by American business in the late thirties but pursued with even greater vigor after World War II to shape the ideas and images that constituted America's political culture.

This was not the first time that corporate leaders had attempted to shape the contours of political discourse. During the Progressive Era and the early twenties, understanding that "what people come to believe and what they happen to do is an effect of a long-term process of persuasion," business struggled for the ideological loyalty of the American working class. As Gary Gerstle has observed, much of this struggle turned on the meaning of Americanism. During this period, business sought to construct a vision of Americanism that emphasized social harmony, free enterprise, individual rights, and abundance. On the eve of the Depression, much of the business community was confident that these values dominated the political and cultural landscape. Business power and autonomy appeared secure.[2]

The Depression of the thirties wrought profound changes in American politics, government, and economy. Business lost enormous prestige and power as it came under increasing public attack and governmental regulation. In turn, having lost trust in the ability of ethnic communities and employers to provide welfare, security, and employment, much of the working class shifted its allegiance to the Democratic party and organized labor. For these workers the values associated with the business definition of the American way receded. Instead of individualism, competition, and free enterprise, workers adopted a vision characterized by equal rights, industrial democracy, economic equality, and social justice. The preferred mechanisms for attaining these goals were collective action at the workplace and an active welfare state authorized to intervene in workings of the economy and, if necessary, to redistribute income.[3]

The demands of World War II continued to challenge business. While the wartime "miracle of production" allowed industrialists to begin rebuilding their reputations, it failed to completely restore their authority within the American polity. Business leaders feared that the war had tightened the bonds between workers and their new protectors, the state and organized labor. Government control and planning played major roles in the wartime economy and wartime regulations. Labor-market shortages enabled organized labor to consolidate its position and to achieve significant gains. Moreover, some union leaders threatened to advance negotiations beyond the standard personnel policy and wage issues into such previously forbidden areas of corporate policy as pricing and investment, essentially demanding a voice in the management of industry. In the realm of politics, the industrial union wing of the labor movement adopted a social agenda featuring a full employment welfare state that promised comprehensive social protection for workers. Business feared that the formation of the CIO's Political Action Committee heralded a more politically aggressive labor movement prepared to exploit workers' dual allegiance to unions and the Democratic party. Thus, as the war ended, such major national issues as the relationship of the government and the economy, the proper size and activities of the welfare state, and the scope of union power in the factory were unresolved.

In 1946, the contentious atmosphere of industrial relations culminated in a strike wave unparalleled in American history. Especially frightening to the business community was Walter Reuther's demand that GM open its books to union contract negotiators in order to link wages, prices, and profits. His demand exemplified the growing threat to management rights both on and off the shop floor. Equally troubling to many companies was the seemingly widespread community support for labor during these struggles. In the aftermath of the strikes, labor appeared so powerful that labor-relations scholar Sumner H. Slichter could easily foresee the United States "gradually shifting from a capitalistic community to a laboristic one—that is to a community in which employees rather than businessmen are the strongest single influence."[4]

Looking back from the vantage point of the 1990s, it seems clear that the threat posed by New Deal liberalism and the trade union movement was more apparent than real. As Alan Brinkley has shown, by the end of the war liberals had significantly lowered their sights. They shifted from demanding that the state control the economy through social planning and extensive business regulation to advocating that the government promote economic growth while only occasionally compensating for the private sector's failures through social welfare and social insurance. An expanding economy, a demand that easily meshed with business's goals, rather than the reform of capitalism became the clarion call of American liberalism and the Democratic party.[5]

Labor historians contend that the union movement underwent a similar conversion on the way to becoming integrated into the newly emerging liberal consensus. Nelson Lichtenstein, for instance, argues that between 1946 and 1948 a full-scale mobilization of business and conservative forces, featuring passage of the Taft-Hartley Act and aggressive corporate collective bargaining, decisively blocked unions from reshaping the postwar political economy along social democratic lines. In the shop, a labor-capital accord emerged with unions abandoning their quest for industrial control in return for periodic wage and benefit increases. In politics, labor shelved its "earlier commitment to economic planning and social solidarity" for a program emphasizing "sustained growth and productivity gain-sharing" with a small expansion of the welfare state. At the same time, an alliance with the Democratic party, which entailed driving out the communists and undermining the militancy of the rank and file, limited labor's ability to act as an independent political force.[6]

By 1948, neither labor nor liberalism appeared to pose much of a challenge to organized business. Indeed most historians in portraying the fifties emphasize the apparent harmony not only between these groups but within society as a whole. It is a period characterized by most historians as a time of consensus that enveloped liberals as well as conservatives. They emphasize that this consensus rested on a common set of assumptions shared by most Americans that included a belief in equality of opportunity for individuals, in the existence of an open, classless society and in the emergence of an economy capable of dynamic growth and change. While inequalities might still exist, abundance promised to deliver all Americans into the "broad, prosperous middle class." The very success many union workers achieved with little overt class conflict helped convince historians that the fifties was an era of consensus.[7]

However, to American business leaders in 1945, or even a decade later, very little of this was self-evident. We should not underestimate their fears, even if from a contemporary perspective they seem unfounded. As Howell Harris observed in his excellent study of the immediate postwar mobilization of industrialists, business leaders may have exaggerated the seriousness of their problems, but they were "players in a power game, with a lot to lose."[8]

It was easy for much of the business community to find evidence for its worries. A great deal of conflict underlay the apparent consensus. Until the mid-fifties unions were still growing and conflict over the pace and organization of work continued to characterize the postwar shop floor. Even in the sectors where the labor-capital accord reigned, few American managers accepted the legitimacy of organized labor and most maintained a deep-seated resistance to unions. At the same time, liberalism's swing to the politics of growth and anticommunism did little to allay corporate hostility. Historian David Brody has observed that "power and interest can be issues of deadly conflict even in a system in which men agree on the fundamentals."[9]

Postwar liberals may have abandoned issues of social and economic control, but their commitment to an expansion of the welfare state, even if at times only rhetorical, roused the ire of all but the most moderate business leaders. Most of the business community still disliked the liberal agenda, even in its modified form, and feared that the New Deal traditions associated with the labor movement and the Democratic party continued to appeal to many American workers.

Important segments of the business community responded to this economic and ideological challenge with an aggressive campaign to recast the political economy of America. They sought to undermine the legitimacy and power of organized labor and to "halt the momentum of New Deal liberalism." The mobilization began in the late thirties but was "at least partially adjourned" during World War II.

The postwar years, however, witnessed an even more powerful remobilization of business as employers stepped forward to shape national social and economic policies. The most visible aspects of the battle for power took place over major policy issues at the national level, pitting executives of large firms and major business organizations, like the National Association of Manufacturers and the United States Chamber of Commerce, against liberal Democratic and union leaders. Business's weapons included such techniques as lobbying, campaign financing, and litigation.[10]

Less obvious, but equally significant, was the struggle led by national business leaders and smaller employers at the local level to reshape the ideas, images, and attitudes through which Americans understood their world, specifically their understanding of their relationships to the corporation and the state. This required reorienting workers away from their new-found loyalties to organized labor and government. It is this struggle to create a more conservative, consensual political climate which undermined the power of labor that is the central concern of this book.[11] Enlightened managers would shape not only national policies but also American values. Accordingly, corporate leaders constructed and sold a specific vision of the reciprocal relationship of businesses and citizens that stressed mutual rights and responsibilities. In this vision, corporate leaders claimed the right to control America's economic destiny without significant interference from unions or the state while acknowledging their responsibility to make the benefits of industrial capitalism available to all. Economic growth rather than the redistribution of income proposed by unionists would allow business to uphold its end of the bargain. The key, as the Committee for Economic Development's research director pointed out in 1947, was productivity. He asserted productivity was "a vitally needed lubricant to reduce class and group frictions. As long as we can get more by increasing the size of the pie there is not nearly so much temptation to try to get a bigger slice at the expense of others."[12] In short, the business vision linked economic success with freedom, individualism and productivity. In projecting this vision, business reached back to the political language of the twenties, once again associating the American way with a harmonious, classless society, with nationalism, individual rights, free enterprise, and abundance rising from ever increasing productivity.

The struggle to undercut organized labor's and the state's ideological hold over the working class and to project this vision took place within a variety of contexts. At the national level, business organizations like the Advertising Council and the National Association of

Manufacturers orchestrated multimillion dollar public relations campaigns that relied on newspapers, magazines, radio, and later television to reeducate the public in the principles and benefits of the American economic system.

Recognizing the need for a more direct connection with the public, employers reached out to workers and their communities. At the workplace, employers sought to undermine unionism and address shop-floor conflict by building a separate company identity or company consciousness among their employees. This involved convincing workers to identify their social, economic, and political well-being with that of their specific employer and more broadly with the free enterprise system. To build allegiance to the firm, employers revitalized mechanisms associated with corporate efforts during the twenties to build a privatized welfare state that emphasized the mutual interests of worker and manager.

Understanding the importance of the outside world in shaping the limits of workplace legitimacy, business leaders also challenged their opponents for power and influence outside the factory gates. Their goals were twofold: first to build good will in the community in order to create a favorable climate for economic expansion; second, to shift political dialogue to a more conservative position in order to weaken organized labor and liberalism. Community, then, took on a renewed importance for business leaders worried about the decline of corporate power.

To achieve these goals, employers tried to construct a favorable image of business as a good neighbor by demonstrating both their social consciousness and the importance of the company to the community. Efforts ranged from publicizing company contributions to the local economy to beautifying plants and opening them to the public. Equally important were local public relations campaigns selling business's political agenda. Exploiting rising anticommunism, business warned of the decline of America's values, morals, and freedoms due to government's and labor's attacks on the free enterprise system. An important component of this campaign was an attempt to reassert business dominance over institutional life by influencing such important community agencies as schools and churches.

It is, of course, misleading to treat business as a monolithic force capable of manipulating people and institutions at will. There were major divisions among business leaders, and they often conflicted over how best to preserve the capitalist system. Historians have analyzed these divisions along structural-functional lines; that is, between large and small, or between newer, mass consumption-oriented firms often with strong international connections and domestic-oriented, labor-intensive, primary goods producers. They argue that these different groups coalesced in competing business organizations, such as the more conservative National Association of Manufacturers, as opposed to the Committee for Economic Development, often characterized as moderately conservative or even liberal. While the NAM and its membership rigidly fought any state encroachment on business freedom, the CED and its supporters are described as welcoming the emergence of industrial unionism and the development of a more powerful governmental role within the economy. While such an analysis is a useful tool for classifying the business community, it tends to leave out considerations of individual inclinations and choices that often do not conform to structural categories. To which wing of the business community employers migrated often reflected less where their firm fit in the market and more whether they were tacticians trying to work within the realm of the possible, or whether they were driven by purely dogmatic or ideological considerations. Finally, as the historian Robert Griffith contends, the "differences among these powerful associations" has "probably been exaggerated . . . given their overlapping memberships, financial support, and shared assumptions."[13] Divisions, then, were often less important than a unity of purpose within much of the business community on certain key issues, in particular, the necessity of halting the advance of the welfare state and of undermining the legitimacy and power of organized labor.

As a result, all the major business organizations, including the Chamber of Commerce, the CED, and the NAM as well as industry-specific bodies like the Iron and Steel Institute, were heavily involved in the campaign to shape America's political culture. So too, were an array of companies that varied in size and crossed industrial divisions. Most firms with extensive economic education, human relations, community and public relations programs were labor intensive, primary goods producers like General Motors, Ford, Caterpillar, or U.S. Steel. But one also finds General Electric, Johnson and Johnson, Standard Oil of New Jersey, and General Foods, companies that according to the structural analysis should have had little interest in these activities.

Diversity in ideological orientation also characterized the business leaders active in reshaping America's political climate. A group of NAM leaders, tending toward extreme conservatism and representing firms that successfully resisted unionization, were among the most committed to changing the political climate. Charles R. Hook of

American Rolling Mill, Henning W. Prentis of Armstrong Cork, J. Howard Pew of Sun Oil, and Jasper Crane of Du Pont, for instance, helped initiate the earliest NAM campaigns against the New Deal. Ardent defenders of traditional business values, they helped form an interlocking network of business leaders that financially supported and provided leadership to numerous organizations promulgating free enterprise ideology after World War II, including Spiritual Mobilization, the Foundation for Economic Education, the Freedoms Foundation, Harding College, and Junior Achievement.

Also, very involved, however, were employers representing unionized firms struggling to contain organized labor. John L. McCaffrey and Fowler McCormick of International Harvester, B. E. Hutchinson of Chrysler, and S. C. Allyn of National Cash Register fell into this category. Finally, not to be overlooked were corporate leaders often characterized as moderates, like Harry Bullis of General Mills or Charles E. Wilson of General Electric. Both were members of the NAM as well as CED trustees and were at the forefront of the CED's efforts to remold education and religion. At times, conservative and moderate business leaders might struggle over the details of the business message, but they agreed on certain fundamental principles, particularly the need to emphasize individualism, freedom, and productivity.

It is also important to understand the ways that business interacted with its opposition, primarily organized labor. Workers and their unions resisted and reshaped employer actions. One segment of organized labor, unions associated with the CIO, actively competed with business in the effort to shape worker consciousness. This study, then, will focus primarily on the industrial unions that most actively contested business for worker loyalty and public sympathy. During the Depression and World War II, unions had become an increasingly potent force not only in the plant and in national politics but also in local communities, establishing connections that grew in the postwar era with important community institutions. Later, particularly as attacks against labor increased during the fifties, unions began to emulate business, conducting their own public relations campaigns. Unions drew on a vision of the American way that emphasized equal rights and social and economic justice. They promoted the notion that worker success and security as well as America's future depended on the collective power of organized labor and on the continued ability of the state to regulate business. As we will see, organized labor had difficulty matching the resources available to the leaders of American business.

To capture and untangle the complex struggle over political culture, this study moves through time and across space. It is organized into five parts. In the first part, I examine in narrative form the ebb and flow of the employer counteroffensive at the national level from the 1930s through the CIO period. I explore the strategic program embarked upon by corporate leaders to regain not only political and economic but also ideological initiatives. Well-orchestrated public relations campaigns helped capital gain strength in the immediate postwar years. Although, business suffered an unexpected reversal in 1948, it regained its footing in the early fifties with major political victories. By mid-decade, with the CIO in disarray, capital appeared well on the way to securing its hegemony.

Business success resulted from national political events only in part, however. In the next three sections, I take apart and analyze the various elements that helped build business's political hegemony. Each part moves back in time and focuses on the various arenas in which employers sought to shape political consciousness during the forties and fifties. In part 2, I examine the competing company and union efforts to reach workers at the workplace. The next section moves beyond worksites to explore the struggle between unions and companies for power and influence in the community. In part 4, I analyze more closely the important role of institutions—particularly those of education and religion—in the struggle for public opinion. Conflict over churches and schools highlights not only the continuing divisions between capital and labor but also the ideological divisions within the business community itself. Conservatives of the NAM and the moderates of the CED promoted different visions of political economy. In these arenas, however, the CED's more moderate message predominated.

In the last part, I return to the narrative and the political arena, beginning with the merger of the AFL and the CIO in 1955. Although business had scored major victories, important elements of the business community were still not satisfied with what they had achieved. In the wake of the merger, the most conservative wing of the business community remained worried about labor and liberalism's apparent continuing strength. As headlines portended the onslaught of a labor juggernaut, the hardline labor policies of the NAM came to the forefront of employers' political agenda. The book concludes by examining the conservative-led drive to redraw the laws governing labor relations at both the state and federal levels. For business and labor, public opinion was a critical element of this struggle.

Assessing the impact of the business community's campaign to shape political culture is a difficult task. Even most companies took it as a matter of faith that the dollars they invested in national educational campaigns and in the workplace or community programs often paid off only in intangible ways. But, by the end of the 1950s, the business community could point to favorable results. Liberal hopes for a fully articulated welfare state had been crushed, while union representation of the labor force had begun its long decline. Meanwhile, the popular image of organized labor shifted from the heroic defenders of the New Deal to just another special interest group. It would be facile to draw a straight line between the subject of this book, business's ideological campaigns, and the social, political, and economic changes that took place during the fifties. Certainly, the impact of such factors as the cold war, high employment, consumerism, shifting sectors of employment, and suburbanization should not be ignored. Nor should we, however, underestimate the significance of the business community's effort to redefine the meaning of Americanism to emphasize individualistic as opposed to mutualistic ways of dealing with inequality.

## Notes

1. "In Our Hands—Workers Talk Economics," *Modern Industry* 22 (July 15, 1951): 41–45; *Latrobe Bulletin*, Apr. 10, 1951.

2. Sarah Lyons Watts, *Order against Chaos: Business Culture and Labor Ideology in America, 1880–1915* (New York: Greenwood Press, 1991), pp. 1–31; Adam Przeworski, *Capitalism and Social Democracy* (Cambridge: Cambridge University Press, 1985), pp. 69–70; Gary Gerstle, *Working Class Americanism: The Politics of Labor in a Textile City, 1914–1960* (Cambridge: Cambridge University Press, 1989).

3. On the impact of the Depression on workers, see Lizabeth Cohen, *Making a New Deal: Industrial Workers in Chicago, 1919–1939* (Cambridge: Cambridge University Press, 1990), pp. 252–89.

4. Slichter quoted in David Brody, *Workers in Industrial America* (New York: Oxford University Press, 1980), p. 174.

5. Alan Brinkley, "The New Deal and the Idea of the State," in *The Rise and Fall of the New Deal Order, 1930–1980*, ed. Steve Fraser and Gary Gerstle (Princeton: Princeton University Press, 1989), pp. 85–112.

6. Nelson Lichtenstein, "From Corporatism to Collective Bargaining: Organized Labor and the Eclipse of Social Democracy in the Postwar Era," in *The Rise and Fall of the New Deal Order*, ed. Fraser and Gerstle, pp. 122–45, esp. 123.

7. See, for example, J. Ronald Oakley, *God's Country: America in the Fifties* (New York: Dembner Books, 1986), pp. 314–19, esp. p. 315.

8. Howell Harris, *The Right to Manage: Industrial Relations Policies of American Business in the 1940s* (Madison: University of Wisconsin Press, 1982), p. 8.

9. Brody, *Workers in Industrial America*, p. 127.

10. For an overview of the business community's mobilization during the Truman years see Robert Griffith, "Forging America's Postwar Order: Domestic Politics and Political Economy in the Age of Truman," in *The Truman Presidency*, ed. Michael J. Lacey (Cambridge: Cambridge University Press, 1989), pp. 57–88, esp. 63.

11. Richard S. Tedlow, *Keeping the Corporate Image: Public Relations and Business, 1900–1950* (Greenwich, Conn.: JAI Press, 1979), and Harris, *The Right to Manage*, have begun to explore corporate efforts to shape the political climate. Tedlow focuses on the history of corporate public relations, especially advertising. Harris addresses similar issues but primarily emphasizes management's efforts to win workers' loyalty within the confines of the shop and argues that business's fight for influence was over by the end of the forties. This study finds a business class shaken by the results of the 1948 election and intensifying its struggle for influence through the 1950s. It moves beyond the factory into homes, schools, and churches and explores organized labor's efforts to challenge business's cultural onslaught.

12. For a cogent analysis of the concept of productivity within postwar political economy discourse, see Charles S. Maier, *In Search of Stability: Explorations in Historical Political Economy* (Cambridge: Cambridge University Press, 1987), pp. 63–69, 121–52, quote from p. 65.

13. I want to thank David Farber of Barnard College for suggestions concerning the various classifications of the business community. Some of his points have been incorporated here. Thomas Ferguson, "Industrial Conflict and the Coming of the New Deal: The Triumph of Multinational Liberalism in America," in *The Rise and Fall of the New Deal Order*, ed. Fraser and Gerstle, pp. 3–24; Maier, *In Search of Stability*, pp. 55–63; Griffith, "Forging America's Postwar Order," p. 67. For a different perspective on unity in the business community, see Colin Gordon, "New Deal, Old Deck: Business, Labor and Politics, 1920–1935" (Ph.D. diss., University of Wisconsin, Madison, 1990).

# PART 1 | The Postwar Employer Counteroffensive

# 1 | *Nothing Less than Catastrophic Civil War*

During the winter of 1945–46, a strike wave of massive proportions swept the United States. To many American employers, these strikes signaled that a grave social, political, and economic crisis threatened the free enterprise system. By January 1946, business writer Whiting Williams proclaimed that what originally seemed "an inconvenient but more or less harmless series of industrial disputes has now become so widespread and so threatening as to look like nothing less than catastrophic civil war."[1] Organized labor's dramatic demonstration of its power to mobilize workers made Williams's analogy of the strike wave as civil war seem increasingly relevant to many in the business community. Since the Depression, labor unions had consolidated and expanded their position in American society. Moreover, during the war, militant workers challenged managerial authority for control of the workplace. Many employers feared that the postwar strike wave augured yet another chapter in labor's growing power within the plant. At the same time, they worried about organized labor's political power and its alliance with New Deal liberals. They saw in this alliance a vivid expression of popular support for the development of a full-employment welfare state. Thus, in 1945 the business community faced the twin challenges of a struggle for control within the workplace and the defense of the free enterprise system from the growing intrusiveness of the federal government.

\* \* \*

Employers did not have to search back too far for a time when challenges from labor and liberalism would have seemed inconceivable. During the twenties, having beaten back the threats of craft unionism, socialism, and Progressive social reform, business reigned supreme over almost every aspect of American society. In 1921, a writer for the *Independent Magazine* characterized the country's mood, proclaiming that "among the nations of the earth today America stands for one idea: Business." In politics, for instance, the corporate community was closely allied with the Republican party and its influence was apparent as the government reduced taxes, cut regulations, and promoted corporate expansion. The celebration of business, though, was by no means limited to the Republican party. By 1928, both major presidential candidates were pledging "their faith to Wall Street and the self-regulating economy." Within the factory, employers asserted their dominance as labor militancy receded and organized labor became increasingly marginalized. Not content with overt control and still fearful of potential working-class militancy, however, some managers moved from repression to experimenting with scientific personnel administration, welfare capitalism, and employee representation in an effort to win workers' loyalty to the firm and the capitalist system.[2]

Business influence and authority extended far beyond the factory and politics. In this culture, the emphasis was on consumption, individualism, and material possessions—values closely linked to business. The Lynd's study of Middletown in the twenties, for instance, describes a community in which public opinion has turned against organized labor with its mutualistic ethos. They suggested that many workers had abandoned the group solidarity of trade unionism for the individualistic rewards of consumption. Americanization campaigns during the early part of the twenties and advertising throughout the decade encouraged this reorientation. Through these means, employers associated the values of business with "traditional" American values. They trumpeted an American way rooted in individualism, independence, freedom, and social harmony. Advertisers made certain that the public equated these ideas with consumption. Increasing consumption, of course, was critical to driving the mass production economy of the twenties.[3]

Business also reached deeply into religious and educational institutions. Within the religious community, especially among Protestants, the emphasis on social reform declined in the 1920s. Instead, elements of the clergy praised business as the source of prosperity, success, and abundance. They attempted to emulate business methods of operation within their churches. Similarly, business values permeated the classroom. Like their clerical counterparts, in their quest for efficiency, educators modeled their schools along corporate lines. By the eve of the Depression, business had become so enmeshed in American culture that historian Thomas Cochran claimed business "enjoyed a degree of public approval unique in American history." During 1929, sixteen business leaders graced the cover of *Time* Magazine; ironically, they included five in a row in the midst of the stock market collapse.[4]

The dramatic economic collapse after 1929, with its devastating unemployment, disastrous drop in wages, and failure of banking and financial systems, shook many Americans' faith in the values of the business community and in corporate leadership. As Lizabeth Cohen has suggested, Depression-era workers lost confidence in the ability of either their employers or their ethnic communities to provide for their "welfare, security, and employment." Business's association of the American way with freedom, independence, individualism, competition, and consumption increasingly had little appeal to workers unable to find jobs. Workers began to define Americanism with such terms as economic equality, social justice, and human rights, in particular the right to a decent wage and to security from poverty, ill health, unemployment, and old age.[5]

To realize these goals, workers rejected the individualistic solutions of business and began looking to the federal government and to organized labor for protection. They called for the government to control capitalism and, if necessary, to redistribute wealth and provide workers their "fair share." By 1935, a *Fortune* magazine survey found the vast majority of employees convinced that the government should assume responsibilities "never seriously contemplated prior to the New Deal." In the survey, 81 percent of those classified lower middle class, 89 percent of those classified as poor, and 91 percent of blacks endorsed the statement that the "'government should see to it that every man who wants to work has a job.'" To employers, such opinions indicated a complete loss in faith among workers in business and the free enterprise system.[6]

The New Deal failed to produce the comprehensive welfare state envisioned by many workers. Nevertheless, the state grew to a degree unprecedented in peacetime and impinged in new and powerful ways on business autonomy. Indeed, the New Deal represented a turning point in the development of governmental control of the economy. The federal government, for instance, assumed a major role in managing the agricultural economy and for the first time provided direct relief to the unemployed through the Federal Emergency Relief Administration, the Works Progress Administration, the Civilian Conservation Corp, and a myriad of other agencies. Through the Tennessee Valley Authority, it dabbled in planning, and legislation like the Securities and Exchange Act of 1934 and the Public Utility

Holding Act of 1935 pushed federal regulation into new areas of the economy. Moreover, the Fair Labor Standards Act of 1938, setting standards for wages and hours, and the National Labor Relations (Wagner) Act, protecting workers' right to organize, enabled the federal government to directly intervene on behalf of employees. With the passage of the Social Security Act in 1935, despite all its shortcomings, America took the first halting steps toward the development of a welfare state.[7]

With the backing of the federal government, organized labor rose up to protect the rights and welfare of workers. As a result, the 1930s and early 1940s produced a virtual revolution in the nation's industrial relations. Because we know that in the late forties and early fifties it was contained and even, in our own times, unraveled, it is easy to forget how enormous a change it represented. Powerful new organizations of workers contested employer control over hours, wages, and the conditions of work. During the war years, they even threatened to intrude upon the board room. Beyond these strategies, workers sought an alliance with Democratic politicians that aimed at refashioning the political economy of modern America.

Organized labor's resurgence began during 1933 when, under the protection of section 7a of the National Recovery Act, workers flooded the federal labor unions of the American Federation of Labor. While the NRA was a significant factor in this upsurge, not to be overlooked was the militancy and determination of a rank and file disillusioned with the promises of the twenties. These same workers soon became disappointed with the government's enforcement of the Act's provisions and triggered a wave of bitter strikes in 1934. At the polls, a new mass political mobilization recruited the urban working class, particularly second-generation immigrant wage earners, into the Democratic party. Although the upheaval collapsed, Democratic victories in the 1934 election and the lingering threat of labor militancy helped push liberals to fight for passage of the Wagner Act over the vigorous protests of corporate leaders.[8]

The Wagner Act provided the foundations for the establishment of a pluralistic industrial relations system. The law essentially made it public policy to promote collective bargaining through independent unions. It established a code of fair practices, outlawing such traditional employer weapons as the blacklist, the yellow-dog contract, and company unions and created a new National Labor Relations Board to determine bargaining rights and to hear charges of unfair practices. If, as later critics would note, the new legislation enfolded unions in institutional structures that would ultimately be used to contain labor's drive for power, it also provided unions with a degree of support and legitimacy that they had never enjoyed before.[9]

Even before the assurance of state support, a group of industrial unionists broke off from the AFL to form the Congress of Industrial Organizations as a vehicle for unionizing the long-ignored mass-production industries. Through a series of bitter strikes, the CIO achieved major victories in the auto, steel, and rubber industries. After initial organizing victories, CIO unions set out to make the work environment more fair and to begin strengthening new members' ties to organized labor. Stung by competition, a newly invigorated AFL expanded its organizing efforts, at times competing head to head with rival industrial unions. This was the beginning of a damaging civil war that the two national labor organizations would wage for much of the next twenty years. Although a new recession that began in 1938 and a conservative backlash temporarily ground organizing to a halt, by 1940 union membership had risen to around 9 million, having increased threefold since the start of the Depression.[10]

Mobilization for defense and America's entrance into World War II had a profound impact on the labor movement. Mobilization ended the Depression and brought a tight labor market that enabled unions to make significant organizational and economic gains. During the conflict, the number of union members again jumped from the 1940 9 million mark to almost 15 million. Moreover, the government's wartime labor policy provided unions with organizational security through maintenance of membership contract clauses. This facilitated organized labor's consolidation of its position by breaking down many of the bastions of antiunionism including the "Little Steel" companies. Governmental guarantees, however, were not without cost to unions. The National War Labor Board demanded not only adherence to a "no-strike" pledge but also union responsibility. Under these pressures unions became increasingly centralized and bureaucratic as they policed discontent on the shop floor through the establishment of formal grievance and arbitration procedures.[11]

Many managers, however, found little comfort in the concept of responsible unionism. From their perspective, they faced an unprecedented challenge from organized labor. Wartime economic conditions, including scare labor, "cost plus" financing, and the necessity for continuous production, contributed both to the growth of unions and to the loss of managerial authority on the shop floor. Wartime wildcat strikes in defiance of the no-strike pledge were just the most dramatic symbols of the decline of managerial power. In many factories, discipline was lax and workers defiant. Aggressive union representatives demanded and received a voice in setting and enforcing production standards. According to employers, all this intervention added up to declining productivity.[12]

As the war ended, managers fretted that the long upsurge of labor had left virtually none of their rights secure. Participants at a 1944 American Management Association round table discussion observed that "management has an uneasy feeling that its prerogatives are slipping from it into the hands of unions." To business writers like Whiting Williams, the National War Labor Board's expansion of the scope of collective bargaining made the government appear to be in "active partnership" with the CIO. Even more ominously, unions were attempting to bargain for such devices as mutual consent clauses, which limited management's right to initiate change, or the establishment of joint committees that would give labor equal voice in planning and decision making. Thomas Roy Jones, president of the American Type Founders, foresaw no limit to the future demands of power hungry labor leaders. "Annual wages, private social security systems, early retirements, long vacations, 25-hour weeks—are completely within the realm of economic possibility." If business did not stop this trend, Roy predicted, "a condition of industrial chaos eventually will ensue."[13]

The end of the war in August 1945 ignited the already explosive atmosphere of labor-capital relations. Massive layoffs swelled the ranks of the unemployed and, for those still working, income dropped as the return to the normal work week resulted in the loss of overtime earnings. In response, unions ended their no-strike pledge, and frustrated workers walked out, initiating one of the largest strike waves in American history. In the year after V-J Day, there were 4,630 work stoppages, involving almost 5 million workers, resulting in the loss of 119.8 million man-days of production. Labor struggles in communities like Stamford, Connecticut; Lancaster, Pennsylvania; and Rochester, New York; took on the characteristics of class warfare, expanding into citywide general strikes.[14]

Most alarming for the business community were the issues raised in the General Motors strike that began in late November 1945. One student of the strike concluded that Walter Reuther "consciously politicized the GM strike by challenging managerial control of product pricing and by emphasizing the stake the consuming public had in the victory of the auto workers." His demand that the auto company open its books to union contract negotiators in order to link wages and prices to profits seemed to employers to strike at the very essence of capitalism. Moreover, by treading on the most sacred of managerial prerogatives, Reuther epitomized the mounting threat unions posed to employer control over their own firms.[15]

By the war's end, some employers charged that not only business but also the entire country was now held hostage by the "monopolistic power" exercised by a handful of irresponsible labor leaders. The National Association of Manufacturers chairman, Ira Mosher, bluntly charged that "Reuther decides whether or not we can have automobiles. Murray decides when we can have steel to build automobiles or refrigerators or homes." Meanwhile, Lewis "determines whether we shall have coal to turn the wheel of our industry, to heat and light our homes." And finally "as if this were not enough, Petrillo decides when and how we can have music."[16]

Labor's threat to business power radiated far beyond the shop floor. The fledgling relationship organized labor began with the Democratic party in 1934 had blossomed into a full blown alliance. As Nelson Lichtenstein has observed, by 1940 "the CIO had built a dense web of political and emotional connections with the Roosevelt administration." At the core of this alliance were workers who looked to the Democratic party to pursue their class interests.[17] The formation of a powerful Political Action Committee in mid-1943 provided the organizational structure to enable the labor movement to play a more decisive role in the nation's political life. During the 1944 election, the PAC supported a broad liberal program and helped revitalize the New Deal coalition. After the election, the CIO seemed to be laying the groundwork for a progressive postwar reconstruction effort. Among the central goals on labor's agenda were full employment, economic planning, and a fuller articulation of the welfare state through an expansion of Social Security and unemployment insurance, and the development of a national health program. Labor's economic vision found legislative expression before the war's end in January 1945 with the introduction of the Full Employment Bill. Written by liberal economists working in wartime regulatory agencies, it promised to institutionalize the wartime state management of the economy and to make Keynesian social planning public policy. The Full Employment Bill had the support of a broad liberal-labor coalition that included the AFL, the CIO, the NAACP, and the National Farmers Union. In early 1945, given the widespread concern reflected in opinion polls about economic readjustment after the war, the measure seemed destined to become law.[18]

While the PAC gained perhaps an undeserved reputation for political power, its attempt to supplement collective bargaining with political activity alarmed the business community. "From the standpoint of the ultimate welfare of the people of the United States," wrote one Missouri business executive, "I think there is no question but that if labor is permitted to consolidate its power," and to use that power to elect more liberals like "Claude Peppers and Wallaces to positions of authority, we shall find ourselves in a position in which labor is stronger than the government of the United States and is able to dictate to it."[19]

* * *

By the late 1930s, some American business leaders were already struggling, often unsuccessfully, against what seemed to them to be a revolution both in their industrial relations and in the larger political economy. Although this opposition would be modified somewhat by the experience and successes of business during World War II, at war's end, much of the business community was convinced that America was in the midst of a serious social, political, and economic crisis. It was against this background that the American business community mobilized vigorously to roll back the power of labor in the factory and to regain control over the larger political process.

Although by 1945 many corporate leaders were uniting in a determination to resist the expansion of labor's power and to refashion the New Deal state, the business community was not monolithic. The solutions to the crisis that corporate leaders posed roughly reflected the division of the business community into two ideological camps. Traditional or practical conservatives, often associated with the National Association of Manufacturers and the Chamber of Commerce, tended to distrust the state and to call for the dismantling of much of the New Deal. They especially denounced the meddling of the government in a peacetime economy through wage and price controls or through Keynesian fiscal policies.[20] Business leaders like Donaldson Brown of General Motors, J. Howard Pew of Sun Oil, and Ernest T. Weir of National Steel Corporation spoke of the centrality of freedom and the value of individual initiative and competition. Abridgement of economic freedom would inevitably lead to such disasters as compulsory state control and possibly even extreme collectivism. Thus, the vice-chairman of the United Aircraft Corporation, Eugene E. Wilson, warned that unless America returned to its fundamental principles, "Christian freedom will give way to atheistic slavery, cooperation to compulsion, hope to fear, equality of opportunity to privilege, and the dead hand of bureaucracy will close the throttle on progress."[21]

Traditional conservatives particularly chafed at the abridgement of their economic freedom in the realm of industrial relations. The growth of unionism in the 1930s and especially under the auspices of the National War Labor Board seemingly imposed strict limits on employer freedom of action. Conservative employers viewed unions as illegitimate, outside forces that fomented trouble and undermined the naturally close relations between worker and employer. Some staunch antiunion firms, such as Weirton Steel and Du Pont, successfully opposed organizing drives. Other companies, like General Motors, forced to recognize unions, still refused to accept their permanence. These companies promoted a strategy that historian Howell John Harris has labeled "realism." It entailed reluctant acceptance of the principle of unionism while actively attempting to restrict the scope of collective bargaining and to contain or weaken the power of organized labor. At the same time, in politics, the owners of these firms backed the NAM in its campaign for the repeal or amendment of the Wagner Act to protect employers against the "monopolistic power" of unions.[22]

At the other end of the spectrum were the more sophisticated conservatives or moderates who joined together during the thirties in organizations like the Business Advisory Council and in the forties, the Committee for Economic Development. These corporate leaders were less concerned with protecting competition. They sought to moderate the New Deal, not destroy it. In contrast with Donaldson Brown, CED founders like Marion Folson of Eastman Kodak, Ralph Flanders, and Paul G. Hoffman of Studebaker Automobile Company, looked to central economic planning, although primarily influenced by business, to ensure prosperity. Hoffman borrowed a line from the NAM conservatives when he dramatically warned in 1943 that collectivism could come to postwar America. However, he certainly shocked conservatives when he claimed that its source would be business's failure to protect against mass unemployment through planning. To Hoffman it would more likely come by default than by "design on the part of revolutionaries."[23]

The CED asserted that America could no longer afford wild economic fluctuations. Instead of "ignorant opposition to change," the business community should help define a new role for the state to promote economic growth and stability. In 1946, Hoffman challenged corporate leaders to "look one important fact squarely in the face— that the Federal Government has a vital role to play in our capitalistic system." NAM conservatives "who claimed that all that is necessary is to 'unshackle free enterprise' are guilty of an irresponsible statement," he went on. "Those who say that the Federal Government's role is only that of an umpire have their heads in the sand." The CED's corporatist message was that enlightened employers should not reject the state but should provide positive policy programs to guide the government in promoting a "recognizable general interest."[24]

Moderates tended to take an accommodationistic attitude toward organized labor. Rather than fearing unions, some welcomed them with open arms. Such progressive industrialists as Henry Kaiser or Eric Johnston believed that if properly directed, unions could "contribute to increased industrial efficiency and social responsibility."[25] They acknowledged unions as legitimate representatives of employees and welcomed the cooperative arrangements that government agencies promoted during the war. Through these means and without giving up real power, these executives hoped to gain organized labor's cooperation in increasing productivity and industrial stability. To these employers, the NLRB was not an enemy but an ally in the development of responsible unionism.[26]

Any attempt to categorize employers into two camps obviously slights many shadings and variations. The business community had many divisions within it and individual employers often demonstrated little ideological consistency. Many members of the CED, like Henning W. Prentis of Armstrong Cork, Harry Bullis of General Mills, Charles R. Hook of Armco and S. C. Allyn of National Cash Register, were also prominent NAM activists. These men might accept an enlightened attitude toward an activist state but scowl at progressive labor policy within their own plants. The CED, in fact, worked hard not to alienate the more conservative employers, and such individuals as Walter D. Fuller, president of Curtis Publishing Company, could direct information committees for both organizations. Fuller seemingly had little difficulty with spreading the apparently contradictory messages of the NAM and the CED to the business community and to the public.[27]

A partial mobilization of the business community actually began in the late thirties. Certainly some "enlightened" business leaders were at the forefront of the New Deal, hoping to use the state to help revitalize the economy. But an equally powerful group of employers were adamantly opposed to reforms like the WPA, Wagner Act and Social Security, which they saw as attacking individualism and freedom. The NAM and the American Liberty League, formed in 1934 and financed by a core of wealthy conservative business leaders, including J. Howard Pew, John J. Raskob and the Du Ponts, led the corporate opposition to the New Deal and the rise of labor. The NAM, for one, lobbied hard against the passage of the Wagner Act. After the Act was declared constitutional in 1937, employers, allied with conservative Republicans, southern Democrats and the AFL, which felt that the NLRB was hostile to craft unionism, attacked the Board demanding balance and equality in the law. While the attack was not entirely successful, it helped create enough public opposition to force Roosevelt to appoint a labor board less sympathetic to industrial unionism. Congress, meanwhile, empowered the Smith Committee to investigate the Board. As they waged war on the NLRB, business leaders also provided key support to a conservative backlash that followed the recession of 1937–38. In this atmosphere, toward the end of the thirties, the legislative agenda of the New Deal was narrowed and a number of industrial states enacted antilabor statutes.[28]

An important part of this early mobilization was an effort to turn public opinion against the New Deal. As criticism of business reached new heights and workers turned to unions and the state for leadership, employers looked to public relations to restore their legitimacy. The NAM argued that industry's problems were primarily the result of public misunderstanding. It appealed to the business community to launch "an active campaign of education" to "tell its story." Business needed to restore the public's faith in its leadership and to promote the corporate vision of the American way. A vision that emphasized freedom, individualism, and harmony between employer and employee.[29]

In the last part of the 1930s, the NAM, other employer associations, and individual firms launched a campaign to convert the American public to the economic goals, ideals, and program of business. The NAM's budget for public relations shot up from $36,000 in 1934 to $793,043 in 1937 representing 55 percent of the organization's total income. The NAM utilized numerous communications media, including weekly radio programs, film strips, educational films, paid advertisements, direct mail, displays for schools and plants, a speakers bureau, and an industrial press service, providing editorials and news stories to seventy-five hundred small papers. By 1940, the NAM was beginning to experiment with methods to more systematically influence the institutions of education and religion and to reach more directly into the community with the story of free enterprise. General Electric and other firms supplemented the NAM's efforts with films, traveling industrial exhibits, merchandise displays, and pamphlets and programs for school children. Some of these corporate efforts, like Westinghouse's *Middleton Family at the World's Fair,* which celebrated the abundance of consumer goods in America, were a fairly sophisticated and subtle rendering of free enterprise ideology. Nevertheless, through the thirties, enough of the corporate campaign was marred by extremist, overt attacks on unions, and the New Deal that it was easy for critics to dismiss the entire effort as mere propaganda.[30]

If World War II enabled the labor movement to grow dramatically, it also offered the business community the opportunity to regain some of its lost power and prestige. The wartime "miracle of production" brought renewed authority as industry's leaders demanded and received the largest voice in establishing policy concerning economic mobilization. Business leaders drew on their new influence with government to encourage the more conservative wartime Congress to begin dismantling some of the New Deal. Finally, in 1943 Congress passed the Smith-Connally War Labor Disputes Act, which aimed at limiting labor's economic and political power.[31]

For corporate leaders, war production symbolized one of the finest hours of the free enterprise system. General Motors Vice Chairman Donaldson Brown attributed successful economic mobilization to the "exercise of individual initiative" and to the efficiency inspired by "long years of competitive effort strengthened by the stimulus and incentive of the profit motive." Similarly, in December 1942 at the NAM's annual meeting, H. W. Prentis, chairman of the NAM's Executive Committee, expressed disdain for the "childlike" faith many had recently put in government. He asserted that "it is not government that has wrought the miracle that is being accomplished today in the production of war materials but the initiative, ingenuity and organizing genius of private enterprise." This was the message that much of the business community wanted the public to take from the wartime experience.[32]

Business leaders worried, however, that wartime economic success sent a different message. Since much occurred within the context of government regulation and regimentation, the war mobilization possibly taught the public that government control, economic planning, and the welfare state were key to continued prosperity. Writing only six months after the bombing of Pearl Harbor, Donaldson Brown already worried that the "public has not come to distinguish between the necessity of centralized planning and regimentation in time of war, and the exercise of corresponding functions on the part of government in the time of peace." Brown feared that those with "ulterior motives" were going to "seize the occasion to contend that the wartime system under which industrial production has worked such wonders could be extended and applied with equal benefit and effectiveness in the post-war economy."[33]

To prevent this from happening, the NAM continued its steadfast support for individualism and freedom from government interference and vowed to "oppose anybody who tries to destroy" these "freedoms when peace comes." The need for wartime unity, however, stopped outright attacks against New Deal liberalism and labor. The NAM's public relations program continued but in more muted, subtle terms. It moved toward refurbishing the negative image the NAM had gained from its Depression-era public relations campaign and toward reinvigorating business leadership. To build up business's reputation, the NAM's radio programs, press releases, pamphlets, and speakers publicized American industries' vital contributions to the war effort. Moreover, they constantly linked production accomplishments to the free enterprise system, reminding the public that they were fighting to preserve "the freedoms and liberties upon which the American way of life has been based." As for the postwar era, the NAM urged that the key to a higher standard of living was increasing productivity, not labor's plan of a government-ordered economy and a state-engineered redistribution of income.[34]

The epitome of this effort was the NAM-initiated community-based program, "Soldiers of Production." Begun in 1943, this program was designed to reach industrial workers through inspirational talks on company time. Over the next two years, hundreds of thousands of workers attended "Soldiers of Production" rallies during which NAM speakers urged greater cooperation between workers and management and a renewed commitment by all to the free enterprise system.[35]

Individual corporations followed in the NAM's steps with advertisements in popular weekly magazines or on the radio, emphasizing protecting America's freedom of enterprise and rugged individualism. A Nash-Kelvinator Corporation piece printed in full color, for example, depicts a young American soldier quietly reflecting on what kind of an America he yearns for when he returns: "I'm not playing for marbles. I'm fighting for freedom. I'm fighting for the things that made America the greatest place in the world to live in. . . . So don't anybody tell me I'll find America changed." Other employers emphasized the same theme of "Don't Change Anything!" The implication was that America should be restored to the status quo of the twenties when private industry rather than government safeguarded the public interest.[36]

Repeating the now familiar dire litany of warnings for the survival of private enterprise, the NAM tried to activate even more of the business community to stand up in its defense. Thus, the organization supplemented its own public relations efforts with a program of public relations forums. These meetings were designed to educate employers about the importance of spreading the kind of message found in the Nash-Kelvinator advertisement and to provide practical lessons on how to reach the public and workers within the plant. Two forums held during the war and one shortly after spoke to the need for a broad, active, conservative business response to the problem of excessive government intervention in the economy.[37]

The NAM was not the only element of the business community publicizing a postwar vision. The CED had as its principal founding goal in 1942 the formulation of a constructive postwar economic policy. It sponsored research into reconversion problems and, through its Field Development Division and Information Department, sought to educate employers and popularize its economic vision. By the end of the war over twenty-eight hundred autonomous CED committees were working to achieve the CED objectives of postwar business expansion and level employment. Remaining nonpartisan, it offered constructive solutions for economic reconversion that included a significant, if circumscribed, role for the government. While differing on the issue of the level of acceptable state involvement in the economy, the CED joined with the NAM in emphasizing the importance of increasing productivity and preserving a free society. Although its focus was primarily on educating the business community, the CED reached out to the public through a weekly national radio program to allay the "fear of fear itself" and to ensure that the people were "informed on what the problems of reconversion are, and how they are being met."[38]

The Chamber of Commerce, at least during the war, pursued goals similar to the CED. In 1942, the Chamber initiated structural changes to reinvigorate the organization. To enhance its political influence, the Chamber of Commerce established a Department of Governmental Affairs to lobby Congress. It also formed eight hundred local-level national affairs committees to mobilize public opinion and apply political pressure. The leadership of the organization temporarily shifted hands from an old guard of traditional conservatives to a new group of cautious moderates led by Eric Johnston. Under Johnston's leadership, the Chamber officially moved closer to the sort of economic policies endorsed by the CED. That is, it accepted the inevitability of government intervention in the economy but was prepared to act decisively in defining the state's role.[39]

Although the CED's economic message certainly conflicted in key areas with that of the NAM, both organizations agreed on the necessity of further mobilizing the business community. The principal point of agreement appeared to be the effort to offset the growing influence of organized labor. Indeed, battles fought in the immediate postwar years over full employment, price controls, and labor legislation drew the groups closer together and encouraged business leaders to seek greater cooperation on at least the basic issues of the postwar economy.

## Notes

1. Whiting Williams, "The Public Is Fed Up with the Union Mess," *FMM* 104 (Jan. 1946): 97.

2. *Independent Magazine* quoted in Paul S. Boyer, et al., *The Enduring Vision: A History of the American People*, vol. 2, (Lexington, Mass.: D. C. Heath, 1990), pp. 833–34; Thomas Cochran, *The American Business System: A Historical Perspective, 1900–1955* (Cambridge: Harvard University Press, 1957), p. 140; David Brody, *Workers in Industrial America: Essays on the Twentieth Century Struggle* (New York: Oxford University Press, 1980), chap. 2.

3. James Oliver Robertson, *America's Business* (New York: Hill and Wang, 1985), pp. 210–15; Robert S. Lynd and Helen Merrell Lynd, *Middletown: A Study in Modern American Culture* (New York: Harcourt, Brace & World, 1956). On advertising see Charles McGovern, "The Political Language of American Advertising, 1890–1940" (Paper presented at the 1991 American Studies Conference, Baltimore, Maryland, Oct. 1991), and Roland Marchand, *Advertising the American Dream: Making Way for Modernity, 1920–1940* (Berkeley: University of California Press, 1985).

4. Rolf Lunden, *Business and Religion in the American 1920s* (New York: Greenwood Press, 1988); Joel Spring, *The American School, 1642–1985,* (New York: Longman, 1986) pp. 222–52; Cochran, *The American Business System,* p. 140; W. A. Swanberg, *Luce and His Empire* (New York: Dell Publishing, 1972), pp. 121–22.

5. Lizabeth Cohen, *Making a New Deal: Industrial Workers in Chicago, 1919–1939* (Cambridge: Cambridge University Press, 1990), pp. 252–89, esp. 268.

6. *Fortune* survey quoted in Cohen, *Making a New Deal,* pp. 281–82, also 267–89.

7. Albert U. Romansco, *The Politics of Recovery: Roosevelt's New Deal* (New York: Oxford University Press, 1983), p. 219.

8. Robert Zieger, *American Worker, American Unions, 1920–1985* (Baltimore: Johns Hopkins University Press, 1986), pp. 26–41; James R. Green, *The World of the Worker: Labor in Twentieth-Century America* (New York: Hill and Wang, 1980), pp. 133–55.

9. Robert Zieger, *American Worker, American Unions,* pp. 40–41. Among critics of Wagner Act, see especially Christopher Tomlins, *The State and the Unions: Labor Relations, Law and the Organized Labor Movement in America, 1880–1960* (Cambridge: Cambridge University Press, 1985).

10. Zieger, *American Workers, American Unions,* pp. 41–61; Howell John

Harris, *The Right to Manage: Industrial Relations Policies of American Business in the 1940s* (Madison: University of Wisconsin Press, 1982), pp. 23–40.

11. Joel Seidman, *American Labor from Defense to Reconversion* (Chicago: University of Chicago Press, 1953), pp. 91–108; Harris, *The Right to Manage*, pp. 41–89; Nelson Lichtenstein, *Labor's War at Home: The CIO in World War II* (Cambridge: Cambridge University Press, 1982), pp. 44–47.

12. Lichtenstein, *Labor's War at Home*, pp. 117–35; Harris, *The Right to Manage*, pp. 60–74.

13. "A New Pattern of Labor Relations: Trends in Union Contract Clauses, A Round Table Discussion," AMA Personnel Series No. 79 (1944), pp. 27–29; Whiting Williams, "Shall Labor Bargain with Government or Employers?," *FMM* 104 (Feb. 1946): 108; Thomas R. Jones, "The Scope of Collective Bargaining," AMA Personnel Series No. 81 (1944), pp. 40–51; Harris, *The Right to Manage*, pp. 44–59, 67–74.

14. David Brody, *Workers in Industrial America*, p. 174; George Lipsitz, *Class and Culture in Cold War America: "A Rainbow at Midnight"* (South Hadley, Mass.: J. F. Bergin, 1982), chaps. 2–4.

15. Lichtenstein, *Labor's War at Home*, p. 225.

16. Ira Mosher, "Labor Legislation—Then What?" (Address before Chicago Industrial Conference, May 24, 1946), Acc. 1412, NAM, Industrial Relations Department Papers, Box 13. Mosher was attacking Walter Reuther, president of the UAW, John L. Lewis, president of the UMW, and James C. Petrillo, president of the American Federation of Musicians.

17. Lichtenstein, *Labor's War at Home*, p. 33. If, as some critics would later argue, this alliance robbed labor of its radicalism and made it vulnerable, it also afforded labor a degree of influence that it had never before enjoyed. On the problematic relationship between labor and the Democratic party see Mike Davis, *Prisoners of the American Dream: Politics and Economy in the History of the US Working Class* (London: Verso, 1986), chap. 2; Brody, *Workers in Industrial America*, chap. 6.

18. James Caldwell Foster, *The Union Politic: The CIO Political Action Committee* (Columbia: University of Missouri Press, 1975), pp. 50–51; Robert M. Collins, *The Business Response to Keynes, 1929–1960* (New York: Columbia University Press, 1981), pp. 99–101.

19. Business executive quoted Christopher L. Tomlins, *The State and the Unions*, p. 248; Foster, *The Union Politic*, pp. 40–48.

20. Collins, *The Business Response to Keynes*, chap. 3.

21. Eugene E. Wilson, "Give the U.S.A. Back to the American People," *FMM* 104 (May 1946): 96; Richard S. Tedlow, *Keeping the Corporate Image: Public Relations and Business, 1900–1950* (Greenwich, Connecticut: JAI Press, 1979), pp. 117–21.

22. Harris, *The Right to Manage*, pp. 23–32, 95–104.

23. Collins, *The Business Response to Keynes*, chap. 3; "Business Plans for the Postwar," *The Republican*, Apr. 1943, p. 4, Box 103, Paul G. Hoffman Papers, HST.

24. Paul G. Hoffman, "The Survival of Free Enterprise," *HBR* 25 (Autumn

1946): 23–24; Thomas B. McCabe, "The Committee for Economic Development—Its Past, Present and Future" (Address before the Semi-Annual Meeting of the CED Board of Trustee, Nov. 17, 1949), pamphlet, Box 78, Lou E. Holland Papers, HST; Collins, *The Business Response to Keynes*, p. 85.

25. Harris, *The Right to Manage*, p. 35.

26. Ibid., pp. 32–33, 135–39; Lichtenstein, *Labor's War at Home*, pp. 217–19.

27. Collins, *The Business Response to Keynes*, p. 73; Richard Tedlow, *Keeping the Corporate Image*, p. 122; Walter D. Fuller to Members of the Committee on Cooperation with Community Leaders, Jan. 19, 1949, Accession 1411, NAM, Series I, Box 109 (hereafter Acc. 1411, NAM I/109); Paul G. Hoffman to Lou Holland, Oct. 14, 1946, Box 162, Holland Papers.

28. Robert F. Burk, *The Corporate State and the Broker State: The Du Ponts and American National Politics, 1925–1940* (Cambridge: Harvard University Press, 1990), pp. 143–277; Anthony J. Badger, *The New Deal: The Depression Years, 1933–1940* (New York: Noonday Press, 1989), pp. 285–98. On attack on NLRB see James A. Gross, *The Reshaping of the National Labor Relations Board: National Labor Policy in Transition, 1937–1947* (Albany: State University Press of New York, 1981).

29. Tedlow, *Keeping the Corporate Image*, pp. 61–63.

30. S. H. Walker and Paul Aklar, *Business Finds Its Voice: Management's Efforts to Sell the Business Idea to the Public* (New York: Harper and Bros, 1938); William Bird, "Enterprise and Meaning: Sponsored Film, 1939–1949," *History Today* 39 (Dec. 1989): 24–30; Tedlow, *Keeping the Corporate Image*, pp. 63–70, 81–105.

31. Joel Seidman, *American Labor from Defense to Reconversion*, pp. 67–73.

32. Donaldson Brown to W. P. Withrow, July 31, 1942, Acc. 1411, NAM I/112; *NAM News: War Congress of American Industry* Dec. 12, 1942, p. 13, Acc. 1411, NAM III/845.

33. Brown to W. P. Withrow, July 31, 1942.

34. *NAM News*, Dec. 12, 1942, p. 32; C. E. Harrison to Mr. Weisenburger, Dec. 18, 1944, C. E. Harrison to N.I.I.C. Staff Executives, n.d., Acc. 1411, NAM III/845; National Industrial Information Committee, *Annual Report*, 1943, Morris Sayre, "Tomorrow's America" (Address before Massachusetts Farm and Industry Conference, Amherst, Mass., May 11, 1944) Acc. 1411, NAM III/842.

35. "Soldiers of Production," n.d. Acc. 1411, NAM III/842; "Soldiers of Production: Industry's 'Double-E' Drive," c. 1943, NAM III/845.

36. Victor H. Bernstein, "The Anti-Labor Front," *Antioch Review* 3 (Sept. 1943): 330; "Advertising in Wartime," *New Republic*, Feb. 21, 1944, pp. 233–36.

37. Tedlow, *Keeping the Corporate Image*, p. 120.

38. *C.E.D. News*, Apr. 1945, p. 4, Sept. 1945, p. 15, Box 29, Hoffman Papers; Collins, *The Business Response to Keynes*, pp. 83–86.

39. Collins, *The Business Response to Keynes*, pp. 88–98.

# 2 | Defending the Free Enterprise System: The National Political Arena

In early 1946 sociologist Robert Lynd observed that "the old liberal enterprise system is on the way out and business must organize and fight for its life." While acknowledging ideological differences within the business community, Lynd asserted that there was broad agreement among employers that their most critical problem was defining the role of the state and of organized labor within the economy. Business, he claimed, was prepared to "spend unlimited money" in search of a solution.[1] In particular, Lynd warned of business's most insidious tactic, the "selling of the 'private enterprise system' on the theory that if you control public opinion you have the government in your hand and labor behind the eight ball."[2]

In the immediate postwar decade, there were a number of major national issues still open to debate. American society had yet to reach a consensus on the relationship of government to the economy, on the proper size of the welfare state, and on the scope of union power in the factory. The two most central actors in this debate, the business community and organized labor, had both reaffirmed the importance of public opinion. Each launched strenuous campaigns to shape national politics and create a favorable climate of opinion for their opposing views. In many respects, these national campaigns framed a debate that would reach into factories, schools, churches, and communities over the next decade. At stake was the future of the American economy.

* * *

Labor, particularly the CIO, had an aggressive political program for postwar reconstruction. With liberal Democrats and the support of the Truman administration, labor's legislative agenda included tax reform, expanded unemployment insurance, price controls, and a higher minimum wage. The legislative centerpiece of a liberal-labor vision of the postwar order, was the Full Employment Bill. Labor demanded that the government assure sufficient employment opportunities for all Americans through support of private investments and, if necessary, by government spending. Full employment was to be the opening wedge for postwar economic expansion and the Keynesian program of using government spending to guarantee prosperity and security.

Factions of the business community mobilized to either oppose or mediate the content of government-guaranteed full employment. To members of the NAM and local chambers of commerce, the bill epitomized the long slide toward state socialism. These business leaders denounced the Full Employment Bill and initiated a lobbying campaign against its passage.[3] Moderate businessmen, equally alarmed, responded in a more sophisticated manner. Adhering to a policy of providing positive guidance, the Business Advisory Council and the Committee for Economic Development disseminated reports on the employment issue that accepted the idea of a limited federal involvement in the economy but rejected compensatory government spending as the solution to unemployment. Moderates like, George M. Humphrey of the M. A. Hanna Company, Ralph Flanders, Paul Hoffman, and Chamber of Commerce President Eric Johnston, worked quietly behind the scenes to provide support for conservative Congressmen who sought to water down but not destroy the bill.[4]

Moderate business leaders enjoyed the most success. When the Employment Act passed in 1946, gone from the final version was the government commitment to full employment and the provisions for mandatory spending. What was left met the specifications of the CED perfectly. The act provided that the government should affirm an interest in maintaining maximum employment through the establishment of research machinery to evaluate the state of the economy. The responsibility for providing employment, however, would continue to reside in the private sector. It was, according to one Business Council activist a "pretty innocuous" bill.[5] Moderates had taken important first steps in shaping the limits of the debate over the role of the state.

If the employment act was a victory for the moderate arm of the business community, conservatives were more concerned about eliminating governmental price controls. The Office of Price Administration had been effective in stabilizing prices during the war, and at the war's end, many liberals joined with organized labor in strongly advocating continuance of the OPA to check inflation. Even the moderate businessmen associated with the CED, while acknowledging their dislike for economic controls in peacetime, stood in fear of the dangers of inflationary pressures generated by the war. Most quietly advocated renewal of the OPA on a temporary basis and gradual relaxation of controls.[6]

Destruction of the OPA became the rallying cry of laissez faire businessmen who chafed under OPA regulations. Its continuance during peacetime symbolized to them America's drift toward collectivism. In late 1945, with the aid of industrial and commercial trade associations, the NAM spearheaded a carefully planned lobbying campaign aimed both at the Congress, which was considering renewal of the agency, and at the public.[7] In a lobbying effort similar to the one conducted against the Full Employment Bill, yet more intense, the NAM and other business groups testified before congressional committees, pressured individual legislators, and the NAM spent over $3 milllion in 1946 to destroy the OPA. Half of that went to newspaper advertising. Full page advertisements directed toward consumers began: "Would you like some BUTTER or a ROAST of BEEF" and alleged that OPA controls had discouraged the production of butter and driven meat onto the black market. Cartoons aimed at educators and clergy warned that the OPA's "artificial prices" along with wasteful government spending and labor strife were the barriers blocking the typical American family from reaching prosperity.[8]

The NAM held a series of meetings with industrialists to whip up local enthusiasm for the drive against price controls. It also sent speakers to make hundreds of talks before civic organizations, women's clubs, and college students. NAM publications barraged over a hundred thousand school teachers, clergy, farm leaders, women's club directors, and over ten thousand weekly newspapers and columnists with anti-OPA statements.[9] "Take the wraps—wartime price controls— off peace production and there will be such an abundance of things to buy as America has never known" the NAM proclaimed. It promised that "if price controls are removed goods will then pour into the market, and then, within a reasonable time, prices will adjust themselves—naturally—as they always have—in line with the real worth of things." Yes, said the NAM, it supported price control but "price control by the American housewife, not by bureaucrats in Washington."[10]

Too late, organized labor mobilized to protect the wartime controls that were due to expire in June 1946. It joined in a liberal alliance of teachers, consumer groups, veterans, and civic organizations to stave off a "joy ride to disaster." A "March of Housewives" paraded into Washington in April 1946, and two thousand women representing consumer groups demonstrated outside the Capitol.[11] UAW president R. J. Thomas warned autoworkers that the removal of price controls threatened recently achieved wage increases. Thomas accused manufacturers of "conducting a strike which makes the labor strikes look puny by comparison. This strike is against the general public, and its objective is higher prices."[12]

Nevertheless, the conservative congressional coalition of Republicans and Southern Democrats gutted the OPA, and the NAM cheerfully took credit. Prices immediately jumped, some as much as 25 percent in two weeks. Labor newspapers acknowledged the effectiveness of the employer campaign, conceding that some of the public and even some trade unionists had fallen for the NAM's "big lie technique." A UAW local paper quoted the editor of a small Pennsylvania weekly: "When we saw that OPA was on the way out, we joined in the snake dance that was led by the National Association of Manufacturers and unwittingly swallowed the platitudes put out by that organization that the end of price control would increase production and lower costs." But, after several weeks of steadily rising prices, "we began to awaken to the fact that the NAM eyewash was irritating rather than soothing."[13]

The struggles against the Full Employment Act and price controls marked the resumption, on an even larger, more comprehensive scale, of the business community's campaign to undermine liberal and left-wing influence on American society, and to shift the political climate in a more conservative direction. The tenacity of liberal support for measures like price controls seemed to demonstrate that the conservative business community's worst fears about the lessons the public would take from the Depression and wartime experiences were not unfounded.[14] Despite these early legislative successes, an expanded role for the state and government guarantees of security for workers through mechanisms like deficit spending appeared to be highly popular. In October 1946, Westinghouse Electric Corporation vice president F. D. Newbury found "no clear demand by the American people, or program from the Washington Administration, for returning to the tested principles and practices of free private enterprise." Instead there were "strong pressures within the Administration to perpetuate as much planning and control as the people would accept."[15]

Conservative business leaders trying to mobilize the business community issued almost hysterical warnings that the American way of life was under attack. One business journal in 1947 found that the world was in "the throes of a cataclysmic conflict . . . the lines of the conflict are clearly drawn. The collectivist system on the one side, the capitalistic system on the other. A test for survival is in progress."[16] Leading the assault on business and the American way of life were trade unions assisted by the "pseudo-liberals, academic busy-bodies, columnists, 'enlightened' newspaper men, radio commentators and a galaxy of associated malcontents." Their "tirades" against free enterprise were not new, but the threat of communism overseas intensified the domestic danger.[17]

From every direction, employers found evidence of the effectiveness of the liberal-trade union indoctrination of the public. Despite industry's war production record, the business journal *Factory* warned that business was headed back into its prewar doghouse.[18] The public tended to be suspicious of industry, and it believed trade union "propaganda" about bloated corporate profits. *Public Relations News* found "incontrovertible" evidence that almost the entire public believed that corporate profits were from double to ten times their actual rate. In contrast, the labor movement "retains the public's good will—or at least its patient indulgence—in spite of stopping the public's trains, planes, boats, trolleys, elevators, and even turning off its lights." According to California businessman James L. Beebe, "the people of the United States have been fed and I think most of them have believed, that the state can provide jobs; that capitalism is on its way out; . . . and that it is the duty of the state to provide security (so-called) for all of its people."[19]

Opinion surveys seemed to substantiate Beebe's fears. *Factory's* 1946 survey found that 47 percent of factory workers thought that the government would do most in providing new peacetime jobs. Similarly, the Opinion Research Corporation discovered that over 70 percent of workers believed that the government should guarantee jobs. For some corporate leaders the most startling revelation in terms of the outlook for business growth and survival was a *Fortune* poll that showed less than half of those interviewed believed hard work would pay off. All these findings seemed to demonstrate a lack of confidence among the public in the free enterprise system.[20]

There were differences within the business community as to the perils facing capitalism. Most alarmist were the traditional conservatives associated with the NAM who had been finding evidence of a coming cataclysm since the days of the New Deal. Fred G. Clark of the American Economic Foundation, a conservative think tank founded in the thirties, asserted that businessmen from across the country agreed "that America is sitting on a volcano." Public relations experts, eager to promote their function in the corporate hierarchy, provided a steady stream of dire predictions to add to the anxieties of these business leaders. One public relations firm, for example, warned in 1947 that "our present economic system, and the men who run it, have three years—maybe five at the outside—to resell our so-far preferred way of life as against competing systems."[21]

Sophisticated moderates, who accepted a growing role for the government, were less likely to shout about America's drift toward statism. They turned for evidence to the findings of opinion pollster Elmo Roper who emphasized the fundamental belief of Americans in the values upon which the free enterprise system was based.[22] But even the leaders of the CED agreed that the business community needed to protect its reputation and ability to decisively influence America's political culture. Paul G. Hoffman argued that it was "high time that we devote time and thought in bringing about public understanding of the role of profits in a free economy."[23]

\* \* \*

In the battle to save the "American way of life," businessmen utilized a combination of attack and persuasion. After World War I, conservative business organizations had exploited public fears of radicalism as a means of attacking organized labor. Ongoing concerns about domestic subversion and the Soviet Union again provided business with the opportunity to utilize anticommunism as a weapon against liberals and labor. In late 1945, business organizations, like the Chamber of Commerce, allied with patriotic groups, such as the American Legion, initiated a propaganda campaign against communism in government and in the labor movement. Warnings of Communist infiltration of American institutions helped foster an atmosphere of intolerance.[24] Symptomatic of their success in changing the political climate was the firing during 1946 (as the result of pressure from business sponsors) of dozens of liberal radio broadcasters. These sponsors also pressured other reporters to "tone down" news sympathetic to organized labor, Russia, or liberal causes.[25]

The flipside of the battle against radicalism was the promotion of an ultrapatriotism. If international communism and domestic subversion threatened American values, what was needed, according to Advertising Council Director Thomas D'Arcy Brophy, was a patriotic campaign that "would help by attacking the root of the evil, which is the loss of faith in our traditions. And it would help by selling the rewards still open to us individually and collectively, if we are willing to put American grit and sweat into our jobs." Such concerns led the business community to sponsor educational-patriotic programs like the Freedom Train, a red, white, and blue train that carried a cargo of historic documents to communities throughout the country. Beginning in 1947, the train emphasized individual rights and freedom from coercion, a subtle attack on the values promoted by liberals and trade unionists.[26]

In Detroit, the campaign to associate patriotism with antiunionism was less subtle. "An American's Pledge of Loyalty" regularly broadcast in 1947 and 1948 over a Detroit radio station, implied that patriotic workers owed their allegiance to more than their flag and country. It read, "I pledge devotion to God and the brotherhood His word proclaims: I offer loyalty to the United Nations and the world order it is maintaining; I vow to defend America and the opportunities it contains; I promise to give my best to America and American Industry and the homes it sustains." UAW Local 600 caustically noted that such sentiments implied that my country right or wrong had become my employer right or wrong. They sarcastically asked workers: "Did you give your best to American industry today."[27]

The business campaign to sell patriotism merged into an equally fervent, if even more intense, campaign of persuasion to sell Americans on the benefits of capitalism. Employers believed in the importance of public opinion. If the public held industry in low esteem, it was because of a general misunderstanding fostered by organized labor through its denunciation of exorbitant corporate profits.[28]

Between 1945 and 1947, new organizations emerged, with the purpose of aiding the business community in restoring "American" values. Among them were the Foundation for Economic Education, formed in 1946; the Industrial Information Institute, established in 1947; the American Heritage Foundation, organized in 1947 to sponsor the Freedom Train; and the Advertising Council, reorganized in 1945 from a wartime agency. Ostensibly nonpartisan, these groups cooperated with such older opponents of New Deal liberalism as the Tax Foundation and the American Economic Foundation. Financial support came from the largest manufacturing corporations and combined firms with ultraconservative outlooks (the Du Pont Company, Sun Oil, and Republic Steel) with others at the somewhat less conservative end of the business political spectrum, such as Ford and U.S. Steel.[29]

There was variety in the messages emanating from these organizations and from individual companies. The most conservative, like the Foundation for Economic Education, emphasized absolute protection of its version of America's freedom, particularly economic freedom. Those representing the more moderate wing of the business community, like the Advertising Council, recognized labor's right to free collective bargaining and acknowledged the necessity of government involvement in economic affairs where private interests proved inadequate. But, there were certain themes common to almost all the business efforts at mass persuasion. Among them were the importance of individual initiative and opportunity, the role of competition, and the necessity for profits. An N. W. Ayer & Son advertisement, for example, linked profits to "the same purposes as the wages a husband brings home Fridays," showing the relationship of profits to investment and the growth of the American economy.[30]

Finally, business groups hammered home the idea that a growing economy depended upon expanding productivity through the application of increased mechanization, power, and efficiency. In 1947, the business journal *Factory* warned that workers "led by mistaken, overzealous, or ignorant prophets, can price themselves out of jobs, and industry along with them out of markets," unless they gave the "cooperation necessary for the production job that must be done." In 1948, a Warner & Swasey advertisement asserted, "It's just that simple: if you want lower prices, a steady job, and more pay, you start with more efficient production. And there's *no other way.*"[31]

At the forefront of the effort to shape public dialogue was the National Association of Manufacturers. At the end of the war, the NAM gave top priority to expanding and intensifying its long-established public relations campaign against what it called collectivism. It asserted that the "battle between the advocates of collectivism and those who believe in freedom and opportunity" had been rejoined after the armistice imposed by all-out war. The NAM believed it had to work quickly, contending that New Deal liberals and the CIO were preparing the American people for a "revolutionary change in the nation's economy." The strike wave, price controls, high taxes, deficit spending, and the "fallacious" principle of ability to pay as a factor in fixing wage scales constituted a "master plan to remake America."[32] In 1946–47, the NAM countered with a multimillion dollar war chest to sell the free enterprise story and to promote the campaigns as opposing the Full Employment Bill and price controls. Financial support from the membership increased each year after the war. While six thousand of the sixteen thousand members of the NAM contributed to its public relations fund in 1946, over eleven thousand contributed the following year.[33]

The NAM revamped its public relations program by hiring the Opinion Research Corporation to field-test potential advertisements for their ability to convey an idea and enlist sympathetic consideration. Members and advertising experts had criticized earlier NAM publicity for being too easily subverted and used by labor to label industry as selfish and greedy.[34] "The story of business economics and philosophy needs to be told," declared NAM vice president for public relations Holcombe Parkes, "simply, understandably, repetitiously and without dilution or distortion—to broad masses of the people." Accordingly, it issued a constant stream of paid advertisements, news releases, speeches, posters, leaflets, and magazines. In 1947, the Industrial Press Service sent free material to 7,500 country papers and 2,500 company journals, while the organization's literature department distributed over 2 million pamphlets. Focusing on the four roadblocks to prosperity—price controls, labor relations, government spending, and taxes—the NAM bought ads in 265 daily papers and 1,876 small-town papers.

Similarly, it ran ads explaining profits in popular magazines like *Harper's* and *Saturday Evening Post.* A typical NAM ad illustrated the role profits played in industry, asserting that business's modest profits paid for the "expansion and improvement that bring more production, more and better jobs, lower prices and greater security for all." Half of the NAM $2.5 million public relations budget in 1947 went to national advertising and publicity. NAM ads spoke to the public's concern over economic security. One ad, for instance, featured Joe Vaughn who ran a food store in High Point, North Carolina. Vaughn wondered if "business firms, today aren't making too much profit." The NAM pointed out that industry profits were much less than the public believed and explained the vital role profits played in the "development and progress that produces more goods, more jobs, and greater security for all." Complementary efforts of other trade organizations to explain the workings of the American economic system gave NAM's program even broader exposure.[35]

The NAM supplemented its written appeals with copy on other media. Its representatives regularly made personal contacts with radio network officers, local station managers, and program directors and it distributed "Briefs for Broadcasters" to a thousand radio commentators. In 1946 it sought, recruited, and trained a staff of full-time radio debaters for participation in the popular forum-style programs like Town Hall, complaining that busy and ill-prepared industrialists had not been particularly effective against opponents "trained in public brawling, armed to the hilt with facts and figures, and bug-eyed with zeal for the Leftist side of any debate."[36] Beginning in 1947, The NAM sought even greater control, sponsoring a radio series, "Your Business Reporter," which reached 3 million homes. Moreover, the organization expanded its motion picture service to develop a wider audience before groups of employees, club members, educators, and students. By 1948, attendance at NAM films had reached over 2.5 million people a year. Films like "American Anniversary" and "Your Town—A Story of America" demonstrated the interrelationship of American freedoms, the value of individual initiative, and the dependence of the community on the industrial payroll. "American Anniversary," for instance, told the story of Joe Karnak, a young immigrant, who, by learning to appreciate the "many freedoms and opportunities America offers," rose to local prominence and affluence.[37]

The barrage of business messages promised to deliver immediate political gains. In the 1946 congressional elections, Republicans seemed poised for victory. Employers viewed this opportunity as evidence of widespread acceptance of their message that liberal government and organized labor were to blame for the constant industrial strife, galloping inflation, and scarcity of consumer goods that frustrated the American public. Exploiting that frustration, Republicans campaigned on the issues of curbing union power and the excesses of federal authority, repeatedly asking, "Had Enough?" Conservative businessmen supported Republicans who linked labor disturbances to the "international Communist conspiracy." The Chamber of Commerce even released a report entitled "Communist Infiltration in the United States" at the height of the campaign. Meanwhile, in cities like Milwaukee, division within the labor movement over communism helped undercut labor's political power.[38]

When Republicans swept to a majority in both branches of Congress for the first time since 1928, the NAM interpreted the triumph as a sign that the public was "tired of government regimentation and boot-strap economics." The mandate, according to the NAM, was that our way of life is better than any other system in the world." To Charles E. Wilson of General Motors the election meant that "America has chosen the fork in the road that leads to freedom and personal liberty," away from government planning, unbalanced budgets, and "organized unemployment."[39]

Conservative political resurgence combined with an apparent decline in labor's public esteem to give the business community a decided edge in management's emerging strategy to restore its lost authority and roll back union power. The NAM figured prominently in this first step toward a successful "recovery of the initiative" in labor relations. To change its greedy image, the NAM abandoned the demand for industrial self-rule, laissez faire, and the repeal of the Wagner Act. Instead, it publicly acknowledged workers' rights to engage in collective bargaining, but called for changes in public policy that would enable the state to intervene on behalf of employers. At a time when a small minority of liberal businessmen were pursuing union-management accommodation, most, even in the moderate camp, joined the NAM conservatives in promoting a strategy of "realism." This was the strategy adopted by General Motors in the late thirties. It entailed reluctant acceptance of the principle of unionism while actively attempting to weaken or contain labor power. By early 1946, it was clear to sociologist Robert Lynd that in labor relations, liberal and conservative businessmen had become "brothers under the skin."[40]

The first part of this multipronged attack on labor involved "the confinement and gradual reduction" of the scope of collective bargaining and union influence within the factory. This effort had begun toward the end of the war and intensified during reconversion, with the auto companies setting the trend during the 1945–46 bargaining round. Determined to save "our American system and keep it from evolving into an alien form imported from east of the Rhine," General Motors refused to negotiate with Walter Reuther over corporate investment and pricing policy. Moreover, it provoked a work stoppage rather than capitulate to labor's attempt to expand the scope of collective bargaining into the realm of management decision making. Henceforth, bargaining would be limited to wages, hours, and working conditions.[41] Similarly, seeking improved control, stability and predictability, Ford Motor Company won freedom to maximize production and security against unauthorized strikes. By late 1946, management had learned to make collective bargaining "a two-sided proposition" forcing unions to "recognize the rights of management and the obligations of employees and union officials."[42]

The second part of curbing union power involved revision of the Wagner Act. The NAM, together with such organizations as the Business Advisory Council, developed a set of legislative proposals that reflected the emerging business consensus on labor. The NAM argued that the business program was not punitive but was designed to make collective bargaining work in the public interest.[43] Under the Wagner Act, former NAM president H. W. Prentis argued, unions had gained unlimited monopoly power without any legal responsibility. They intimidated their members and the public through mass picketing, boycotting, and violence, and crippled the country's economic progress through restrictive practices that undermined productivity. Even more fundamentally troubling to Prentis was the "ominous rise of class consciousness, engendered by legalized labor union activity."[44] The "House of Labor," intoned Detroit manufacturer Frank Rising, had become "a nuisance in the neighborhood."[45] What business spokesmen demanded was legislation that would bring balance between labor and management. The failure to protect employees and the public from unions resulted in ever increasing levels of industrial strife.

Beginning in February 1946, the NAM aired its proposals to protect employees by guaranteeing employer free speech, prohibiting union security clauses that interfered with the right to work, and regulating internal affairs of unions. The proposals guarded the public rights by regulating strikes that threatened the nation's safety and by outlawing sympathetic and jurisdictional strikes as well as secondary boycotts. In addition, requirement of proof that union officers were not communists would help rid the labor movement of subversive influence, while bans against union contributions to federal political campaigns would limit organized labor's political power. Finally, the exclusion of foremen from collective bargaining would provide safeguards for the rights of management and help offset the union challenge to managerial prerogatives.[46]

In the spring of 1947, the conservative business community threw its full strength behind the Taft-Hartley Bill, the labor reform legislation that came out of the Republican-dominated Eightieth Congress. Industrialists combined an intense lobbying campaign in Washington with a commitment to obtaining public support through its newly expanded public relations mechanisms. The NAM alone spent over $3 million in the public relations drive that featured full-page ads in 287 daily papers in 193 key industrial centers. Always, employers couched their arguments for labor reform constructively, "in the public interest."[47]

A compliant press aided business in mobilizing public opinion. The weekly *Quincy Record* of Illinois, for example, engaged in a blitz of pro–Taft-Hartley coverage, reprinting the bi-weekly talks of Henry J. Taylor, the General Motors sponsored radio commentator. Playing on public fears of radicalism, Taylor labeled opponents of labor reform as Communist fellow-travelers who weakened America by "hamstringing our individual effort through lopsided labor law . . . through sponsoring false economic doctrines that can bust us, along with political action dedicated to tying up management so that it cannot possibly manage." The newspaper added that Taft-Hartley was not antilabor. If workers would only look beyond their narrow class interests, they would see that the legislation would fight inflation by lifting arbitrary union rules "which exploit the worker in his other role as a customer of goods and services." Arguments such as these flooded the newspapers and airways. In June 1947 conservatives and the business community celebrated victory when Congress passed the Taft-Hartley Act over a presidential veto.[48]

\* \* \*

The labor movement did not just surrender before this managerial onslaught. Its defense centered on two strategies. First, trade unionists, the labor press, and their allies tried to counter employer propaganda efforts. In late 1947, for example, Senator Harley Kilgore blasted the NAM before the Senate. He exposed the various techniques used by the organization to "soften up the country," and denounced its role in killing price controls, wrecking the Wagner Act, and attempting to "emasculate" the wage and hour law.[49] Similarly, labor papers warned workers that business was funding "a vast outpouring of propaganda" designed "to convince the American people that labor is a 'monopoly' and that its organizations should be weakened to give business an even break." Indiana State CIO president Neal Edwards, sent letters to the membership seeking their help with "our efforts to expose the NAM for what it is, . . . industrialists organized for the sole purpose of protecting their profit-bursting pocketbooks." Labor papers joined in the exposé with cartoons lampooning the NAM's propaganda campaign. The employers' organization was invariably represented as an overweight man in a top hat, who through the judicious use of money, controlled a compliant Congress.[50]

Particularly alarming were the seemingly nonpartisan campaigns to sell free enterprise. While the Advertising Council's campaign was in its planning stages in early 1948, the labor press pointed out that the project was an "audacious billion-dollar plan" designed to "sell the American people on the virtues of big business." Trade unionists chortled with glee when Marshall Adams, a director of the Association of National Advertisers, denounced the campaign, which boiled "down to an effort to cover up the evils of the private enterprise system and to propagandize against changes to improve that system." Similarly, the Railway workers journal, *Labor*, ridiculed these efforts: What is wrong with free enterprise, the paper asked, if "after having its own way all these years, it must now be 'sold' in this lavish way?"[51]

Trade unionists asserted that the class nature of mass communications prevented fair coverage. *The CIO News* charged that most daily newspapers and radio stations had close ties to an interlocking web of large corporations. It was only natural that the press would follow a policy of "damming labor at every opportunity while carefully glossing over the sins of the banking and industrial magnates who really control the nation."[52] In 1946, the Greater Buffalo Industrial Union Council, infuriated at the "anti-labor" and "anti-CIO" coverage of the *Buffalo Evening News,* resolved to expose the paper's intent to destroy the public's civil liberties and legal rights.[53] Similarly, Pennsylvania unionists warned members against newscasters like Fulton Lewis, Jr., a propagandist in the employ of the NAM and the Republican party. UAW foundry worker Leroy Krawford, cautioning workers against the antilabor Detroit newspapers, simply urged: "Believe only our union press and radio hookup which is paid for by you and staged by you to tell you the score."[54]

"Watch out," organized labor also told its members, for those "phony" opinion polls that provide ammunition to employers. A 1947 Opinion Research Corporation poll, for instance, apparently showed that while most workers opposed the Taft-Hartley Act, they supported ten of the most important provisions of the act when presented separately. These findings were publicized in a *Look Magazine* article, in corporate-sponsored full-page advertisements, and among factory employees and editorial writers. *Labor and Nation* charged that this poll was simply "planned confusion."[55]

In an effort to undercut the political uses of these polls in 1948, the Building Services Employees Union engaged pollster Robert C. Myers who reported that "much of the polling reported in today's newspapers and magazines is unscientific, biased, and slipshod." Meanwhile, the AFL accused pollsters of the "worst kind of fraud. They are big business organizations which are used to influence rather than measure public opinion." Trade unionists also pointed to sociologist Arthur Kornhauser's 1946 study of major public-opinion polling agencies, which found that the questions on labor were biased toward a management point of view. Not surprisingly, since polling was a profit-making enterprise, according to the *Pennsylvania Labor News,* procorporation pollsters were featured speakers at a NAM public relations conference.[56]

The second part of the labor union defense against business aggressiveness involved publicizing the union point of view. In general, however, unions reacted to an agenda set by the business community. A great deal of effort, for example, went into refuting employer calls for higher productivity. Walter Reuther declared that the employer propaganda campaign on productivity was an "effort by management to swell already scandalously high profits by sweating still more profits out of workers."[57]

Even more union literature sought to disprove employer charges that wage increases led to inflation. Following Keynesian reasoning, the CIO argued that rather than harming the economy, wage increases were necessary to sustain mass purchasing power and prevent a depression. In 1946, it widely publicized the Nathan Report, which demonstrated that wages could be increased 38 percent without price increases and without affecting profit levels.[58] The CIO asserted that inflation actually came from shortages manufactured by employers to drive up prices and profits. To prove this, labor papers constantly charted increases in corporate profits in articles like one published in the *United Automobile Worker* entitled "Golden Goose Hangs High, Profit Orgy Paves Way to Depression."[59]

Unions did not have the means to offset biased newspapers nor could they compete with business groups in purchasing extensive newspaper advertising. Consequently, the labor movement looked increasingly toward radio as a means of gaining support for union programs. In 1939, the National Association of Broadcasters had adopted a code that prohibited the discussion of controversial issues except for political broadcasts on the radio. Many radio stations used the code to effectively bar unions from the airways while providing time to business groups. Succumbing to pressure from the AFL and the CIO, however, ABC began providing airtime in 1945 to the CIO's weekly program, "Labor-U.S.A."[60] The program used music, stories, and interviews as "a good antidote to the antistrike poison you get from newspapers and from many radio commentators." Surprisingly, *Variety* reviewed competing business and labor radio programs and found that "'Labor' is warm, ingratiating, and human," while the "exact antonyms characterize the 'business's pitch.'" When the "voice of ex-NAM president Ira Mosher was pitted against Tom Glaser singing a ballad like 'Money in the Pocket,'" it was impossible to "expect anyone to cheer for the NAM."[61]

To gain greater exposure, the CIO asked affiliates to urge their local radio stations to broadcast the program as well as a second network program sponsored by CBS, "Cross-Section—CIO." In January 1948, the CIO even tried to broaden its appeal, producing the first weekly labor quiz show. "It's in the Family" featured two rank-and-file families competing for a savings bond by answering questions about labor, the CIO, and current events.[62]

As the antilabor assault intensified, unions began to aggressively challenge the coverage of labor on commercially owned stations. In

1946, the UAW petitioned the FCC for a hearing on censorship, charging that a Cincinnati station had refused to broadcast a program by the Catholic church regarding its position on organized labor. When commentator H. V. Kaltenborn "beat his gums too freely one night about the Allis-Chalmers strikers," the local drew upon the fairness doctrine to force NBC to give it time on his program to "speak the truth." Two years later, the Geneva Federation of Labor, incensed at Fulton Lewis, Jr.'s attacks on social security and the labor movement, tried to drive him off the air by boycotting his local sponsor, the Geneva Federal Loan.[63]

The trade union public relations efforts, however, lacked the resources and the sophistication of the business community's free enterprise campaign. Of the national unions, the UAW and the United Electrical Workers were perhaps the most active. The class-oriented nature of the left-wing UE program partially backfired, however, for it provided fuel to business claims of Communist indoctrination of the working class. The UE's activities included the establishment of the first union weekly news broadcast, the distribution of a modest amount of literature, including a guide to community action and pamphlets directed at the public schools, and the production and distribution of motion pictures. The business journal, *Public Relations News*, characterized "Deadline for Action," the UE's first picture, as an "exceptionally well made and compelling movie which *castigates business and industry as a gang of profiteers, war mongers and slave drivers.*" The film became almost as popular among businessmen as among workers as business groups bought copies to demonstrate the dangers facing America.[64]

The struggle against the passage of Taft-Hartley revealed the limitation of union persuasion. In early 1947, unions lobbied furiously in Washington, organized a massive letter writing campaign, and held huge public protest rallies against the specter of antilabor legislation. The CIO promoted a publicity campaign entitled "Defend Labor Month" in an effort to mobilize local communities against the legislation. CIO publicity director, Len DeCaux, urging affiliates to obtain radio time to present labor's position, distributed radio spot announcements and scripts for speeches and interviews.[65] Emulating the NAM, the AFL ran five advertisements in one hundred leading newspapers warning, "Don't be a NAM fool." Appealing to antiradical sentiments, the AFL contended that "by prohibiting free bargaining among free men," Taft-Hartley "would wreck our nation's position as the defender of democracy and the champion of freedom in the fight to halt further expansion of Communism." In the last weeks of the campaign, the AFL topped off its written appeals with a daily soap opera that began, "Lady, down in Washington they're trying to push through a slave-labor bill that will slice your husband's envelope right down the middle," and with weekly variety shows featuring such popular stars as Milton Berle and Jimmy Durante.[66]

Despite labor's efforts, the Taft-Hartley Bill became law. The business community seemingly had helped shape public opinion more effectively than the unions. According to one commentator, "the words 'radical labor leaders' have been linked together in people's minds as ineradicably as the phrase, 'damn yankees,' is in Georgia."[67] Similarly, local UAW leaders found that thousands of their fellow workers had "been stampeded into making grave mistakes due to the vast propaganda arms of the corporations." Critics charged that labor's effort had been too little, too late. The liberal journal *Labor and Nation* argued that the crucial period of political maneuvering before the introduction of the Taft-Hartley Act was distinguished "by a general passivity on the part of labor."[68] Only at the very last minute did unions actively resist the congressional drive, and then their campaign was not effectively organized. Moreover, the split in the house of labor between the AFL and CIO meant unions never "united in a positive statement of aims" while industry presented a well-coordinated front.[69]

The passage of the Taft-Hartley Act and the success of conservative initiatives during the Eightieth Congress seemed to bode well for the Republican party and their business supporters as they approached the 1948 election. The splintering of the Democratic party with the emergence of two third-party candidates, combined with the nomination of the unpopular Harry Truman, also added strength to the predicted guarantee of a Republican victory.[70]

The Taft-Hartley Act, however, had galvanized the labor movement against the "reactionary" Eightieth Congress. In January 1948, CIO Secretary-Treasurer Emil Mazey sounded the clarion for action. Declaring that gains achieved on the picket line could be easily erased by political action, he asserted: "Organized labor must not and will not take these political and legislative defeats standing still. Organized labor must develop new and more effective political weapons, not only to repeal vicious antilabor legislation, but to remove from office those lackeys of big business responsible for its passage."[71]

More effective political action entailed the AFL's formation of Labor's League for Political Education and its formal participation for the first time in a presidential campaign. Wedded to the emerging anticommunist liberalism, the CIO rejected Henry Wallace's Progressive third-party candidacy and joined in an alliance with Truman, who had mended his fences with labor by vetoing the Taft-Hartley Act. The alliance with the Democrats was so intense that in some states, like Michigan, the CIO's Political Action Committee actually took over the party.[72]

The PAC broadened its appeal for the 1948 campaign, carefully divorcing unions from communism and emphasizing that labor's objectives were "shared by the overwhelming majority of Americans." These included guaranteed full employment, adequate housing, health care, education, social security, and the assurance of full political rights and equal economic opportunities for all "men and women in our country of every race, creed or color."[73] But more important was labor's need to overcome rank-and-file apathy and get out the labor vote. Low turnout by workers frustrated with Truman had been a decisive factor in the 1946 defeat. Unions distributed literature, sponsored radio programs, and fielded an army of precinct workers to avoid repeating their mistakes in 1948.[74] Another key was setting aside the bitter struggle between the AFL and CIO. In Massachusetts, for instance, faced with three "vicious anti-labor referenda," the AFL, the CIO, and the liberal organization, the Americans for Democratic Action, formed a "historic pact" to overcome the disunity in the ranks of organized labor that had contributed to the 1946 "debacle."[75]

Truman in turn appealed for working-class support by conducting a slashing antibusiness campaign. He charged that the Republican party was in the hands of big business. Speaking before a group of farmers, he accused those Wall Street "gluttons of privilege" of attacking the structure of agricultural price supports. Truman also warned that collectivism was not the only threat to the American way of life; "powerful reactionaries were also silently undermining our democratic institutions." Behind these forces were men "who are striving to concentrate great economic power in their own hands." These men controlled the Republican party, which recently had delivered gains to the private power, big oil, railroad, and real estate lobbies. Wrapping himself around the image of the New Deal, Truman reminded the public that in 1933, it was the Democratic party that "drove the money-changers out of the temple and brought new life to our democracy."[76]

In one of the sharpest class votes in American history, Truman won an unexpected victory over Thomas Dewey, his Republican opponent, and the Democrats regained control of Congress. Labor played a special part in that victory. Massachusetts CIO President J. William Belanger, who headed the coalition that helped defeat that state's anti-labor referenda, concluded that organized labor united with liberal forces, had overcome the power of "selfish wealth." Despite, the "great powers of their minion press, the persuasive voices of their radio hirelings, the inaccurate minds of the political pollsters," Belanger continued, "the sound and patriotic common sense of the little men and women" had triumphed. Trade unionists celebrated the victory as a call for the extension of the New Deal. According to a Pennsylvania labor paper, the election "delivered a mandate for free labor unions, for extended social security, for increased education opportunity for all Americans, for civil rights for all, for the end to dangerous profits and for control of inflation."[77]

* * *

The results of the 1948 election stunned the business community. It indicated the tenuous hold conservatives had over the public. Business ideologues apparently had not convinced voters that freedom from "government paternalism" was more important than the economic security promoted by both labor and the Democratic party. Indeed, Truman had campaigned effectively for the repeal of the Taft-Hartley Act, the restoration of price controls to protect earnings, and the expansion of government spending. To a shaken business community, it was not inconceivable that many of their achievements would be lost. General Foods Vice President Thomas G. Spates, observed that "when the smoke of last November's election had cleared away there was revealed a . . . rededication to the policy of achieving the more abundant life through more taxes, more spending, more controls and less liberty, and a clear declaration that the government should stand for the welfare of the people."[78]

Moreover, the critical role of labor in the campaign convinced Spates and other businessmen that unions were even more politically powerful than they had feared. *Business Week* editor Merlyn Pitzler warned a United States Chamber of Commerce gathering that the passage of the Taft-Hartley Act had "committed the unions to political activity on a scale and at a pace never before approached." The Taft-Hartley Act, designed in part to weaken labor politically, had seemingly backfired.[79]

What then, asked businessmen, was the lesson to be learned from the 1948 election? Was it impossible for the business community to sell its values and its world view to the American public? "No," thundered speaker William McMillen to the December 1948 convention of the National Association of Manufacturers. The election showed that "you just haven't done enough of what you have been doing." Businessmen, McMillen demanded, must intensify their efforts "to convince those Americans who are confused that the road to statism, tyranny, and slavery is paved with good intentions and lighted with great 'welfare' schemes." Freedom, indivisible and unimpaired, he continued, was "the only fertilizer of well-being," and "teamwork based on mutual understanding is the only guarantee of either individual or collective happiness." Thomas G. Spates added urgency to McMillen's call for a renewed commitment from the business community; time was short, he declared, but there still was "a fighting chance" to save "this nation as a democracy."[80]

Both moderate and conservative business organizations vowed to redouble their efforts. The first major campaign, emanating from the moderate wing of the business community was already prepared. Fearful that ignorance of the benefits of the American economic system increased the public's susceptibility to Communist subversion, the Advertising Council had started planning an economic education campaign as early as 1947. The Council's Industries Advisory Committee, led by General Foods and General Electric donations of $100,000, spearheaded fund-raising. Other substantial donors included General Motors, Johnson and Johnson, Procter and Gamble, Goodrich, Republic Steel, and Remington Rand, while four advertising agencies volunteered their services to create the campaign.

The Advertising Council's message stressed the need for free enterprise to expand productivity through mechanization and increased efficiency. For six months, beginning one week after the 1948 elections, radio spots barraged the public, and the four major networks pledged half-hour special programs on economic education. By 1950, the Council had placed before the public over 13 million lines of newspaper advertising, over 600 pages of magazine ads, 300,000 car cards, 8,000 billboards and 1.5 million pamphlets extolling the virtues of capitalism. Corporations ran Advertising Council–approved ads during the campaign. One Republic Steel advertisement, for instance, showed three men attacking a piano. It acknowledged that while the American way wasn't perfect, it beat "anything that any other country in the world has to offer." To help "tune it up" rather than "chop it down," Republic Steel called upon readers to vow to "work more effectively every hour I am on the job" and to send away for a free booklet entitled, "The Miracle of America." In it, Uncle Sam explained "Why Americans live better," "How machines make jobs," and "Why freedom and security go together." *Look, Opportunity,* and forty-one company publications either reprinted or summarized the pamphlet. Even the publisher of *Junior Scholastic* magazine incorporated the complete "Miracle of America," in its March 1950 issue, making it the "main subject of discussion" in fifteen thousand junior and senior high schools.[81]

Moderate business leaders were not alone. The NAM was joined by several trade associations, including the American Petroleum Institute, the National Association of Electric Power Companies and the American Medical Association, in an effort to derail Fair Deal programs on such issues as natural resources, public power, and health care. J. Warren Kinsman, chairman of the NAM's Public Relations Advisory Committee and vice president of Du Pont, reminded businessmen that "in the everlasting battle for the minds of men" the tools of public relations were the only weapons "powerful enough to arouse public opinion sufficiently to check the steady, insidious and current drift toward Socialism."[82]

In part, the business effort relied on intensifying earlier efforts. The NAM, for instance, increased its production of pamphlets from 2.5 million in 1948 to 6.5 million in 1949, to nearly 8 million in 1950. It also began new initiatives, including a new $1.5 million radio program featuring singers and interviews with business leaders. In 1950, the NAM turned to television, launching a weekly program, "Industry on Parade," which showcased companies, explained how products were made, and demonstrated what industry gave to individuals, communities, and the nation. Adopting a more subtle approach than its radio programming, the goal was to make industry "the symbol of progress and hope for the majority of people." The program had an immediate impact. In early 1952, Oklahoma City reported that the series ranked among the first five programs in popularity, and Milwaukee gave "Industry on Parade" a higher audience rating than "Meet the Press," telecast in the same time segment.[83]

Corporations as well as the NAM saw advantages in movies and television. Since the thirties, companies like Ford, Du Pont, U.S. Steel, and Firestone had sponsored highly prestigious classical music and serious drama programs designed both to improve the corporate image and to promote ideas. Ford, for example, laced its "Ford Sunday Evening Hour" with attacks on New Deal programs and government interference in business. In the late forties and fifties, corporations shifted this kind of programming into television. The Bohn Aluminum and Brass Corporation's NBC program, for instance, regularly warned the public about the dangers of "Socialistic schemes" that looked safe but in reality were a "deadly poison" that limited "individual rights and freedom." Other firms dramatically expanded their production and distribution of movies to clubs, schools, churches, and theaters as well as to television. These movies ranged from simple company promotions to sophisticated attacks on what business viewed as a growing socialistic economy. By late 1951, business-sponsored movies reached an audience of 20 million people every week, more than one-third of the nation's weekly attendance at commercial movies. That represented a 30 percent larger audience than in 1950 and a 500 percent increase since 1946.[84]

Corporations also sought more personal contact by creating a nationwide legion of articulate business spokespersons. In 1949, a joint committee of the Association of National Advertisers and the American Association of Advertising Agencies instituted "Freedom Forums," which were held on a regular basis at Harding College in Arkansas. At the first meeting, over 100 industrialists from companies like Armco, J. I. Case, General Electric, General Mills, Kohler, Quaker Oats, and Chrysler sat through "long sessions of indoctrination in the fundamentals of our economic system." They discussed "the most effective channels of communication needed to give an understanding of America to those who are confused or apathetic," and left "determined to interpret the system in understandable terms to both management and labor."[85]

Although unions continued the activities that had worked so well in the 1948 election, domestic and foreign policy events combined to help create a more receptive audience for business, inexorably shifting the political center of gravity from liberalism. Anticommunism rapidly became the primary political motif. Between 1948 and 1950, Communist revolution in China, Soviet development of the atomic bomb, espionage cases, and McCarthy's accusations of Communist infiltration of the government created an atmosphere of crisis and tension. With the outbreak of the Korean war, Truman, who had met stiff resistance to the expansion of the welfare state from a coalition of southern Democrats and Republicans, sacrificed what was left of the Fair Deal on the altar of anticommunism. All this and the renewed inflation touched off by the war lent credibility to the business warning that something was fundamentally wrong with America.[86]

Contributing to the nation's drift to the right was labor's own internal anticommunism. In 1949, after years of struggle between left and right, the CIO expelled eleven allegedly Communist-controlled unions. An internecine battle ensued that crippled the unions of the electrical and farm equipment workers among others. The feuds and anti-Communist purges also played a role in the collapse of "Opera-

tion Dixie," the CIO's Southern organizing drive. Within the broader context of Southern racism and antiunionism, the CIO internal
struggle over communism and the continuing rivalry between the AFL
and the CIO ensured the failure of any significant organizing in the
South.[87]

In this political atmosphere, labor began to narrow its political
vision. Labor's hopes for a sweeping expansion of the welfare state
and for the repeal of Taft-Hartley receded but was not totally abandoned. Unions, for instance, promoted a national health care program long after other elements of liberalism had given up on the issue. Still, unable to immediately achieve security for all workers
through politics, CIO unions pushed for worker security through collective bargaining. In 1949 and 1950, unions like the UAW and the
Steelworkers achieved significant victories on the issues of wages and
fringe benefits. But they also conceded much to the employer drive
to increase productivity at the expense of union rights on the shop
floor.[88]

The 1950 elections revealed just how much American politics had
changed. In Maryland, California, North Carolina, and elsewhere,
Republicans rode the issue of anticommunism to victory. In Ohio,
the struggle was even more clearly one of business against labor. In
late 1949, the business journal *Factory* had warned that unions
planned to punish those politicians who had opposed Fair Deal legislation; 1950, it opined, "promises to be a year of decision of American industry." Only through collective action, and "by molding the
opinions of large groups" could business prevail. Top on labor's list
of enemies was Robert Taft, leader of the conservative branch of the
Republican party and coauthor of the Taft-Hartley Bill. Business leaders rallied around Taft, who successfully appealed to rank-and-file
workers. Wage earners, according to political analyst Samuel Lubell,
supported Taft's candidacy to voice a protest against being told how
to vote by national union leaders and because they bought the Republican argument that a PAC victory implied that labor was "running the country."[89]

Determined that the conservative cause should not lose momentum as it had after the 1946 election, business leaders moved to select a Republican candidate who could win in 1952. Dwight Eisenhower seemed the perfect choice. A World War II hero, he had broad
popular appeal. Although, his political and economic ideas meshed
closely with the moderate wing of the business community, his concern over "the insidious inclination toward statism" made him acceptable to corporate conservatives. Moderate businessmen led by

Paul Hoffman of Studebaker, Thomas J. Watson of IBM, and Harry A. Bullis of General Mills helped mobilize the initial grass-roots support for Eisenhower's candidacy. Adlai Stevenson won the support of liberals and organized labor.[90]

The most heralded issues of the election were communism, corruption, and Korea. The business community, however, continued to stress the threat "Big Labor" and "Big Government" posed to American liberty and freedom. In late September 1952, NAM President William J. Grede charged that "dictatorial union bosses" sought to "establish in Washington a government which will be a Labor Government in *name*—as well as in fact." Business-sponsored advertisements in popular magazines inveighed against the dangers of government dictation asserting that the welfare state crushed freedom. One ad began, "THEY DON'T KEEP FEEDING YOU CHEESE AFTER THE TRAP IS SPRUNG," and cautioned that "to vote into office a welfare state is to 'find you have voted away your freedom.'"[91]

Eisenhower struck a responsive chord with the American public, winning in a landslide and carrying the Republicans to control of the House and Senate. For the first time in twenty years, friends of business dominated government in Washington. The business community joined in the victory celebration and looked forward to a more favorable political and economic climate. "Business," observed the journal *Steel,* was "no longer on the outside looking in." Contemplating the implications of the election, Henry Ford II wrote in the *Saturday Review:* "This is an opportunity that we in business must not fail to meet. For years we have talked glibly of the superiority of the American way and of our ability, if given the chance, to correct many of the evils which beset us and the other peoples of the world."[92]

\* \* \*

Over the next eight years with the Republican party at the presidential helm and with a government committed to working closely with the corporate sector, the business community counted significant political and economic victories. Initially, Eisenhower's failure to mount a campaign to dismantle the New Deal disappointed the most conservative business leaders, but they cheered as the administration successfully put brakes on further growth of the welfare state. Tax cuts in 1954, the abolishing of the Reconstruction Finance Corporation, the decline of antitrust activity, and the passage of legislation giving business access to oil-rich coastal lands all testified to the emergence of a more probusiness political climate.[93]

Business's national level ideological campaign to win the allegiance of Americans continued, if at a somewhat less intense level. The NAM, emphasized the importance of a continuing effort, pointing out that Eisenhower's election should be viewed more as a "reprieve than an acquittal from the Fair Deal." Similarly, a Warner and Swasey advertisement advised that "one day of feeling better doesn't mean you're cured . . . a relapse could kill us." To prevent such a relapse, Warner and Swasey, among other firms, continued sponsoring advertisements reminding the public that the "more abundant life" came not from government ownership of the means of production or from the welfare state but from the "opportunity for profit."[94]

In this environment, organized labor took a beating. Business succeeded in defeating efforts to revise Taft-Hartley, and the rulings of the Eisenhower-appointed National Labor Relations Board made the law more and more restrictive of unions. Violence associated with bitter strikes at Kohler in Wisconsin and Perfect Circle in Indiana demonstrated a growing recalcitrance among some employers and blackened the reputation of labor. So too did the findings of congressional probes during 1953, 1954, and 1955 on labor "racketeering, extortion, and gangsterism." Moreover, weakened by internecine struggles over communism and by its competition with the AFL, the CIO was faltering, leading conservative labor columnist Victor Riesel to predict in early 1954 that the "odds are that the CIO may not survive the year." Enough of the fire had been extinguished from the CIO's social unionism that in 1954 it began negotiating a merger with the AFL. Public opinion also appeared to be tilting away from labor. A *Look Magazine* survey found that three times as many Americans were concerned about the power of big labor as opposed to that of big business and two-thirds felt that unions were "getting out of hand."[95]

At the national political level, business had scored major victories. Still it worried about how much labor had already won. Through 1955, despite the CIO institutional troubles, the labor movement continued to grow and to win major collective bargaining concessions. Over the howls of much of the business community, the UAW won supplemental unemployment benefits for its members, taking the union a step closer toward its goal of a guaranteed annual wage.

At the same time, committed to contesting business domination of political discourse, labor maintained a strong national voice. The AFL's news and commentary program, featuring Frank Edwards, reached 7 million listeners a week over 176 stations. Its goal was to provide "intelligent interpretation of the news from the liberal point of view." Not to be overshadowed, in 1953, the CIO appropriated $1 million for a public relations program that featured a daily news commentary by John W. Vandercook and commercials promoting labor's political and economic vision. Broadcast over 150 stations, it offered an "additional liberal voice on the nation's airwaves" and sought to convince the public that labor was "not another public economic pressure group" but that it sought "solutions of the problems of all of the people."[96]

All this left many in the business community with a continuing sense of insecurity. Who knew what impact the proposed merger of the AFL and CIO might have on union power? Were workers genuinely willing to turn away from the security offered by an expanding welfare state? Certainly the business community took nothing for granted. Beneath the apparent business-dominated consensus of the 1950s much contention remained. To gain a better understanding of that contention, as well as the effort of both business and labor to shift political discourse, we need to move from the national level to the struggle that took place within communities and at worksites to define the meaning of Americanism.

## Notes

1. Robert S. Lynd, "We Should Be Clear as to What Are the Essentials and What are the Historic Trappings of Democracy," *L&N*, Feb.–Mar. 1946, pp. 34–35.

2. Robert S. Lynd, "Labor-Management Cooperation: How Far, to What End?" *L&N*, Jan.–Feb. 1948, pp. 36–38.

3. Nelson Lichtenstein, "From Corporatism to Collective Bargaining: Organized Labor and the Eclipse of Social Democracy in the Postwar Era," in *The Rise and Fall of the New Deal Order, 1930–1980*, ed. Steve Fraser and Gary Gerstle (Princeton: Princeton University Press, 1989), pp. 125–28; Robert M. Collins, *The Business Response to Keynes, 1929–1964* (New York: Columbia University Press, 1981), pp. 99–109.

4. Kim McQuaid, *Big Business and Presidential Power: From FDR to Reagan* (New York: William Morrow, 1982), pp. 131, 125–32.

5. McQuaid, *Big Business and Presidential Power*, pp. 130–32; Collins, *The Business Response to Keynes*, pp. 105–9.

6. Robert J. Donovan, *Conflict and Crisis: The Presidency of Harry S. Truman, 1945–1948* (New York: W. W. Norton, 1977), p. 198; "What Price Controls?" *Fortune*, May 1946, p. 100.

7. Joel Seidman, *American Labor from Defense to Reconversion* (Chicago: University of Chicago Press, 1953), pp. 94–96; Karl Schriftgeisser, *The Lobbyists: The Art and Business of Influencing Lawmakers* (Boston: Little, Brown, 1951), pp. 94–96.

8. Schriftgeisser, *The Lobbyists,* pp. 95–96; "The Shape of Things to Come," *Nation* 162 (May 11, 1946), 559; Seidman, *American Labor,* pp. 238–39.

9. *PLN,* Mar. 29, 1946; Schriftgeisser, *The Lobbyists,* pp. 94–96.

10. *Trends,* Mar. 1946, p. 8; "Renovation in N.A.M.," *Fortune,* July 1948, pp. 167–68.

11. Donovan, *Conflict and Crisis,* pp. 198–99; James Boylan, *The New Deal Coalition and the Election of 1946* (New York: Garland, 1981), pp. 55–63.

12. R. J. Thomas to the Presidents of all Local Unions, UAW-CIO, Feb. 28, 1946, Box 1, UAW Local 686 Records, Buffalo, N.Y., LMDC.

13. *New Era,* Reading, Pa., May 1, 1947; *FF,* Jan. 3, 1948; R. Alton Lee, *Truman and Taft-Hartley: A Question of Mandate* (Lexington: University of Kentucky Press, 1966), p. 16.

14. Millard C. Faught, "Its Your Story—You Tell It," *NB* (Journal of the United States Chamber of Commerce), Mar. 1947, pp. 47–49.

15. F. D. Newbury, "Wages and Productivity—The Problems Involved," AMA Personnel Series No. 103 (1946), p. 4.

16. "What the Surveys Show," *Stet,* Aug. 1947, p. 1.

17. "Business Tells its Story," *Stet,* Nov. 1945, pp. 1–2.

18. "Let's Take the Lead in Giving Workers Economic Facts," *FMM* 104 (June 1946): 124.

19. *PRN,* Jan 20, 1947; "Let's Take the Lead," p. 124; James L. Beebe to Leonard E. Read, Nov. 14, 1946, Box 34, Jasper E. Crane Papers, HML.

20. "What the Factory Worker Really Thinks," *FMM* 102 (Oct. 1944): 85; "Powwow in Pittsburgh," *Stet,* July 1950, p. 1; "The Fortune Survey," *Fortune,* May 1947, pp. 9–12.

21. Fred G. Clark to Jasper E. Crane, July 14, 1947, Box 1, Crane Papers; Richard S. Tedlow, *Keeping the Corporate Image: Public Relations and Business* (Greenwich, Conn.: JAI Press, 1979), pp. 59–73; Faught, "Its Your Story," p. 49.

22. Howell John Harris, *The Right to Manage: Industrial Relations Policies of American Business in the 1940s,* (Madison: University of Wisconsin Press, 1982), p. 183.

23. "The Role of Profits," *Stet,* Oct. 1947, p. 3.

24. Peter H. Irons, "American Business and the Origins of McCarthyism: The Cold War Crusade of the United States Chamber of Commerce," in *The Specter: Original Essays on the Cold War and the Origins of McCarthyism,* ed. Robert Griffith and Athan Theoharis (New York: New Viewpoints, 1974), pp. 72–89.

25. Bryce Oliver, "Thought Control—American Style," *New Republic,* Jan. 13, 1947, pp. 12–13; Allen W. Sayler to Walter P. Reuther, Mar. 12, 1947, Box 146, Walter Reuther Papers, ALUA.

26. Robert Griffith, "The Selling of America: The Advertising Council and American Politics, 1942–1960," *Business History Review* 57 (Autumn 1983): 398; "Our American Heritage," *Stet,* Oct. 1947, pp. 5–6.

27. *FF,* Jan 24, 1948.

28. "Challenge," *Stet*, Oct. 1946, p. 4; "Many Private Opinions," *Stet*, Oct. 1946, p. 1; Harris, *The Right to Manage*, pp. 177–99.

29. Lucille G. Ford, "A Survey of Organizations Active in Economic Education" (Ph.D. diss., Western Reserve University, Sept. 1967), pp. 115–18, 128–29, 211–13, 224–26; Harris, *The Right to Manage*, pp. 196–98.

30. Francis X. Sutton, et al., *The American Business Creed* (Cambridge, Mass.: Harvard University Press, 1956), pp. 74–89; "Teaching Workers the Facts about Profits," *AB*, Feb. 1948, pp. 28, 52; James W. Prothro, "Public Interest Advertising—Hucksterism or Conservatism?" *Social Studies* 45 (May 1954): 172–78.

31. "The Only Road to Worker Security," *FMM* 105 (Apr. 1947): 49; Sutton, *The American Business Creed*, pp. 125–29.

32. *PRN*, Dec. 9, 1946; "An Integrated Public Relations Program for the National Association of Manufacturers, Confidential Report," Jan. 14, 1946, Accession 1411, NAM, Series I, Box 110, (hereafter Acc. 1411 NAM I/110); Alfred S. Cleveland, "NAM: Spokesman for Industry?" *HBR* 26 (May 1948): 354–56.

33. *PRN*, Dec. 9, 1946; *CIO News*, Dec. 16, 1946, Dec. 15, 1947; Richard W. Gable, "NAM: Influential Lobby or Kiss of Death?" *Journal of Politics* 15 (1953): 263.

34. *NAM News*, Nov. 15, 1947, Apr. 3, 1948; Eugene Whitmore, "Business Talks Back to Politicians," *AB*, Feb. 1948, p. 9.

35. *NAM News*, Apr. 3, 1948; National Association of Manufacturers, *The Public Relations Program of the National Association of Manufacturers*, pamphlet (New York, 1946), pp. 14–16; "Salesletter, Jan. 17, 1949, #15, Acc. 1411, NAM I/110; NAM advertisements included "What Do You Need to Go into Business—and *Stay* in?" *Saturday Evening Post*, Sept. 13, 1947, p. 135, "There's More Than Dollars in Your Pay Envelope!" *Saturday Evening Post*, Nov. 8, 1947, p. 127, "Do You Think You Can Build a Better 'Mousetrap'?" *American Magazine*, Mar. 1948, p. 3, "How Big a Portion is Profit," *American Magazine*, Aug. 1948, p. 63.

36. "An Integrated Public Relations Program."

37. *NAM News*, Apr. 10, 1948; *Understanding*, June 1948, p. 6; "An Integrated Public Relations Program," *NAM News*, Aug. 2, 1947; NAM Salesletter, #15, Jan 17, 1949.

38. Lee, *Truman and Taft-Hartley*, pp. 18, 46–48; Donovan, *Conflict and Crisis*, pp. 229–38; James Caldwell Foster, *The Union Politic: The CIO Political Action Committee*, (Columbia: University of Missouri Press, 1975), pp. 67–69; Irons, "American Business and the Origins of McCarthyism," pp. 80–81; Stephen Meyer, "The Allis-Chalmers Strike of 1946–1947: Milwaukee Labor, Urban Politics, and the Rise of Joseph McCarthy" (Paper presented at the 1988 Lowell Conference on Industrial History), in author's possession.

39. *CIO News*, Sept. 22, 1947; Wilson quoted in Herman Kroos, *Executive Opinion: What Business Leaders Said and Thought on Economic Issues, 1920–1960* (Garden City, N.Y.: Doubleday, 1970), p. 211.

40. Thomas R. Jones, "The Scope of Collective Bargaining," AMA Person-

nel Series No. 81 (1944), p. 48; Harris, *The Right to Manage*, pp. 109–25; Richard W. Gable, "NAM: Influential Lobby or Kiss of Death," *Journal of Politics* 15 (1953): 270–73; Robert S. Lynd, "We Should Be Clear as to What Are the Essentials and What Are the Historic Trappings," p. 34.

41. Harris, *The Right to Manage*, pp. 139–42; Charles E. Wilson, "The American Way," *FMM* 106 (May 1948): 128; Gwilym A. Price, "Right to Manage Reestablished by Strike," *FMM* 104 (Sept. 1946): 280–82.

42. Harris, *The Right to Manage*, pp. 143–49; John S. Bugas, "Looking Ahead in Labor Relations" (Address before the Chicago Association of Commerce, Apr. 29, 1946, Box 55, AOF I, LMDC; Ralph A. Lind, "Salient Characteristics of Postwar Union Agreements," AMA Personnel Series No. 97 (1946), pp. 20–21.

43. Harris, *The Right to Manage*, pp. 109–27; Kim McQuaid, *Uneasy Partners: Big Business in American Politics, 1945–1900* (Baltimore: Johns Hopkins University Press, 1994), chap. 1.

44. H. W. Prentis, "The Citizen's Stake in the Labor Union Problem" (Address before the General Federation of Women's Clubs, Chicago, Ill., June 19, 1946), pamphlet (New York, 1946), pp. 3–19, esp. 11.

45. Frank Rising, "What's Ahead for the Unions," *FMM* 105 (Apr. 1947): 53.

46. Ira Mosher (Address before Chicago Industrial Conference, May 24, 1946), Acc. 1412, NAM, Industrial Relations Department Papers, Box 13; Harris, *The Right to Manage* pp. 114–18, 120–23.

47. Lee, *Truman and Taft-Hartley*, pp. 49–57, 64–66; Harry A. Millis and Emily Clark Brown, *From the Wagner Act to Taft-Hartley: A Study of National Labor Policy and Labor Relations* (Chicago: University of Chicago Press, 1950), pp. 286–91; Harris, *The Right to Manage*, p. 123.

48. Philip Ash, "The Periodical Press and the Taft-Hartley Act," *Public Opinion Quarterly* 12 (Summer 1948): 266–71; *Quincy Record* (Illinois), Mar. 11, May 15, June 4, 19, July 3, 10, 17, 1947.

49. *PLN*, Jan. 2, 1948.

50. *CIO News*, Dec. 16, 1946, Feb. 24, Dec. 15, 1947, Mar. 15, 1948; *Guild Reporter*, Jan. 11, 1946; *PLN*, Feb. 20, 1948; *CIO News*, July 26, 1948.

51. *PLN* Feb. 6, 27, Apr. 2, 1948; *Labor*, Feb. 6, 14, 1948.

52. *CIO News*, Feb. 17, Feb. 24, 1947; *UAW*, Jan 15, 1945; *PLN*, May 24, 1948, June 11, 1948; *Labor*, Jan. 1, 1948.

53. Buffalo Evening News Resolution, c. 1946, Greater Buffalo Industrial Union Council Records, Box 2, LMDC.

54. *PLN*, June 11, 1948; *FF*, May 29, Sept 25, 1948.

55. Hazel Gaudet Erskine, J. Bernard Phillips, and Ruth Harper Mills, "Polling Opinion—Or Planning Confusion: The Taft-Hartley Law, Mr. Claud Robinson and the ORC," *L&N*, Nov.–Dec. 1947, pp. 8–12; *PLN*, Apr. 16, 1948.

56. *PLN*, Mar. 6, May 7, 1948; Arthur Kornhauser, "Are Public Opinion Polls Fair to Organized Labor?" *Public Opinion Quarterly* 10 (Winter 1946): 484–500.

57. *UAW*, Sept. 1947.

58. "A Summary of the Case for Wage Increases" c. 1946, Greater Buffalo Industrial Union Council Records, Box 6, LMDC; George Soule, "Who's Right—Nathan or NAM?" *New Republic* 116 (Jan. 20, 1947): 27–29.

59. *UAW,* Aug, Oct. 1945, July, Dec. 1946, Mar., Dec. 1947; *CIO News,* Feb. 23, July 26, Dec. 27, 1948; *PLN,* Mar. 26, 1948; *FF,* May 29, 1948.

60. Llewellyn White, *The American Radio* (Chicago: University of Chicago Press, 1947), pp. 70–82; *UAW,* Aug. 1, Sept. 15, 1944, Jan. 15, Feb. 1, 1945; "C.I.O. on the Air," *BW,* Oct. 20, 1945; Alan Lomax, "A Right to the Airwaves," *Ammunition,* May 1944, pp. 21–22.

61. *Variety,* Jan. 16, 1946; *CIO News* Jan, 28, Dec. 30, 1946, Feb. 17, 1947.

62. Len De Caux to CIO Affiliates, Jan. 11, 1946, Box 3, Greater Buffalo Industrial Union Council Records, LMDC; *CIO News,* Jan. 5, 1948.

63. "Suffering from Commentators? Snap Back with a Comeback," *Ammunition,* Jan. 1947, p. 36; Geneva, New York, Federation of Labor Minutebook, 1939–53, p. 187, Oct. 27, 1948, LMDC.

64. UERMWA, *Telling the Town: UE Guide to Community Action* (New York, 1946) in AUF, Box 166, LMDC; UERMWA, *Proceedings,* 1946, pp. 187–92; UERMWA, *Proceedings,* 1947, pp. 58–59, 306–11; *PRN,* Nov. 11, Dec. 26, 1946.

65. Lee, *Truman and Taft-Hartley,* pp. 80–85; Len De Caux to Regional Directors, May 20, 1947, (enclosed Radio Scripts, "The Danger That Confronts America" and "Radio Spot Announcements on the Taft-Hartley Bill"), Box 6, Greater Buffalo Industrial Union Council Records.

66. *PLN,* May 9, 1947; Lee, *Truman and Taft-Hartley,* p. 82; "No NAM Fools," *New Republic* 116 (May 26, 1946): 34–35.

67. Melton S. Davis, "Public Opinion—The Court of Last Resort," *L&N,* Jan.–Feb. 1947, p. 24.

68. *FF,* Jan 31, 1948; "From Issue to Issue—Report by the Editor," *L&N,* July–Aug. 1947, pp. 5–6; Erskine et al., "Polling Opinion," pp. 8–9.

69. "From Issue to Issue," pp. 5–6; Erskine et al., "Polling Opinion," pp. 8–9, 12; *Guild Reporter,* Feb. 13, 1948.

70. Alonzo L. Hamby, *Beyond the New Deal: Harry S. Truman and American Liberalism* (New York: Columbia University Press, 1973), pp. 209–19, 224–33, 260–63.

71. *UAW,* Jan. 1948.

72. Lee, *Truman and Taft-Hartley,* pp. 110–13; Foster, *The Union Politic,* pp. 111–30; Fay Calkins, *The CIO and the Democratic Party* (Chicago, 1953), pp. 112–46.

73. "Political Action in the 1948 Campaign," (Recommendation of the Executive Officers to the meeting of the CIO Executive Board, Washington, D.C., Aug. 30–31, 1948), Box 4, Greater Buffalo Industrial Union Council Records.

74. "Labor Day Release" (press release), Sept. 1, 1948, Box 1, Greater Buffalo Industrial Union Council Records; J. M. Gambatese, "What Labor Did in the Election—and What It Will Do," *FMM* 107 (Jan. 1949): 134–36.

75. United Labor Committee of Massachusetts, *The Massachusetts Story,* (Boston, n.d.); "Leading Citizens Say Vote No! on Referenda 5, 6, and 7," pam-

phlet, William Belanger Papers, Manuscripts and Archives, University of Massachusetts, Amherst, Mass.; *Christian Science Monitor* Sept. 25, Oct. 27, Nov. 3, 1948.

76. *Evening Bulletin,* Providence, R.I., Oct. 26, 27, 1948; Hamby, *Beyond the New Deal,* pp. 247–55; Donovan, *Conflict and Crisis,* pp. 418–31; Lee, *Truman and Taft-Hartley,* pp. 136–43.

77. Foster, *The Union Politic,* p. 130; Lee, *Truman and Taft-Hartley,* pp. 146–53; *Massachusetts CIO News,* Dec. 1948; *PLN,* Nov. 5, 1948.

78. Wheeler McMillen, "The Miracle of 1948," *Vital Speeches* Jan. 1, 1949, p. 182; Thomas G. Spates, "The Competition for Leadership in A Welfare Economy," AMA Personnel Series No. 124 (1949), pp. 4–5.

79. *Organizer,* Feb. 14, 1950.

80. McMillen, "The Miracle of 1948," p. 183; Spates, "The Competition for Leadership," p. 6.

81. Robert Griffith, "The Selling of America: The Advertising Council and American Politics, 1942–1960," *Business History Review* 57 (Autumn 1983): 399–401; Theodore S. Repplier to Charles W. Jackson, Mar. 23, 1950, Box 17, Charles W. Jackson Files, Harry S. Truman Papers, HST; "How to Tune a Piano," *Time,* Jan. 3, 1949.

82. *PRN,* Nov. 14, 1949; *NAM News,* Dec. 16, 1950, Feb. 17, 1951.

83. "NAM Propaganda," *New Republic,* Mar. 5, 1951, p. 9; *NAM News,* Mar. 22, 1957, July 8, Oct. 21, 1950, Feb. 17, 1951; "NAM Scores a Hit on TV—Soft-Pedaling Commercials," *BW,* Apr. 19, 1952, pp. 86–88.

84. Erik Barnouw, *The Golden Web: A History of Broadcasting in the United States, Volume II—1933 to 1953* (New York: Oxford University Press, 1968), pp. 34, 89–92; *WSJ,* Sept. 29, 1951; "Transcripts," Bohn Aluminum & Brass Corp. advertisements, Apr. 13, June 29, 1952, Box 132, National Broadcasting Corporation Papers, SHSW.

85. C. C. Carr, "Translating the American Economic System," *PRJ* 5 (June 1949): 2–3; *NYT,* June 5, 1949; "An Invitation from Harding College of Searcy, Arkansas to the Third Freedom Forum," July 11–15, 1949, Box 14, Jackson Files, HST.

86. Among the interesting surveys of this period are Hamby, *Beyond the New Deal;* Robert J. Donovan, *Tulmultous Years: The Presidency of Harry S Truman, 1949–1953* (New York: W. W. Norton, 1982).

87. Zieger, *American Workers, American Unions,* pp. 123–34; Barbara S. Griffith, *The Crisis of American Labor: Operation Dixie and the Defeat of the CIO* (Philadelphia: Temple University Press, 1988), passim.

88. Zieger, *American Workers, American Unions,* pp. 147–58; Brody, *Workers in Industrial America,* pp. 173–211; Lichtenstein, "The Eclipse of Social Democracy," pp. 140–44.

89. "How Not to Give Away Your Right to Manage," *FMM* 107 (Sept. 1949): 108; Foster, *The Union Politic,* pp. 133–54; Samuel Lubell, *The Future of American Politics* (New York: Harper & Row, 1965), pp. 183–89.

90. Robert Griffith, "Dwight D. Eisenhower and the Corporate Commonwealth," *American Historical Review* 87 (Feb. 1982): 96–100; Herbert S. Parmet,

*Eisenhower and the American Crusades* (New York: Macmillan, 1972), pp. 33–44; McQuaid, *Big Business and Presidential Power*, pp. 171–72.

91. William J. Grede, "Big Labor—Enemy of Itself" (Address before the Niagara Falls Industrial Club, Sept. 30, 1952); James W. Prothro, "Public Interest Advertising—Hucksterism or Conservatism?" *Social Studies* 45 (May 1954); 172–77, esp. 175.

92. "How Industry Can Be a Better Neighbor," *Steel*, Feb. 23, 1953, p. 60; Henry Ford II, "Business is on the Spot," *Saturday Review*, Jan. 24, 1953, pp. 22–23.

93. On Eisenhower's administration see Griffith, "Dwight D. Eisenhower and the Corporate Commonwealth," pp. 103–22.

94. "Analysis of the Operations of the National Association of Manufacturers"; "Summary of Recommendations with Respect to Opinion Research Surveys," c. 1953, Box 69, *Washington Bulletin* (NAM newsletter), Nov. 11, 1952; Box 24, William Grede Papers, SHSW; Warner & Swasey advertisement, *Newsweek*, Dec. 21, 1953, p. 1; Warner & Swasey advertisement, *U.S. News & World Report*, Jan. 30, 1952, p. 1.

95. *'New' Labor Board—Even Worse Than Taft-Hartley*, pamphlet reprinted from *Economic Outlook*, Feb. 1955, Box 4, Greater Buffalo Industrial Union Council Records, LMDC; *Congress and the Nation: 1945–1964, A Review of Government and Politics in the Postwar Years* (Washington, D.C.: Congressional Quarterly Service, 1965), p. 1717; Victor Riesel, "Inside Labor," Feb. 25, 1954, Box 133, David J. McDonald Papers, USA; "Report to National Association of Manufacturers on a Market Study Made by Opinion Research Corporation," Feb. 23, 1955, John Stuart to Members of the Opinion Research Corp. Report Committee, Oct. 11, 1954, both in Acc. 1411, NAM I/46.

96. Sara U. Douglas, *Labor's New Voice: Unions and the Mass Media* (Norwood, N.J.: Ablex Publishing, 1986), p. 30; Gerald Pomper, "The Public Relations of Organized Labor," *Public Opinion Quarterly*, 23 (Winter 1959–60): 485; CIO Executive Board Minutes, June 4, 1953, ALUA.

# PART 2 | In the Factory

# 3 | *Building Company Consciousness*

The economic and political struggles between capital and labor in the 1930s and 1940s as we have seen, raised fundamental questions of power in society. Inside the factory, such challenges raised questions about who would make the critical decisions affecting hours, wages, and the conditions of work? Who would control the shop floor? Some labor leaders, such as Walter Reuther, raised the specter of codetermination of investment and pricing. As the historian Charles Maier has explained, the outside social and political environment had entered the factory. Managers in the postwar era, then, were increasingly expected to help shape national policies and values in order to restore their authority in the plant. A narrow focus on the company's concerns no longer seemed adequate.[1]

Altering national economic and social priorities inevitably began with a struggle over the consciousness and loyalties of American workers. The rise of labor unions had mobilized workers around new and powerful loyalties. These unions, business leaders complained, had drenched the minds of workers "in a reckless propaganda of distortion, deceit, and phoney [*sic*] economics."[2] Fearing that in the new loyalties of their workers lay threats to their control of the workplace and to the future shape of America itself, businessmen not only sought victory at the bargaining table and in the halls of Congress but also sought to win the hearts and minds of American workers. To accomplish this latter task, managers drew heavily upon such earlier mechanisms as human relations and welfarism. However, employers changed the character of these devices to serve a new purpose— to send a message that business had solved the fundamental ethical and political problems of industrial society, the basic "harmony between the self interest of our economic institutions and the social interests of society."[3]

* * *

Control of the shopfloor was an important goal for postwar business. To cut costs and to restore the productivity necessary to meet rising consumer demand, employers developed several responses to the labor problem. A significant number of businesses, including those located in the sunbelt as well as companies involved in extremely capital-intensive, continuous flow production, like chemicals and oil refining, continued to resist unions. Alternatively, a small group of progressive employers, primarily in the garment and electrical industries, along with some smaller steel-making and fabricating firms, looked to union-management cooperation or accommodation as a means of gaining control over the labor force.[4]

The majority of large corporations, however, tended to take a moderate, "realistic" approach to industrial relations. They reluctantly accepted organized labor but hoped that an aggressive collective bargaining strategy would enable them to contain union power and achieve productivity goals. Contract negotiations in the auto industry that confined the scope of collective bargaining to wages, hours, and working conditions were the first steps in this direction. In 1948, General Motors proposed linking wage rates to increased productivity. At least at the national level, unions were to trade job control for periodic wage increases and benefits. The inclusion of no-strike clauses in postwar contracts and an increasingly elaborate grievance system were designed to ensure that union leaders shared responsibility with management to tighten up worker discipline and prevent interruptions to production. By 1950, the historian Howell Harris concludes, large corporations like GM, Ford, U.S. Steel, and Westinghouse Electric had made significant progress toward achieving stable and efficient labor relations.[5]

It is tempting to draw broader generalizations from the willingness of some corporations to concede higher wages and benefits. However, it neither signaled the formation of a "social contract" between capital and labor nor ended genuine conflict, as many historians have argued. Employer intransigence in the area of managerial prerogative had forced unions to give up some power, but the fight for economic security continued to galvanize workers for serious struggle. Only the threat of strong union action brought increased wages and benefits. Dramatic, long strikes in 1945–46 were necessary to allow labor to begin to catch up with wartime inflation. Furthermore, new benefits required sacrifices. Over half of the strikes in 1949 and 70 percent during the first half of 1950 were over health and welfare issues, and General Motors' concession of pensions in 1950 came only after a longstanding UAW campaign for old-age security.[6]

National collective bargaining agreements, moreover, did not put an end to an ongoing struggle to control the shopfloor. Quickly, the business community discovered the inadequacies of collective bargaining to solve all managerial problems. In late 1949, labor analyst Edward T. Cheyfitz observed that "Labor-management relations in America are continuing in the pattern of a power struggle. That is the outstanding fact characterizing industrial relations today." Local unions and management fought endlessly over the pace and organization of work. Seniority and grievance systems, which could at times stifle worker militancy, also placed substantial constraints on managerial discipline and personnel deployment.[7] Even in plants where the collective bargaining system was weak and the union nonconfrontational, informal work groups served to challenge managerial authority. These cohesive units of workers, protected by the grievance system, stymied efforts to increase productivity through a variety of tactics, including informal bargaining with foremen, slowdowns, work-to-rule campaigns, and wildcat strikes.[8]

Continuing conflict evoked two sharply divergent interpretations within the business community. A small core of moderates accepted as inevitable the idea that significant differences of interest and social philosophy separated employees and management. Business leaders like Paul Hoffman of Studebaker, Robert Wood Johnson of Johnson & Johnson Pharmaceuticals, and Meyer Kestenbaum of the garment firm Hart, Schaffner & Marx recognized organized labor as legitimate representatives of workers' interests. They believed that unions served as the channel and instrument, but not source, of worker protest and discontent.[9] Dependent upon each other for survival, unions and management needed to find a way to overcome their differences. "We must develop a relationship between management and union which is neither based on the assumption of permanent industrial warfare, nor on the equally false hope that we can eliminate all the conflicts within enterprise," asserted railway executive Charles R. Hook. Instead, we must, "find a way to make the conflict itself constructive and fruitful."[10] Collective bargaining was a workable, practical, and democratic vehicle for resolving conflicting interests. Through the collective bargaining process, progressives hoped to make the union an "integral part of a program of teamwork, communication and participation."[11]

For progressive employers like Robert Wood Johnson, no contradiction existed between workers' loyalty to both company and union. He observed that life "is full of multiple loyalties which can be adjusted by common sense."[12] Similarly, a Raytheon Company executive contended that employees could have "dual loyalties, just as a foreman must have loyalty to his employees as well as to the management. This duality need not present serious conflict or create adversaries." Workers could be promanagement and pro-union at the same time. Continuing conflict, then, simply symbolized the expression of divergent opinions and perspectives. When capital and labor achieved mutual accommodation of their legitimate differences then industrial peace would become a reality. Industrial relations professionals applauded and encouraged this vision of labor relations.[13]

Most conservative businessmen, in contrast to the small core of liberals, had a harmonious, consensual vision of society. To them, no inevitable conflict existed between labor and management. Workers and management were partners in a community of interest directed by employers.[14] Thus, in 1946 industrial relations expert E. Wright Bakke found that managers viewed employees as "'our men,' not workers in general, not members of the union," and certainly not organized labor.[15] "We are all workers," declared NAM President Wallace F. Bennett in 1949, "we are all capitalists." Employers, not unions, were the natural allies of workers, and yet, Bennett continued, "we have allowed our detractors to put over on us their symbols, with certain words spelled with capitals to spell out classes which compartmentalize us."[16]

The detractors, of course, were typically trade unions. Unions had successfully challenged the business leadership of American society during the Depression. In the postwar years, labor was expanding the scope of that challenge in the workplace, especially in the modern, mass production factories that seemed so hierarchical, rigid, and alienating. Businessmen felt that unions were responsible for an "artificially created" ideological chasm between employers and their workers.[17] Labor's collectivist philosophy and its challenges to managerial authority exacerbated the problems inherent in the labor process and contributed to continuing turmoil on the shop floor. Labor relations consultant Martin Dodge accused unions of poisoning the minds of workers with a "barrage of irresponsible invective, false economics, distorted statistics, and general accusations that front offices are largely filled with a conspiring coterie of lying leeches."[18]

Particularly galling to business leaders was a 1950 *Harvard Business Review* article by Solomon Barkin, director of research of the Textile Workers Union, which asserted that a fundamental conflict existed between workers and management. The source of this conflict was the helplessness of the individual worker in the face of the economic and social power of the employer. Unions, representing workers as a group, empowered employees, fulfilling their aspirations and reflecting their needs. Accordingly, Barkin contended, the worker's primary loyalty was to the union, not the firm.[19] NAM managing director Earl Bunting, challenged Barkin's assumptions, asserting that approaching industrial relations "on the basis of mass and class is repugnant to our ideals," for the United States has "attained a classless society which other countries dream of." He declared that trade unionists had finally shown their true colors with Barkin's "frank and open acceptance of the class conflict approach."[20]

Yet there appeared to be ample evidence that large numbers of workers accepted Barkin's interpretation of class relations. Opinion polls concluded that many workers distrusted their employers and doubted the virtue of the free enterprise system itself. Surprisingly large numbers of workers favored government ownership or control of the economy and even greater numbers wanted governmental guarantees of economic security. In 1946, the Psychological Corporation found that 43 percent of surveyed workers believed they would do as well or better if American manufacturing firms were run entirely by the government. A 1950 Opinion Research Corporation sample of industrial workers found that over 30 percent believed that the government should control prices and limit profits, 26 percent wanted to see the government limit salaries of top executives and 21 percent would vote for government ownership of four key industries.[21]

The same workers who trusted the government had little faith in management's concern for their welfare. Attitude surveys reflected a rejection of the traditional managerial philosophy that individual effort rather than collective action led to success and advancement. As a result, skeptical, group-minded employees were suspicious of employer appeals for greater productivity. Fifty-eight percent of manual workers surveyed by ORC responded to a call for increased effort, with the answer: "That's the SPEED UP. Means they want more work for the same pay." A similar number rejected the idea that workers benefited from increased productivity, and over a third of these workers believed that labor-saving machinery destroyed jobs.[22]

Polls demonstrating that over half of American workers believed that corporations earned profits topping 25 percent each year alerted industrialists that significant economic misunderstandings clouded the relationship between worker and employer. "No partnership can be expected to work very well," Henry Ford II told United States Chamber of Commerce in 1947, "when 75 percent of industry's employees think stockholders and top management of corporations take more out of business than employees." In reality, according to the automaker, industry profits averaged less than 5 percent and employees received almost six times as much as the amount paid to stockholders.[23]

Employers believed that these negative attitudes toward the American economic system intruded onto the shop floor. Workers who felt that they only received the "crumbs" had little incentive to work hard. Within this context traditional managerial complaints about low productivity assumed a new, more ominous significance. In 1946, 73 percent of executives surveyed by *Mill and Factory* blamed "a general indifference on the part of the workers" as the prime cause of declining labor productivity.[24] Similarly, American Thread Company executive Guy B. Arthur, Jr., noted that employees, who "years ago were as regular as the sunrise," routinely skipped work or produced as little as necessary, feeling no obligation to "trade a fair day's work for a fair day's pay." Part of the problem, continued Arthur, was that the worker no longer accepted responsibility for his security, expecting "the government to take care of his future." Most disquieting, however, was the "subordination of the individual to the group" as workers relied on seniority rather than ability or merit for advancement.[25]

Across the spectrum of business associations, leaders awakened to the dangers a misled working class posed to each firm as well as the future welfare of America. By exploiting employer silence, organized labor was winning the battle for the loyalty of workers, which enabled increasingly powerful unions to undercut business influence. Management, declared General Foods president Austin S. Ingleheart, "has left open a wide hole through which its adversaries are driving half-truths and falsehoods."[26] In a 1949 article, associate editor of *Factory*, M. J. Murphy, described the results of employer reticence to challenge unions at every level. Continuing union power over the shop floor, he charged, was gained primarily through ideological manipulation of employees. Organized labor's ability to limit output through its influence over the work force threatened the economic viability of every firm.[27] The labor columnist Victor Riesel admonished businessmen at the 1950 NAM convention, "You are not competing [effectively] for the creditability of your company with your working people, and I say that with the rush to the left, you will get washed aside in the years to come."[28]

In response to these warnings, particularly after the 1948 election, business mobilized to protect its interests by selling the free enterprise system in its factories. More than creative collective bargaining was needed to gain worker acceptance of the business agenda and thereby thwart the power and influence of unions on and off the shop floor.[29] A large segment of the business community responded to the ideological and economic challenge posed by unions by attempting to create a separate company identity or company consciousness among their employees. This involved convincing workers to identify their social, economic, and political well-being with that of their specific employer and more broadly with the free enterprise system.[30] A company conscious worker, rather like the idealized boy scout, was not only productive but also took pride in his job and demonstrated loyalty and allegiance to the firm. One component of company consciousness drew from the insights of human relations. Through human relations, managers planned to gain the willing cooperation of workers in expanding productivity and to restore "the natural and sincere friendship that should exist" between worker and employer.[31]

* * *

The origins of the human relations theory of management are well known. It developed from the Hawthorne experiments conducted by the sociologist Elton Mayo and his Harvard Business School associates beginning in the mid-1920s and from the theories published by the psychologist Abraham H. Maslow during and after World War II. The Hawthorne researchers discovered the influence that informal work groups exerted over worker behavior and productivity. Informal organization grew out of the employee's social needs, the desire for recognition and dignity, as well as the natural camaraderie of the shop floor. Using these insights, sociologists challenged the dominant managerial ideology that treated workers simply as a source of labor driven by economic incentives. Instead, each worker needed to be treated as a "social being related to others in a complex social organization." Increased productivity depended on securing the cooperation of the small work group through participation in decision making, better communication, and improved supervisory training, and by providing employees with greater social and psychological satisfaction on the job.[32]

In an influential article published in 1943, Maslow contributed a more sophisticated understanding of motivation to human relations. He identified five sets of needs, including physiological, safety, affection, esteem, and self-actualization, or accomplishment. When the most basic drives were satisfied, they no longer motivated behavior. Drawing on Maslow's findings, social scientists in the field of human relations contended that employers could not depend on higher wages alone to substitute for fulfilling the entire range of workers' needs. They linked employee discontent and falling productivity to the failure to meet workers' higher needs on the job and asserted that these problems could be alleviated only through the enhancement of the social aspects of the workplace.[33]

Mayo's and Maslow's work had great appeal to the business community. Like many employers, Mayo assumed that company and employee formed a community that reflected homogeneous interests. Conflict was not natural but simply the result of misunderstanding. If management could gain the cooperation or control of the informal groups of workers then the need for trade unions would disappear.[34] The flood of social science literature on these topics provided "scientific" verification that collective action was not a natural phenomenon. Reflecting this interpretation, General Foods vice president Thomas G. Spates argued that the "militancy and the crusading spirit of the labor movement" was nurtured by the "failure of management to satisfy the *non*-economic needs" of workers. Demands for higher wage rates were simply an expression of worker discontent at their firm's failure to meet their higher needs. Fulfilling such noneconomic wants was the key to industrial peace in the factory and beyond.[35]

Practical application of human relations theory in the firm grew slowly. Even before the Hawthorne experiments there had been some discussion but little sustained effort to improve morale and supervision. But the rise of industrial unionism during the thirties and the demands of wartime production triggered experimentation with employee morale and job satisfaction. What employees thought about their company assumed a growing importance in the context of the broader contention over national economic and social priorities. Companies conducted attitude surveys, initiated counseling programs, and began instructing foremen on the application of human relations supervision.[36]

The postwar labor crisis widened the audience for human relations. One scholar notes that after 1946 "the managerial conviction that problems of human relations were important knew virtually no bounds."[37] That same year, Henry Ford II asserted that one of the greatest problems confronting American industry concerned "human relationships—relationships which can either aid or impede our efforts to achieve greater industrial efficiency."[38] Fowler McCormick, chairman of the board of International Harvester Company, predicted more devastating results if managers continued to overlook the human element, contending that "the very existence of American industry depends on the success of its human relations." Unless the people of this country believe in industry, he continued, "American industry will not last."[39]

By the late forties, human relations became the dominant managerial theme. Commitment to human relations transcended the divisions within managerial ranks. With its promise of winning worker loyalty to the firm, it touched a responsive chord among both nonunion employers and those unionized employers committed to containing the scope of industrial relations. Its potential to enhance productivity, however, also attracted more moderate employers. Courses, bulletins, and even national meetings devoted to human relations reflected its widespread appeal. In 1952, *Time* pronounced that a second industrial revolution, "quieter but more profound, is sweeping through U.S. industry; its name: Human Relations in Industry." The new corporate mottos were "understanding" and "togetherness." In 1948, Cloud Wampler, head of Carrier Corporation, for instance, determined that "happy relationships shall prevail between the Corporation and its employees."[40] The central goal of the movement was to reforge a personal relationship between each worker and the company by appealing to his or her nonfinancial, social needs.[41]

Getting workers to believe in industry was intimately connected to the operation of the shopfloor. Human relations oriented personnel administration emphasized effective supervision in the belief that worker identification with the firm and possibly with the free enterprise system itself was intimately linked to the employee's relationship with their supervisor. Following the war, many firms increased the size of their supervisory force and negotiated reductions in the number of stewards to strengthen foremen's shopfloor leadership. Supervisory training programs proliferated as firms like GE, Armstrong Cork, Alcoa, and Ford sought to increase the prestige, effectiveness, and loyalty of their foremen whose status had been severely shaken by the rise of industrial unionism. A few firms had initially offered these courses after World War I and during the late thirties to combat rising unionism. Employers also offered foremen greater job security and established a sharp differentiation between supervisors and the rank and file by placing foremen on salary, inviting them to special meetings and dinners, and giving them offices and special parking privileges.[42]

Supervisory development promised to boost the foremen's ability to serve more effectively as the first line of defense against unionism. This appealed both to large nonunion firms and unionized companies committed to a realistic approach to industrial relations. Courses taught foremen how to use their own personality to develop discipline and instill loyalty among workers. They were instructed to compete with the union steward for worker allegiance by personally greeting each employee every day and by providing a sympathetic ear for on-and-off the job problems. In 1947, General Electric, for instance, attempted to strengthen supervisory-employee relationships by establishing fifteen thousand cells of five to twenty-five people grouped around a single supervisor. The corporation urged foremen to find out what each employee "likes and dislikes about his job, what he thinks we can do to help him have a job and a personal association with us that is more rewarding materially and spiritually." The NAM praised these efforts, arguing that the ability of workers to confide in their supervisor "builds confidence in and loyalty to the company."[43]

Participation, another fundamental concept associated with human relations, also promised to wrestle the loyalty of workers away from the unions. The Hawthorne studies had demonstrated that allowing workers to participate raised morale and productivity by promising to address employees' higher needs through making work more meaningful. The goal of postwar participation programs was to "make workers feel they are participating" without restructuring work or the line of authority within the shop.[44]

In some firms, participation involved increased use of conferences during which supervisors "consulted" with employees on decisions that affected them. Management thereby aimed to "get workers to accept what management wants them to accept *but* to *make* them feel they made or helped to make the decision." More commonly, employers relied on suggestion programs to secure greater employee involvement. Suggestion systems enabled employers to gain greater access to workers' knowledge of the work process by giving employees a direct monetary reward for ideas on how to cut waste, eliminate unnecessary motions or prevent safety hazards while making the employees feel that the company was interested in their ideas. Although they dated back to the 1880s, it was not until the postwar era of human relations that suggestion systems began to flourish. Ford Motor Company, for example, established an employee suggestion plan in 1947 as part of its new human relations effort. By 1953, four thousand firms received more than 2 million ideas from workers and paid out over $15 million in return. The National Association of Suggestion Systems, organized in 1942 by four companies to promote suggestion programs, had grown to a membership of over a thousand firms twelve years later.[45]

Companies frequently had to counter worker complaints that rewards were too meager or that labor-saving suggestions might lead to job loss. Elaborate contests offered one way to overcome such resistance and raise the level of worker involvement. In 1949, Goodyear Tire and Rubber Company conducted a five-week campaign devoted to waste reduction suggestions. It doubled awards and held weekly drawings for merchandise prizes. A "villainous looking hunchback named Weasel Waste" roamed through the plants criticizing good work and praising any waste he observed. During 1956, "Mr. Check" strolled daily through the Westinghouse Columbus plant tapping employees on the shoulder and giving them five silver dollars if they successfully answered three questions on improving quality.[46] Sylvania's 1952 "Operation Sharp" contest stressed group spirit to improve worker performance in the areas of safety, housekeeping, reduction of scrap, and product improvement. The company publicized the campaign with streamers, posters, floats, a circus parade, and the crowning of "Miss Sharp" before an audience of twelve thousand. To ensure fullest participation, the contest divided workers into groups named after college football teams, which competed in various categories, for a grand prize of a three-day luxury weekend in New York City.[47]

As all of these activities attest, human relations systems trumpeted the company's sincere and personal concern for the individual employee. Name plates, awards for long service, birthday greetings and merit awards provided individual recognition and acknowledged that the most menial job, however minor, was important to the company.[48] One manager whose company began sending birthday cards in 1946 attested that: "One of my men is going around walking on air, saying that for the first time in thirty-five years with the company he has been recognized as an individual rather than a cog in the machine. He says that birthday card is worth more to him than a ten dollar bill."[49] Firms like the Frigidaire division of General Motors, Union Carbide and Carbon, and 3M provided dinner at a hotel, flowers, music, and entertainment to honor employees "who have proved their worth and loyalty over a long period of years." To enhance the worker's prestige in the community, many companies broadcast service award ceremonies over local radio stations or released pictures to local newspapers.[50]

Firms that employed large numbers of women believed that these kinds of activities were especially important. Their approach, however, reflected the gender relations of the dominant culture and served to reinforce its assumptions. Hughes Aircraft stressed making women feel at home at work, encouraging supervisors to act as a "handholder" when necessary. Other employers believed that it took little more than a "big mirror, perfumed soap, hot water" and an occasional kind word to "keep the girls happy." The GE Schenectady Works' paper featured women's contributions to the plant by focusing on the "Woman of the Month." In other firms, however, recognition was based more on women's physical attributes. Standard Oil held beauty contests while McDonnell Aircraft Corporation plants annually elected a "Sky Queen" to "reign over company activities."[51]

Although human relations included improving personnel management through supervisory training and participation, the most intriguing aspect of human relations for postwar employers was direct communication with their workers. To get the people on the shop-floor to believe in industry, managers relied on a sophisticated, if politically loaded, understanding of communications, a key to building "company consciousness." Effective communications would help fulfill workers' higher needs by giving them a "sense of 'belonging' in the plants where they work" and by creating a new kind of cooperative interaction between employer and employee.[52]

Companies earlier had used various communication techniques to forestall unionization in the decades before the New Deal.[53] The passage of the Wagner Act, however, made this an unfair labor practice. For a decade employers found their communications restricted. In 1947, the passage of the Taft-Hartley Act brought employers greater freedom of expression within their firms. J. P. Woodard, Director of Industrial Relations for the Johns-Manville Corporation, observed that "perhaps the principal advantage granted to the employer by the new Act lies in the opportunity for top management—directly, through management authority channels to convey its opinions and advice to all employees." Within months of the law's passage, *Modern Industry* observed that companies were "taking the offensive against the attacks made upon the American economic system by the Communists and by their propagandists within the unions."[54]

The National Association of Manufacturers, established communication conferences and clinics around the country. Other groups, including the Chamber of Commerce and local employer associations quickly followed suit. Between 1948 and 1950, the NAM conducted a thousand clinics and distributed thousands of communication manuals. The Employers Association of New Jersey in promoting its NAM co-sponsored communications clinic emphasized the importance of communicating with workers, pointing out that

> sixty million people in this country spend nearly half of their waking hours under management's collective roof; next to their families, most

of them are more interested in their jobs than in any other subject. They are the same people who vote, who join unions and who use your products. And what the people who work for you think about you and your company largely determines their opinions about industrial management as a whole, and consequently about the amount of economic freedom under which they think you should operate.

In 1953, the Association established a special task force devoted to increasing the quantity and quality of information available to employees. Its efforts in this area continued through the 1950s.[55]

The Chamber of Commerce's work meshed with that of the NAM, sponsoring 227 meetings during the first eight months of 1950 alone. Each organization also issued monthly newsletters devoted to communications transmission, complete with ideas, suggestions, and case histories. In 1956 Champion Paper and Fibre Company produced a film focusing attention on the importance of communication to happiness and well-being. The story was placed in an industrial setting and dramatized how a communication failure at the top of the firm led to misinformation and misunderstanding among the employees. As one of the characters of the film pointed out, solving communication problems suggested "the basic answer to every problem is mutual understanding, from how to get along with your wife to international peace." More than six hundred prints of *Production 5118* circulated among firms like Du Pont, Ford, IBM, and International Paper Company.[56]

Reflecting the growth of the movement, private management communications consultants emerged, offering to design tailor-made programs for firms. The Employers Labor Relations Information Committee (ERLIC), formed in 1953, convinced managers at such firms as B. F. Goodrich, GE, Ford, Westinghouse, Standard Oil, Sears, Monsanto, Kennecott Copper, United States Steel, and Goodyear that it could design programs to draw "the corporate family together." ERLIC promised to win the "emotional allegiance" of a client's workers and aid companies in overcoming the "songs of class struggle and fear" emanating from unions. It asserted that the failure of employers to correct misunderstandings propagated by labor was the cause of most shopfloor conflict and the reason for America's drift toward "alien ideologies."[57]

The antidote was direct communication with the individual worker. In reducing the influence of unions, nothing was more important than reaching the individual. The biggest mistake a company could make, according to Ford's John Bugas, was to conflate the individual employee with the union. Similarly, William B. Given of American

Brake Shoe declared: "We must stop thinking of them as union members, or as a group, and think of them as individuals." Accordingly, in 1950, Ivan Willis, International Harvester's vice president for industrial relations, vowed

> we are finished with the idea of letting unions tell our story to our people. We are going to do that for ourselves and we are going to do it in competition with a union or any other agency which attempts to do it. We recognize the rights of a union as the employees' spokesman, their lawyer if you like, on a specific topic. But we do not consider our employees the union's employees. They are our employees. We are attempting to establish a relationship directly with our people so that regardless of what union they belong to . . . our story will reach our people consistently and continuously.[58]

Herman Steinkraus, president of Bridgeport Brass bluntly declared that while an employee may belong to the union, he "belongs to the company first."[59]

Firms bombarded their workers with pamphlets, comic books, posters, bulletin boards, letters home, company annual reports, magazines, newspapers, films, and even matchbooks. In 1949, for instance, General Motors became the first company to install information racks in its plants. It distributed 7 million pamphlets in a single year. By 1958, three thousand companies utilized reading racks.[60] But the mainstay of communication was the employee magazine. Some of these publications dated to the Progressive Era, but many were discontinued during the thirties. The postwar campaign to build company consciousness sparked the revival of this medium of communication. The number of titles multiplied more than six-fold in the 1940s, reaching more than 80 million employees. So fast was the growth that universities began offering training for company editors and several professional journals appeared.[61]

The messages management communicated had two interrelated parts. The first part was a timeless industrial message concerning managerial authority and worker morale. Moderate as well as conservative employers portrayed the individual firm's financial position, operations, products, and problems to give employees a feeling of closeness to the firm. Explanations of the significance of each operation to the finished product were designed to help create a sense of purpose, pride, and dignity even among those frustrated by subdivided and alienating labor. Moreover, information about the company was to clarify for workers the mutual aims and shared interests of the "employee-company family."[62]

In 1946 the NAM spent over three million dollars on a public relations campaign to end price controls. Reprinted from *Trends in Education*, May 1946; courtesy of Hagley Museum and Library.

# Do you think you can build a better "mousetrap"?

**1.** Suppose you felt sure you could make a better mousetrap—or any other product—and you began to think about risking your savings to start up a business of your own.

**2.** First, you'd want to make certain you could turn out this product at a price that would enable you to meet or beat your competition.

**3.** Next, you'd check very carefully to be sure there was a "market" for your type of product. In other words, would enough people want to buy it to give you the volume you'd need to keep going?

**4.** And, of course, good management would be another "must." You'd have to know how to run the business, or be able to hire someone to do it for you. For only with good management could you keep on meeting your material costs, your payroll, your rent, your taxes, and all the other costs of doing business.

**5.** Finally, you'd have to see an opportunity to make a fair profit. The firm that can't earn a profit soon folds up! And, like other progressive firms, you'd want to put part of your profits back into the business. For, a large share of the reasonable profits earned by industry pays for the development and expansion that bring more goods, more jobs—and greater security for all.

**N**ATIONAL **A**SSOCIATION OF **M**ANUFACTURERS

*Composed of 16,500 large and small manufacturing companies.*

*Most Americans say they think 10 to 15 cents out of each dollar of sales would be a fair profit for business to make. Government figures show that industry averages less than half that much profit! And about half of that is plowed back by industry to pay for the progress and development that give Americans more good things than any other people on earth!*

This typical NAM advertisement explained the importance of profits in the American economic system. Reprinted from *American Magazine*, Mar. 1948; courtesy of the National Association of Manufacturers.

# How to tune a piano!

The piano's out of tune. So we'll chop it up. Then we'll get a tin horn instead.

Sure, these men are crazy.

But they're using the same kind of thinking a lot of people have been using on the American economic system lately.

Our American way isn't perfect. We still have our ups and downs of prices and jobs. We'll have to change that. But even so, our system works a lot better than the second-rate substitutes being peddled by some countries we could mention.

It works better because of a few simple things. We are more inventive, and we know how to use machine power to produce more goods at lower cost. We have more skilled workers than any other country. We believe in collective bargaining and enjoy its benefits. And we Americans save—and our savings go into new tools, new plants, new and better machines.

Because of this, we produce more every working hour . . . and can *buy* more goods with an hour's work than any other people in the world.

We can make the system work *even better,* too: by *all* of us working *together* to turn out more for every hour we work—through better machines and methods, more power, greater skills, and by sharing the benefits through higher wages, lower prices, shorter hours.

It's a *good* system. It can be made *better.* And even now it beats anything that any other country in the world has to offer.

So—*let's tune it up, not chop it down.*

### Want to help? Mail this!

*I want to help.*

*I know that higher wages,* lower prices, shorter hours and larger earnings can all result from producing more goods for every hour all of us work.

*Therefore, I will ask myself* how I can work more effectively every hour I am on the job, whether I am an employee, an employer, a professional man or a farmer.

*I will encourage those things which* help us produce more and add to everyone's prosperity—things like greater

use of mechanical power, better machines, better distribution and better collective bargaining.

*I will boost the good things in our* set-up, and help to get rid of the bad.

*I will try to learn* all I can about why it is that Americans have more of the good things of life.

*Please send me your free booklet,* "The Miracle of America," which explains clearly and simply, how a still better living can be had for all, if we all work together.

> Republic Steel Corporation,
> Republic Building,
> Cleveland 1, Ohio.
>
> Name_____
>
> Address_____
>
> Occupation_____

The Advertising Council's economic education campaign, begun in late 1948, emphasized that the solution to America's economic problems was not radical change but expanded productivity through mechanization and increased efficiency. Reprinted from *Time,* Jan. 3, 1949; courtesy of the LTV Corporation.

Organized labor charged that business used its control over the mass media to sell not only its products but its ideology. Reprinted from *CIO News,* Feb. 17, 1947; courtesy of the George Meany Memorial Archives.

General Electric, a leading advocate of human relations in industry, barraged its employees, their families and neighbors with books, pamphlets, cartoons and articles in plant newspapers promoting corporate profits. Reprinted from *General Electric Commentator,* Mar. 3, 1950; courtesy of the General Electric Company.

On opening day of the Quaker Oats Company's "I'm Gonna Holler about Taxes" campaign, letter-writing stations were set up throughout the Cedar Rapids, Iowa, plant, and employees were encouraged to write their representatives in Washington urging support for legislation reducing the tax burden. Reprinted from *Public Relations Journal*, Oct. 1953; courtesy of *Cedar Rapids Gazette*.

Boeing Airplane's Fishing Derby was part of the recreation program run by Boeing employees with the sponsorship of management. The 1952 contest was so popular that over five thousand employees participated in a ticket drawing from which fifteen hundred contestants were selected. Reprinted from *Recreation*, Feb. 1953.

# How Many Homes Would Your Taxes Buy?

Concerned that few employees understood their tax burden, DuPont dramatized the impact of "hidden taxes" in the company journal. Reprinted from *Better Living*, Mar.–Apr. 1952; courtesy of the DuPont Company and Hagley Museum and Library.

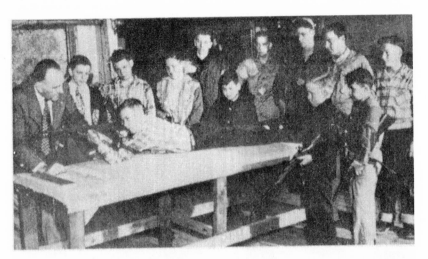

Olin Industries, which produced Winchester Arms and Ammunition, sponsored an extensive array of recreation activities for their employees' children. Not surprisingly, rifle clubs were the featured activity. If the guns were too big for the children, employees sawed off the barrels. Reprinted from *Industrial Sports and Recreation*, Feb. 1954.

Summer picnics featuring free T-shirts, hot dogs, soda, games, and prizes helped build employee and family identification with the company. Reprinted from *Industrial Sports and Recreation*, Feb. 1954.

UAW Local 600 responded to Ford's human relations campaign by advising workers to dump company communications into specially marked trash cans in each department. Reprinted from *Ford Facts*, July 3, 1948; courtesy of the Archives of Labor and Urban Affairs, Wayne State University.

In this cartoon, the UAW lampoons Allis-Chalmers' mandatory economic education program. Allis-Chalmers' workers filed grievances, complaining that "forced listening" was a violation of their rights. Reprinted from *United Automobile Worker*, Jan. 1950; courtesy of the Archives of Labor and Urban Affairs, Wayne State University.

# They Visit the Sick

## When a man is sick and is attacked by loneliness, a visiting union brother is very welcome

If you work at Ford's in Windsor and during January you had the flu, the way many people did, about the second week you were in bed your kid answered the door and then called upstairs, "Daddy, somebody's here to see you."

The next thing you knew a pleasant little man with gray hair and squint eyes and a rather large nose was standing in the door with a package wrapped up under his arm. . . .

"Hello, brother," he said, "my name is Don Kelton and I'm chairman of the Sick and Welfare Committee of UAW-CIO Local 200. Thought I'd come over and see how you were."

And then he walked over beside your bed and sat down. Before he began to talk he put his package on the bedside table and remarked, "Here is a little something for you the local sent you to say we all want you to get well pretty soon."

FEBRUARY, 1949                                            Page Seventeen

Visiting sick members was one way UAW Local 200 of Windsor, Canada, helped build loyalty to the union. Reprinted from *Ammunition*, Feb. 1949; courtesy of the Archives of Labor and Urban Affairs, Wayne State University.

Organized labor directly competed with corporate welfare capitalism by sponsoring recreational activities. The UAW promoted recreation as a vehicle for breaking down racial barriers between workers. Olga Madar Papers; courtesy of the Archives of Labor and Urban Affairs, Wayne State University.

Organized labor's community service activities served as an antidote to business propaganda. Reprinted from *AFL-CIO News;* courtesy of the George Meany Memorial Archives.

The second part spoke more specifically to current political and economic issues. Particularly before the election of Eisenhower, companies engaged in a propaganda campaign to teach general lessons on the importance of free enterprise to the American economic system. Careful not to attack unions too openly for fear that such boldness could alienate workers, conservative employers nevertheless emphasized the idea that only freedom from government regulation could prevent a drift toward statist collectivism. The Allis-Chalmers Company paper, for instance, published an employee poem entitled "My Name Is Profit" that began, "I have been maligned and I have been praised. / My name is hallowed where Industry and Commerce prosper. / Where I am unknown Enterprises cease and Bankruptcy takes over." Similarly, magazine racks, such as those at the American Steel and Wire Company carried titles like Sherman Rogers' *The Three Headed Monster,* an attack on government spending and high taxes.[63]

Successfully meshing these messages with human relation objectives required company journals to build readership by integrating news about the firm and economics with recreational and educational activities, department gossip, and announcements of special events in the lives of employees. Reading rack services mixed innocuous literature on hobbies and home improvement projects with those carrying an explicit economic message to encourage employees to form the habit of picking up every booklet from the racks and taking them home.[64]

Employers also used more direct means, such as letters, to personalize communications with individual employees. *The Public Opinion Index for Industry* found that the proportion of surveyed firms writing to employees increased from 28 percent in 1947 to 82 percent in 1955.[65] "It's warm," asserted James Black, the Director of Public Relations for the Associated Industries of Cleveland, "It goes right into the home of the worker and his family, and it takes the company with it." Beginning in 1946, Henry Ford II annually sent Christmas letters to every employee and his family. To encourage both loyalty and productivity in the work force, companies wrote to employees about competing firms, customers, future business prospects, and new methods and machinery. Letters, like many other forms of corporate communication, bypassed organized labor. Especially in times of conflict, employers felt these letters served as an important bridge to employees; International Harvester and Chrysler, among others, wrote almost daily to employees during strikes.[66]

Some firms went to great lengths to ensure that workers listened to their messages. In 1956, Kaiser Steel Company put its annual report in a motion picture film and then showed it along with a Hollywood premiere at company-sponsored theater parties to thirty thousand people. Other companies recorded their presidents' reports and sent the phonograph records to the employees' homes.[67] General Aniline & Film Corporation conducted a game called Qunch (quiz-at-lunch), testing workers on their knowledge gained from annual reports, booklets, magazines, and plant papers, of company economics, products, people and history.[68]

Managers argued that two-way communication was essential for verifying if workers were absorbing the employer's message. Attitude surveys were one means for determining what was on employees' minds. One thirty-minute survey developed in 1952 at the University of Chicago was used by Sears, Campbell Soup Company, and others to determine "what keeps the worker happy, enthusiastic, and loyal to his employer." By the mid-fifties, one in five firms was surveying its employees.[69] Meetings, particularly in small and medium sized firms, complemented surveys by providing a forum for face-to-face contact with management. Weekly "Understanding Luncheons" provided an "open forum" at such companies as Stanley Home Products, while Timken Roller Bearing Company invited all eleven thousand employees during 1953 to lunch in small groups with management. Many other firms utilized lunch and dinner meetings to explain their company's condition and outlook.[70]

Some firms combined meetings with plant tours, enabling employees to integrate their jobs into the firm's overall operation. Luncheon meetings with a ranking company officer after the tour dealt with such "touchy subjects" as job ratings and specific grievances.[71] One Chicago company, employing fifteen hundred workers, ended its tour with a conference with the general manager. The employee-tourists, timid at first, soon were "talking openly and with feeling about matters that are of deep concern to them." Enthusiastic responses from veteran workers who gained a new understanding of the company and a sense of pride in their work paid significant dividends, but few companies outdid Lockheed's 1950 tour, which dramatized the value of good workmanship. It ended with chartered flights over Southern California in company-built Constellations for eleven thousand employees on company time to enable them to see how the planes they built performed in the air.[72]

Companies devised some of the most innovative communication techniques to convince employees of the danger of big government and high taxes. Concerned that few employees understood their tax burden, Du Pont dramatized the impact of "hidden taxes" by having an employee and his family pick out all of the merchandise they might have purchased with the money they had paid in taxes between 1947 and 1954 and photographing the collection for its journal.[73] Other companies specifically mobilized workers to demand lower taxes and the creation of a "better business environment." On March 5, 1953, Quaker Oats Company initiated the "non-partisan" Ighat (I'm Gonna Holler About Taxes) campaign in seventeen major plants. Employees circulated Ighat petitions that they sent along with letters and postcards to their Congressmen urging support of legislation to reduce the tax burden. William Kohs, a Quaker Oats maintenance man, who won a contest by collecting antitax petition signatures, shouted "IGHAT" at Senator Everett Dirksen over the telephone.[74]

In the postwar decade, industrialists added a greater sophistication to the selling their version of the American economic system. A dozen educational and business organizations and over thirty large firms, ranging from progressives like Johnson & Johnson to such staunch antiunion conservatives as IBM and Du Pont, developed economic education programs, many of which were distributed nationwide to other firms. These entailed taking workers or supervisors off the shop floor for one or more days for a period of three to fifteen hours to participate in discussion classes. Approximately 105,000 Westinghouse, 180,000 U.S. Steel and 20,000 Swift Company employees were among the first to be exposed to this new technique. GE demonstrated its commitment to promoting "a better understanding of our American way of life" by assigning an executive full time as "Manager of Economic Training." In early 1951, a leading management consultant observed in the *Harvard Business Review* that "practically every prominent leader of business in the United States today is talking about teaching economics to employees. Many of the largest corporations have launched economic-education programs."[75]

Two of the most popular courses, "How Our Business System Operates" (HOBSO) and "In Our Hands," were initially created by the Du Pont Company and the Borg Warner Company and Inland Steel for their employees but then given to the National Association of Manufacturers and the American Economic Foundation for national distribution. The NAM conducted eight-day institutes for the training of HOBSO discussion leaders at sites throughout the country. By the mid-fifties over five hundred firms had participated in training sessions and were equipped to present the program and its sequel, HOBSO II, to their workers.[76] Beginning in 1950 the American Economic Foundation began distributing "In Our Hands," the Inland Steel and Borg Warner course. Within three years, 1.5 million workers had participated in this program. Nineteen firms in Latrobe, Pennsylvania, for example, co-sponsored the AEF program enabling half the workers of that town to "study economics." The *Latrobe Bulletin* observed that "we still cannot get used to hearing economics being casually discussed on buses, on street corners, and in the lunchrooms and taverns." Both these programs emphasized the importance of worker participation, because "conclusions reached through participation are understood, accepted, believed, and remembered." To facilitate participation, "In Our Hands" limited group size to fifteen and relied on "unsupervised" discussion led by rank-and-file workers. But the movies and flipcharts utilized by both programs tended to steer discussion to the conclusions desired by management.[77]

In terms of content, economic education fell into three groups—evangelistic, academic, and company oriented. Although there were significant differences in approach, all ultimately led to the goal of generating support for free enterprise. Evangelistic programs, like HOBSO and "In Our Hands," taught "Free Enterprise Economics" by focusing on the accomplishments of the American business system and by exploiting the fear of losing its benefits to encroaching socialism. HOBSO also emphasized the importance of profits, competition, and individual freedom and defended the "capitalistic standard of living against central government control." After the HOBSO sessions one Du Pont worker commented, "I realize what could happen under a socialistic government and now I am going to do all I can to prevent our Government from going socialistic."[78]

Academic programs, like the one developed by the University of Chicago for three thousand Republic Steel supervisors, shunned emotional appeals about the dangers of socialism for a more subtle approach. Such programs purported to teach the basic principles of economics, including issues like costs, stock investment, and the banking system, in order to provide a framework for analyzing economic and social problems. After participating in fifteen educational sessions, Republic Steel foremen were to have developed "an appreciation of the values, benefits and rewards to the individual as part of the Corporation and the Economic system" and an ability to correct workers' misconceptions. Foreman Chris Cutropia reported that the course enabled him to effectively respond to a disgruntled worker who snapped, "Why should I knock myself out for Republic? They make $75 out of every billet of steel and I get nothing." Cutropia, who took the "griper" aside and convinced him that the company would be lucky to make seventy-five cents a billet, recalled that "three months ago I wouldn't have been able to say anything."[79] Sears and Standard Oil courses typified company-oriented economic education. They presented to all their employees information specifically about the company—including its history, products, and financial outlook to enhance organizational rapport in the belief that the best way to generate approval of the economic system was to create feelings of identity with the firm.[80]

Economic education advocates pointed to the opinion polls conducted before and after the presentations to demonstrate how they reshaped worker attitudes. In 1951, before participating in the "In Our Hands" discussions, half the rank-and-file workers of Sharon Steel Corporation believed, among other things, that there was no real danger to personal freedom if the government took over industry, that the way to increase prosperity was to circulate more money, and that a strong union was the best protection for job security. The postcourse survey showed only one quarter of the workers agreed with these propositions. "In Our Hands" also seemingly changed workers' ideas about the best way to improve their standard of living. Exactly 53 percent compared with 33 percent of a precourse audience agreed that the solution was greater production.[81] Similarly, an informal survey of Latrobe workers showed that workers like Paul Palmer of the Toyad Company had learned that "People benefit when the tools of production are in the hands of private individuals rather than under the control and supervision of the government." Without the profit motive, he continued, "inefficiency is bound to creep into our industrial pattern and the loss would be passed on to the taxpayers."[82]

Often, economic education programs had more immediate political goals. In the early fifties, mobilizing support for the Republican party drove many programs. One example is the program developed by the arch-conservative Harding College and presented to workers at General Motors and Swift Company and throughout the Midwest, which openly attacked the Democratic party. The growth pattern of economic education programs reflected this political use. While economic training increased steadily after 1948, the biggest jump occurred during the year before the 1952 presidential election, when the percentage of participating firms increased from 20 to 44 percent. After the Republican victory, the number of active firms receded back to one in five. NAM president Charles Sligh, pleaded against backsliding, warning "the spirit of peace and sweet reasonableness is not going to descend automatically" just because of a political change in Washington. But an Opinion Research Corporation vice president later admitted that "the Republican victory in the national elections has removed the need for explaining so thoroughly the basis of the enterprise system and the threats to its continuation."[83]

In these ways, overtly political communications blended with employers' efforts to develop closer ties with their workers through human relations. Awakened to the growing interaction of the social environment and the factory atmosphere, employers with widely differing ideological perspectives adopted at least some of the language and mechanisms of human relations. Nonunion employers hearkened back to earlier uses of human relations to stifle labor organizing drives. Companies that had already succumbed to unions and collective bargaining expected improved employee relations programs and sophisticated communications to sap the strength and militancy of the unions in their plant. Liberal businessmen tended to be less interested in these mechanisms as tactics for stealing the worker's loyalty back from unions but nevertheless liked human relations prescriptions for enhancing worker productivity by responding to noneconomic needs.[84]

Whatever the desired results in any particular plant, treating the worker with greater dignity and respect was expected to yield bigger payoffs in the society at large. Being able to point to "instances where workers are so well satisfied . . . that union leaders have not been able to organize them," not only had significance for those instances but assured the American people that business, and not unions, was capable of caring for the average working man or woman. Doing what was necessary "to make the individual honor the privilege of being part of the enterprise" was likely not only to boost that individual's productivity but also to make that individual more prone to accept business's postwar attack on government interference and labor activism.[85] Consequently, unlike earlier attempts to use human relations strictly for a particular firm's narrow interests, the sweeping human relations movement of the postwar years had broad implications for the country's social and economic policies.

* * *

All the attention given to the noneconomic factors leading to the satisfaction and motivation of employees was never a complete substitute for improved wages and benefits. Even in the 1920s, human relations was tied to the worker's material well-being. The Depression, however, uncoupled the link attaching the employee's material standard of living to the company. Workers began to shift their loyalties, increasingly focusing on labor unions and government to guarantee their security and prosperity. In the postwar decades, companies sought to recapture the allegiance of their employees by revitalizing an older corporate concern for worker's welfare, a concern that included profit sharing and recreation. To these, business added an intricate web of benefits, including pensions, vacations, health plans, and educational assistance. Even in unionized plants, employers fought hard to claim credit for benefits that labor won through collective bargaining. Like human relations, the postwar version of American welfare capitalism had several purposes. In the narrow sense, recreation, health plans, and profit sharing boosted the worker's company consciousness, hopefully resulting in loyalty and improved productivity. At the same time, welfarism had implications for business's political agenda. If companies were truly providing for their workers' security and prosperity, the New Deal innovations of industrial unionism and the welfare state were unnecessary aberrations.

Welfarism's deep roots in the American economic system gave it a special resonance for postwar employers. With links to the paternalistic relationships between employer and employee in the earliest factories, more systematized welfare programs emerged in the early twentieth century to combat problems caused by the advent of mass production, Taylorism, and unionism. Particularly after the labor turmoil at the end of World War I, progressive employers began to address these problems by developing bureaucratic personnel programs in which welfarism played an important part.[86]

Underpinning welfare capitalism was the concept of management's obligation to secure the well-being of its employees. Employers improved conditions in their factories through safety campaigns, lunchrooms, and even beautified plants, and alleviated many of the hazards of industrial life by providing doctors and insurance plans. Through stock purchasing, pension, and home-ownership plans, managers sought to bind workers closer to the company and decrease the costly turnover rates, while work councils and shop committees encouraged workers to believe that they had a voice in determining wages and working conditions or in settling grievances. Finally, in recreational activities like sports teams and hobby clubs, employers linked company imperatives to the worker's leisure time and offset the monotony of factory work.[87]

The welfare capitalism of the 1920s achieved mixed results. Welfarism played at least some part in the precipitous decline in labor activity and the greater stability of the work force during that decade. But employees never passively accepted management's policies;

instead, corporate loyalty implied a negotiated compact between management and worker, based on the employer's willingness to compromise on significant issues. While companies achieved a degree of consent, they paid for it through wages and shopfloor concessions.[88]

The Depression, however, severely damaged the notion of mutual responsibility between worker and company. The prolonged economic slump forced most firms to drop expensive programs, while other companies faced competition for control of welfare programs from newly unionized workers. Equally important, government entitlement programs and unionized collective bargaining appeared to promise that business was not the only source of economic security. The company no longer had a free hand to dispense wages and benefits.[89]

Although in disarray, welfarism survived. Companies like Endicott Johnson, NCR, Sears, and Goodyear Tire and Rubber, combined welfare capitalism with a degree of intimidation to combat labor-organizing drives. A few others implemented new benefit schemes to contain the industrial union upsurge.[90] The outbreak of the Second World War brought changes in state policy that breathed new life into welfare capitalism. The drive to promote wartime productivity and industrial harmony led state agencies to support traditional welfare programs like corporate-sponsored industrial recreation. The government also altered corporate tax laws and instituted wage control policies that encouraged the development of employee benefit plans in the private sector. Finally, some firms struggling with labor militancy, turnover, and absenteeism looked to welfarism with renewed favor.[91]

By the late 1940s, management's effort to recapture their employees' loyalty led to an explosion in private-sector welfarism, underwritten by high corporate profits and postwar prosperity. But welfare capitalism had changed. State-sponsored public housing, for instance, limited employer interest in providing homes, which had been a common component of earlier welfare capitalism. Moreover, benefits like pensions, vacations, and health insurance came under the regulation of federal and state law or became meshed in the collective bargaining system. Still, employers hoped that providing an array of benefits and services would translate into greater productivity, higher morale, and increased employee loyalty. They also hoped to weaken worker reliance on unionism and the state.

One program that expanded rapidly following the war was profit sharing. Previously, a small number of companies had distributed profits, usually in the form of cash, shares, or deferred payments to encourage worker loyalty and productivity. All but disappearing in the 1930s, union criticism of high corporate profits in the postwar years renewed employer interest in the plans. The number of profit sharing plans formally approved by the U.S. Treasury Department grew from thirty-seven in 1940 to over twenty thousand in 1960.[92]

Firms resisting unionization were particularly attracted to a policy that promised to eliminate the "dividing line," and made workers "feel they belong, that they're not just another cog in the impersonal machine." Not surprisingly, then, in 1950 only 30 percent of the members of the Council of Profit Sharing Industries had contracts with organized labor. Some large nonunion firms like Sears, Procter and Gamble, and Dow Chemical offered profit sharing or stock ownership. Most often, however, smaller companies were behind the programs. Indeed, for many small and medium sized firms, profit sharing anchored a paternalistic personnel program designed to raise productivity while resisting unions.[93]

Beyond its immediate practical benefits, profit sharing generated great excitement among employers because it appealed to their broader class interests. Business leaders, who feared for the future of capitalism, believed that profit sharing's significance lay in strengthening the "spirit of capitalism" in the American social and political system. Strange J. Porter, personnel director of a Syracuse machine company, contended that profit-sharing plans, when combined with other evidence of "sincere appreciation and respect" for the worker, "will go farther in establishing his inherent identity with free enterprise . . . than anything we merely preach about."[94]

While profit-sharing plans attracted new interest, private benefit programs were far more significant and far-reaching. In part, offering benefits was an ingredient of a broader corporate strategy within primary sector firms to stabilize tight labor markets through changes in personnel policy.[95] But they also served as weapons in the battle to undermine worker allegiance to unions and reliance on public sector welfare programs.

Organized labor, of course, contested business's claim for credit in the massive growth in private sector benefits. Unions, in fact, had turned to private benefits only after their failure to expand the welfare state to include such reforms as national health insurance. Then, most employers resisted union demands, fearful of the cost and the loss of managerial prerogatives.[96] Business leaders charged that union-negotiated plans tended to "glorify the union at the expense of the employer," throwing the "obligation entirely on the one, the credit on the other." Instead, employers wanted the goodwill generated from voluntarily provided benefits and the freedom to administer such programs independently of unions. Several companies even tried to preempt union demands or government involvement by immediately instituting employee benefit plans.[97] However, union militancy and NLRB insistence that benefits were subject to collective bargaining forced companies to deal with union demands on these issues.[98]

Forced to concede to union demands, unionized firms tried to claim credit for the new benefit policies. In 1950, General Motors president C. E. Wilson contended that employers had been attempting to improve wages, working conditions, and benefits. He complained about what he believed was the false impression that improvements for workers "are brought about only by a union beating an employer over the head." Nonunion firms had an equally large stake in ensuring that benefits came willingly and without outside prodding. Both union and large nonunion firms came to believe that benefits, if properly handled, could "be turned into investments that bring a rich return in the form of a more efficient, more cooperative, and more stable work force."[99]

To assure the best return, the National Association of Manufacturers advised "a continual selling job of how well the employee is being treated." Employers used their developing communication channels, including booklets, movies, letters and personal conferences, to disclose the "hidden" value of the company's fringe benefit package.[100] Especially useful were individual stories demonstrating corporate concern. In August 1950, for example, Allis-Chalmers pointed to the experience of employee Steve Kalan. The company helped him rebuild his home after it was destroyed by fire. Allis-Chalmers, which was in the midst of a battle with UAW Local 248, trumpeted Kalan's observation that "I found out who my real friends are at a time like this." He advised, "be 100% with the management and they will be with you."[101]

Like profit sharing, then, private welfare plans carried a political message. To business leaders, the free enterprise system adequately met security needs, making unnecessary any expansion of the welfare state. Standard Oil executive J. W. Myers believed that private social security systems provided important means by which employers could reach their workers and "create a better understanding of how they may share in the fruits of private capitalism by each becoming a capitalist and having a stake in our economic system."[102]

Less costly forms of welfarism complemented employer efforts to build company consciousness. In 1949, a survey of new plants by the business journal, *Factory Management and Maintenance*, found progressive managers committed to a good physical environment, including gardens, air conditioning, escalators, and x-ray rooms. Minor changes, like improving lighting, and maintaining a decorous plant exterior, not only increased productivity but stimulated feelings of pride toward the plant and the company. Similarly, nice touches, like coffee breaks, plant nurses, financial counseling, holiday parties, and clubs for retirees enabled companies to assert that they treated workers like family; families, unlike the state, had a responsibility for caring for their own.[103]

A more pervasive link to earlier welfare capitalism was industrial recreation. Management's positive experience with recreation during the war led to a tremendous expansion of corporate-sponsored leisure activities in the 1950s.[104] In 1953, thirty thousand firms spent $800 million on recreation, a 50 percent increase over the previous five years. The National Industrial Recreation Association, which jumped from eleven founding members in 1941 to over nine hundred in 1957, estimated that industry spent more money on sports equipment than all the schools in the country combined.[105]

By the mid-1950s, industrial recreation had become such an important part of industrial relations programs that it was a business in itself. The Industrial Recreation Company of New York planned, coordinated, and packaged programs for such corporations as General Electric and Lever Brothers, while companies set out to convince workers that recreation did not simply mean "getting exhausted on your own time." Despite the growing competition from commercialized leisure, large numbers of workers took part in the recreation program; 94 percent of 3M's fifty-nine hundred St. Paul employees, for instance, participated in company classes, picnics, clubs, athletics, carnivals, and musical events. A 1949 *Factory* survey found that 75 percent of both union and nonunion workers approved of industrial recreation.[106]

Recreation addressed many of the same problems as human relations, and many company executives believed that it, too, would give alienated workers the individual recognition and sense of achievement lacking on the job. At the same time, it promoted the teamwork essential to industrial success. In 1952, General Motors personnel director W. J. Mahoney repeated a truism of the industrial recreation movement when he asserted that "employees who can play well together can work well together, too." As in the case of other welfare programs, advocates foresaw recreation paying off in increased productivity, resulting from improved morale and efficiency, and reduced fatigue, absenteeism, and turnover.[107]

Perhaps, more importantly, recreation was a crucial component in the effort to forestall or undermine unionism. Large nonunion firms like Eastman Kodak, Du Pont, and Scott Paper combined recreation with systematic welfare programs that included pensions, vacations, and insurance to successfully combat organized labor. Small paternalistic firms openly boasted that their picnics, parties, and clubs helped create a "nice, friendly attitude" that kept out union organizers.[108] In unionized firms, where organized labor competed with employers for credit for the implementation of benefits, employers hoped recreation would offset organized labor's influence. It helped give workers a new group identity that stemmed from the enterprise alone. Thus, after the war, new recreation programs anchored Ford's, International Harvester's, and Allis-Chalmers' efforts to win back the allegiance of their workers after more than a decade of bitter conflict.[109]

Large numbers of business leaders felt that recreation was a crucial means of breaking down social barriers that were often exploited by unions. A. H. Spinner, director of employee activities at Armstrong Cork Company, found that recreational activities promoted a company rather than a class orientation. "Class consciousness," he contended, "fades out of the picture when people are engaged in the pursuit of common interests."[110] Employers felt that corporate-sponsored leisure time also improved loyalty to the firm. In 1951, the personnel director of one firm reported to *Factory* that during a recent strike the firm reopened the plant to workers willing to cross the picket line. It discovered that while only 30 percent of plant workers regularly participated in the recreation program, over 60 percent of the strike-breakers were active in the company-sponsored activities. The personnel director justified recreation expenses this way: "We certainly don't consider recreation programs as strikebreaking tools . . . and don't feel recreation programs make company 'stooges' either. Its just that those who are active in recreation programs seem to be the employees who are mostly likely to stand on their own feet and rely on their own judgement."[111]

Recreation meshed with another corporate welfare goal of integrating families into the company. Historians, of turn-of-the-century welfarism, have explored the importance of families in shaping attitudes toward work, but the continuing significance of the relationship between the family and the workplace has been largely ignored.[112] Yet, in 1950, a business newsletter pointed out that "the family is the major influence in determining the course of any member of the group—including the worker." It advised that the employer who "realizes this fact, and works with it, will reap the long run benefit of a kinder feeling toward the company."[113]

Following this advice, many postwar employers reached out to families in a variety of ways. They sent letters and company publications home, opened recreation centers to workers' relatives, and built company parks to make the company a social center for workers' families. Particularly through mass activities, like summer picnics, or Christmas parties, managers attempted to bring the entire company together, including executives, supervisors, workers, and families, as a way of creating feelings of interdependence. Two such mass gatherings attracted sixty thousand Goodyear employees and families to a 1957 picnic and forty thousand workers and family members to the Consolidated Vultee Aircraft Corporation's free circus. Similarly, General Motor' 1949 preview of its new auto line for the GM family brought out fifty-three thousand people.[114] Joseph Losito gave General Motors the kind of endorsement it expected for its efforts when he stated, "my family looks forward to the BLC picnics and shows each year—we haven't missed a performance yet."[115]

After World War II, companies increasingly utilized open houses, plant tours, and family days to personalize the factory and to teach more explicit economic and political messages to relatives. In 1948, the Burroughs Adding Machine Company's 133 branches held a series of Family Nights, which provided information on the company's products and included talks by company officials. Burroughs also presented a company-made film, showing the American enterprise system in action and explaining how profits were good for business and the public.[116] In 1952, those touring the Foote Brothers Gear and Machine Corporation of Chicago "saw what dad did at the plant, the machine he operated and what he made. They shook hands with his foreman, his supervisor, union steward, and other fellow workers." Other companies used family factory tours to display their human relations programs, excellent working conditions, and many benefits to employee relatives.[117]

Direct contact with workers' families, companies felt, could enhance the corporate message and tighten employee identification with the firm. The Crucible Steel Company of America posted weekly safety slogans and phoned the homes of employees during work hours. Family members who could recite the slogan won a five-dollar prize. The company found that the "wives and children are flattered when the call comes to them . . . The company, once just a cold, impersonal name, is now a neighbor who calls on the telephone." Even vacations provided opportunities to promote family identification with the company. During the mid-fifties, Caterpillar and 3M employees pasted stickers with company slogans on their cars and luggage to enable traveling workers to recognize fellow employees.[118]

Firms tried to convince employees that the company took a human interest in their families. During the Korean War, Victor Adding Machine of Chicago sent corsages on Mothers Day to the mothers of fifty employees serving in the armed forces. The card read, "If your son were home, we know he would personally bring your favorite flowers. However, in his absence, please accept this token as a remembrance of him on Mothers Day." Other gestures targeted children; the General Electric recreation department in Schenectady ran a babysitting service to help harried parents. Firms often sent presents and cards to acknowledge new arrivals. The Ferro Corporation of Cleveland gave a sterling silver teething ring engraved with the baby's date, time, and weight at birth, while Timken Roller Bearing sent banks containing ten dimes "to start your youngster's first savings account."[119] Other firms began providing more substantial help through the establishment of college scholarship funds for employee children.[120]

Increasingly, employers developed recreational programs specifically for workers' children, both to engender workers' loyalty and to develop a relationship with potential employees. IBM and Eastman Kodak, among others, set up children's clubs and provided arts and crafts classes, while such firms as Caterpillar, Goodyear, and North American Aviation established instruction in various sports.[121] Special summer events brought children to plants throughout the country. In 1948, the first Ford Rouge day camp, which included a plant tour, attracted eight hundred children and six years later attendance had increased to over four thousand. Ford found the program "effective because it reaches into the home." Thousands of 3M and Timken Roller Bearing employees also brought their sons and daughters to work for day-long programs highlighted by a visit to the department where "Dad or Mom" works and the presentation of a shirt with the company emblem. To ensure attendance, the Timken personnel office sent a list of children's names, generated through their records, to foremen, who notified parents of the invitation to camp.[122] In 1954, the *Industrial Sports and Recreation Journal* observed that children who participated in corporate-sponsored activities upon reaching adulthood would surely "look upon the industry which has given them some of the best sports and recreational years of their life with a warmth and respect no company can buy."[123]

Spouses, particularly wives, remained the principal focus of company welfarism, however. In 1946, Whiting Williams wrote an article entitled "Who's Got Momma's Ear?" warning that labor leaders were giving special attention to selling wives on the importance of union membership. He contended that unions understood that wives were "a silent but important partner in all industrial relationships." Conversely, a 1951 survey of industrial workers' wives in Cleveland found that 62 percent of wives opposed strikes. Moreover, the more women knew about the company, the more they thought along management lines. However, the survey warned that where unions filled the gaps in company communication with the home, women tended to influence husbands along union rather than company lines.[124]

These observations powerfully influenced employers to court the "invisible" employee. In 1950, *Quotes Ending*, a newsletter for company editors, noted increasing use of features and news stories directed solely to the home, mainly at women. Editors believed that special pages with household hints and recipes attracted female readers to the company paper. Similarly, letters addressed to the spouse explained the firm's position during contract negotiations and attempted to enlist "mom" in the drive for quality, safety, and productivity.[125] In 1953, convinced that enthusiasm for the company could never be maintained "unless they are shared and nurtured by the distaff public," International Harvester invited the wives or female relatives of seventy thousand workers to a plant tour, lunch, and a meeting with top executives. The tour emphasized International Harvester's benefit program and taught that increased production meant progress and security for all.[126]

Companies gave wives special recognition for their "loyalty and devotion" to the firm. Armco Steel Corporation and Victor Adding Machine presented wives of long-term employees with gold broaches. With suggestion awards worth over $1,000, Westinghouse Corporation also gave the employee's spouse a gift. In 1951, the general manager of a small paternalistic firm in Denver explained why his company sent birthday cards and bouquets to employee wives, notified them of changes in hours, and handed them the profit-sharing checks at the company's annual Christmas party: "A man's wife has a powerful influence over her husband's reaction to his job and his company... if you do it properly, you can mold that influence so it does you and the employee a lot of good."[127]

In times of crisis, some employers tried to draw on the reservoir of goodwill developed through their attention to workers' wives. "You would be surprised," contended Timken Roller Bearing executive R. L. Frederick "at the pressure that a woman can place upon her husband if he is considering going out on strike for half a cent an hour, or vested right... Mrs. Employee will often make it clear that she doesn't care for that." To overcome a worker slowdown in 1949, the

Lionel Company sent home a series of cartoons called "Talking it Over with the Wife." The cartoons stated that if husbands were making less, they probably were "fighting the rate," which had been agreed upon with the union. According to Forbes, Lionel "did not underestimate the power of a woman. In a few weeks the laggards were back in stride, and production has hummed ever since."[128]

Profit sharing, benefits, recreation, and the integration of the family into the firm, these were the building blocks of the corporate attempt to build company consciousness. These mechanisms often blended with those associated with human relations in linking workers to the company and the free enterprise system. A core of American industry, led by firms like IBM, Du Pont, Sears, and Endicott Johnson, relied on human relations and welfarism to maintain their nonunion status. But, company consciousness cannot be dismissed as a strategy pursued only by the nonunion sector. Firms openly fighting with their unions, such as General Electric and Timken Roller Bearing, as well as those that had supposedly reached an accord— General Motors for one—utilized company consciousness to confine the political and economic horizons of both organized labor and liberal proponents of the welfare state.

## Notes

1. Charles S. Maier, *In Search of Stability: Explorations in Historical Political Economy* (Cambridge: Cambridge University Press, 1987), pp. 53, 63–69.

2. John W. Hill, "Industry's Iron Curtain," *PRJ* 2 (Nov. 1946): 3.

3. "Basic Elements of a Free, Dynamic Society—Part I, A Round Table Discussion Sponsored by the Advertising Council, Inc." *HBR* 29 (1951): 57.

4. On postwar managerial labor strategy, see Howell John Harris, *The Right to Manage: Industrial Relations Polices of American Business in the 1940's* (Madison: University of Wisconsin Press, 1982), passim.

5. Ibid., chap. 5; David Brody, *Work in Industrial America: Essays on the Twentieth Century Struggle* (New York: Oxford University Press, 1980), pp. 173–211.

6. On the accord, see, among others, Mike Davis, *Prisoners of the American Dream: Politics and Economy in the History of the US Working Class,* (London: Verso, 1986), p. 104; David M. Gordon, Richard Edwards, and Michael Reich trace the formation of an accord featuring union accommodation with management but acknowledge that the postwar labor management system reflected a compromise between labor and capital. *Segmented Work, Divided Workers: The Historical Transformation of Labor in the United States* (Cambridge: Cambridge University Press, 1982), pp. 170–89, esp. 189. Sociologist William Foote Whyte has observed that in the 1940s and 1950s the "prevailing relationships between unions and management were sharply adversarial." "From

Human to Organizational Behavior: Reflections on the Changing Scene," *ILRR* 40 (July 1987): 49. Similarly, Thomas A. Kochan, Harry C. Katz, and Robert B. McKersie argue that management never accepted unions as legitimate partners and that "deep-seated resistance towards unions" historically has been "embedded in the belief system of managers." They contend that an understanding of the post-1960 decline in union membership and collective bargaining coverage requires "a reconceptualization of managerial strategies, structures, and policies that were unfolding, often quietly" during the fifties and sixties. *The Transformation of Industrial Relations* (New York: Basic Books, 1986), pp. 3–38.

7. Edward T. Cheyfitz, "Show-Down Decade Ahead" (Address before the fifty-fourth annual Congress of American Industries), Hagley Library, Wilmington, Delaware. Unlike Brody and Lichtenstein, who emphasize the extent to which management successfully constrained union power, Tolliday and Zeitlin contend that the centralized and contractual collective bargaining that developed during the postwar limited management's freedom of action to a significant degree. Steven Tolliday and Jonathan Zeitlin, "Shop Floor Bargaining, Contract Unionism, and Job Control," in *On the Line: Essays in the History of Auto Work*, ed. Nelson Lichtenstein and Stephen Meyer (Urbana: University of Illinois Press, 1989), pp. 229–36, esp. 235.

8. James W. Kuhn, *Bargaining in Grievance Settlement: The Power of Industrial Work Groups* (New York: Columbia University Press, 1961).

9. Harris, *The Right to Manage*, pp. 135–36; Meyer Kestenbaum, "The Human Element in Productivity," AMA Personnel Series No. 172 (1948), pp. 28–33; Robert Wood Johnson, "Human Relations in Modern Business," *HBR* 27 (Sept. 1949): 533–34.

10. Charles R. Hook, Jr., "Profits and People: The Personnel Function of Management," AMA Personnel Series No. 132 (1950), p. 7.

11. Johnson, "Human Relations in Modern Business," p. 533.

12. Ibid., p. 533.

13. Lois R. Dean, "Union Activity and Dual Loyalty," *ILRR* 7 (July 1954): 526–36.

14. William H. Ruffin, "Management and Government in Human Relations" (Address before the Blue Ridge Conference of Southern Industrial Executives, July 18, 1951), Accession 1412, NAM, Industrial Relations Department Papers, Box 12 (hereafter Acc. 1412, NAM, Box 12).

15. E. Wright Bakke, "Labor and Management Look Ahead," AMA Personnel Series No. 98 (1946), p. 11.

16. Wallace F. Bennett, "The Bridge" (Address before a Regional Meeting of the Denver Rotary Club, the Manufacturers Association of Colorado and the NAM, June 2, 1949), Accession 1411, NAM, Series I, Box 5 (hereafter Acc. 1411, NAM I/5).

17. Bennett, "The Bridge"; "Employee Loyalty—How and When," *Communicator*, June 28, 1956, reprint in Acc. 1412, NAM, Box 14; Hill, "Industry's Iron Curtain," p. 5.

18. Martin Dodge, "Does Management Get Its Message Across to Employ-

ees?" AMA Personnel Series 102 (1946), p. 4; "Job of Communications," *Stet*, Aug. 1947, p. 5.

19. Solomon Barkin, "A Trade Unionist Appraises Management Personnel Philosophy," *HBR* 28 (Sept. 1950): 59–64.

20. Earl Bunting, "The Employee as an Individual" (Address before the Twentieth NAM Institute on Industrial Relations, Oct. 30, 1950), pamphlet (New York, n.d.), pp. 7–9.

21. Hill, "Industry's Iron Curtain," pp. 3–4; "Trends in Employee Thinking on Simple Economics," *POII* 8 (Feb. 1950): 5. See also Harris, *The Right to Manage*, pp. 184–89, for more extensive discussion of the business interpretation and concern over worker attitudes after the war.

22. Hugh L. Rusch, "Management's Obligation to Disseminate Economic Facts," in *Proceedings of Thirty-Second Silver Bay Conference on Human Relations in Industry, July 19–23, 1950* (New York, 1950), pp. 19–20.

23. Henry Ford "Obligation of Business Management" (Address before the Thirty-fifth Annual Meeting of the Chamber Commerce of the United States, Apr. 30, 1947), Box 29, AOF 1, LMDC.

24. Rusch, "Management's Obligation to Disseminate Economic Facts," p. 20; *M&F* quoted in S. Avery Raube, "Nonfinancial Incentives," *MRec* 8 (Dec. 1946): 395.

25. Guy B. Arthur, Jr., "The Status of Personnel Administration in Management," AMA Personnel Series 102 (1946), pp. 32–34.

26. Austin S. Ingleheart, "Management Must Sell Itself," *FMM* 106 (Sept. 1948): 212.

27. M. J. Murphy, "Why Unions Cry 'Speed-Up'—and How Management Can Answer," *FMM* 107 (July 1949): 122–25; M. J. Murphy, "Must Big Unionism Mean Labor Monopoly?" *FMM* 107 (Oct. 1949): 125–28.

28. Victor Riesel, "Remarks" at the 55th Annual Congress of American Industry, Dec. 6, 1960, NAM Press Releases, Neilson Library, Smith College.

29. James J. Nance, "Top Management Views the Job Ahead in Industrial Relations," AMA Personnel Series No. 124 (1949), pp. 32–34; J. M. Gabatese, "What Labor Did in the Election—and What It Will Do," *FMM* 107 (Jan. 1949): 134–37.

30. In 1961, Textile Research Director Solomon Barkin tried to explain the decline in the growth of unionism, contending that one of the most serious obstacles was "the unwillingness of employers to accept unions and collective bargaining as an integral part of the industrial system." He contended that important segments of the business community fought unions through a theory of personnel management designed to build allegiance among employees to their companies. Solomon Barkin, *The Decline of the Labor Movement and What Can Be Done About It* (Santa Barbara, Calif.: Center for the Study of Democratic Institutions, 1961), pp. 5–20, 39–40.

31. William H. Ruffin, "Management and Government in Human Relations."

32. There is a vast contemporary literature on the origins and development of human relations. Among the classic descriptions is Loren Baritz, *The Servants of Power: A History of the Use of Social Science in American Industry* (Mid-

dletown, Conn.: Wesleyan University Press, 1960). For a more recent discussion, see Richard Gillespie, *Manufacturing Knowledge: A History of the Hawthorne Experiment* (Cambridge: Cambrige University Press, 1991).

33. A. H. Maslow, "A Theory of Human Motivation," *Psychological Review* 50 (Sept. 1943): 370–96; Keith Davis, *Human Relations in Business* (New York: McGraw-Hill, 1957), pp. 38–44.

34. Baritz, *The Servants of Power*, pp. 202–3; Henry A. Landsberger, *Hawthorne Revisited: Management and the Worker, Its Critics, and Developments in Human Relations in Industry* (Ithaca: Cornell University Press, 1958), pp. 30–43.

35. Thomas G. Spates, "The Competition for Leadership in a Welfare Economy" (Address Before the Midwinter Personnel conference of the American Management Association, Chicago, Illinois, Feb. 15, 1949), Acc. 1412, NAM, Box 13.

36. Welfare workers during the Progressive Era had discussed the problem of worker alienation. Also there were early efforts at foreman training during World War I. Sanford M. Jacoby, *Employing Bureaucracy: Managers, Unions, and the Transformation of Work in American Industry, 1900–1945* (New York: Columbia University Press, 1985), pp. 99–104, 258–59, 269–73; Baritz, *The Servants of Power*, pp. 139–66.

37. Baritz, *The Servants of Power*, p. 169; Davis, *Human Relations in Business*, pp. 7–8.

38. Henry Ford II, "The Challenge of Human Engineering," pamphlet c. 1946 in Box 55, AOF 1, LMDC.

39. Fowler McCormick, "American Business and Its Human Relations," AMA Personnel Series No. 106 (1947), p. 3.

40. Among firms formally adopting systematic human relations programs on the heels of the postwar strike wave were the George D. Roper Company, Ford Motor, General Electric, ALCOA, Steel Improvement and Forge Company, Borg-Warner Company, Monsanto Chemical Company, and International Harvester. "Human Relations: A New Art Brings a Revolution to Industry," *Time*, Apr. 14, 1952, p. 96; Cloud Wampler to H. M. Dirks, June 28, 1948, Box 27, AOF I, LMDC; "Communication Methods at Carrier," *MRec* 10 (Sept. 1948): 441–43.

41. Leo Teplow, "It's the Individual Who Counts" (Speech delivered before the Toledo Foreman's Club, Dec. 21, 1949), Acc. 1412, NAM, Box 13.

42. For a more extensive treatment of the changing role of foremen, see Jacoby, *Employing Bureaucracy*, chaps. 1, 5, 6, 7, and 8; Harris, *The Right to Manage*, pp. 63–69, 74–87, 143–48, 162–67, 171–74; Nelson Lichtenstein, "'The Man in the Middle': A Social History of Automobile Industry Foreman," in *On the Line: Essays in the History of Auto Work*, ed. Nelson Lichtenstein and Stephen Meyer (Urbana: University of Illinois Press, 1989), 153–89.

43. Jacoby, *Employing Bureaucracy*, pp. 269–72; Corning White, "Humanizing Management," *PJ* 30 (Oct. 1951): 168–72; Lukens Steel Company, "Industrial Relations Division Annual Progress Report for the 1950 Fiscal Year and Forecast of Special Projects for the 1951 Year," Jan. 15, 1951, Box 31,

AOF III, LDMC. For more references on the origins and development of a softer supervisory style see works cited by Harris, *The Right to Manage*, pp. 267–68; Lemuel R. Boulware, "How Big is Our Job?" AMA Personnel Series No. 116 (1948), pp. 39–41; *Supervisor's Guide to General Electric Job Information*, pamphlet (1947), Box 57, AOF 1, LMDC; National Association of Manufacturers, "Improving Human Relations in Industry," p. 10, HML.

44. Baritz, *Servants of Power*, pp. 186–88; James C. Worthy, "Democratic Principles in Business Management," *MRec* 14 (Mar. 1949): 19; William Foote Whyte, "From Human Relations," p. 492.

45. Lewis Corey, "Human Relations Minus Unionism," *L&N* Spring, 1950, p. 50; William B. Wolf, *The Management of Personnel* (Belmont, Calf.: Wadsworth Publishing, 1961), pp. 248; "Suggestions Are Good For the System," *AB*, July 1949, p. 28; "The Suggestion Box: Treasure Chest for Industry," *Time*, Nov. 26, 1956.

46. For worker reaction to the suggestion system at Remington Rand, see Marc Steven Kolopsky, "Remington Rand Workers in the Tonawandas of Western New York, 1927–1956: A History of the Mohawk Valley Formula" (Ph.D. diss., University of New York, Buffalo, 1986); E. W. Hamlin, "Waste Reduction Campaign Hits Million-Dollar Jackpot," *FMM* 107 (May 1949): 102–3; "Silver Dollars for Quality," *FMM* 114 (Sept 1956): 140.

47. A. L. Chapman, "Use Showmanship to Get Better Plant Performance," *FMM* 110 (Feb. 1952): 84–89.

48. "Presentation of Employee Awards," pamphlet, 1950, Box 56, AOF I, LMDC; "Industry Honors Its Best," *MRec* 14 (June 1952): 225–32.

49. "'Happy Birthday'—from the Company," *MRec* 16 (Jan. 1954): 3–11, 34–35, esp. 3.

50. "Making a Production of the Service Club Dinner," *MRec* 14 (Mar. 1952): 96; "How to Make Service Awards Mean More," *FMM* 108 (Dec. 1950): 108.

51. "How One Company Fits Women to Jobs," *FMM* 115 (Feb. 1957): 125; Francis M. Bogert, "Keeping the Gals Happy," *PJ* 28 (Apr. 1950): 412–13; *PRN*, Mar. 3, 1952; June 13, 1955; "Planning a Company Picnic?" *MRec* 13 (Sept. 1951): 132.

52. Anna M. Rosenberg, "A New Industrial Citizenship for America's Workers," *FMM* 106 (Aug. 1948): 111–12; Harris, *The Right to Manage* pp. 189–92.

53. Jacoby, *Employing Bureaucracy*, p. 253.

54. Even before the passage of Taft-Hartley, the NLRB and the courts had begun to broaden the parameters of allowable employer speech. Taft-Hartley codified this trend. "How Practical Personnel Men Think the Labor Law Will Work," *FMM* 105 (August 1947): 91; "Economic 'Facts of Life' for Your Workers," *MI* 14 (Dec. 15, 1947): 40.

55. Harold Hawkey, Memo, "Management's Hottest Problem," Apr. 7, 1952, Acc. 1411, NAM I/11; Ira Mosher, "Producing for Freedom" (Address before the 55th Annual Congress of American Industry, Dec. 6, 1950), NAM Press Release, Neilson Library, Smith College; the Quarterly Reports of the NAM Employee Relations Division trace the organization's involvement in the drive

to promote employee communications, Acc. 1411, NAM I/13, Carroll E. French, "Evaluation of Communication Methods" (Address before Estes Park Conference on Human Relations In Industry, July 14, 1950), Acc. 1412, NAM, Box 6.

56. Walter Petravage, "The Chamber of Commerce Does Something about It!" *PRJ*, Nov. 1950, pp. 6–8. The Chamber of Chamber of Commerce files at the LMDC contain programs of "Explaining Your Business Seminars" conducted by the CCUS, Box 30, AOF 1, LMDC; "How to Be Understood," *Stet*, Nov. 1956, pp. 1–4.

57. ERLIC, *Communications and the Issues of Our Times*, pamphlet, 1958, ERLIC, *Purposeful Communication with Your Employees*, pamphlet, n.d., both in Box 51, AOF I, LMDC.

58. John S. Bugas, "Labor Relations and Productivity," AMA Personnel Series No. 112 (1947), p. 57; William B. Given "Freedom to Manage" (Address before the American Management Association meeting in Chicago, Nov. 15, 1946), pamphlet, Box 4, AOF I, LMDC; Ivan L. Willis, "Basic Principles for Effective Communications," *AM* 15 (Sept. 1950): 9.

59. Steinkraus quoted in "Management's Quid Pro Quo," *MRec* 16 (Feb. 1954): 62.

60. "GM's New 'Booklet Cafeterias' Open Information Channel Between Top Management and Employees," *AB*, Jan. 1950, p. 53; "Information Racks: A New Communications Medium," National Industrial Conference Board Conference Report No. 125 (New York, 1952); *New York Tribune*, Nov 8, 1959.

61. See Stuart D. Brandes, *American Welfare Capitalism, 1880–1940* (Chicago: University of Chicago Press, 1970), pp. 62–65, for origins of the employee magazine; Robert Newcomb, "Modern Administration of Employee Publications," AMA Personnel Series No. 108 (1947), pp. 25–29; "Survey Shows Big Gains," *Stet*, Jan. 1952, pp. 4–5; *WSJ*, Oct. 23, 1962.

62. Harris, *The Right to Manage*, p. 191; "Many Private Opinions," *Stet*, Oct. 1946, pp. 1–4; "Help 'em Like the Job," *Stet*, May 1952, pp. 4–5.

63. Harris, *The Right to Manage*, p. 191; "For New Understanding," *Stet*, Feb. 1950, pp. 1–4; *A-C Views*, June 4, 1949; Pamphlets distributed by the American Steel & Wire Co. Rack Service ca. 1950 in Box 11, AOF IV, LMDC; "How A S & W Does It," *Stet*, Apr. 1950, pp. 2–3.

64. *New York Herald Tribune*, Jan. 8, 1959; John Cameron Aspley and Eugene Whitmore, *The Handbook of Industrial Relations* (Chicago: Dartnell, 1952), pp. 825–45.

65. "How to Make the Communications Dollar Work Harder," *POII* 14 (1956): 4.

66. James M. Black, "How to Write Better Letters to Employees," *FMM* 111 (Sept. 1953): 84–89; Wells Norris, "Keeping 185,000 Ford Employees Informed," *AB*, June 1954, pp. 16–17, 44; "The Battle for Men's Minds," *Explaining Your Business*, May 1953.

67. "AFT President Records Message for Employees," *AB*, July 1948, p. 59; "Sure-Fire Way to Get Employees to Listen to Your Company Story," *FMM* 114 (Dec. 1956): 124–25.

68. "New Qunch Game Keeps Employees Informed about Company Products and People," *AB*, Sept. 1948, p. 59.

69. For a more extensive discussion of attitude surveys, see Baritz, *The Servants of Power*, pp. 149–55; Sanford M. Jacoby, "Employee Attitude Testing at Sears, Roebuck and Company, 1938–1960," *Business History Review* 60 (Winter 1986): 602–32; "New Morale Meter Measures Employee Attitudes," *AB*, Apr. 1952, p. 56.

70. "How to Make the Communications Dollar Work Harder," *POII* 14 (1956): 8; M. J. Murphy, " A Little Paternalism Makes a Lot of Sense," *FMM* 108 (Apr. 1950): 55; "Lunch with the Bosses," *FMM* 111 (July 1953): 138. The Thompson Products Records provide a good record of the numerous meetings held by the firm. See, for example, *Friendly Forum*, June 21, 1946, Oct. 11, 1946, Case 15, Thompson Products Company Records, Baker Library, Harvard University, Boston, Mass.

71. "Two Way Communication Builds Employee Co-operation," *AB*, July 1959, pp. 34–35.

72. Robert Newcomb and Marg Sammons, "Plant Tours for Employees," *M&F* 52 (Jan. 1953): 102–4, esp. 104; "Let 'em Fly in the Finished Product," *FMM*, 108 (Apr. 1950): 83.

73. "Impact of Taxes is Revealed in Unusual Picture," *AB*, Jan. 1954, p. 40.

74. The following year Avco, GE, International Harvester, Quaker Oats, and Sears sponsored a similar campaign entitled IGHUGS (I'm Gonna Howl 'bout Unnecessary Government Spending); *PRN*, Apr. 20, 1953, Feb. 8, 1954; "Quaker Oats Fights High Taxes with 'Ighat' Plan," *AB*, Apr. 1953, p. 56.

75. Several studies published during the fifties examined the development and content of various in-plant economic education programs. See Blaine M. Cooke, "Economic Education in Industry" (Ph. D. diss., University of Minnesota, 1954); Richard Stanton Rimanoczy, *Adult Economic Education in Industry* (New York: Lincoln Foundation, 1954). All Westinghouse employees underwent two separate programs of economic education between 1951 and 1953; "Westinghouse Promotes American Way in Program," *AB*, Oct. 1951, p. 64; *PRN*, Jan 23, 1953; "Highlights of the General Electric Economic Education Program," pamphlet, n.d., Box C8, Acc. 1631, AISI; Fred G. Clark to J. Howard Pew, Sept. 20, 1951, Box 213, Pew Papers; Swift Uses 'Slapboard' Talks for Dramatic Emphasis," *AB*, Jan. 1950, p. 54; William H. Stevenson, "Economic Education for Employees," *HBR* 29 (Jan 1951): 75.

76. The records of the Education Department of the NAM trace the development, spread, and content of the HOBSO program, Acc. 1411, NAM I/ 62-70, for a listing of firms involved in HOBSO see Box 67; *NAM News*, Sept. 9, 1950, Jan. 6, 1951.

77. "In Our Hands—Workers Talk Economics," *MI* 22 (July 15, 1951): 41–45; Stevenson," Economic Education for Employees," p. 77; *Latrobe Bulletin*, Apr. 10, 1951; James M. Underwood, "A Program of Community Economic Education" (pamphlet), (c. 1951), Box C-8, AISI.

78. For a good analysis of the content of the major programs, see Cooke,

"Economic Education in Industry"; H. K. Breckenridge, "Freedom or Social-ized Industry?" *PJ* 30 (Mar. 1952): 376–79, esp. 377; "Comments Concern-ing 'HOBSO' Program" (Du Pont Company) Acc. 1411, NAM I/64.

79. Cooke, "Economic Education in Industry," pp. 19–20, 27–45; "Republic Steel Teaches Economics to Supervisors," *BW,* Sept. 8, 1951, p. 88; Foreman-ship Foundation, *Survey of Economic Education,* AMA Management Develop-ment Series (1951), pp. 33–34; "Teaching Foremen the Economic Facts of Life," *MRev* 40 (Dec. 1951): 742.

80. Cooke, "Economic Education in Industry," pp. 113–28; "Esso Exam-ines Economic Education," *MRec* 12 (Sept. 1950): 334–37.

81. "How the 'In Our Hands' Program Affected Employee Thinking at Sharon Steel Corporation," Survey for Sharon Steel Corporation prepared by the Public Opinion Index for Industry, Opinion Research Corporation, Feb. 1952, Box 213, Pew Papers; "Company Courses in Economics—Test Results On," *POII* 10 (Jan. 1952).

82. *Latrobe Bulletin,* Apr. 10, 1951.

83. Foremanship Foundation, *Survey of Economic Education,* pp. 7–8; "Changing Fashions in Economic Education," *MRec* 22 (Oct. 1960): 18–20; "How to Make the Communications Dollar Work Harder," *POII* 14 (1956): 9; New York State School of Industrial and Labor Relations, "In-Plant Commu-nication Seminar," July 11–15, 1955, p. 63.

84. Wallace F. Bennett, "We Must Learn How to Manage Our 'Phantom Factories,'" *FMM* 107 (Aug. 1949): 94–96; James J. Nance, "Top Management Views the Job Ahead in Industrial Relations," AMA Personnel Series No. 124 (1949), p. 38; Robert Wood Johnson, "Human Relations in Modern Business," pp. 521–41.

85. "Industry and Public Relations Program of Columbia Steel and Shaft-ing Company," c. 1948, Box 39, AOF I, LMDC; L. C. Morrow, "Industrial Peace Can be Speeded by Working from the Bottom Up," *FMM* 107 (Apr. 1949): 49.

86. Stuart D. Brandes, *American Welfare Capitalism, 1880–1940* (Chicago: University of Chicago Press, 1976).

87. Company-level studies of welfare capitalism include Stephen Meyer, *The Five Dollar Day: Labor Management and Social Control in the Ford Motor Company, 1908–1921* (Albany: State University of New York, 1981), and Ger-ald Zahavi, *Workers, Managers, and Welfare Capitalism: The Shoeworkers and Tanners of Endicott Johnson, 1890–1950* (Urbana: University of Illinois Press, 1988).

88. Brandes argues that American workers failed to accept welfare capi-talism, finding its paternalism intrinsically demeaning. In addition, the rise in popularity of the automobile and the extension of community services undercut the demand for plant-based activities and services. It was, he con-tends, a passing phase of American industry. David Brody asserts, however, that companies practicing welfarism won the loyalty and goodwill of most of their workers and that welfarism would have persisted untransformed had it not been for the extraordinary turn in the business cycle. Brandes, *Ameri-*

*can Welfare Capitalism*, pp. 30–37, 135–48; David Brody, *Workers in Industrial America: Essays on the Twentieth Century Struggle* (New York: Columbia University Press, 1985), pp. 60–78. For more subtle interpretations of welfare capitalism's impact, see Lizabeth Ann Cohen, *Making a New Deal: Industrial Workers in Chicago, 1919–1939* (Cambridge: Cambridge University Press, 1990), pp. 159–211, and Zahavi, *Workers, Managers and Welfare Capitalism*, passim.

89. Cohen, *Making A New Deal*, pp. 238–46; Brody, *Workers in Industrial America*, pp. 66–78; Gordon, Edwards, and Reich, *Segmented Work, Divided Workers*, pp, 176–82.

90. Sanford Jacoby discusses the persistence of welfarism in the 1930s and beyond, *Employing Bureaucracy*, pp. 207–85. See also Zahavi, *Workers, Managers and Welfare Capitalism*, pp. 99–125. Despite its welfare program, Goodyear lost its battle against unionization in 1936. Daniel Nelson, "The Company Union Movement, 1900–1937," *Business History Review* 56 (Autumn, 1982): 354–57.

91. Elizabeth Fones-Wolf, "Industrial Recreation, the Second World War, and the Revival of Welfare Capitalism, 1934–1960," *Business History Review* 60 (Summer 1986): 242–50; Jacoby, *Employing Bureaucracy*, p. 266; Beth Stevens, "Blurring the Boundaries: How the Federal Government Has Influenced Welfare Benefits in the Private Sector," in *The Politics of Social Policy in the United States*, ed. Margaret Weir, Ann Shola Orloff, and Theda Skocpol (Princeton: Princeton University Press, 1988), pp. 130–34.

92. Brandes, *American Welfare Capitalism*, pp. 83–91; B. L. Metzger, *Profit Sharing in Perspective* (Evanston, Ill.: Profit Sharing Research Foundation, 1964), p. 6; "Sharing the Profits: Businessmen Get a New Religion," *Time*, Dec. 6, 1954, p. 104.

93. "Profit Sharing," *MI* 20 (July 15, 1950): 52–56; *Financial Post*, Oct. 7, 1950; "Motorola Profit Sharing Plan Paid $4.41 for Each Employee Dollar," *AB*, Apr. 1951, pp. 10–11. For profit sharing in unionized firms, see Dwight G. Baird, "Profit Sharing Doubles Production," *M&F* 52 (May 1953): 133–36; Clarence A. Wimpfheimer, "The Importance of Being Important Together," *AM* 16 (Mar. 1951): 8–10.

94. *WSJ*, Dec. 5, 1949; "Profit-Sharing Industries Organize," *FMM* 105 (Oct. 1947); 234–36; Strange J. Palmer, "Labor-Management Partnership Through Profit Sharing," AMA Personnel Series No. 140 (New York, 1951): 43.

95. Jacoby, *Employing Bureaucracy*, pp. 232–74; Edward Berkowitz and Kim McQuaid, *Creating the Welfare State* (New York: Praeger, 1980), pp. 135–37.

96. Some employers were not opposed to the expansion of benefits, finding advantages in the tax breaks and the ability to pension off older employees. This group also envisioned improvements in morale and loyalty from the voluntary provision of benefits. Jill Quadagno, *Transformation of Old Age Security: Class and Politics in the American Welfare State* (Chicago: University of Chicago Press, 1988), pp. 159–62; Beth Stevens, "In the Shadow of the Welfare State: Corporate and Union Development of Employee Benefits" (Ph.D. diss., Harvard University, 1984), pp. 116–25.

97. "Royalties for Unions," *FMM* 103 (Sept. 1945): 92; Stevens, "In the Shadow of the Welfare State," pp. 121–22; Gustave Simons, "Controlling the Cost of Employee Benefits," *N.A.C.A. Bulletin*, Jan. 15, 1946, p. 464; "The Greatest Opportunity on Earth," *Fortune*, Apr. 1949, p. 68.

98. Stevens, "In the Shadow of the Welfare State," pp. 122–36; Jacoby, *Employing Bureaucracy*, p. 23.

99. David B. Cornfield, "Declining Union Membership in the Post–World War II Era: The United Furniture Workers of America, 1939–1982," *American Journal of Sociology* 91 (Mar. 1986): 1112–53, explores the implications of union-corporate competition over benefits. "Correcting the Wrong Impression," *FMM* 108 (Aug. 1950): 224; "The Neglected Side of Fringes," *MRec* 21 (Apr. 1959): 120.

100. "Confidential Report of the N.A.M. Institute of Industrial Relations," Mar. 11–15, 1957, Box 9, USA District 30 Records, USA/A; "Getting Across the Value of Employee Benefits," *MRec* 21 (Oct. 1959): 332–41.

101. Robert Newcomb and Marg Sammons, *Employee Communications in Action* (New York: Harper and Brothers, 1961), pp. 116–17; *A-C Views*, Aug. 31, 1950.

102. J. W. Myers, "Governmental and Voluntary Programs for Security," *PJ* 28 (Mar. 1950): 35–36.

103. Alonzo Flack, "Provide Favorable Working Conditions," *FMM* 107 (Oct. 1949): 73; "Medical Help at Home," *FMM* 117 (Dec. 1959): 125; "Retirement with a Future," *FMM* 113 (June 1955): 124–26; "Pensions Alone Are Not Enough," *MRev* 41 (Aug. 1952): 280–81.

104. For the impact of World War II on employee recreation, see Fones-Wolf, "Industrial Recreation."

105. In 1952, McCullough Motors Corporation of Los Angeles spent over $1,000,000 on its recreation building. Even the annual picnic could require a significant financial commitment from the company. Timken Roller Bearing, for example, spent $50,000 for its annual picnic; *PRN*, Aug. 7, 1950; "The Big Boom in Employee Recreation," *MRev* 41 (May 1957): 27–29; "Industry Investing $800 Million This Year in Sports, Recreation for Employees," *ISR* 14 (June 15, 1953): 7.

106. *NYT*, Nov 12, 1956; A. H. Spinner, "Industrial Recreation—What It Is—and What It Isn't," *ISR* 15 (May 1954): 9; "You Say Recreation Won't Pay Off!" *FMM* 115 (June 1957): 140; "What the Factory Worker Really Thinks," *FMM* 107 (Nov. 1949): 108–9.

107. W. J. Mahoney, "Oldsmobile Management Finds Recreational Teamwork Carries Over Smoothly into Work Production," *ISJ* 13 (Oct. 15, 1952): 30; Jackson M. Anderson, *Industrial Recreation: A Guide to Its Organization and Administration* (New York: McGraw-Hill, 1955), pp. 3–34; John B. Clark, "Employee Recreation: A Potent Contribution to Plant Morale," *ISR* 13 (Apr. 15, 1952): 19–20.

108. "Playing at the Plant," *BW*, Feb. 20, 1954, pp. 74–80; "Employee Policies and Practices in American Organizations: Eastman Kodak," *Journal of Chemical Engineering* 27 (Apr. 1950): 200–201; Dwight G. Baird, "Employee Club Prevents Labor Trouble," *AB*, Jan. 1954, pp. 18, 24.

109. Ford's recreation program grew rapidly with annual participation increasing from 286,000 in 1946, the first year of operation, to 2,156,000 in 1956. Ivan L. Willis, "American Industry and Its Human Relations" (Address before the State Layman's Advance, Roberts Park Methodist Church, Indianapolis, Indiana, May 22, 1949), Acc. 1412, NAM, Box 12; "Allis-Chalmers Recreation Program," Nov. 11, 1963, Box 6, AOF IV, LMDC; "Employee Recreation at Ford Motor Company," May 26, 1949; Ford executives discussed their hopes for the recreation program at a management meeting in late 1948. They noted that at the Rouge participation jumped from four thousand during the program's first month in operation to forty-five thousand a month two years later. "Report of Management Meeting," Ford Motor Company, Oct. 1948, both in Box 54, AOF I, LMDC.

110. Spinner, "Industrial Recreation," p. 10.

111. "Recreation vs. Strike," *FMM* 109 (Apr. 1951): 79.

112. See, for instance, the work of Virginia Yans-McLaughlin, *Family and Community: Italian Immigrants in Buffalo, 1880–1930* (Ithaca, N.Y.: Cornell University Press, 1977).

113. *Quotes Ending: An Information Letter to Management on Employer-Employee Publication*, May 1950, p. 2; Edward J. Condon, "Management's Relations with Employees and Their Families," AMA General Management Series No. 170 (1956), pp. 18–27.

114. "How to Take Care of Everyone," *ISJ* 14 (June 15, 1953): 10; "Sixty Thousand Goodyear Folks Have Themselves a Picnic," *ISJ* 15 (Sept. 15, 1953): 26–27; "Convair Goes to a Circus," *ISJ* 11 (July 1950): 15, 25–26; *General Motors Folks*, Feb. 1949, p. 10; "Christmas Greetings for Employees," *BW*, Dec. 19, 1953, pp. 120–24.

115. General Motors Corporation, *The Worker Speaks: My Job and Why I Like It* (1948), p. 137.

116. Dwight G. Baird, "Family Nights at Burroughs," *AB*, Jan. 1949, pp. 20–21, 48.

117. F. C. Minaker, "What Open House Can Accomplish," *AB*, Feb. 1952, pp. 36–38; Norge Machine Products Division, Borg Warner Corporation, "Planned Activities Program," 1948, Box 26, AOF IV, LMDC.

118. *PRN*, Apr. 7, 1952, May 9, 1955; "Safety Contest for Children Draws Management and Goodrich Employees Closer Together," *AB*, Nov. 1949, p. 54; "Spread the Word," *FMM* 115 (Oct. 1957): 144.

119. *Exchange* (NAM newsletter), Jan. 1950, Acc. 1411, NAM I/122; *PRN*, Jan. 15, 1952, May 25, 1953; "Kid Stuff," *M&F* 53 (Nov. 1953): 103; "Well Fed Babies," *M&F* 50 (Apr. 1952): 108.

120. "Off to College—On Company Funds," *MRec* 13 (June 1951): 210–12, 235–36; "Company Scholarship Programs Broaden," *MRec* 14 (May 1952): 172.

121. "Company Recreation Programs for Children," *MRec* 22 (Mar. 1960): 5–9; "Dad's Boy Taught Baseball as Peoria Caterpillar," *ISJ* 14 (Mar. 15, 1953): 18, 31; "Industry Expands 'Small Fry' Activity," *ISJ* 13 (Nov. 15, 1952): 12–13.

122. "Summer for the Small Fry," *ISR* 16 (May 1955): 9–12, esp. 10; *PRN*, Sept. 28, 1953; "Recreation in Industry," *Recreation* 43 (Feb. 1950): 530–31.

123. "Get the Kids Into the Act," *ISR* 15 (Feb. 1954): 12–16, esp. 14.

124. Whiting Williams, "Who's Got Momma's Ear," *NB* 34 (June 1946): 41–43, 110–11; "And Eve Told Adam," *MI* 21 (May 15, 1951): 45–47.

125. *Quotes Ending*, May 1950; "Making Full Use of the Employee Publication," *MRev* 39 (Apr. 1950): 201; "Letters to Wives," *FMM* 113 (June 1955): 136–37.

126. *PRN*, Nov. 9, 1953; "For Employees' Wives Only," *FMM* 109 (Aug. 1951): 111.

127. "Women Again . . . And Again," *FMM* 112 (Sept. 1954): 132; "Power Behind the Throne," *FMM* 116 (Jan. 1958): 74; E. H. Van Delden, "A Service Recognition for the Family," *MRev* 39 (Jan. 1950): 20; "For Employees' Wives Only," p. 111.

128. Lawrence Stessin, "Management Speaks Its Mind," *Forbes* 63 (Feb. 15, 1949): 18; "How Far Should Management Go in Talking with Employees about Union Demands?" *MRec* 21 (Apr. 1959): 116–17.

# 4 | *The Lighted Union Hall:*
*Building Union Consciousness*

In the decade after World War II, the vitality and union conscious-ness of the rank and file waned. Scholars seeking explanations, jour-nalists, and even some labor leaders blamed unions for a compla-cency emerging from the labor-capital accord. Combined with demographic trends, the rising affluence of unionized workers ap-peared to sap organized labor's energy. However, one perceptive ob-server, Textile Workers Union research director Solomon Barkin, pointed to a different source to explain labor's decline. For Barkin, business strategies were the most telling factor. In 1950, he assert-ed that management's "humanistic" personnel policies and welfare practices contrived to encourage "loyalty to the enterprise and weave the worker into the employer's social and economic fabric." These programs were simply a bald attempt "to fight a rear-guard action against the union."[1]

If less vocal, other labor leaders, nevertheless, recognized the dan-ger company consciousness posed to organized labor. They attempt-ed to expose the ulterior motives behind the seemingly benign mech-anisms associated with human relations and welfarism. Moreover, to varying degrees, unions sought to actively contest business for worker loyalty and to provide an alternative vision. Unions drew on a vi-sion of the American way that emphasized equal rights and social and economic justice. They promoted the notion that worker suc-cess and security depended on the collective power of organized la-bor and on the continued ability of the state to regulate industry. That labor ultimately waged a less successful struggle than business should not obscure the fact that a conflict occurred.

\* \* \*

For many unions, particularly within the CIO, company conscious-ness was a serious threat to a much newer and more fragile union consciousness. The leading industrial unions worried about the growth of programs designed to "coax workers into accepting management policies." The UE recognized GE's communications program as an effort "to destroy our union so that you will have a free hand in speedup, rate-cutting, and working conditions," and vowed "it is not our intention to let that happen." Where employers established successful recreation programs, the UAW and the Steelworkers charged "the company has had a comparatively easy time dividing the loyalty of our workers in the shop" and reducing the number of dues paying members. Moreover, company propaganda frightened union officials. In 1961, Ben Segal of the International Union of Electrical Workers condemned managerial communications programs that aimed at "belittling the union and undermining it and its leadership."[2]

Recognizing the danger company consciousness posed to the labor movement, unions fought to maintain worker loyalty. In part, they responded defensively, relying on ridicule and warnings to alert members of management's underlying goals. Henry Staffer, president of a Decatur, Indiana, UE local lampooned the goals of General Electric's newly implemented human relations program: "We call upon you to quit worrying about what might be in our minds and instead give some consideration to what's in our pocketbook."[3] The UAW, also consistently scorned human relations, calling efforts to communicate "baloney" and dismissing supervisory training as ineffective. In 1949, the UAW's journal, *Ammunition*, noted derisively that "foremen are attending schools throughout the country to receive training in the art of convincing workers that they are really deeply beloved by the boss." Instead, these special classes taught supervisors to forget everything they had learned as workers and to adopt as their favorite song "My Company, 'Tis of Thee." On the subject of company welfare work, the Federated Press, a labor news agency, found laughable the Container Corporation of America's claim that cheerier colors in the shop alone made workers happy. It quoted one old union carpenter who agreed, "Sure, its all a matter of color. Labor's black and blue from the beating it's taking, but every time it fights for a little more of that green stuff, they call us red."[4]

Communication programs were favorite targets for ridicule. In 1952, the Steelworkers local at the Fairbanks Morse Company renamed the company's pamphlet service the "trash rack" and thanked the firm for providing more fodder for the union paper to refute. The CIO mocked the early economic education programs by attaching labels like "Freedom Forum Fascist Front" or "Operation Gas Chamber." Later, with "exultant humor," the CIO set up a "Captive Audience Department."[5]

Underlying the ridicule, however, was the fear that unless workers were forewarned, human relations and welfarism might succeed in weakening their attachment to the union. UAW Local 600 leaders at Ford's River Rouge plant admonished workers not to be misled by friendly foremen for the "trend of thought by 'management' is to sugar and salve" employees. Similarly, in 1949, R. S. Black of the Rouge Rolling Mill warned new employees: "Don't be fooled by a supposedly friendly arm about your shoulder. They've got an arm around your neck at the same time!" Committeeman Alex Semion cautioned fellow Rouge workers that human-relations-oriented supervision was an integral part of a "new scientific method to control and discipline the masses of workers."[6]

Watch out, advised local union leaders, for programs promoted by foremen that boosted productivity at the expense of union solidarity. In 1955, UAW Local 842 warned that the Pangborn's Corporation's newly implemented practice of publicly comparing production records of workers on opposite shifts was an example of the "latest company psychological trick!" to speed up production. Most worker participation programs also fell into the category of schemes that injured workers. In 1948, Machinists' president Harvey W. Brown advised employers that they could not gain workers' "full-fledged cooperation" in efforts to improve production methods unless a union representative was involved "at every phase of the plan's development." Similarly, in 1956, Steelworkers Local 2601 warned workers against participating in a management-sponsored safety program. The real goal, the union charged, was to get workers into the foremen's office to answer personal questions without union protection.[7]

UAW Local 600 voted against cooperating with the Ford suggestion plan, charging it ignored suggestions for improving working conditions and paid "peanuts" for ideas that ultimately cost other workers their jobs. Warnings were not always effective. The Ford plan continued to pay out hundreds of thousands of dollars in awards each year. Local leaders engaged in a long campaign patiently explaining to the membership "the damage they are doing to themselves and others by participating in the much glorified 'Suggestion Plan.'" With less patience, others labeled the awards "blood dollars," and snapped "Wise up, it won't work, you won't get anything but contempt from your fellow workers" for suggestions that eliminated jobs and intensified the pace of work.[8]

Unions insisted that all forms of company communication were propaganda. The UAW education department regularly published exposés of the methods utilized by employers in their "secret struggle" to change workers' ideas. It warned that posters appearing in the shop with slogans, like "We've Got a Job to Do," or letters, discussing "Last Year This Is How We Did," sought to trick workers into identifying too closely with the corporation. Employee magazines also attempted to confuse workers with their homey, intimate appeal. General Motors, for instance, used in its journal an "old codger," who "looks like everyone's grandfather," to mouth glittering generalities about free enterprise. According to the UAW, the idea was "to get the corporation curse off what the company is telling you, and to make it look as if it were just your old man giving you the benefit of his years of experience."[9]

The labor press served as a bulwark against the business community's drive to shape worker ideology. Industrial unions' papers analyzed the content of company reading racks and condemned them for subtly trying to undermine unionism and promote "reactionary Republican viewpoints." *The CIO News*, which was distributed to millions of workers, tried to counter employer economic and political education through a constant stream of articles exposing the organizations and goals behind the movement. In the same way, *The Packinghouse Worker* advised that, "hiding under the camouflage of freedom," these courses were simply "a wicked, smear-ridden attack on every type of progressive legislation enacted or proposed since the New Deal." The *Wisconsin CIO News* revealed that Harding College, which created one of the economic education programs, was a front organization for a nationwide business propaganda campaign. In a January 1950 radio broadcast, the UAW commentator Guy Nunn warned Detroit area workers of this "highly organized and systematic attempt to poison the minds of workers against liberal government."[10]

Union leaders tried to minimize the damage created by company welfarism and propaganda by responding quickly in kind. The UAW reacted to the automakers' efforts to take credit for the growth of fringe benefits by reminding workers that benefits came from union solidarity rather than business generosity. Steelworkers Local 1400 rushed to inform workers of the union's role in the development of a new insurance plan "before any member of management breaks their arm patting themselves on the back taking full credit."[11]

Similarly, unions responded promptly to the employer letters to their members. Local 600 advised dumping Henry Ford II's letters into specially marked trash cans in each department. It urged "don't be fooled" by this "paternalistic propaganda," which sought "to lull workers into believing that Henry Ford II is the Great White Father who will lead the worker—misled by those nasty old union leaders—

from the morass of exploitation and despair." The union at the John Deere Plant in Waterloo, Iowa, met the general manager's Christmas message of goodwill with a reminder that workers were facing the new year with a pay cut. During 1948, UE locals held meetings to "tear apart the curtain of company propaganda" issued by General Electric. More specialized communication mechanisms, like economic education, also brought a sharp response. Swift Company locals answered the "phony claims and arguments" of management with mimeographed leaflets prepared for distribution immediately after the classes. The UAW education department conducted a series of discussions to arm Allis-Chalmers' stewards with answers for questions raised by the company economic education program.[12]

At times union-staged counteractions subverted company intentions. A union organizer, for example, asked unauthorized questions at a Thompson Products company dinner, while stewards disrupted GE employee meetings by firing half-a-dozen difficult questions in a row. Although uninvited, UAW Local 887 helped reshape North American Aviation's 1953 Family Day. Before reaching the plant gates to view a "bunch of Company exhibits" emphasizing management's story, sixty thousand workers and family members met clowns, a band playing hillbilly music, and trade unionists distributing balloons with union slogans, and a special edition of the local paper. The company later carefully blocked out the balloons from their pictures of the Family Day. Finally, some unions undercut profit sharing or employee stock ownership schemes by demanding that they be included in the collective bargaining agreement.[13]

Union struggles against company consciousness, particularly in the area of economic education at times went far beyond the plant. Forced to participate or lose pay, Swift and Allis-Chalmers workers filed grievances complaining that "forced listening" was a violation of their rights. Allis-Chalmers responded with a declaration that it would continue to exercise its rights of freedom of speech. Unable to gain relief through the grievance system, in 1951, the Wisconsin State Industrial Union Council, with the support of the AFL, advocated passage of a bill by the state legislature outlawing captive audiences. At a hearing, State Senator William Proxmire, one of the bill's sponsors, explained that it "would guarantee the fundamental freedom not to listen." A Republican majority controlling the Assembly Labor Committee, however, killed the measure and employers retained a free hand in the area of economic education.[14]

One of the more effective tactics utilized by unions involved turning the language and principles of company consciousness against employers. Trade unionists compared the promises of human relations and welfarism with the reality of the shop floor to demonstrate the emptiness of the employer's commitment to the worker. CIO columnist Max Ruskin observed that employers spoke often of the partnership between managers and workers but when the union representative asked, as a partner, to examine the company books, the employer snapped, "No" they're "confidential." Partnership, then, was a misleading concept that failed to include workers in decision making that affected their work lives.[15]

Unions asserted that the principle of freedom, a central tenet of employer economic philosophy, also failed to carry over into the factory. UAW Local 248 observed that Allis-Chalmers emphasized freedom during its economic education program, but when workers sought to exercise their "American freedom" to use the grievance system the General Foreman resorted to threats of layoff. In 1951, William H. Harvey, a GM industrial relations manager, in the best human relations tradition, declared that "The most valuable asset of Electro-Motive is their employees." If so, asked UAW Local 719, why were grievances over working conditions ignored? UAW Local 600 also exposed the limitations of the Ford Motor Company's commitment to human relations at the River Rouge. Union representatives complaining of health hazards and abusive supervision demanded that Ford "practice what you preach." Following layoffs in 1948, workers at the Gear and Axle department asked, "where is this big happy 'human-engineering' teamwork and cooperation stuff that we are supposed to be (a part of), or are we just not pals anymore?"[16]

* * *

Labor realized that weaning workers away from company consciousness required more than rebuttals and ridicule. Indeed, organized labor needed to pose a positive alternative. Some unions, most notably the United Automobile Workers, the International Ladies Garment Workers, the Textile Workers, and, to a lesser degree, the Steelworkers, sought to resist the new cultural politics of the workplace by revitalizing and expanding activities originally begun in the thirties. Hoping to create what the historian Lizabeth Cohen calls a "culture of unity," many unions reestablished the recreational, educational, and social activities that had been disrupted by the war or, in some cases, co-opted by management. Labor sought to reclaim the initiative in creating a shared culture that reinforced workers' common ground on the union's turf rather than in the company-built facilities.[17]

Labor education was an important element of the union effort to build loyalty among the rank and file. It certainly had significant shortcomings. Critics have emphasized that postwar labor education tended to serve the narrow, utilitarian needs of the labor leadership. In some cases, it involved "very little education and a sizable chunk of training and information." Moreover, it was often a "political football" in internal union struggles for power. In some unions, these internal political struggles reduced labor education's effectiveness.[18]

Nevertheless, its development needs to be examined within the broader context of the ongoing struggle between capital and labor. From this perspective, despite its shortcomings, labor education emerges as a weapon against the employer campaign to shape worker ideology. In 1954, the Steelworkers' Education Department observed that to a "shocking extent" the millions spent annually on business-sponsored educational activities were "sheer propaganda efforts to win over the minds and hearts of worker-employees to follow a narrow and selfish philosophy centered around the principle of the free enterprise system." The Education Department viewed itself as part of "a fight for the minds of men" and foresaw the future success of the union movement depending "upon the kind of educational programs which are offered to those who work and toil, and likewise, exercise their franchise at the polls."[19]

Labor education grew rapidly after World War II. Through their national and state organizations, the AFL and particularly the CIO encouraged affiliates to devote resources to education and also directly promoted educational activities through publications and conferences. In 1946, the Amalgamated Clothing Workers revived its education department. At the same time, the UAW, the ILGWU and the Steelworkers began expanding their educational activities. By 1957, the UAW could boast that sixty thousand students were involved in local classes, summer school activities, and weekend institutes. The Steelworkers' summer programs began in 1946 with several hundred workers attending two university-based institutes. Twelve years later over six thousand workers attended summer institutes based at thirty-two universities.[20]

These classes and institutes focused primarily on the training of stewards and local officers. In a sense, they were the counterpart to the rapidly proliferating supervisory and management training programs that were an integral part of human relations. Through labor education aimed at the secondary leadership, unions hoped to develop a core of local leaders equipped to compete with management in both the economic and political marketplaces. Most programs provided training in the tools of trade unionism, including such subjects as speaking, writing, parliamentary procedure, grievance settlement, and job evaluations, or helped officers with the issues arising from the increasingly complex contracts. Classes in economics, however, challenged the underlying assumptions of corporate economic education, offering labor's interpretation of the workings of the American economic system and emphasizing that security came not just from individual but from group effort. CIO classes, for instance, repeatedly asserted that increasing productivity alone would not improve the condition of workers or promote economic growth, as argued by management. Instead, workers should draw on the strength of their unions to demand their fair share of the gains from rising productivity, thereby improving the buying power of millions of families and bolstering the economy's mass consumption base. Redistribution of income and increased consumption by the masses of people, then, were the keys to economic progress.[21]

Many of the more progressive unions integrated labor education with political action. Unlike the worker education movement of the twenties, postwar labor education downplayed a fundamental economic restructuring of society or the promotion of a third party. However, unions recognized the dependence of labor on a sympathetic state and argued that coupling labor's political and economic strength would not only increase its power but improve the welfare of all Americans. Consequently, political action classes were sharply pragmatic, mobilizing local union leaders to mount campaigns in support of Democratic party candidates or specific legislative issues. Organized labor emphasized that its support for progressive politics and for an activist government promoting "the general welfare" stood in sharp contrast to the employer free enterprise ideology.[22]

Unions hoped that labor education classes would prepare stewards to infuse the rank and file with the union's economic and political goals. In 1949, UAW assistant regional director Frank Sahorske called upon the stewards at Allis-Chalmers to "talk unionism and talk Local 248" to the members. Stewards were to remind members that the CIO stood not only for full employment, maximum production, and a constantly expanding standard of living but also "believed that slums can be eradicated, civil liberties extended, social security broadened, and health and educational services increased." Eight years later, UAW education director Brendon Sexton, contended that informal plant discussions by stewards were one of the most significant means of educating the rank and file.[23]

Reductions in the number of union shop floor leaders mandated by postwar contracts, however, limited the political effectiveness of stewards. Sheer numbers made it difficult, if not impossible, for stewards or committeemen to compete with foremen at a personal level for workers' attention. In 1948, Ford Rouge committeemen apologized for their inability to personally contact each new employee and "explain the real meaning of unionism and its progress and benefits." Similarly, officers of a New Jersey GM local expressed frustration that only thirteen committeemen were available to protect twenty-five hundred members "while keeping an eye on several hundred foremen at the same time." While in 1946, the UE discussed building up the steward organization so that "our stewards have the answers inside the plant for our people," by 1952, it conceded that companies reached new workers "immediately and were able in many instances to influence them before they were even contacted by a union representative."[24]

Given the structural limitations of the steward system, unions sought more direct avenues of communication with workers. Their goal was to raise the level of union consciousness among an often indifferent rank and file. There were a number of forces operating to produce this indifference, including the changing nature of unions and of the working class. Rank-and-file apathy was in part a response to an increasingly bureaucratized labor movement. To many workers, long-term contracts and complex grievance procedures made participation in the union inaccessible. Moreover, the very success of the labor movement in bringing economic security to workers and in orienting them away from production and toward consumption undermined the bases of labor solidarity. Unions were thus forced to compete for workers' attention with the "distractions" that these union successes had made possible. Newfound prosperity enabled many workers to move to suburbia where they adopted middle-class leisure pursuits if not middle-class values. As sociologist Richard A. Lester observed, "in this era of suburban living and thinking," it seemed nearly impossible "to preserve a sense of dedication to the ideals and traditions of organized labor."

Union leaders worried about declining significance of unions in workers' lives. In 1952, UAW officer Emil Mazey lamented that "too many people in our plants today don't know the difference between unionism and rheumatism." Again and again, unions like the UAW called for mass education to teach workers facing a "barrage" of corporate propaganda the meaning of unionism and the way in which "the union constitutes the major safeguard of the individual worker's dignity." In 1952, the CIO observed that "one of the most serious problems facing union leadership today is how to reach the rank and file with the message and program of the union," and how to generate member participation.[25]

To build ties to the rank and file, the ILGWU and the Building Service Employees, as well as some UAW locals, sponsored new membership classes aimed at those who had "no memory of the role the union has played in building that sense of security and dignity which they enjoy today." Others tried to create an infrastructure of local union education committees to inform and encourage rank-and-file participation in union activities. Education committees held lectures and classes, showed movies, and distributed leaflets at the plant gate that reminded workers of labor's history and achievements. Even more critical were the current issues in the state and national politics. Union education committees argued that decisions made by Congress, state legislatures, and government officials on such issues as the union shop, taxes, unemployment insurance, health care, housing policy, and civil rights had a major impact on workers. Time and time again, Mike Novak, as president of Dodge Local 3, explained to members that to solve "our Union problems we must participate in Political Action. It is as important as our homes; the furniture in our homes, the food on your tables." Despite the best intentions of some union leaders, however, labor education programs often reached few rank-and-file workers. The fact that in 1954 two hundred international unions employed only fifty full-time labor educators reflected the limits of union commitment to education.[26]

Unions had somewhat better success at communicating with workers. During the fifties, there were about eight hundred labor papers with a circulation of 20 to 30 million. Local unions also produced newsletters or small-scale shop papers. The union press consciously competed with both company journals and the commercial press for the attention of workers. The shop paper was "the union's most intimate speech to the union member." It talked in the language of the shop and with the familiarity of one's co-workers, revealing "the meaning of trade unionism and progressive political action in terms of the work and activities" in which the member participated. According to the UAW, labor journalism had the "special job of putting the finger on sowers of racial hatred, exposing all kinds of anti-democratic words and deeds," and of providing "antidotes for the worst poisons of the kept press." While, company journals usually refrained from endorsing specific legislative issues or candidates in favor of more general economic lessons, the union press was openly partisan in drumming up support for its liberal political agenda. There were certainly variations between unions on their level of commitment to public affairs and their political stands, but both AFL and CIO papers tended to devote considerable space to legislation and political action.[27]

Labor also turned to radio and television in an effort to keep in touch with the rank and file. Union leaders hoped that workers, who ignored labor education programs and the union press, might be attracted to a program that mixed union-building, politics, and popular culture. In the late forties, unions pursued two radio strategies, one focusing on owning FM stations, the other purchasing programming on commercial AM stations. In 1949, the UAW and the ILGWU obtained FCC licenses and launched labor stations in Detroit, Cleveland, Chattanooga, Los Angeles, and New York City. The UAW's noncommercial station, WDET, mixed news of the union with "decent music and intelligent discussions of community and national problems." The weekly program, "Brother Chairman," took listeners into a different union each week, introducing the officers who discussed the local's history and activities. According to *Ammunition,* when "some of the people start to talk on this program, you can almost hear the foreman coming up behind you in the shop, it brings your shop experiences so close to you." The UAW worked hard to promote its stations among workers, even offering low-cost FM converters. Despite this, only about one quarter of autoworkers owned FM sets. Moreover, without support from advertisers, labor's noncommercial stations proved too costly to the CIO. By 1952 the Detroit, Cleveland, and New York stations had folded.[28]

But, as *Factory* observed, labor's voice was still "on the air waves, plenty," for unions also brought their message to the membership via commercial AM radio and television. Following World War II, CIO unions organized radio councils at the city and state levels to provide support for the development of labor programming. By 1950, there were fifteen CIO radio programs in Michigan alone. UE locals in Evansville, Indiana, and Rock Island, Illinois, sponsored daily newscasts with UE news and the union's interpretation of current events. In May 1950, Toledo UAW programs concentrated on explaining the newly negotiated pension and health security provisions to members. In Waterloo, Iowa, UAW Local 838's daily program sandwiched ten minutes of popular songs around announcements of union meetings and news of the local. Utilizing a similar format, by the mid-fifties, more than forty stations broadcast a half-hour UAW program, "Eye Opener," directed at day shift auto workers on their way to work and "Shift Break," for second shift workers. A check of automobile radios in a parking lot of a UAW organized plant one morning showed 87 percent of them with the dial set on the Eye Opener station.[29]

Radio promised access to the unorganized as well. Seeking a new way to penetrate "the iron curtain of reaction" that existed in the South and Southwest, in 1950 Operation Dixie sponsored a series of radio programs over seventy-five stations to present the policies and purposes of the CIO to Southern workers. The program consisted of folk music played by a well-known singer and a short period of dialogue designed to overcome "the vicious and distorted propaganda" of employers. Similarly, the American Federation of Hosiery Workers' thirteen-week series, "Your Stake in Unions" argued that labor unions fought for the good of the "common man" through their collective bargaining activities. Moreover, their support for full employment, Social Security, price controls, fairer tax laws, higher minimum wages, increased unemployment compensation benefits, and better housing was leading "the march of the dispossessed toward a decent standard of living."[30]

During the fifties, television became an increasingly popular medium for unions. CIO unions in Elkhart and Evansville, Indiana, attempted to undercut NAM and Chamber of Commerce programming with a television series directed at "Mr. and Mrs. Wage-Earner." Beginning in 1951, the UAW's weekly program, "Meet the UAW-CIO," and later the daily "Telescope" programs carried union and general news and interviews. The IUE used television during a 1957 organizing campaign at a Garden City, New York, plant. *Factory* observed that "there was no denying its ability to get attention, not only from every worker who tuned in, but from his whole family as well." Such was the hope of the Steelworkers union, which countered both rank-and-file indifference and a grassroots insurgency movement in 1957 with the program "TV Meeting of the Month" to bring the union to its members.[31]

\*　\*　\*

Undergirding this union campaign to influence workers' economic and political ideas was a more subtle attempt to build worker allegiance to the union as an institution. Unions, like employers, hoped that by addressing workers' social and economic needs beyond the realm of the factory they would strengthen their organization, while improving workers' lives. Traditions of union involvement in the health and welfare of their members reached back to the nineteenth century. Elizabeth Faue, examining the community-based unionism of the thirties, noted "consumer concerns, family and community networks, and education."[32] During the postwar period, a core of unions that included the UAW, the ACWA, and the ILGWU tried to make organized labor a way of life for their members. At times, they competed directly with employers seeking to build company consciousness.

Some unions challenged the individualism of employer free enterprise ideology by urging workers to rely on their own collective institutions in meeting their material needs. In this way, organized labor sought to politicize consumption while strengthening unionism. The inflationary wave immediately after the war initially stimulated widespread union interest in cooperative buying. The UAW sold low-cost food at local union halls to prove the effectiveness of "buying solidarity." Indeed, the UAW built member loyalty by appealing to workers as consumers. Autoworkers eagerly snapped up the outboard motors, refrigerators, and coats the union sold at wholesale rates.[33]

The UAW and the Rubber Workers were at the forefront of a movement to channel worker protest against high prices into a consumer-run democratic system of distribution. In 1948, they joined with representatives of AFL and CIO unions, including the Pennsylvania Federation of Labor, the Steelworkers, and the Sleeping Car Porters, to form the Council for Cooperative Development to promote cooperativism within the labor movement. By 1949, Detroit had four large cooperative food warehouses backed by one hundred union locals, and union cooperatives were operating in other cities across the country. At the same time, Racine, Wisconsin, South Bend, Indiana, and New York City trade unionists were building cooperative housing. Within three years, 250 UAW locals had formed cooperative credit unions run by workers "interested in the welfare of their union brothers and sisters." The UAW urged members to support a movement that fought monopoly and worked to create "a world organized to serve the needs of the many and not the profits of the few." When the Flint, Michigan, co-op opened, Roy Reuther declared that it was a symbol of labor's "unity and solidarity." It would make Flint a co-op city "where people live happily—instead of a GM town."[34]

Provision of services that improved or eased members' lives reinforced the notion of the centrality of the union to workers. In the early fifties, Toledo autoworkers could pay their utility bills, borrow money, and pick up hunting licenses or driving licenses and plates at Local 12's five-story union hall. The local's Flying Squadron visited the sick and furnished pallbearers and "a committee that will mourn your passing sincerely." For UAW Local 200 of Windsor, Canada, visiting ill members provided proof that "all this business about brothers and sisters really means something," creating a "deep sense of loyalty the members feel toward their local."[35]

Union concern for health went beyond visiting the ill. Most workers received their health care from commercial insurance secured through collective bargaining. In some cases, unions stipulated that claims pass through the local office to ensure proper adjustment and to give workers a greater feeling of union involvement in their health care. A group of unions, however, directly provided medical care to workers. After World War II, the ILGWU, the United Mine Workers, the ACWA, and the Hotel Workers began offering health services, while St. Louis and Philadelphia labor organizations established medical centers open to local unions through subscription.[36]

Generally, limited resources prevented the development of such elaborate union health and welfare programs. Still, the CIO envisioned a labor movement that reached out to workers with personal problems having nothing to do with collective bargaining issues. Frequently, this meant serving as a liaison between the rank and file and the greater resources of the community. The CIO's National Community Services Committee, which emerged during World War II to help members cope with wartime dislocations, grew rapidly thereafter. Following the merger of the AFL and CIO, it became an AFL-CIO department. The Community Services program trained counselors who directed fellow workers in need to appropriate community agencies and then ensured that workers received full access to the health and welfare services they supported through taxes and voluntary contributions. Counselors dealt with the problems of unemployment, illness, debt, and housing that often struck workers and their families with catastrophic consequences. They aided workers through the often confusing task of applying for unemployment benefits or public assistance. By 1954, twenty thousand workers, representing a wide range of CIO unions, had graduated from union counselor training courses. Three years later the number of union counselors had doubled.[37]

The CIO used the Community Services program to encourage workers to turn first to their union with their problems. One of the early union counselling classes, conducted in 1944, stressed that counselling represented the glue that kept the union strong. Harry Block, of the Philadelphia Industrial Union Council, charged that management had spent large sums of money on "so-called counselling services" that often were used to combat labor. Unions, he contended, needed to perform these "services themselves." Instructor Anne Gould, declared that labor "must do a far greater job than collective bargaining" and advised that if you "help your members with their domestic problems it will help to hold the union together." We now have, she continued, "a tremendous influx of workers who are not used to unions or to industrial life. It is your job to make the union a vital thing in their lives."[38]

Community services provided organized labor an entry into workers' homes. Unions had long recognized the importance of family support and participation, particularly that of wives. In the early twentieth century, craft unions had women's auxiliaries that organized union label campaigns; during the thirties, the "emergency brigades" of women workers and wives provided critical support to emerging CIO unions.[39] After World War II, the AFL regularly passed resolutions supporting the activities of its auxiliaries. But, AFL interest was more form than substance. In 1948, the vice president of the American Federation of Women's Auxiliaries complained of "neglect" on the part of the labor movement, and the Massachusetts Federation of Labor substantiated this charge, finding only one AFL auxiliary in the state.[40]

Like employers, many CIO unions sought to court the family. During the thirties, promoting family-oriented activities had contributed to the CIO's emerging "culture of unity." In the postwar period the CIO again turned to families. Taking what *Business Week* called a "cradle to grave" approach to union organization, auto, clothing, and New York City retail worker locals invited wives and children to meetings and ran classes or movies for "toddling CIOers." Union papers, like those of companies, published special women's pages to attract family readership. In 1949 UAW Local 600's *Ford Facts* declared that "today the Union needs 'Union Home's as well as Union Shops. Today the Union needs the support of wives and families, who will read Union, buy Union, and vote Union!" It asked "will you carry the message by word and action. Are you a member of a Union family?"[41]

CIO auxiliaries, organized in the Congress of Women's Auxiliaries, taught the principles and ideals of trade unionism. Most performed stereotypical women's work within the local, organizing social events and refreshments. But, like their sisters of the thirties, postwar auxiliary members bolstered their husbands and brothers during times of labor conflict. In 1955, autoworker Ben Michel's wife, who was marching on a Harvester picketline with her husband and son, declared, "If my husband didn't get out on the picket line and help fight for better wages and conditions . . . I would lock him out." The UAW credited the Windsor auxiliary for exposing and defeating a back-to-work movement during a 1954 strike and in 1956 asserted that Sheboygan, Wisconsin, wives played a key role in the long running boycott against the Kohler Company.[42]

As early as 1944, the CIO recognized the political potential of auxiliaries. But, the 1952 election made clear that organized labor's political message was not getting through to most women. Union wives, in contrast to their husbands, tended to favor the Republicans. A steelworkers' survey showed that during the campaign, 87 percent of members' families failed to receive union political literature, and political problems were not a topic of family discussion. Beginning in 1954, the CIO's Political Action Committee began making special appeals to CIO women. The CIO issued "A Call for Mom" to attend "family participation conferences" to activate women voters. Workshops, like "Does Politics Affect Our Family Life?" tied current political issues with the bread and butter problems facing the average homemaker. Effective political action, declared the CIO, was a family affair that required "the integration of husbands, wives and other voting members of the family into a working group."[43]

Following the merger, the AFL-CIO set up a Women's Activity Department within its Committee on Political Education at both the national and local levels. Like auxiliaries, WADs provided support to local COPE political initiatives. Lack of interest in women at the local level, however, often undercut the national organization's efforts. In 1960, COPE director James L. McDevitt admitted that too often unions ignored members' families; "We are fighting with one hand behind our back so long as we don't make this a family fight with every member of a trade union family on the team."[44]

Expanding the union to include the retired workers also enhanced organized labor's political as well as economic power. A UAW program launched in 1953 included three Detroit "drop-in" centers in local union halls, a newspaper, monthly information-recreation meetings, and two citywide parties that kept upward of ten thousand retirees connected to organized labor. By 1959, the autoworkers operated drop-in centers in thirty cities open to all elderly workers. The Garment Workers, the Textile Workers, and the Clothing Workers ran similar programs for their retirees. The UAW encouraged retirees to retain their union membership, viewing their continued activity as a crucial link to the struggles of the thirties. UAW Secretary-Treasurer Emil Mazey asked a 1953 gathering of retirees to "tell the younger men and women what conditions were like before the union, what you saw with your own eyes. Tell them about the long, bitter struggles to reach the standards we have now." Militant retirees bolstered the union in its ongoing struggles. During the 1958 negotiations, UAW retirees from across the country "slow marched" in considerable strength around the General Motors Administration Building to express their solidarity with the union. Unions also recognized that retired workers, like women, represented an important political force. During the fifties, retired workers in Michigan were mobilized in special campaigns for liberalizing Social Security, housing legislation, and the development of a state program of services for the elderly.[45]

After World War II, like their corporate counterparts, unions again looked to recreation as a means of earning the loyalty of workers and their families. Recognizing the danger the growing company-sponsored recreation movement posed to unions, segments of the labor movement contested business leadership in the realm of leisure. The CIO urged its affiliates to promote more systematically recreational activities in an effort to draw workers from the company orbit. CIO recreation councils and sports leagues emerged in many cities. City central bodies, like the Milwaukee Industrial Union Council, frequently sponsored tournaments in softball, bowling, or golf that at times attracted thousands of workers. Local unions also established activities committees. United Electrical Workers Local 450 formed its committee in 1948, and during its first year of operation organized a bowling league and sponsored a Christmas party, horseback riding club, and the local's first annual picnic.[46]

In 1946, the United Steelworkers established a recreation program to compete with the company-sponsored industrial leagues. It promised athletes participation in a "sports program sponsored exclusively by our union," and assured the rest of the membership of the opportunity to root for "union made" baseball or basketball. In response to the postwar managerial offensive, the UAW revived its moribund recreation department and developed the labor movement's most extensive program. When employers said to workers, "Look at the recreation program we have for you!" the union wanted its members to reply, "Thanks just the same. We're not interested in your paternalism. Our local has a great recreation program, too."[47]

The Autoworkers' recreation department hoped to infuse members and their families with the spirit of unionism. It encouraged the formation of local union recreation committees and regional recreation councils and provided training for volunteers at workshops and conferences. By 1953, the UAW asserted that four hundred golfers and twenty-four hundred bowlers matched skills in UAW International Championships. One fourth of the union locals sponsored interdepartmental basketball, softball, or bowling leagues, while nine hundred locals fielded industrial league teams. Moreover, family "fun nites" and three UAW summer camps gave children a "union view of the world."[48]

The "lighted union hall" was a central tenet of UAW recreation.

Locals reported that open bars (or in the case of Lockport, New York, a night club, complete with floor shows, movies, dancing, and a ballroom) made the union hall "the social center of activity" for many workers. All the CIO locals in Pottstown, Pennsylvania, supported UAW Local 644's club. In 1949, Windsor autoworkers, instead of going inside "beautiful plants" to find a more fulfilling and stabilized recreation, went to the union hall. "There, within his union, he is finding his own ways of building a more satisfying social life."[49]

Like other unions, the UAW looked to recreation to unite the membership. One of the primary wedges dividing workers was racial prejudice. In contrast with the AFL, the mass-production oriented CIO unions had actively recruited black workers during the organizing drives of the thirties and forties and sought to develop a close cooperative relationship with the black community. The CIO national office encouraged its affiliates to pursue egalitarian racial practices within their unions while fighting discrimination and prejudice within society as a whole. By the end of World War II, the UAW had emerged as one of the most racially egalitarian labor organizations in the country. It had earned the respect of the black community in many northern cities by championing black political and social causes including Fair Employment Practices legislation and public housing. As part of the union's commitment to racial equality, the UAW recreation department encouraged social interaction between black and white workers. UAW newspapers regularly published pictures of integrated bowling and basketball teams as testimony of the union's success in promoting integrated recreational activities. The recreation department also vigorously fought discriminatory practices. It condemned management programs that condoned racial discrimination, observing that "there are no black and white home runs," and in the factory "there is no black production or white production." The recreation department vowed to bring together workers in a "situation in which runs scored, or pins knocked down, or strikes taken, not the color of a man's skin nor the altar at which he kneels will be the criteria for acceptance." Accordingly, the UAW led the CIO in a five-year boycott of segregated American Bowling Congress tournaments. It ended in 1951 with the elimination of the "whites only" rule.[50]

At times, union and company programs directly competed for worker participation. Such was the case at the River Rouge, where UAW Local 600 clashed repeatedly with the Ford Motor Company. Indeed the struggle over recreation symbolized the larger conflict between company and union. With sixty thousand members, a large percentage of them African Americans, Local 600 had one of the

UAW's most fully developed recreation programs, offering a wide variety of activities ranging from ballroom dancing classes and bridge tournaments to an annual water carnival. While thousands participated in the union-sponsored activities, however, even more turned to the company, which boasted a more elaborate and better funded and segregated program. In 1950, for example, the union sponsored one bowling league with twenty teams, while Ford had sixty men's leagues and thirteen women's leagues. Union officers pleaded with the members for support. R. S. Black of the Rolling Mill asserted: "We can call it loyalty for a good union member to confine his sport likes to his Local Union activities." In the Plastic Plant, Bill Jackson asked why "some workers prefer to participate in the company sports plan even when they are contacted by their own union brothers."[51]

Department picnics were another arena of contention. In July 1951, plastic department foremen were encouraging worker attendance at an upcoming Family Day Picnic. Union officials warned that it was "strictly a company affair" and a ruse to gain employee consent to intensifying production by improving relations between worker and supervisor. Unionist James Simmons asked, "how can you go to a picnic one day and feel good about the mean tricks those very same fellows play on you and your fellow workers?" The union countered with its own picnics. That summer the Stamping Plant contended that despite a small budget, its picnic, which excluded supervision and featured greased pole climbing, chicken catching, and a jitter bug contest, "was just as successful and well or better attended as any put on by the Company." If company picnics boosted production and enhanced company consciousness, union picnics enhanced union solidarity. Following the union-sponsored Rouge stamping plant picnic, a Local 600 member observed that "events of this nature do more to weld friendship and promote unionism than all the speeches our politicians feed us" but lamented "too bad, we don't have picnics more often."[52]

Unions, however, had difficulty competing with management over recreation. One problem, actually shared with employers, was competition from commercialized leisure, particularly television, which encouraged workers to remain in their homes for recreation. Moreover, many unions had neither the means nor commitment to contest employers for worker loyalty in this realm. For many locals, recreation consisted mainly of occasional picnics or Christmas parties for children or a baseball team fielded in the local industrial league. At the national level, only the Clothing Workers, the Ladies Garment Workers, and the Textile Workers matched the UAW's commitment to recreation. Even the UAW's program suffered from underfunding. In 1952, Walter Reuther admitted that the "entire recreation program of the UAW must operate on a budget so low its total would appall the average person connected with industrial recreation." Few unions had the recreation buildings or facilities that were a common feature of corporate-sponsored recreation. Local 600 was unusual in employing a recreation director. In contrast, a staff of fourteen ran the Ford Company program at the Rouge.

Recreation also mirrored the internal contradictions within the CIO on the issue of race. At the national level, CIO unions embraced a racially egalitarian ideology, but at the local level segregation and racial discrimination in seniority and promotion continued. Union leaders moved more slowly and inconsistently when it came to fighting discrimination within their own organizations because they were "constrained by the prejudices of the white rank and file." In recreation, for instance, the UAW's national recreation department constantly struggled against racial prejudice. From the origins of the union in the 1930s, black participation in the locals' social activities had always been a "touchy matter." In some locals, the presence of a large number of black workers had postponed the development of social programs. In 1948, UAW officials were still chiding members who didn't participate in the union social affairs on the grounds that they couldn't bring their families "out in that kind of group . . . with all races, creeds, and different types of religious training."[53] These workers, perhaps, felt more comfortable in company programs some of which separated black and white workers.

*　*　*

The overwhelming advantages of wealth and power business brought to its campaign to build company consciousness made labor's opposing efforts seem insignificant. Indeed, the social unionism of the CIO has been almost forgotten as historians have tended to dismiss the social consciousness and social vision of the postwar labor movement. It has been too easy to read the rise of business unionism and the steady decline of organized labor back into the immediate postwar era. But, this was no foregone conclusion. Well into the fifties, despite the efforts of business, the inhospitable political climate of the cold war, and labor's internal divisions, a segment of organized labor embraced social unionism and defended a liberal, democratic vision, which placed the social needs of the people above profits. Their efforts to make labor's voice heard among workers contributed to organized labor's maintenance of a significant level of status and power in postwar America. That the lighted union hall began to dim in the late fifties should not diminish organized labor's struggle against the managerial onslaught of the postwar years.

## Notes

1. Solomon Barkin, "A Trade Unionist Appraises Management Personnel Philosophy," *HBR* 28 (Sept. 1950): 60, 64.
2. "The Secret Struggle to Change Your Ideas," *Ammunition*, Sept. 1955, p. 6; *UE News*, Nov. 13, 1948; UERMWA, *Proceedings*, 1952, pp. 250–51; Melvin G. West to R. J. Thomas, Feb. 18, 1946, Box 2, Series II, UAW Recreation Department Records, ALUA; "United Steelworkers Proposed Recreation Program," 1946, Phillip H. Scheidling to David J. McDonald, Mar. 27, 1946, Box 133, David J. McDonald Papers, USA/A; Ben D. Segal, "A Unionist's View of Economic Education," *Challenge*, Apr. 1961, pp. 23–27, esp. 27.
3. *UE News*, Nov 13, 1948.
4. "Deep Therapy on the Assembly Line," *Ammunition*, Apr. 1949, pp. 47–51; *719 News* (GM Electro-Motive Diesel UAW Local 719, Brookfield, Ill.), Jan. 1949, Nov. 1951; *FF* (Ford Motor Company UAW Local 600, River Rouge Plant), Feb. 28, Mar. 13, 1948. Christmas edition, 1952; Federated Press quoted in *Reading Labor Advocate*, Jan. 27, 1950.
5. *SS* (Fairbanks-Morse Company, USA Local 1533, Beloit, Wis.), Aug., Dec. 1952, Feb. 1953; *UAW*, Jan. 1950; *719 News*, July 1950; William H. Whyte, *Is Anybody Listening* (New York: Simon and Schuster, 1952), p. 8.
6. Rouge union leaders urged workers to ignore the company's suggestion that they take their troubles to their supervisor rather than to their committeeman. *FF*, Feb. 7, 1946, Jan. 3, 24, 1948, July 16, 1949, Feb. 24, 1951, Feb. 9, 1952.
7. *Unionaire* (UAW Local 842), Dec. 1955; Harvey W. Brown, "What Labor Expects of Management," AMA Personnel Series No. 117 (1948), pp. 26–27; USA Local 2601 (Buffalo, N.Y.) Minutes, May 7, 1956, Reel 2, LMDC.
8. *FF*, Aug. 21, July 9, Sept. 3, 10, Dec. 10, 1949, Jan. 21, Feb. 18, 1950, July 14, 1951, Oct. 3, 1953. For other examples of union reaction to suggestion plans, see *SS*, June 1955, and *Hod Rod*, May 29, 1959.
9. "The Secret Struggle to Change Your Ideas," pp. 6–10; "Propaganda Methods I," *Ammunition*, Dec. 1950, pp. 2–7, esp. 4; "The Reading on the Racks," *Ammunition*, July 1953, pp. 2–3; "How Corporations Get Their Propaganda Over" (leaflet), c. Dec. 1952, Box 19, UAW Education Department Records, 1952–56, ALUA.
10. "The Reading on the Racks," *Ammunition*, Nov. 1950, pp. 2–3; "Propaganda—Cafeteria Style," *Machinists Monthly Journal*, Dec. 1953, pp. 374–75; *SS*, Aug. Dec. Feb. 1953; *CIO News*, constantly linked economic education to business organizations like the NAM, the Chamber of Commerce, and Opinion Research Corporation and to right-wing business-financed bodies,

including the Foundation for Economic Education and the Committee for Constitutional Government. The findings of the House Lobby Investigating Committee fueled labor's attack on economic education. See, among others, *CIO News*, July 3, 24, Aug. 14, Oct. 30, 1950, June 4, 1951, Oct. 27, 1952; *Packinghouse Worker*, June 30, 1950; *WCN*, Jan 6, 13, June 9, 1950; Wisconsin State Industrial Union Council, "If You Don't Listen, You'll Lose Your Job: An Exposé of the Freedom Forum" (pamphlet), c. 1950, Box 58, AUF, LMDC; "Captive Audience and Labor," Guy Nunn Radio Script, Jan. 7, 1950, Box 146, Walter Reuther Papers, ALUA.

11. *UAW*, May 1955; UAW Local 248 (Allis-Chalmers) Administrative Letter, Dec. 13, 1951, Box 7, United Automobile Workers Local 248 Papers, ALUA; *719 News*, May 1949.

12. *FF*, Feb. 7, 1948, Aug. 6, 1949; *Hod Rod*, Mar. 24, 1953, Mar. 10, 1955; *UE News*, Apr. 10, 1948; *WCN*, July 17, 1950; "Leaflet" enclosed in Lewis Carliner to all Education and PAC representatives, Oct 16, 1950, Box 5, Reuther Papers.

13. *Recorder*, Dec. 1946, case 15, Thompson Products Company Records, Baker Library, Harvard University, Boston, Massachusetts; *General Electric Employee Relations Newsletter*, June 24, 1949, *UAW*, Aug. 1953; *Ithaca Labor Union Review*, June 1955.

14. *WCN*, Feb. 24, June 23, 1950, May 11, 21, 1951; *Organizer*, Mar. 6, May 21, 1950; *CIO News*, July 17, 1950, May 21, 1951; Wisconsin State Industrial Union Council, "Legislative Letter," May 4, 11, 1951, Box 51, AUF, LMDC.

15. *WCN*, Dec. 9, 1949.

16. *Organizer* (UAW Local 248), Jan. 31, 1950; *719 News*, Feb. 1951. *FF*, Jan. 31, Feb. 2, Apr. 10, 1948, also Jan. 24, Mar. 13, May 15, July 24, 1948, June 12, Dec. 9, 1950, Sept. 1, 1951.

17. Elizabeth Fones-Wolf, "Industrial Unionism and Labor Movement Culture in Depression-Era Philadelphia, *Pennsylvania Magazine of History and Biography* 109 (Jan. 1985): 3–26; Lizabeth Cohen, *Making A New Deal: Industrial Workers in Chicago, 1919–1939* (Cambridge: Cambridge University Press, 1990), pp. 324–68.

18. Frank Marquart, *An Auto Worker's Journal: The UAW from Crusade to One-Party Union* (University Park: Pennsylvania State University Press, 1975); Kenneth D. Carlson, "Labor Education in America," *Review of Educational Research* 41 (Apr. 1971): 115–29, esp. p. 119.

19. In 1950, UAW Local 719 editor Herman Rebhan noted that "the G.M. Corporation has an educational program for the workers. The Corporation spends a fortune on pamphlets, movies, employee activities councils, forced lectures, etc. If we want to make sure that we not only preserve our union but build a stronger and better organization. . . . We must devise some better techniques to bring home the union's ideas on economics and political action." *719 News*, June 1950; USA, *Report of Officers to the Seventh Constitutional Convention*, Sept. 20–24, 1954, pp. 21–29, esp. 21–22.

20. M. Mead Smith, "CIO Training for Active and Effective Local Leadership," *Monthly Labor Review* 74 (Feb. 1952): 140–44; "Planning for More Edu-

cation," *Ammunition*, May 1946, pp. 10–11; Joyce L. Kornbluh and Mary Frederickson, *Sisterhood and Solidarity: Workers Education for Women, 1914–1984* (Philadelphia: Temple University Press, 1984), p. 56; Thomas E. Linton, *An Historical Examination of the Purposes and Practices of the Education Program of the United Automobile Workers, 1936–1959* (Ann Arbor: University of Michigan School of Education, 1965), pp. 187–305; USA, *Report of Officers to the Ninth Constitutional Convention*, Sept. 15–19, 1958, pp. 122–26.

21. Joseph Mire, "Recent Trends in Labor Education" (Paper presented at the Thirty-Fifth Anniversary of School for Workers, Nov. 20, 1959, Madison, Wisconsin), Box 99, McDonald Papers, USA/A; Jack Barbash, *The Practice of Unionism* (New York: Harper and Row, 1956), pp. 269–76; Congress of Industrial Organizations, *The CIO: What It Is and What It Does*, n.d., pamphlet.

22. A. A. Liveright, "A Long Look at Labor Education," *Adult Education* 4 (Feb. 1954): 102–3; "Report of Education Department," c. 1950, Box 180, Michigan AFL-CIO Records, ALUA; Linton, *An Historical Examination*, pp. 221–56.

23. "Minutes," Oct. 24, 1949, Joint Council Meeting, Box 3, UAW Local 248 Records, ALUA. For Brendon Sexton, see Linton, *An Historical Examination*, pp. 198–99; "The Stewards are the Brains of the Union," *Ammunition*, June 1948, pp. 18–21.

24. *FF*, Jan. 24, 1948; *UAW-CIO Assembler* (Linden, New Jersey, GM Local 595), Apr. 1951; *Proceedings*, Twelfth Annual Convention, UERMWA, 1946, p. 189; *Proceedings*, Seventeenth Annual Convention, UERMWA, 1952, p. 250.

25. Robert Zieger, *American Workers, American Unions, 1920–1985* (Baltimore: Johns Hopkins University Press, 1986), pp. 138–41; Kenneth D. Carlson, "Labor Education in America," p. 119; Richard A. Lester, *As Unions Mature: An Analysis of the Evolution of American Unionism* (Princeton: Princeton University Press, 1958), pp. 44–45; *UAW*, Apr. 1952; *FF*, Sept. 29, 1951; CIO Department of Education and Research, "How to Reach the Rank and File—Some Suggestions for Union Officers," Feb. 1952, Box 39, AUF, LMDC.

26. *FF*, July 15, 1950; Joseph Mire, *Labor Education: A Study Report on Needs, Programs and Approaches* (Chicago: Inter-University Labor Education Committee, 1956), pp. 49–53; USA Executive Board Meetings, Apr. 5–6, 1954, pp. 32–40, Box 5, USA/A; "At UAW Local 370: They 'Took It,' Then They Gave," *Ammunition*, Apr. 1956, pp. 27–29; "Minutes of All Day PAC Conference, Wayne County CIO Council," July 15, 1950, Box 33, Michigan AFL-CIO Records, ALUA. On union indifference to education, see A. A. Liveright "A Long Look at Labor Education," pp. 101–2; Barbash, *The Practice of Unionism*, p. 272.

27. J. B. S. Hardman and Maurice Neufeld, eds., *The House of Labor* (New York: Prentice Hall, 1951), pp. 185–95, 202, 213–14, 224–25; International Union of United Automobile, Aircraft, and Agricultural Implement Workers, *Shop Paper Handbook* (1951), pp. 1–2; Booton Herndon, "Labor Tells Its Story," *NB*, June 1954, pp. 66–72; Lewis H. Spence, "Dollars and Sense of Employee Communications," *AM* 22 (Feb. 1957): 26–27.

28. Sara U. Douglas, *Labor's New Voice: Unions and the Mass Media* (Nor-

wood, N.J.: Ablex Publishing Corporation, 1986), pp. 26–29; "Report of the Radio Stations Committee to the Executive Board, UAW-CIO," Mar. 17, 1947, Box 146, Reuther Papers; "UAW-CIO FM Sets Cheap," *Ammunition*, Nov. 1947, p. 36; "The Electrons Are Organizing," *Ammunition*, July 1948, pp. 12–13; "Turn it On," *Ammunition*, May 1950, p. 10.

29. "Looking Ahead in Labor," *FMM*, 110 (May 1952): p. W-1, "Suggested Outline for Remarks on the Work of the Radio and Press Councils," c. 1951, Bill Friedland to Ivan Brown, July 13, 1950, Box 188, Michigan AFL-CIO Records; *Proceedings*, Sixteenth Convention, UERMWA, 1951, p. 190; "Dialing Union on the Radio," *Ammunition*, Mar. 1948, p. 16; Jack Stieber, *Governing the UAW* (New York: John Wiley & Sons, 1962), pp. 120–21; "Bid for Power: Labor Leaders Seek More Influence," *NB*, May 1960, p. 75.

30. George Baldanzi to David J. McDonald, Jan. 19, 1950, Box 142, McDonald Papers. There are Operation Dixie radio scripts in Box 1560, John Ramsay Papers, SLA; Radio Scripts, Box 19, Series 3, American Federation of Hosiery Workers Papers, SHSW.

31. Dallas Sells to All Locals and Councils in the Evansville Television Area, Oct. 1, 1954, Box 8, USA District 30 Records, USA/A; UAW International Executive Board Minutes, Feb. 6, 1952, Box 5, IEB Minutes, 1947–58, ALUA; *Pittsburgh Sun-Telegraph*, Nov 9, 1957; USA Executive Board Minutes, Dec. 3, 1957, Box 6, USA/A.

32. Elizabeth Faue, *Community of Suffering and Struggle: Women, Men and the Labor Movement in Minneapolis, 1915–1945* (Chapel Hill: University of North Carolina Press, 1991); Labor's efforts to reach workers beyond the workplace and in the community have been largely overlooked in the scholarly literature. A recent exception is Arthur B. Shostak, *Robust Unionism: Innovations in the Labor Movement* (Ithaca, New York: ILR Press, 1991).

33. "Flint Rehearses for the Future," *Ammunition*, Nov. 1947, pp. 3–9; "Cutting Living Costs Cooperatively," *Ammunition*, May 1949, p. 36.

34. Victor G. Reuther to Philip Murray, Mar. 15, 1948, C. J. McLanahan to Vincent Sweeney, June 22, 1948, Box 1, USA Public Relations Department Records, USA/A; Congress of Industrial Organizations, *Unions and Co-ops* (pamphlet), c. 1947; "Co-ops in Action," *Ammunition*, July 1946, p. 21; "The Spadework Is Almost Over," *Ammunition*, Sept. 1947, pp. 28–31; *UAW*, Oct. 1948; *CIO News*, June 29, 1953.

35. "Toledo is a Good Town for Working People," *Ammunition*, Mar. 1950, pp. 6–7; "They Visit the Sick," *Ammunition*, Feb. 1949, pp. 17–19.

36. Joseph A. Langbord, "The Union Health Center Fosters Employee Health: The Philadelphia Experience," *Industrial Hygiene and Occupational Medicine* 6 (Dec. 1952): 474–76; Albert Deutsch, "A New Union Health Plan," *Nation*, Sept. 20, 1952, pp. 232–33; "A Health Program that Prevents Illness," *Ammunition*, May 1947, pp. 20–22.

37. "President's Murray's Report on the National CIO Community Services Committee," Nov. 30, 1949, National CIO Community Services Committee, "Union Counsellor's Casebook," n.d., Box 7, all from Greater Buffalo Industrial Union Council Records; "Good Advice for Bad Times," *Ammunition*, May

1948, pp. 20–21; National CIO Community Services Committee, *Action for a Better Community,* (c. 1951); *Christian Science Monitor,* Sept. 21, 1957.

38. For the UAW, counselling represented the "expanding philosophy" that "anything which affects the welfare of our members is a concern of the union. It is projecting the needs of our members into the community where they live." "Union Counselling Notes," *Ammunition,* July 1946, p. 23; "Minutes of first Union Counsellor Training Course Session," June 21, 1944, Philadelphia, Pa., Box 49, AUF, LMDC.

39. Majorie Penn Lasky, "'Where I was a Person': The Ladies' Auxiliary in the 1934 Minneapolis Teamsters' Strikes," in *Women, Work and Protest: A Century of US Women's Labor History,* ed. Ruth Milkman (Boston: Routledge & Kegan Paul, 1985), pp. 181–205.

40. AFL-CIO, *History Encyclopedia and Reference Book,* vol. 3 (Washington, D.C., 1960), p. 2708; *Reporter* (Education Committee of the Massachusetts Federation of Labor), June 1948.

41. "Unions Start Them in the Cradle," *BW,* Oct. 25, 1947, p. 104; *FF,* Jan. 3, Mar. 13, May 29, 1948, Oct. 15, 1949 and Aug. 18, 1951; *Organizer,* Sept. 5, Oct. 15, 1951; "Stewards' Meeting with Kids," *Ammunition,* July 1948, p. 39.

42. *UAW,* Sept. 1955, Sept. 1956; *CIO News,* July 2, 1947, Dec. 12, 1949, Nov. 27, 1950, Sept 1955; "Our Men Need Us," *Ammunition,* Mar. 1947, pp. 30–34.

43. James B. Carey, R. J. Thomas, Reid Robinson to CIO Internationals and Industrial Union Councils, Dec. 5, 1944, Bertha Perrin to Allan S. Haywood, Sept. 21, 1950, both in Box 78, CIO Office of the Secretary-Treasurer Papers, ALUA; James Caldwell Foster, *The Union Politic: The CIO Political Action Committee,* (Columbia: University of Missouri Press, 1975), pp. 178–81; USA Executive Board Proceedings, Apr. 5–6, 1954, p. 34, Box 5, USA/A; "A Call for Mom and All Other Women of CIO," c. July 1954, Dallas Sells, George Coldwell, Mary Salisbury to James Robb, Apr. 27, 1954, Box 8, USA District 30 Records, USA/A. The AFL also slowly became concerned with involving women in labor politics. James L. McDevitt, "Enlist the Ladies," *American Federationist,* Feb. 1952, p. 5.

44. "Keeping in Touch" (WAD newsletter), Feb. 1, 1960, Box 446, AUF, LMDC. On resistance from local unions to involving women and families, see, for example, Brendon Sexton to All Local Union Presidents in Regions 1 and 1-A, UAW-CIO, May 21, 1952, Box 3, UAW Education Department Records, 1948–55.

45. "Look Back, Look Forward," *Ammunition,* Aug. 1953, p. 15; *AFL-CIO Education News and Views,* May 1956; John Fitzpatrick to Walter P. Reuther, July 2, 1958, Ken Morris, et al. to Detroit Area Local Union Presidents of Regions 1 and 1A, July 14, 1958, Box 152, Reuther Papers; UAW Older and Retired Workers Department, "Handbook on Retired Workers," c. 1959, Box 100, AUF, LMDC; *UAW,* June 1954.

46. *WCN,* Jan. 24, 1946, Aug. 5, 1949; *UE Shop News* (Local 450), Aug.–

Sept. 1949, Box 165, AUF, LMDC; *Connecticut CIO Vanguard,* Sept. 1949, "Plan a CIO Christmas party for Kids—Here's How to Do it," n.d. (leaflet) Box 4, *Local 246 Chatter* (United Rubber Workers), June 1949, Box 3, both in Greater Buffalo Industrial Union Council Records.

47. *Steel Labor,* Sept. Dec. 1946; "District 27 USA-CIO Picnic Committee Report," Nov. 9, 1947, USA District 27 (Ohio) Records, "United Steel Workers Proposed Recreation Program, 1947, Philip H. Scheidling to David J. McDonald, Mar. 27, 1946, Box 133, McDonald Papers; *Ammunition,* May 1948, p. 34.

48. "UAW-CIO Recreation Program," leaflet, c. 1955, Box 102, AUF, LMDC; "The Members of the Committee," *Ammunition,* June 1952, pp. 18–19; Olga M. Madar to Frank Winn, Oct. 1, 1947 (UAW-CIO Recreation Dept. Annual Report), "Report of the Recreation Department Activities, November, 1947–October, 1948," Box 2, Series II, UAW Recreation Department Records; *UAW,* Sept. 1951, July 1952.

49. "Toledo Is a Good Town for Working People," *Ammunition,* p. 6; William S. Hilger to Earl Brown, Feb. 15, 1949, Box 1, UAW Local 686 Records, LMDC; "Air-Conditioned Idea Center," *Ammunition,* Aug. 1949, p. 12; "Anomie? No, Organization," *Ammunition,* May 1949, pp. 47–49, esp. 49.

50. August Meier and Elliott Rudwick, *Black Detroit and the Rise of the UAW* (Oxford: Oxford University Press, 1979); Olga M. Madar, Victor G. Reuther, and William H. Oliver to Casell M. Miles, June 5, 1947, Box 1, Series I, UAW Recreation Department Records; Walter Reuther and George F. Addes to All Recording Secretaries Affiliated with the UAW—CIO (RE: Bowling Program for 1947–48), Box 148, Reuther Papers; *WCN,* Jan. 3, Feb. 3, Mar. 3, May 19, 1950; UAW Recreation Department, "A Summary of the Recreation Program of the United Automobile, Aircraft, and Agricultural Implement Workers of America, UAW-CIO," c. 1954, Box 102, AUF, LMDC.

51. Local 600 measured the success of its 1948 Field Day against the attendance at the company ceremony that unveiled the "New Look Ford" to plant workers. It pleaded for a turnout that would exceed the two hundred thousand workers and family members who came to "give a look at the New Look." "You're Invited to the Biggest Local Union Field Day," *Ammunition,* July 1948, p. 10; *FF,* Aug. 20, 1949, May 27, 1950; "Employee Recreation at the Ford Motor Company," May 26, 1949, Box 54, AOF I, LMDC.

52. *FF,* Sept. 27, July 1, 1950, June 30, July 14, July 21, Aug. 25, 1951.

53. Walter P. Reuther, "Recreation and the Auto-Workers," *ISR* 13 (Mar. 15, 1952): 19; C. E. Brewer, "Recreation in Labor Unions," *Recreation* 44 (Sept. 1950): 219–21; Meier and Rudwick, *Black Detroit,* pp. 3–4, 52–53, 73–74; 207–22. Despite the UAW boycott, many local union teams still bowled under the auspices of the ABC, which unlike the UAW league, provided a money guarantee in tournaments, bonded officials, and other services. Similarly, although the UAW condemned the Detroit Baseball Federation for prohibiting blacks from participating in their league, some locals continued to enter teams in the Federation league. "Report of the Recreation Department Activities, No-

vember, 1947–October, 1948," Olga M. Madar to George F. Addes, June 10, 1947, Box 148, Reuther Papers; Proceedings of First Annual State Recreation Conference; *FF*, Sept. 18, 1948.

# PART 3 | In the Community

# 5 | *Meet Your CIO Neighbors*

More than ever before, events in the year 1946 taught organized labor the importance of public support. At the beginning of the year, unions waged a long battle for much-needed pay increases. By the summer, they were locked in a losing struggle to maintain price controls while launching attacks against their own members who deviated from the liberal political line. A decisive Republican victory in the congressional elections in November culminated a frustrating year for unions and prepared the ground for the passage of the Taft-Hartley Act. A labor movement that had come to rely on liberal government awoke to the fact that its public support was diminishing rapidly.

The labor press issued repeated calls for union members to recapture the good will of their local communities. Wisconsin CIO vice-president Malcolm Lloyd, UAW leader Victor Reuther, and International Ladies Garment Workers Union education director Mark Starr all suggested better labor-community relations was the first key step in reversing trade unionism's political and economic fortunes.[1] Minneapolis mayor Hubert Humphrey put it most emphatically: "Labor must first become a part of its community—of all the organizations and enterprises that go to make up the life of a community—the PTA's, the Community Chest, the School Boards, the City Planning groups, and all the rest. Labor must show that it wants a good community." Unions must also remember, continued Humphrey, that "they must sell themselves to the farmers, the white collar workers and businessmen. This requires work and education not only in the union hall, but in the clubs and farm meetings."[2]

Despite the gloomy events of 1946, organized labor had a solid community base upon which to build. Indeed, the mixed reaction of many towns and cities to the postwar strike wave sent no resounding message to either labor or business. Unions still had a reservoir of good will from their wartime community activities. Furthermore, many local unions and labor councils had plans to expand the range of their services and increase the level of their participation in their home towns. Labor's efforts at the community level, then, complemented its program to develop a union consciousness among its rank and file.

* * *

The community support labor received during the strike wave of 1945–46 dramatized just how far unionism's influence had spread since the emergence of the New Deal. In many towns and cities, groups that had formerly been friendly to industry ignored the inconveniences caused by work stoppages and took the side of the workers. Allegheny Ludlum Steel Corporation reported that in one of its plant communities, small businessmen aligned themselves with the strikers. Up and down almost every business street, placards placed in saloons, stores and shops proclaimed sympathy for the men on strike. Similarly, in Three Rivers, Michigan, over one hundred businessmen and professionals signed advertisements supporting workers in their struggle against the Fairbanks Morse Company. Fifty prominent Cleveland citizens marked the one-hundredth day of the Westinghouse strike by sending telegrams to the company urging settlement, and the traditionally conservative *Newark Evening News* held the company alone responsible for the continuation of the struggle.[3]

These strikes revealed the limitations of corporate industrial relations policies that relied on the community to discipline recalcitrant workers. During the thirties, the Remington Rand Company's Mohawk Valley Formula had defeated strikes with a strategy that combined police intimidation and court injunctions with propaganda campaigns that turned local communities against workers. In 1947, however, the company discovered a change in the political and social climate of its plant cities. For the first time, Tonawandas, New York, local leaders failed to support Remington Rand's policies; community officials refused to blame workers for strikes, and police authorities denied assistance to the company's attempts to cross the picketline. Aware of labor's increased political clout, the mayor dramatically reversed his predecessor's practices and maintained a strictly neutral position. The normally antiunion *Evening News*, which in past struggles had forecast dire predictions of plant shutdowns, was also unusually restrained in its editorial policies.[4]

Elsewhere, local officials moved beyond neutrality. The mayors of

Pittsburgh and Cleveland publicly backed organized labor against the Westinghouse Corporation. Cleveland city Councilman Richard Masterson and mayoral aide James McSweeney participated in a mock funeral burying a rejected Westinghouse offer, leading the United Electrical Workers Union to express delight at the "most unusual display of public support for a strike."[5] In Anderson, Indiana, Mayor C. D. Rotruck employed financially strapped UAW strikers in the city park department, furnished lighting for the picket stations, and appointed UAW members to two vacancies on the city council. In many communities, public and private welfare agencies also provided assistance to strikers. When Francis H. Wendt, mayor of Racine, Wisconsin, interceded on behalf of J. I. Case Company workers, the company president, L. R. Clausen, accused him of "partisanship" and decried his "failure to act as a public official in behalf of all the citizens of Racine."[6]

Hostility from the community during the 1946 strike was a "shocking surprise" to General Electric. The company had felt secure in the belief that it ranked high as a good employer and good neighbor. But at many strike sites, clergymen joined the picket line while local merchants ran ads criticizing the firm for prolonging the strike. Several stores even removed GE products from their shelves. In some locations, city councils passed resolutions on behalf of the United Electrical Workers Union. General Electric believed that these unfriendly acts resulted from widespread distrust and misunderstanding not only of General Electric but of business in general. A survey conducted during the strike confirmed the company's fears. Community neighbors charged that "wages are as low as G.E. can possibly keep them; prices are kept as high as G.E. can push them; G.E. profits are unwarranted or excessive; G.E. has no concern for the welfare of its employees; G.E. has no interest in its plant communities." Finally, and most troubling, the company discovered that its plant communities believed that "G.E.'s motives are dishonest and contrary to public interest."[7]

Labor's wartime patriotic activity as well as a lingering distrust of business help explain support for strikers. Participation in war bond drives, scrap salvage drives, and Red Cross and United War Chest campaigns boosted the presence of organized labor in communities across the country. Philadelphia unions, for instance, dedicated themselves to the war effort. Union leaders, as well as thousands of members of the rank and file, gave generously of their time and money on behalf of wartime charitable agencies. Built and operated by trade unionists, the USO-Labor Plaza, one of the city's most popular recreation centers for service personnel, served as a visible example of labor's commitment to victory. These efforts won the local labor movement numerous accolades from community leaders and the press.[8] Similarly, in Tonawandas, New York, the site of the Remington Rand strike, the AFL and the CIO formed a new organization, the United Labor Council, to facilitate trade union voluntary activity. This organization helped give labor an increased voice in the town's civic affairs. In early 1946, after evaluating labor's behavior during the war, Charles Cooper, a UE Local 308 officer, declared that "labor in Tonawandas has earned a right to community support."[9]

During the war, the development of closer cooperation between labor and social welfare agencies enhanced the effectiveness of union patriotic activity while strengthening organized labor's prestige within the community. Previously, organized labor often had little contact with these agencies. In most communities, business and professional people controlled the policy-making boards of governmental and voluntary organizations. In 1940, for instance, only ninety CIO representatives served on the boards of the many thousands of local, state, and national health and welfare bodies in America. Business leaders also took credit for most of the funds contributed to such voluntary agencies as the Community Chest and the Red Cross through either private donations or corporate fund-raising campaigns. Workers, meanwhile, resented both the solicitation process, which in many companies was largely a "shake-down" affair with a foreman ordering employees to "fork over," and management's claims of full credit for their gifts. Antagonism typically characterized the relationship between workers and the social service agency staffs, who often identified with the business and professional classes and assumed an attitude of paternalistic benevolence toward those in need, barely hiding their suspicion and distaste for unions.[10]

Mobilization for war began to break down old barriers. Just before the United States' entry into the conflict, the CIO and the AFL developed war relief committees to aid workers in countries fighting Fascism, to provide special services for America's armed forces, and to meet the needs of America's defense workers. In 1942, the government's War Relief Control Board encouraged combining all war-related appeals into one coordinated drive administered by a single, newly created agency, the National War Fund. With the assistance of the National War Fund, the Red Cross, the Community Chests and Councils of America, and numerous smaller agencies began pooling fund-raising and relief efforts.[11] Labor committees reached a national agreement to cooperate with the Community Chests and Red Cross in return for substantial funds to the AFL and CIO committees to facilitate their work. This agreement also called for labor representation on all governing boards, campaigns, and allocation committees. The agencies promised to publicly credit unions for worker contributions and to encourage solicitation by joint employer-union committees.[12]

The war, then, provided the labor movement with the opportunity and resources to begin integrating itself into community service networks. At the national level, the AFL and the CIO built a cooperative relationship with the top leadership of important health and welfare agencies, in particular the Community Chests and Councils, Inc. At the local level, AFL and especially CIO committees, working closely with their community counterparts in fund-raising campaigns, gained representation on community and war chest boards of directors. By 1945, for instance, Ohio unions led the country in board participation with 109 CIO representatives.[13]

National War Fund agencies provided the CIO's War Relief Committee with an annual operating budget of almost $600,000, enabling the committee to move beyond fund-raising to establish an outreach organization, the Division of Community Services. This division set up regional offices throughout the country and organized fifty state and city industrial union council community services committees, which were responsible for working with community agencies on programs of service to industrial workers on nonfactory local problems. These committees initiated the union counselling programs, discussed in an earlier chapter, which were expanded after the war. During the 1945–46 strike wave, unions drew on the relationships established with both public and private agencies to secure health and welfare services for strikers. At the request of the United Steel Workers, for example, the Buffalo and Erie County Council of Social Agencies provided a counselling and information service in union halls during the steel strike.[14]

The wartime rapprochement of labor and community agencies augured well for the CIO's postwar plans. In late 1945, the national Community Chest's Committee on Future Relations with Organized Labor proposed that local chests support labor community services committees in the same way they funded organizations like the YMCA. The report argued that health and welfare agencies could not afford to ignore labor, for unions were "a basic sociological necessity in a free society such as ours, not merely a colossal 'grab bag.'" Moreover, their "permanency may well prove to be a very vital feature of the continuing health and stability of our industrial progress."[15] Encouraged, in early 1946, the CIO proposed a yearly budget of $240,000 for its National CIO Community Services Committee. The Chest's National Budget Committee gave tentative approval to the CIO's request and then passed it on to be considered by local community chests, which would actually raise and allocate the funds.[16]

The commitment of local community agencies to the CIO, however, was more fragile than an alarmed business community realized. Despite strong support from the National Chest's board, president and staff, the majority of local chest leaders refused to endorse the national organization's plan. Leo Perlis, national director of the CIO's Committee, disappointedly acknowledged that although community chests and organized labor had come to know each other better during the war, "some very real fears and some deeply ingrained prejudices still remain." He also suspected that lurking behind the local chests' refusal to fund the CIO Community Services Committee were business leaders. The professional social workers who comprised local chest staff routinely reported to boards of laymen often controlled by industrialists. Perlis charged that some "financially powerful lay leaders," disturbed by recent industrial unrest and by the assistance given strikers by some social service agencies, had brought "great influence . . . to bear upon the insecure shoulders of some community chest leaders." As a result, Perlis bitterly concluded, "doubts, fears and prejudices won out—at least for the present."[17]

Out of this impasse between the national and local bodies of the Community Chest over the form and level of the institutional relationship with labor came a compromise. The national organization agreed that rather than provide direct financial support to the CIO's Community Relations Committee, it would set up a small Labor-Employee Participation Department. The department would serve as a liaison between the National Chest and organized labor and would promote the active participation of unions in the health and welfare activities of local communities. In addition, the National Chest encouraged local chests or councils of social agencies to hire special labor staff to set up advisory labor participation committees. Furthermore, the department gave unions the power to choose labor staff persons who would represent the interests of the AFL and the CIO, but the Community Chest would pay their salaries. The Community Chests and Councils Inc. launched the Labor-Employee Participation Department in January 1947, but as late as 1955 local coordinating councils for private social agencies employed only fifty-two full-time labor representatives.[18]

During 1946, without the financial support of the Community Chests and Councils, Inc., the CIO had to practically dismantle its

National Community Services Committee. The Committee's budget dropped from its wartime peak of over $500,000 a year to $12,500. Limited funds forced it to liquidate all its regional offices. Leo Perlis later recalled, "We had to start, in a very large sense, from scratch."[19]

\* \* \*

Starting from scratch meant defining the broad goals that would characterize the CIO's community service program for the next decade. First, the CIO wanted to ensure that all workers gained access to health, welfare, and recreational services. Second, the CIO hoped to establish a positive image of labor in the community. Extending trade unionism beyond the plant gates and job-centered objectives would help establish unions as important mainstream civic organizations. Moreover, by integrating itself into the community, the CIO hoped to demonstrate that unions were not like selfish special interest groups but instead were concerned "about the welfare of the community" as a whole. A strengthened, more politically powerful union movement would be the byproduct of labor's improved image. Joseph A. Beirne of the Communications Workers contended, "looked at most crassly, community service is one way of convincing one's fellow citizens that a union's economic program, legislative program, political action program or organizing program is deserving at least of thoughtful consideration if not outright support." Community service, he continued, might "make our political action and legislative work a little easier, and thereby make our collective bargaining and grievance work a little easier."[20]

Without its large wartime budget, the national CIO Community Services Committee acted primarily as a policy-making and facilitating body. It served as a liaison between the CIO and the national organizations in the health and welfare field such as the chests and the Red Cross. The committee emphasized mobilizing local trade unionists for civic activism and acted as a clearinghouse for information and guidance on programs and policies. Initially, despite the gains made during the war, it was difficult to interest some labor officials in social welfare services. They viewed the CSC as being removed from the mainstream of union activity. But, gradually during the late forties, under the leadership of the National CIO Community Services Committee, city level industrial union councils and local unions across the country began to set up community services committees.[21]

Community services committees pursued a variety of programs that promoted unions in the community. Illinois labor activities can serve as an example of the growing presence of organized labor. In 1947, Chicago United Packinghouse Workers Local 28 organized a Boy's Club that was operated out of the union hall. At the same time, in a Chicago neighborhood, UAW CSC members formed a Community Council that succeeded in improving street lighting, reducing traffic hazards, and industrial smoke nuisances. Locals across the state established blood banks and held blood procurement drives. During times of crisis, the local committees stepped in to aid their fellow citizens; in the spring and summer of 1952, when major floods hit East Moline and Rockford, Illinois, local CSCs aided in evacuation, housing, and collection of food, money, clothing, and furnishings. The Rockford social service agencies publicly commended the trade unionists for their actions. Elsewhere in the country, unions participated in similar activities, sponsoring little league teams, operating dancehalls for teenagers, and giving Christmas parties for needy community children.[22]

Fund-raising for voluntary health and welfare agencies helped organized labor demonstrate good citizenship. At the national level, leaders of major trade unions, like David J. McDonald of the Steelworkers, served on national fund-raising committees. At the city level, local industrial union councils set up labor participation committees that cooperated with business committees and agency personnel to decide on labor's fair share of the fund-raising campaign goal and to work out campaign procedures. Where good labor-management relations existed within the plant, union counselors often worked with supervisory staff in soliciting funds or pledges. In all cases, unions were committed to giving without coercion but, in turn, demanded full credit for labor's role in raising money.[23]

With organized labor's assistance, the level of workers' contributions to charity increased significantly. In 1950, Detroit UAW Local 600 alone raised 10 percent of the city's $8 million Torch Fund Campaign. That same year, Akron workers' gifts totaled 36 percent of all money collected. The 1953 National CIO Community Services Committee annual report proudly announced that CIO members had over the past twelve years contributed more than $400 million to voluntary agencies.[24]

To ensure that workers had access to the health and welfare services that they supported, local community services committees sought labor representation on the boards and committees that governed social agencies. These ranged from the tax-supported public welfare and health departments to the community chest-supported family and children's agencies, settlement houses, Red Cross and Salvation Army chapters, Boy and Girl Scouts, and the YW and YMCA. The CIO argued that since workers supported these agencies with their tax dollars and their voluntary contributions, labor had a right to participate directly in the policy-making and budget decisions of these organizations. Essentially, union members would represent the consumer of welfare services. Their participation would help "democratize" social agencies, making them more representative of the community and more responsive to popular needs.[25]

Unionists believed that labor's participation would help reduce the influence of business over social agencies. On the one hand, unions could protect sympathetic social workers from undue pressure applied by the large donors from the business community. In 1950, the Ohio CIO's CSC observed that "sometimes social workers, who are liberal in their view or friendly to Labor, are subjected to coercive treatment by reactionary givers and the presence of Labor representation can assure them a greater measure of security." On the other hand, union community activism could help develop an appreciation of the labor movement among indifferent or even hostile social workers. In 1953, for example, Treva Berger, the chairman of the Illinois Lake County Community Services Committee, recalled that her committee had worked closely with a director of the Public Aid Commission. Impressed with the CIO CSC program, this director had helped change "entirely" the minds of the members of the Council of Social Agencies "about people in unions and in [the] CIO in particular."[26]

Unions succeeded in increasing labor representation on social and welfare agency boards and committees. Whereas only 90 CIO members sat on agency boards at the beginning of World War II, by 1953, 15,000 CIO members served in various capacities with national, state, and local welfare organizations. To a lesser degree, AFL unions also provided representatives to the agencies. Still, even this level of representation was only a beginning. In 1953, in Chicago alone, 5,000 citizens made up the agency boards, making the 140 CIO volunteers seem almost insignificant.[27]

The CIO hoped that increased participation in the administration and funding of community agencies would pay off during labor conflict. Even financially strong unions were unable to fully support strikers. A cooperative social service sector, however, could strengthen immeasurably labor's ability to sustain a long-term work stoppage by providing relief for workers. The CIO National Community Services Committees sought to ensure that assistance was given on the basis of need, regardless of the cause, as "a community responsibility to its citizens."[28] The CIO recognized, however, that the extent to which community welfare agencies within their legal and financial means willingly gave assistance to strikers was a measure of the community's acceptance of the principle of the strike as a lawful step in the collective bargaining process. Here the changing image of labor and the degree to which unions had established prior relationships within the community came into play. The CIO increasingly found that social agencies were more "responsive to a union which is a vital and integral part of the fabric of daily community life."[29]

As strikes approached, the CIO Community Services strike assistance program swung into action. At the plant level, a strike steering committee appointed and arranged for the training of strike counselors who referred workers in need to appropriate social agencies. In some plants the work of strike counselors meshed with the established union counselling program, another important CSC activity. Union representatives then met with local public and private agencies to set up procedures for relief and to make certain that social workers understood their responsibility to workers on strike.[30] In 1952, the Labor Participation Department of the Community Chest asserted that "to the credit of many social agencies" many communities accepted the principle of need as the basic eligibility for assistance. Unions, like the Amalgamated Clothing Workers, the UAW, and the Steelworkers credited the CSC's strike programs for sustaining prolonged labor struggles. The United Steelworkers, for instance, noted that the strike relief program contributed to the successful conclusion of its 1952 strike, until then, the longest in the union's history.[31]

Although the CIO did not intend for its CSC to be a political force, the quest to improve community welfare or to gain access to services at times pushed local committees into the political arena. While supporting voluntary agencies, the CIO contended that security for all could be achieved only through an activist government. Moreover, it considered government agencies responsible for the major burden of financial assistance during unemployment and strikes.[32] Again, the example of unions in Illinois suggests the range of CSC political activity. During 1952, faced with Korean-War induced inflation, community service committees in such Illinois towns as Alton, Moline, and Galesburg led the political struggle to maintain rent control. In Chicago, the CSC fought for increases in workmen's compensation, for funds to build a tuberculosis sanitarium, for a liberalization of residency requirements for public assistance, and for state aid for slum clearance and public housing. The CIO CSC in East Moline helped guarantee access to public relief for the unemployed by electing six CIO people to the Town Board responsible for approving relief expenditures. During strikes, political power was even more important. In 1953, Kenawee, Aurora, and Freeport township supervisors initially refused to provide assistance to needy strikers and their families. Pressure from community services committees eventually reversed the policy. Chester Winski of the ACWA reported a change "after the Township Supervisor had been properly educated."[33]

* * *

Community services was the core of labor's slowly growing local-level public relations campaign. Political failure in the 1946, 1950, and 1952 national campaigns had convinced many trade unionists that they were laboring "in a climate that is completely hostile to our point of view." By the early fifties, both the AFL and the CIO believed that unions needed to change the climate of opinion in America.

Consequently, both houses of organized labor launched national-level public relations programs to promote labor and liberalism. The CIO, in particular, complemented national efforts by targeting more localized public relations activities. It believed that business penetration into the community helped shape the political atmosphere. The CIO urged local unions to compete with business by trumpeting labor's contributions and point of view within the community.[34]

Community services served as a public relations function by transmitting a subtle message to the community, one that attempted to establish unions as useful, responsible, and civic-minded organizations. For the CIO, the beauty of this program was that it allowed unions to demonstrate through their actions the "mutuality of interest" between labor and the public. Henry Fleisher, National CIO Director of Publicity, consistently urged local unionists to take advantage of all the potential goodwill that could be generated by publicizing their community service work. He advised CSC representatives at a 1953 institute to "cultivate newspaper [sic] and radio contacts" and furnish them with "good human interest stories." Union insistence on receiving credit for its fund-raising activities and contributions was another manifestation of labor's drive to gain community goodwill and acceptance.[35]

As part of its efforts to alter the local community's perception of unionism, organized labor realized the potential benefits of communicating directly with the public. The UAW encouraged its districts to organize speakers' bureaus and offered the services of the national union's Education Department in providing resource materials and training. International Harvester UAW Local 6 of Melrose Park, Illinois, energetically attacked the task of changing public opinion; its officers spoke regularly before high school social sciences classes, college groups, and gatherings of ministers. In June 1950, as part of its public relations program, the Michigan CIO Council began mailing CIO literature on economic and political issues to key people, including ministers and educators, throughout the state. Reverend Walfred Erickson of the First Baptist Church in Lawton, Michigan, admitted that his sympathies were not "one hundred per cent pro-union," but appreciated receiving material which represented "fairly and fully the union viewpoint on the issues which confront us as citizens." Another Baptist minister, Reverend Robert D. Hotelling of Midland, Michigan, found it "healthy to hear of a different viewpoint than that consistently maintained by the NAM and the Chamber of Commerce."[36]

The CIO Council in Grand Rapids, Michigan, worried about the "many misrepresentations about the CIO," introduced itself to the community through a widely distributed pamphlet entitled "Meet Your CIO Neighbors." The pamphlet pointed out that the "CIO isn't just a bunch of initials. It isn't something far away. CIO is your neighbor, or the fellow who lives down the block; the family next to you at church, your friend in the club, or your fellow straphanger on the bus."[37] Similarly, beginning in 1949, CIO unions across the Midwest began reaching out to neighboring farmers by sponsoring exhibits at highly popular state and county fairs. Relief from the hot sun or rain, free cold drinking water, movies, "gimmicks," including quiz shows and raffles, and giveaways, like shopping bags or balloons with a union imprint, promoted attendance at the CIO fair tents. In one tent, Michigan CIO Council representatives strategically placed near the drinking fountain a large display chart illustrating the comparative incomes of farmers, big businessmen and the "middle men." The unionists reported that "this chart caused considerable comment." Farmers left the CIO exhibits with literature pointing out the close relationship between farm income and high wages for workers. One CIO Education Committee Chairman summed up his comments on his union's fair booth this way: "We don't feel that we can expect to convert people to CIO thinking in the few minutes we can hold them in the tent. For that reason, we feel that the entertainment we provided was important as a means of breaking down prejudice and preparing the way for a little more sympathetic feeling toward [the] CIO" and for a "more receptive audience to a year-round program of public relations."[38]

In most cases, however, unions equated public relations principally with the mass media. Radio and later television provided a point of contact not only with the union membership but with the broader public as well. Increasingly, as the postwar corporate antilabor assault intensified, AFL and CIO locals and city councils began sponsoring programs "geared at showing the ordinary citizen just what unions are and how they benefit the community." In 1946, for example, Lansing, Michigan, UAW locals began a radio program "Labor Speaks," initially to support the autoworkers' strike against General Motors. Maintained as a regular offering after the struggle, it brought labor's point of view on economic and political issues to union members and the public. In 1950, the Michigan CIO Council contended that the sixteen labor programs broadcast throughout the state were beginning to have an effect "upon the political picture in Michigan." According to the Council, letters from listeners indicated that for the first time many people were hearing labor's point of view.[39]

A television program served as the core of a public relations campaign in Cincinnati. In early 1952, as the Ohio labor movement geared up for the forthcoming election, the Cincinnati CIO Council broadcast a thirteen-week television program, "What's Your Answer?" In it, labor representatives debated opponents on subjects including price controls, civil rights, academic freedom, and farm supports. At the same time, Cincinnatians saw advertisements in the local press depicting the role of the CIO in the community and listened to spot radio announcements explaining how the CIO helps workers and their families. Local papers also featured the CIO contributions to the polio fund, while the public library ran an exhibit demonstrating the influence of thirty thousand unionists on the city's life.[40]

Even more ambitious in terms of public relations were the labor-operated FM radio stations. As noted earlier, during the late forties, unions launched stations in Detroit, Cleveland, Chattanooga, Los Angeles, and New York City to guarantee unions, which had experienced difficulty in purchasing air time, access to a mass audience. The UAW, which vigorously promoted labor radio, envisioned that these stations would "enhance the cause of our political, economic, and social democracy through affording to all groups and classes such freedom of speech and opportunities for discussion as to be unparalleled in the history of the radio broadcast industry." Walter Reuther believed that the UAW could make its Detroit station, WDET, "a powerful instrument for propaganda free news." The UAW president asserted that impartial coverage "cannot be overestimated," especially "in a city like Detroit where the daily newspapers consistently distort the news." In the same vein, the ILGWU's station in New York

City, which symbolically took the call letters, WFDR, promised upon its debut in 1949 to be a voice for labor and liberalism. Indeed, labor's FM stations featured five liberal news commentators, several of whom had been fired from commercial stations. They also typically carried the AFL and CIO's national news commentary programs and local union messages.[41]

In their appeal for public support, unions promised to devote their stations to community service. This stood in sharp contrast to commercially run AM stations that emphasized profits over public interest programming. The ILGWU intended to make WFDR "the most articulate town-meeting hall, the outstanding music hall, the most attractive cultural center in the community." Similarly WDET was to be the "people's station, where all the problems, social, political, economic—which affect labor and the community generally can be talked about openly and honestly."[42] Indeed, labor FM stations provided a significant amount of educational and cultural programming while serving as an outlet for communication with union members. In 1950, WDET's schedule, for instance, included "Community Clinic" and "Let Freedom Ring," both designed to combat discrimination and bigotry; the "WDET Roundtable," a panel discussion of national and local legislative and economic issues; several children's educational programs; a show produced in cooperation with the city's health department; and a daily musical series featuring the Detroit Public Library Symphony.[43]

\* \* \*

All of this suggests that labor appeared to pose a real threat to business's domination of local communities. But often labor's influence was more shadow than substance. Labor's widely heralded FM radio stations folded after only a few years, the victim of both the manufacturers' and broadcasters' unwillingness to embrace FM and of wariness from advertisers that the stations would be union propaganda outlets.[44] Moreover, in the late forties and fifties, the cold war atmosphere of suspicion and intolerance toward liberal causes impeded union access to outlets of mass communication. Particularly in politically conservative communities, local television and radio stations at times refused to sell air time to unions. Stiff resistance from advertising agencies and television stations almost kept the Cincinnati CIO television series off the air.[45]

Even in the realm of community services, there existed many barriers to labor's attainment of community recognition and power. Until the merger of the AFL and the CIO in 1955, division within the labor movement impeded the growth of the community services program. Although some AFL members served on the labor staff of the national and local community chests, they did not officially represent the Federation. It wasn't until 1953 that the AFL even enunciated a policy on community activities. Continuing hostility and competition between the AFL and the CIO also hindered the development of a unified labor program.[46]

Following the merger, the AFL-CIO committed itself to an expanded community services program. By 1957, the number of labor representatives on voluntary boards and committees had increased to 75,000 and the number of full-time labor staff on community agencies to 125.[47] But, as labor educator Alice Cook observed in 1959, "judged by a variety of standards . . . this representation is small— small in proportion to the number of workers in these communities and of the contributions they make in support of these agencies." She continued that "while labor representatives had been readily accepted in a few communities, generally they have won only grudging acceptance." Leo Perlis admitted at the AFL-CIO's inaugural convention that agencies viewed labor as a "junior partner."[48] Contemporary studies of community agencies revealed that trade unionists were often letterhead or token representatives with little impact on policy making. On the whole, they failed to present a new set of interests, a new program, or a new ideology.[49] In part, this reflected resistance from social workers and the business leaders who often dominated board membership. In 1959, the Indiana State AFL-CIO observed that although labor contributed millions to agency coffers, the "leaders always look at us as something aside from the community." Furthermore, agency boards and committees made participation difficult for workers by scheduling board meetings during the day or by creating an atmosphere at the meetings that made the labor representatives "so uncomfortable that they no longer wished to attend."[50]

Labor's own ambivalence about its role in the community also helps explain its failure to gain a more significant level of influence. Lack of interest was one factor. Joseph Beirne of the Communication Workers Union, who became chairman of the CIO's Community Services Committee in 1953, complained repeatedly of the refusal of unions to "exploit part of the opportunities that exist in the Community Services field."[50] Participation on the boards, itself, created contradictions for organized labor. Unions presented their representatives as advocates of the community's broader interests. Indeed, labor's manifesto was "The Union member is first and foremost a citizen of his community." To prove their nonpartisanship, labor representatives frequently yielded to other groups and failed to consistently promote the needs of organized labor. By emphasizing the common interests of labor, business, and the middle class, unions tended to lose their class identity. Those few employers who recognized this contradiction welcomed labor's involvement in community affairs, believing that participation brought a cloak of respectability and responsibility to union leaders that might have a moderating influence on their behavior during times of industrial conflict.[51]

For all these reasons, then, labor's community services failed to tap the potential public support that prevailed in the strike wave of 1945–46. Facing a generally conservative social atmosphere in the 1950s, contemporary commentators like the sociologist C. Wright Mills even denied that local communities still had important influence. A bureaucratized mass society had rendered citizens voiceless and small towns powerless, according to Mills; labor could compete as a less potent large-scale institution, but it was unlikely to enjoy much success through a community-based strategy.[52]

There is, of course, another explanation for labor's inability to attain power and political influence from its community activities. Business leaders were neither dismissive of community relations nor sanguine about labor's inability to compete. Indeed, the National Association of Manufacturers' chairman of the board, Cola G. Parker, asserted that it "is in the local communities that the work must be done, and the union leaders know it. . . . This kind of community activity pays off in politics too. It makes the union leader an important and influential figure, and it helps the union machine do the job at the polls."[53] Rather than dismiss local community efforts, employers and corporate managers in the postwar era embarked on an aggressive campaign to shape a probusiness environment in the nation's cities and small towns.

## Notes

1. *WCN*, Mar. 7, 1948; Victor G. Reuther, "Education for Survival," *Ammunition*, July 1946, pp. 4–5; Mark Starr, "The ILGWU—Leader in Educational Work," *L&N*, Summer 1950, p. 57.

2. *PLN*, Sept. 24, 1948.

3. *UE News*, Mar. 30, May 11, June 22, 1946; Lamar Kelly, "A Grass-Roots Public Relations Program," in Metropolitan Life Insurance Company, *Community Relations: Selected Cases*, (New York, 1950), p. 45. On community sup-

port for autoworkers see Martin Halpern, *UAW Politics in the Cold War Era* (Albany: State University of New York Press, 1988), p. 78. Support for labor in some communities, such as Akron, reached back to the thirties. Samuel Lubell, *The Future of American Politics*, 3d ed. (New York: Harper & Row, 1965), p. 187.

4. Marc Steven Kolopsky, "Remington Rand Workers in the Tonawandas of Western New York, 1927–1956: A History of the Mohawk Valley Formula" (Ph.D. diss., University of New York, Buffalo, 1986), pp. 194, 230, 365–67, 388–408.

5. *UE News*, Mar. 30, Apr. 6, 1946.

6. Claude E. Hoffman, *Sit-Down in Anderson: UAW Local 663, Anderson, Indiana* (Detroit: Wayne State University Press, 1968) p. 97; *CIO News*, Jan. 21, Feb. 11, 1946; L. R. Clausen to Francis H. Wendt, June 4, 1946; L. R. Clausen to Milton F. LaPour, July 12, 1946, Box 28, AOF I, LMDC.

7. John T. McCarty, *Community Relations for Business, Operations Manual* (Washington, D.C.: BNA, 1956), pp. 16–18; John T. McCarty (Consultant-Groups Relations, General Electric Co.), "Plant Community Relations" (Address before the 29th NAM Institute on Industrial Relations, Hagley Library, Wilmington, Delaware); General Electric Company, *The GE Plant Community Relations Program* (New York, 1952), pp. 10–12.

8. William H. Form and Delbert C. Miller, *Industry, Labor, and Community* (New York: Harper & Brothers, 1960), p. 84. For examples of coverage of labor activity in Philadelphia, see *Evening Bulletin*, (Philadelphia) July 15, 1941, Mar. 6, Dec. 22, 1942, Nov. 20, 1943, Sept. 11, 1944, Oct. 29, 1945.

9. Cooper quoted in Kolopsky, "Remington Rand Workers," p. 365; see also pp. 335–45.

10. Orville C. Jones, "Organized Labor's Concern for Community Welfare," *Religious Education* 43 (Sept.–Oct. 1948): 291; Outline for CIO Secretary-Treasurer James B. Carey from National CIO-CSC, Oct. 13, 1950, Box 59, Walter Reuther Papers, ALUA; Daniel Bell, "The Worker and His Civic Functions," *Monthly Labor Review* 71 (July 1950): 68.

11. Outline for CIO Secretary-Treasurer James B. Carey from National CIO-CSC, Oct. 13, 1950; John R. Seeley, *Community Chest: A Case Study in Philanthropy* (Toronto: University of Toronto Press, 1957), pp. 22–23.

12. "United War Chest, Report of Executive Director to Executive Committee," Apr. 26, 1943, in Minutes of Executive Committee, Box 4, Philadelphia United War Chest/United Fund Records, UA; Outline for CIO Secretary-Treasurer James B. Carey from National CIO-CSC, Oct. 13, 1950.

13. *Citizen CIO* (National CIO Community Services Committee), Dec. 1945, Box 36, AUF, LMDC; *National Newsletter*, Labor-Employee Participation Dept., Community Chests and Councils, Dec. 1947.

14. Leo Perlis to Joseph A. Beirne, CIO-CSC Today—A Report with Recommendations, Apr. 21, 1955, Box 55, CIO Washington Office Files, CIO Records, ALUA; *Community Services News Letter*, Mar.–Apr. 1945, Box 7, Greater Buffalo Industrial Union Council Records, LMDC; Nat Klein to James Miller, Jan. 2, 1946, Box 4, Buffalo and Erie County Council of Social Agencies' Re-

port on Emergency Liaison Between Families of Strikers and Social Services, Apr. 24, 1946, Box 3, both in Greater Buffalo Industrial Union Council Records.

15. Community Chests and Councils, "Report of Committee on Future Relationships of Chests and Councils with Organized Labor," Sept. 14, 1945, Box 31, David J. McDonald Papers, USA/A.

16. Leo Perlis to Joseph A. Beirne, Apr. 21, 1955; Community Chests and Councils, Committee on Future Relations with Organized Labor, Report and Recommendations as amended and adopted by the Executive Committee, July 12, 1946, Box 10, USA Department of Education Records, USA/A; Irving Abramson to E. A. Roberts, Apr. 29, 1946, Box 31, McDonald Papers.

17. Leo Perlis to E. A. Roberts, July 11, 1946, Box 36, McDonald Papers.

18. "Minutes," National CIO Community Services Committee, Sept. 19, 1946, Leo Perlis to Irving Abramson, Mar. 19, 1947; CIO-CSC Today: A Report with Recommendations, Apr. 21, 1955.

19. CIO-CSC Today, A Report with Recommendations, Apr. 21, 1955; Nat Klein to Industrial Union Councils, Oct. 15, 1946, Box 3, Greater Buffalo Industrial Union Council Records.

20. Emil Reive, "Labor Acts for a Better Community," reprint, *Survey*, Sept. 1948, Box 49, AUF, LMDC; "Proceedings," Institute on Community Services, Washington, D.C., June 4–8, 1950, Box 37, McDonald Papers; Joseph A. Beirne, *Challenge to Labor: New Roles for American Trade Unions* (Englewood Cliffs, N.J.: Prentice-Hall, 1969), p. 75.

21. Leo Perlis to Irving Abramson, Apr. 30, 1946, Box 10, USA Department of Education Records, Perlis to Beire, CIO-CSC Today, A Report with Recommendations, Apr. 21, 1955; Proceedings, Twelfth Annual CIO Community Services Institute, May 17–23, 1953, Box 55, CIO Washington Office Records, ALUA.

22. Myrna S. Bordelon, "Everyman Has the Power," (pamphlet), Mar. 1948, Box 58, AUF, LMDC; Illinois State Industrial Union Council CIO Community Services Committee, Annual Activities Report, 1952, Box 46, Series 1, Michigan AFL-CIO Records, ALUA; "Facts Bared on Wilkes-Barre UC Activities," c. 1953, Box 55, CIO Washington Office Records; Milton Derber, *Labor in Illinois: The Affluent Years, 1945–80* (Urbana: University of Illinois Press, 1989), pp. 338–39.

23. Proceedings, Twelfth Annual CIO Community Services Institute; Fred Koppers to David J. McDonald, Nov. 27, 1956, Box 149, McDonald Papers.

24. Bell, "The Worker and His Civic Functions," p. 68; National CIO Community Services Committee, A Report to the National CIO Executive Board (mimeograph), June 4, 1953, Box 46, Series 1, Michigan AFL-CIO Papers.

25. National CIO Community Services Committee, *Action for a Better Community* (n.p.: CIO, n.d.), pp. 8–10; *National Newsletter*, Labor-Employee Participation Dept., Community Chests and Councils, Dec. 1947; "Proceedings," Institute on Community Services, Washington, D.C., June 4–8, 1950.

26. Ohio CIO Council, *CIO Community Services Committee in Action*, (Columbus, Ohio CIO Council, 1950), p. 5, Box 36, AUF, LMDC; "Lake County

CIO CSC Report to the State (Illinois) CIO Convention" (mimeograph), Dec. 1953, Box 116, Bessie Hillman Papers, ACWA.

27. "Minutes," Health and Welfare Advisory Council to the National Community Services Committee, Dec. 15, 1953, Box 116, Hillman Papers.

28. James Carey, "The Opportunity of Labor in Social Welfare" (Address before the National Conference of Social Work, Atlantic City, May 12, 1954), Box 55, CIO Washington Office Files; National CIO Community Services Committee, A Report to the National CIO Executive Board, June 4, 1953.

29. National CIO Community Services Committee, "Case Histories of the Strike Assistance Program, 1952 Steel Strike," Box 36, AUF, LMDC.

30. J. C. Pierce to Leo Perlis, Oct. 6, 1949, Andy Brown to Leo Perlis, Oct. 7, 1949, Robert L. Kinney to Leo Perlis, Dec. 6, 1949, all in Box 37, McDonald Papers.

31. Report of the CIO Field Staff for the Fifth Anniversary Meeting Labor Participation Department Advisory Committee, Jan. 15, 1952, Box 10, USA Department of Education Records; Union Counseling Notes, *Ammunition*, July 1946, pp. 23–24; National CIO Community Services Committee, "Case Histories of the Strike Assistance."

32. *Citizen CIO*, National CIO Community Services Committee newsletter, May 18, 1954; Carey, "The Opportunity of Labor in Social Welfare."

33. *Labor-Welfare in Our Community*, Chicago Industrial Union Council CSC and the Community Fund and Council of Social Agencies of Chicago newsletter, May–June 1947, July 1947, Aug.–Sept 1949, Box 59, AUF, LMDC; Illinois State Industrial Union Council CIO Community Services Committee, Annual Activities Report, 1952; "Four County Council CIO CSC Report to the State CIO Convention, East Moline Illinois," Dec. 1953, Statewide CIO CSC Report to the (Illinois) State CIO Convention," Dec. 1953, both in Box 116, Hillman Papers, ACWA.

34. Darrell Smith, Address to the Statewide PAC Conference, Feb. 9, 1952, Box 8, USA District 30 Records, USA/A; "Proceedings," Twelfth Annual CIO Community Services Institute; CIO *Proceedings*, 1953, p. 444.

35. CIO, *Proceedings*, 1954, pp. 501–2; "Proceedings," Twelfth Annual CIO Community Services Institute.

36. Victor G. Reuther to All Education-PAC Representatives, Oct. 3, 1950, Box 5, Victor Reuther Papers, UAW Education Department Records, ALUA; "Speakers' Bureau," *Ammunition*, Apr. 1948, p. 38; UAW Local 6, "Report to Membership," 1952, p. 11, Box 91, AUF, LMDC; August Scholle and Barney Hopkins to Dear Friend, June 26, 1950, Walfred Erickson to August Scholle and Barney Hopkins, July 20, 1950, Robert D. Hotelling to August Scholle, July 6, 1950, Box 177, Michigan AFL-CIO Records.

37. *Meet Your CIO Neighbors in Grand Rapids*, pamphlet, Box 52, AUF, LMDC.

38. "Report of 1951 County Fair Program," Marvin Meltzer, "Report on County Fair Project," Marvin Meltzer to Don Stevens, Nov 28, 1951, Box 166, Michigan AFL-CIO Records; *Education at Work*, CIO Department of Education and Research newsletter, 1949, Box 4, Greater Buffalo Industrial Union Council Records.

39. Bill Kemsley to All County CIO Councils in Michigan, Sept. 6, 1951, Box 7, Mildred Jeffrey Papers, ALUA; *UAW*, Feb. 1947; Report of Education Department, c. 1950, Box 180, Michigan AFL-CIO Records.

40. Melvin J. Brisk, "The Cincinnati C.I.O. Tries Television," *Nation* 175 (Sept. 6, 1952): n.p.; *Ohio CIO Council News Letter*, Feb. 22, 1952, in Box 54, AUF, LMDC.

41. "Unions Seeks FM," *BW*, Dec. 9, 1944, p. 102, "Union Network," *BW*, Dec. 17, 1949, pp. 92–93; *UAW*, Dec. 15, 1944; Walter P. Reuther and Emil Mazey to All Local Union Officers in the WDET-FM Reception Area, June 10, 1949, Box 146, Reuther Papers; "Laboring Voice," *Time*, June 27, 1949, pp. 64–65.

42. "On the Air: WFDR," *New Republic*, July 4, 1949, pp. 20–21; Untitled two page news release, c. 1950, Box 15, "Policy Statement of the UAW-CIO Broadcasting Corporation of Michigan," c. 1948, Box 13, both in Jeffrey Papers.

43. Pat Petermen, Untitled report regarding labor-owned radio stations, Nov. 1950, Box 8, "Statement of Program Service" (WDET), c. 1949, Box 13, Jeffrey Papers.

44. Mildred Jeffrey to Bob Miller, Nov. 23, 1949, Box 4, Unsigned letter to T. J. Slowie, c. Mar. 1952, Box 13, Jeffrey Papers; Sara U. Douglas, *Labor's New Voice: Unions and the Mass Media* (Norwood, N.J.: Ablex Publishing Corporation, 1986), pp. 26–29.

45. "The Cincinnati CIO Tries Television"; on the difficulty of obtaining air time in Rochester where the UAW hoped that television programming might "neutralize some of this community's anti-union feeling," see the following correspondence: Frank Wallick to Mildred Jeffrey, Oct. 26, Nov. 19, 1951, Frank Wallick to Joe Rauh, Nov. 19, Dec. 29, 1951, Box 18, Jeffrey Papers.

46. Irving Abramson to Philip Murray, Apr. 22, 1949, Box 37, McDonald Papers; Edwin F. Hallenbeck to George Meany, Oct. 21, 1953, Box 26, George Meany Papers, GMA; AFL-CIO, *American Federation of Labor: History, Encyclopedia and Reference Book*, vol 3, part 1 (Washington, D.C., 1960), pp. 439–44.

47. "Need More Community Activity, Reedy Tells Parley," *AFL-CIO American Federationist*, June 1957, p. 28; "People at Work," *Christian Science Monitor*, Sept. 21, 1957; AFL-CIO, *Proceedings*, 1957, pp. 287–89.

48. Alice H. Cook, "Education of Workers for Public Responsibility in Community and Public Affairs" (Paper presented to the conference on Labor's Public Responsibility, Nov. 17–20, 1959, Madison, Wis.), Box 99, McDonald Papers; *Proceedings*, First Annual AFL-CIO Community Services Conference, Mar. 4–9, 1956, pp. 2–3, Neilson Library, Smith College.

49. Vaughn Davis Bornet, *Welfare in America* (Norman: University of Oklahoma Press, 1960), pp. 126–27, 144–45; William H. Form, "Organized Labor's Place in the Community Power Structure," *Industrial and Labor Relations Review* 12 (July 1959): 526–39; Harold L. Wilensky and Charles N. Lebeaux, *Industrial Society and Social Welfare* (New York: Free Press, 1965), pp. 276–81.

50. In 1953, Community Chest Council Executive Robert MacRae of Chicago admitted that the word "'partner' is not always realistically used in describing labor's role in health and welfare. Too often 'partnership' gets lip

service comparable to that sometimes accorded the phrase 'opportunity for Negroes,'" *Community* (Community Chests and Councils of America newsletter), Feb. 1953, pp. 106–7; "Minutes," Executive Board Meeting, Indiana State AFL-CIO, Mar. 18–19, 1959, Box 7, USA District 30 Records, USA/A; *Ithaca Union Labor Review,* June 1954, AUF, Box 30, LMDC; Alice H. Cook to Ralph N. Campbell et al., Nov. 7, 1952, Box 11, Series 3, Inter-University Labor Education Committee Records, LMDC.

51. "Minutes," CIO Executive Board Minutes, June 4, 1953, Oct. 5, 1954; Alice Cook interview, July 12, 1989, Ithaca, N.Y.; New York State School of Industrial and Labor Relations, Third Annual Seminar in Community Relations for Business and Industry, Dec. 1, 1952, Box 10, Series 3, Inter-University Labor Education Committee Records.

52. Irving Louis Horowitz, ed., *Power, Politics and People: The Collected Essays of C. Wright Mills* (London: Oxford University Press, 1967), pp. 353–73.

53. Industrial Relations Division, National Association of Manufacturers, *Spotlight on Union Activities—Their Impact on Individuals, the Economy and the Public* (New York: NAM, 1958), p. 16.

# 6 | A Beachhead in the Community

During 1950, several top International Harvester executives traveled across the South and Midwest to participate in town meetings. The purpose of these company-sponsored gatherings was to introduce International Harvester management to community leaders and to encourage the exchange of information and attitudes between company and community. Typically, the company invited about two hundred local people to a luncheon meeting. Guests included public officials, county agents, local business and professional people, teachers, clergy, members of women's clubs and civic groups, labor leaders, and representatives of the press and radio. Local and divisional management officials sat scattered among the guests, serving as hosts at each luncheon table. International Harvester President John L. McCaffrey or Chairman of the Board Fowler McCormick began the meetings with a short talk outlining the company's place in the community and the current state of business. What followed was an opportunity for community leaders, in a "no-holds barred" atmosphere, to ask questions of the "highest authority in the company" about issues ranging from Harvester's attitude on social security to soil conservation.

According to the company, these forums helped "create an impression of neighborliness" that went far in correcting misunderstandings "commonly held about corporations." After one such community forum, McCaffrey explained that "industry has made a terrible mistake over the years in its failure to interest itself more in the community in which it operates—we want to tell the people in the twenty-four communities where we have plants that their problems are our problems." Industry, he declared "can no longer continue to ignore the community in which it operates."[1]

International Harvester's interest in its plant communities arose from a widely shared fear among postwar employers that they had lost authority not only on the shop floor but also beyond their factory gates. Community sympathy for workers in the 1945–46 strike wave as well as the growing union presence in community agencies sent business alarming signals of public support for liberal values and organized labor. Community, then, took on a new importance for business leaders worried about the decline of corporate power. At the 1948 Congress of American Industries, National Cash Register Company President S. C. Allyn rallied fellow business executives to the struggle, declaring that the community had become "a beach-head for the recapture of American ideals; for the acceptance of industry in its true and ordained role as leading citizen."[2]

Business strategy in the community followed two intertwined paths. One path was an aggressive public relations effort threatening the decline of American values, morals, and freedoms due to government's and labor's attacks on the free enterprise system. This effort was especially vigorous in the period from 1945 to 1952 and was the product of national organizations, in particular the National Association of Manufacturers. However, other business groups and individual firms also joined the crusade against collectivism and state intervention. A second path emphasized business's effort to shape community relations in a more positive fashion. Employing in the community, programs akin to the welfarism and human relations used in the plant, individual companies constructed a more favorable image of business as a good neighbor. Together, these two facets of community relations aimed to create the proper climate for corporate America.

\* \* \*

Business took labor's community activities much more seriously than subsequent historians have. In the years immediately after World War II, business felt besieged by labor's political and economic power. The community response to the strike wave confirmed employers' fears, epitomizing the crisis facing the continuation of the "American way of life," as they perceived it. The growing presence of labor in the community, even if at times only a form of tokenism, served notice to the business community that unions had become a force to be reckoned with in their own backyards. Employers feared that greater union prestige would mean increased union power in the plant. One industrial relations handbook warned of the danger posed by labor's public relations, which sought, it charged, "to keep the community class-conscious." Unions, it contended, wanted to make the public believe that "employers as a class are out to skin the shirts off the backs of workingmen," and that business was "as cold-blooded as a fish in a cake of ice."[3]

Faced with this challenge, the public opinion of the local community became immensely important to business leaders. The community, they believed, was crucial in shaping attitudes and in determining the economic and political environment. Government, which played an increasingly intrusive role in the operation of the economy, started at the grass roots in towns and cities. In early 1946, C. C. Carr of Alcoa warned that "public opinion of industry takes root where industry lives, and from this root will stem the freedoms granted to industry . . . or the restrictions imposed upon it." Similarly public relations consultant James W. Irwin reminded employers that "in our industrial communities we may be made or broken. With the support of our neighbors, who regard industry as a good neighbor, we can win many battles. Without the support of our neighbors, we stand to win none."[4]

Employers matched their efforts to influence the ideas of their work force with a pledge to restore community confidence in business. This required teaching the public about the centrality of the company and the free enterprise system to community well-being. Indeed, these two efforts were closely interrelated; employers saw industrial relations and community relations as overlapping spheres. Worker attitudes toward employers served as the base from which communities formed their opinions of business. Advocates of human relations argued that an employer's reputation and influence beyond the plant gates could be built on the goodwill generated by a contented and loyal work force. In turn, they believed that a community favorable to the company could set the boundaries for acceptable worker activism within the plant. In a sense, they saw corporate community relations as a form of company consciousness writ large.[5]

Not surprisingly, many of the same business leaders who promoted human relations and welfarism stood behind the dramatic growth in corporate community relations. Most active were the umbrella business organizations like the National Association of Manufacturers, the Chamber of Commerce, the American Petroleum Institute and the American Iron and Steel Institute. The NAM's community relations program, designed to "merchandise" the business story to the public, was the most ambitious and far reaching. It overlapped with community relations campaigns devised by city and regional business associations, like the Associated Industries of Cleveland, which urged its members to "sell the principles of free enterprise as a real and living force."[6] Both national and local business organizations provided guidance and support to the many firms who established their own community relations activities in the ensuing decade.

The drive to sell the free enterprise system at the local level also gained momentum from a campaign to arouse communities in defense of Americanism. In the late forties and fifties, the major threat was communism. After the war, business had latched upon anticommunism as a way of strengthening its own appeal and legitimating its attack on liberals and organized labor, whom it tarred as collectivists. Business groups joined with veterans organizations, patriotic societies, civic clubs, and religious bodies to battle communism at home. The American Legion, the General Federation of Women's Clubs, the American Bar Association, and others formed Americanism departments, charged with exposing and rooting out subversion in communities across the country. In 1948, the Chamber of Commerce contributed to the struggle by publishing a *Program for Community anti-Communist Action*, which included directions on how to compile a filing system on local suspects.[7]

If one part of defending Americanism involved exposing its detractors, the other part encompassed promoting the values associated with the American way of life. Key were the concepts of individual freedom and liberty. Community organizations mobilized to reaffirm the public's commitment to these values. In 1951, the Elmira (N.Y.) Freedom Committee, born in the Elmira Association of Commerce but including civic, religious, veteran, farm, fraternal, youth, and patriotic associations, organized a massive demonstration of community solidarity for "freedom in America." In a community of forty-nine thousand, twenty-five thousand people joined in a mass "Pledge of Allegiance to the Constitution." The pledge read: "Before God and in the sight of my fellow men I reaffirm my devotion and loyalty to the rights and obligations of freedom under law granted by the Constitution of the United States of America, and reassume my personal responsibility to cherish the blessings of liberty and to preserve them undiminished for posterity."[8]

According to defenders of Americanism, communist ideology was the most obvious threat to freedom. Ranking second was economic illiteracy. The often unthinking, apathetic, and misguided citizens that populated America's cities and town were unable to fend off the attacks on industry by labor and government. These attacks undermined the whole economic order and ultimately the American way of life, business asserted, because the loss of economic freedom and individualism inexorably led to the loss of political and social freedom. Thus, protecting American freedom became intertwined with protecting American business. The General Federation of Women's Clubs sought to cooperate with such business groups as the NAM to orchestrate a defense of industry through education, particularly in communities. "There," according to GFWC President Mrs. Hiram Houghton, was "where the danger must be met."[9]

The NAM certainly intended to fulfill the GFWC's mandate. Its prewar interest in community relations had consisted mainly of mailings and a few regional meetings. But at the end of the war, the NAM began paying increased attention to organizing local communities in support of private enterprise. In 1947, it formed a national Committee on Cooperation with Community Leaders. Goodyear president, E. J. Thomas, a member of the NAM's Public Relations Advisory Committee, stressed the significance of this change in NAM policy: "No amount of activity at the national level—radio talks, advertising, or even 'personal appearances' by a national figure—can take the place of hard work in the home town by local talent." That advice, he argued, "applies to selling a political ticket or selling a product—or industry's point of view."[10]

The NAM's program had two closely linked methods. One stressed bolstering business leadership within the community; the other aimed at aiding these reinvigorated business leaders in shaping the local climate of opinion. In mid-1947, the Association launched an Industry Leaders Program, designed to mobilize business leaders as shapers of public opinion in their local communities. The program gave local employers the "factual ammunition and platform techniques to become better champions of the American way." To accomplish this, the NAM formed teams consisting of two experts, one in the field of economics and labor relations and one in the field of public speaking. At the invitation of local employer associations, the NAM representatives offered two-day invitation-only seminars to key industrial leaders. Advance men preceded the team to aid in making local arrangements for the conference.[11]

NAM experts began each conference by distributing an Industry Leaders Manual, which was to serve as the local business spokesperson's "bible," providing sources for speeches and panel discussions aimed at local audiences. This loose-leaf "sales kit," was essentially a guide to the NAM's economic and political philosophy and its position on legislation. It explained the nature and philosophy of the "American Individual Enterprise System" and, through a series of discussion outlines, provided explanations of issues like prices and profits, the relationship between wages and productivity, monopoly in collective bargaining, and the growing pressure toward centralization and government controls. To keep employers current on the changing political scene, the NAM sent all conference participants updated material with which to amend their guidebooks.[12] The manual also included instructions on how to sell the free enterprise philosophy. It suggested that appeals should be made to the heart so strongly "that it is not inconsistent with intelligence to act upon it." Indeed, according to the Industry Leaders guide, people needed to "be led through a thinking process" on the value of contending philosophies.[13]

While the manual provided the "factual" ammunition, the meetings whipped up employer enthusiasm and provided practical lessons. NAM experts pointed to opinion polls revealing a crisis. One team member then dramatized "with some wild soap box forensics . . . 'The Voice of the Opposition,'" while the other exposed the fallacies of collectivist philosophies. After discussing issues raised in the manual, the participants used it to compose and deliver short speeches. NAM experts and fellow conference members provided businessmen with "coaching in the art of meeting the forensic tirades of the left-wingers with the truth about what has made this nation great."[14]

Testifying to business support of the Industry Leaders program was the participation by over nine thousand businessmen in 260 cities during the first two years. The secretary of the Janesville, Wisconsin, Chamber of Commerce reported that program participants were almost evangelically enthusiastic, "feeling that at last they have been given the weapons with which to do an effective job in the community." The group, he continued, was "now anxious to follow up as missionaries of the free enterprise system." Similarly, reports from the field convinced NAM official T. M. Brennan that participants were "instilled with an inspired fervor to spread the message of private enterprise."[15]

In many communities, the program's graduates followed up the seminar by forming speakers' bureaus. The appearance of manufacturing executives at grass roots gatherings of organizations like the YMCA and YWCA, Rotary and Exchange clubs, Parent-Teacher Associations and church groups not only facilitated the spreading of the free enterprise message but also served to strengthen the influence of the local business community. The Tristate Industrial Association of Pittsburgh, for example, formed a bureau of twenty-eight business representatives who had offered their services to "combat false propaganda with facts." Similarly, within days of their Industry Leaders conferences, employers in Davenport, Iowa; Bridgeport, Connecticut; and San Diego, California, established speakers' bureaus and reached out aggressively into their local communities. By the end of 1949, 195 local employer associations had developed speakers bureaus.[16]

A second, closely related NAM program, also launched in 1947, helped local employers' associations establish comprehensive community public relations programs. Upon request, NAM representatives mapped out a plan of action and aided local employers in such communities as Quincy, Illinois; San Diego, California; Tacoma, Washington; and Lynchburg, Virginia. To learn where industry stood in each locale, the program began by recruiting local college students to conduct an opinion survey of the local population.[17] In Reading, Pennsylvania, the Manufacturers Association drew upon the information generated to organize popular opposition to unions and the local Socialist city administration. To promote a positive image of local industry, the Association created a sports league and encouraged members to respond to complaints about factory noise, dirt, and unsafe working conditions. To show that employers were more interested than union officials in the community, a Community Social Progress Committee publicized the extent of management involvement in civic and charitable organizations. Within six months of its implementation, Frederick H. Klein, president of the Manufacturers Association, claimed that local newspapers long partial to labor "now see that all stories about enterprise that are in any way controversial contain management's side of the case."[18]

The NAM encouraged employers to direct their message at those groups considered by public relations experts to be the key to molding public opinion. These "thought leaders" included educators, clergy, professionals, local officials, and women's leaders. The NAM began publishing periodicals directed at opinion molders: *Trends* (aimed at educators), and *Program Notes* (women's club leaders), each had a circulation of forty-six thousand; *Understanding* (clergymen) had a circulation of twenty-six thousand. Recognizing that women's clubs were an audience of "inestimable potential," the NAM provided package programs to club directors designed to stimulate discussion on issues like federal spending and taxation or the Taft-Hartley Act. The packages included speeches, hints on speaking effectively, sample invitations, and publicity releases.[19]

One of the more ambitious of NAM's community-oriented programs attempted to build consensus among large numbers of local opinion leaders through a nationwide series of town meetings. Begun in June 1948, the meetings combined the initiative of local business groups with the organizational support of the national body. The theme of the gatherings was, "Is the System Under Which We Have All Grown-up Worth Saving?" Seven hundred clergymen, educators, women's leaders, students, youth leaders, and businessmen from Reading, Lancaster, York, Harrisburg, and Lebanon attended the first town meeting in Hershey, Pennsylvania. A panel of local businessmen discussed the challenges facing American society and afterward fielded questions from the audience. Over nine hundred of the "most influential leaders of community life and opinion" of Providence, Rhode Island, attended the next meeting, which was broadcast over the radio. Audiences at these meetings raised questions about why industry opposed the guaranteed annual wage, how taxes could be cut when necessary government expenses were so great, and why businessmen denied that organized labor promoted a better standard of living for workers. These questions indicated the work still facing the business community. Nevertheless, the NAM concluded that "these local leaders of thought" left the town meetings having rededicated "themselves to the traditional concepts of American liberty."[20]

On the eve of the 1948 election, the NAM was convinced that its community relations program was reshaping America's political landscape. But Truman's reelection stunned the NAM, leading it to question its public relations strategy. Reflecting the members' despondency, Thomas J. Bannan, association director, asked NAM President Wallace F. Bennett "whether we were so far down the road to socialism that there was no return or whether freedom still existed?"[21] Some public relations experts argued, however, that Truman's campaign provided proof of the significance of communication efforts targeting individuals at the local level. The Democrat's victory, they asserted, could be attributed to Truman's whirlwind "whistle-stop" train tour and to organized labor's effectiveness in influencing individual members. These were grassroots, face-to-face interactions with the people. According to *Public Relations News*, Truman's success proved that public relations campaigns could change attitudes.[22]

After a period of study and reevaluation, the NAM's Board of Directors and staff vowed to cast aside "defeatist" attitudes. Particularly at the community level, the only place where "genuine confidence in industry [can] be engendered," they planned to redouble efforts to convince "the American people that only through the operation of a competitive capitalistic economy can lasting national prosperity and the basic freedoms of the individual citizen be assured."[23] The NAM enlarged the Committee on Cooperation with Community Leaders from 250 to 2,000 leading industrialists in hundreds of cities and towns. These business leaders formed local task forces devoted to reshaping public opinion. The NAM's expanded community program featured more town meetings and an intensified industry leaders program, with four instead of two teams of experts in the field.[24]

Beginning in 1949, Truman's legislative proposals in the fields of agriculture, housing, and health brought a special urgency to the NAM's warnings about state interference in the economy. The Davenport, Iowa, speakers bureau presented a panel discussion on "What Price Security?" before the YMCA Men's Club of that city. As a direct result, the club went on record with a resolution "opposed to any legislation which subsidizes government in business or which is designed to reapportion the wealth of the nation for the benefit of special interest groups." The national YMCA then sent this resolution to over three hundred YMCA's Men's Clubs throughout the United States. In Lakewood, Ohio, the NAM town meeting kicked off a "Free Enterprise Week," during which citizens "were given many evidences of the blessings of the system to community and nation."[25]

In early 1950, the NAM launched one of its most successful community relations efforts in the Southern states, partially in response to the CIO's Operation Dixie, the last major effort to organize Southern workers.[26] The growing public fear of domestic Communist subversion also contributed to the urgency of effectively reaching the public at the community level. Called the "Roanoke Plan" after the city of its origins, the program was a year-long integrated campaign that brought together tested community relations techniques with the goal of reaching every segment of society. In early January 1950, several business organizations, aided by NAM staff, formed the Roanoke American Way of Life Committee. From February through November, it scheduled weekly activities to create economic understanding throughout the area. An Industry Leaders workshop opened the schedule and was followed closely by the organization of a speakers bureau, which heavily promoted its offerings among civic clubs. Next came a five-week radio round-table of business and economic problems. Spring brought Economic Education Months, featuring a Town Hall Meeting, the distribution of NAM pamphlets and posters to schools, factory tours, and the showing of NAM films to schools, churches, and colleges. During May, the close relationship between community relations and company consciousness became clear as the Roanoke Plan moved into factories, offering NAM-run Employer-Employee Communications Clinics. June was Church Month, with a luncheon for the city's clergy and an introduction of the NAM's journal, *Trends*. July and August activities included an industrial exhibit, more radio programs, and films for youth summer camps.

Winding up in the fall, the committee sponsored a Business-Industry-Education Day, a new program developed by the NAM and the Chamber of Commerce. On BIE day, schools closed while teachers toured local plants and learned at luncheons or dinners about the part that business played in the welfare of their community. October was School and College Month, during which local businessmen participated in vocational guidance forums and spoke to local Roanoke college students about national economic and social trends. The year's program climaxed in November, the "Thanks for Freedom" month, with communitywide meetings, newspaper, radio, church activities, and special school assemblies with business speakers. The program ended with "Thanks for Freedom Sunday" in all Roanoke churches on November 26.[27]

Such elaborate programs were the exception rather than the rule, but the committee applauded its results: "Roanoke people are talking to their fellow Americans about the values of freedom and the American way of life." Moreover, the Roanoke Plan provided a model of what could be accomplished by business groups.[28] Other organizations such as the conservative-moving Chamber of Commerce followed the NAM lead in expanding local public relations. In 1949 the Chamber began its "American Opportunity Program" and later followed it with "Explaining Your Business." These programs provided training, resources, and plans to local chambers for community relations campaigns. Then, in 1954, the Chamber of Commerce began promoting Economic Discussion Groups, which, like the NAM's earlier Industry Leaders Conferences, aimed at developing "articulate, persuasive spokesmen" for business. Between 1955 and 1960, fifteen hundred groups of businessmen—including some organized by such large companies as Caterpillar, Eastman Kodak, and Alcoa—met weekly for eighteen weeks to discuss economic problems using materials supplied by the Chamber of Commerce.[29]

Other employer groups believed they could promote their free enterprise vision more effectively if organized independently of established business organizations. In the immediate postwar years, many of these groups were particularly effective in pushing anticommunism and linking it to any ideas that business could define as subversive. In 1947, for instance, the New Jersey Manufacturers Association quietly formed the "Work and Unity Group," then denied any connection with it. Believing that Communist cells were burrowing throughout the country spreading "poisonous misinformation," the Group vowed to "fight fire with fire." Local businessmen formed "cells" at private luncheons to provide an antidote to left-wing ideas.

Manufacturers Association Director Robert W. Watt explained that his organization was working underground "to set off a chain reaction of public opinion." The group sponsored meetings before church, consumer, and veterans groups, provided speaker kits, and passed out fifty thousand copies of a pamphlet called *Free Men or Slaves*, which denounced government planning and excess profit taxes.[30]

Similarly, in 1947 Syracuse, New York, employers formed the Citizen's Foundation to avoid being "labeled with any name the public was familiar with." Financial support came from such businessmen as Cloud Wampler of Carrier Corporation, but the Foundation asserted that it represented "public spirited citizens," rather than employers. These citizens were appalled by the "apathy" of the general public about America's economic, political, and moral freedoms, which were being swapped "for promises of a life of less personal responsibility." Its active enemies were "communists, their allies and their dupes"; its passive enemies were "ignorance and indifference."[31] Working behind the scenes, the Foundation's Anti-Subversive Committee stopped the proposed broadcast of "communist-front" programs on a local radio station and exposed the "misuse and abuse" of the names of a score of prominent Syracuse citizens in connection with a Henry Wallace campaign meeting. It also distributed "The Red Package," a folder explaining the evils of Communism to fifty thousand workers. Finally, in a campaign tarring the International Union of Mine, Mill and Smelter Workers as subversive, the Foundation convinced Precision Casting Company workers to reject unionism altogether.[32]

The full range and scope of the business community's public relations efforts can only be suggested here. Included were such campaigns as "Forward Hamilton," organized by Hamilton, Ohio, employers and quietly financed by General Motors, Ford, the Lima Hamilton Company, and Champion Coated Paper Company. Forward Hamilton mobilized to defeat Mayor Eddie Beckett, a UAW member, and to restore business dominance of the city council. It poured $20,000 into the city election, trumpeting its free enterprise message with car cards, radio time, and an intricate network of small meetings. Similarly, Anderson, Indiana, business leaders, supplied with $90,000 by General Motors, organized a group called the American Guard. The Guard claimed to be a "non-partisan patriotic group" formed to "obtain good government and worthy office holders by education of the voter," but by late 1949, the American Guard sponsored two radio programs a week attacking socialism and a proposed liberal unemployment compensation bill.[33]

In addition, individual firms contributed to business's public relations campaigns. *Public Relations News* found that 77 percent of surveyed firms were committed to increasing their community relations budgets for 1948.[34] For many, the immediate impetus for action was "the continuing threat to Free Enterprise in our country, the growth of ideas leading to the Welfare State, creeping Collectivism and a continuation of high taxes." For others, like Allegheny Ludlum Steel Company, community support for labor fostered an interest in community opinion. Allegheny Ludlum Steel Company attempted to restore its reputation by conducting an intensive two-week campaign that included meetings between the entire executive staff of the company and the local "opinion creating people" as well as a series of full-page advertisements touting the company's contributions to the community in all the local papers.[35]

Although Eisenhower's election in 1952 removed some of the urgency from the business community's campaign to sell the free enterprise system to its neighbors, alarmists remained. In early 1953, *Public Relations Journal* reminded employers that the "long, hard battle against socialism was all but lost by business's neglect of its public relations opportunities and obligations for many years prior to the depression and for a long time after that." It warned that if business slackened "in its well-organized efforts to keep the public informed, nothing better can be expected than a swing again to the left—for the forces of bureaucracy and socialism are forever at it—and they are masters of propaganda." But in general, the business message in the community was less hysterical by mid-decade. However, business interest in community relations, albeit in a slightly different form, continued to grow. One 1956 survey revealed that 70 percent of companies had designated an executive in charge of plant community relations.[36]

* * *

The flip side of the aggressive selling of the free enterprise system was a community relations strategy emphasizing in a more positive way the need to create a more sympathetic political and economic environment for business. Company involvement in communities was not new to the mid-twentieth century; from the earliest mill villages business had been intimately linked to the communities that produced its labor force and customers. What distinguished the postwar corporate community relations programs was the "degree of conscious commitment, initiative, organization, and sophistication which companies were now prepared to pour into them."[37]

Industry's bid to become a good neighbor looked very much like the campaigns to build company consciousness within the plant. One part, the equivalent of welfare capitalism, consisted of philanthropic and welfare activities that provided tangible evidence of company concern for the community. A second part, akin to human relations, emphasized the importance of direct communication with the public. "We must" declared Frank W. Abrams, chairman of the board of Standard Oil, during a 1950 meeting of the CED's Board of Trustees, "reestablish the common touch with our fellow men. We must reappear in the role of warm-hearted human beings—which is what we are." Companies could draw upon the reservoir of goodwill and understanding generated by effective community relations to reestablish, in Abrams words, "genuine public acceptance" of the business community's economic leadership.[38]

A wide range of companies participated in this drive to improve community relations, yet there is no simple formula to predict which firms would develop community programs. Union as well as nonunion, large and small, single and multiplant companies practiced community relations. Shortly after the war, for instance, Bigelow-Sanford Carpet Company, Keystone Steel and Wire, Ford Motor Company, International Harvester, General Foods, and General Electric, to name but a few, organized community relations departments or embarked upon their first planned community relations program.[39]

One common factor linking companies with community relations programs was a commitment to human relations within the plant. Companies developing human relations programs saw community relations as an extension of their in-plant activities. In 1948, John L. McCaffery, chairman of International Harvester, advised one works manager that "our community relations are important not only from the standpoint of good public relations but also from the standpoint of good industrial relations within the plant. The general attitude of the community colors, and helps to shape, the attitude of employees themselves towards us." Employers like McCaffery sought to recapture the sense of identification and common interest that they believed business used to share with its employees and its neighbors.[40]

Company size and plant location were also factors determining level of commitment to community relations. Large multiplant firms created programs hoping to alleviate hostility, which they feared existed toward "foreign owned" branch plants. General Foods found that the "bugbear" of absentee ownership was the attitude of local people who felt that "outfits like ours are big, remote, impersonal money-making machines that take all they can from the community, care little about the individual worker's well-being, and less about the community welfare." A 1953 Bureau of National Affairs survey also found that the level of company community activity varied with the size of the community. While both large and small firms (large defined as over a thousand employees) were likely to develop full-scale programs in mid-size or small cities, generally only large companies with greater resources operated community relations programs in metropolitan areas. Small firms doubted their ability to have an impact in large cities like New York or Chicago.[41]

The new concern with human and public relations contributed to a growing interest in the decentralization of production away from major industrial cities. Many employers believed that dispersing plants among smaller communities would increase their ability to influence what both workers and the public thought about American business. In 1946, *Factory* pointed out that factory decentralization promised to solve not only production and distribution problems but also industry's social problems. People in smaller centers were "closer to realities and understand that they cannot have what they do not produce." Many companies further hedged their bets by locating in southern and western states where unions had yet to make much headway.[42]

So fundamental was the concept of integrating company into community that it affected the appearance of the factory itself. Believing that unsightly plants might irritate neighbors, firms like Bethlehem Steel and the Borden Company began extensive programs of landscaping and beautification. The Bournville Works of Cadbury Brothers Ltd. created a "suburban landscape" around its factory with "masses of crocuses, daffodils, and flowering trees" that not only lent color to the immediate surroundings of the plant but also made "the grounds one of the beauty spots of the community." Many companies, particularly when building near residential areas, designed new plants so that they blended into the surrounding landscape and architectural patterns. The streamlined look of the factories of the fifties was part of this effort to create within the community a more visually pleasing image of industry.[43]

Companies often attempted to curry public favor by providing services and gifts directly to the community. Ansul Chemical Company's community program, begun shortly after World War II, for instance, featured a volunteer emergency rescue squad, trained, equipped and operated at company expense. Yale and Towne Manufacturing Company made its auditorium available to Stamford civic groups for meetings. Similarly Caterpillar Tractor Company of Peoria, Illinois, loaned its trucks to the city for clean-up drives and to the Post Office to assist in the department's Christmas rush.[44]

Business routinely won friends by supporting local recreation programs. Many companies gave, or leased at a nominal charge, park land to local communities. In 1949, the Peerless Woolen Mills of Rossville, Georgia, the town's leading industry, began a project to build an eight thousand seat stadium, softball and baseball fields, a running track, a field house, and other sports facilities for use by the community as well as company employees. Dow Chemical Company also generated goodwill by opening its facilities and programs for use by the community. The West Point Manufacturing Company of Alabama made "itself responsible for the recreational activities and general welfare of the 25,000 residents of the area, known as 'The Valley.'" It provided lighted playing fields, swimming pools, gymnasiums, tennis courts, and croquet lawns, in addition to other facilities, to the five towns where West Point mills were located.[45]

Programs for children built goodwill with the local communities of the present and of the future. In 1946, *Factory* advised management to learn more about children. "Kids," it contended, "are the biggest common denominator of community life." Nearly everything revolves around the "community's kids." Local industry would do well to get into the orbit if for no other reason than "today's kids are tomorrow's workers."[46] Sports was a special focus. The Wyandotte Chemicals Corporation conducted a sports program that offered basketball, volleyball, wrestling, boxing, tumbling, weight lifting, and gymnastics in its gymnasium at Wyandotte, Michigan. Companies like General Electric, Olin Industries, Motorola, and North American Aviation, among many others, became closely associated with the developing youth sports movement in the areas of baseball, basketball, football, and soccer. In 1947, United States Rubber Company stepped into the Little League baseball picture, promoting the activity nationwide and picking up the cost of the annual World Series in Williamsport, Pennsylvania.[47]

Social programs complemented this outreach to community youths and their families. In 1950, a Bloomfield, New Jersey, Westinghouse plant sought "firmer acceptance of the company as one of the community's good neighbors" by running a Teen Canteen with dancing, games and free refreshments.[48] About the same time, the Falk Corporation and the Allis-Chalmers Manufacturing Company, located in Milwaukee, Wisconsin, each began sponsoring post-prom parties for area high school students, treating them to a midnight supper, professional entertainment, and dancing.[49] Raybestos-Manhattan, Incorporated "carved a solid niche in the town of Stratford," Connecticut, when in 1947 it formed the Knot Hole Gang, a club for all children in the neighborhood of its plant. The club met three times a week under the supervision of volunteer workers from Raybestos. The company also sponsored a Sea Scouts program and eight Little League teams, complete with special field, uniforms, and a banquet at the end of the season featuring a major league ball player as the principal speaker.[50]

Companies not only sponsored activities but also encouraged employee participation in community affairs to promote community acceptance of business and its values. General Electric maintained a file of employees active in civic projects that enabled supervisors to personally congratulate workers on their accomplishments. In some firms, leadership of community organizations was seen as a prerequisite for professional advancement. Keystone Steel and Wire of Peoria, Illinois, expected its junior executives to take an active role with local groups.[51] The Iron and Steel Institute explained the importance of Keystone's activity. In local social organizations, company representatives became better acquainted with the community's "thought leaders"—doctors, clergy, merchants, educators, and others. The Institute claimed that through the resulting friendships "much of the mystery about what goes on within the walls of the company plant will gradually be dispelled. More important, these people will become missionaries for the company in the community."[52]

Companies expected their senior executives to sit on the governing boards of community agencies. Business representation on these boards was hardly unique to the period after World War II. As individual philanthropists, local business leaders had always been the major force in private welfare activities. During the twenties, however, participation shifted from individuals to corporate representatives acting as officials of the company. In the postwar decade, this practice increased in the face of labor's challenge. Representation on policy-making boards ensured decision making congenial to business interests and served as a device for changing attitudes in the community toward business.[53]

Fund-raising provided corporations with a means to acquire greater influence over voluntary agencies while increasing their community prestige. During and after World War II, corporate giving expanded dramatically. Giving rose from 0.35 percent of profits in 1941 to 1.08 percent in 1960. In dollars, this represented a jump from $239 million to $555 million in the decade after 1948. In part this was a result of war-born profits and tax incentives, but desire for an improved public image was also an important factor.[54] Corporations, like unions, had played a major part in the National War Fund and were drawn into the fund-raising drives of the Community Chest and other voluntary social welfare agencies. Facing multiple appeals, in the late forties, companies like Ford and U.S. Steel began promoting United Fund drives. Despite some labor participation, businessmen felt these drives consolidated the giving process and provided even greater opportunity for business control. As these federated fund-raising drives grew larger, executives representing the largest companies assumed leadership by providing both the largest donations and most of the staffing. In 1956, Humble Oil Company lent a full-time staff of one hundred people to organize the United Fund drive in Houston, Texas.[55] Corporations exacted a price for their high levels of support. In most cities, business leaders overwhelmed labor participation and gained a larger voice in the allocation process. Central financing, then, provided "a channel for the expression of business interests in the spending of welfare funds."[56]

Through corporate philanthropy and other welfare activities, companies tried to create the image of themselves as benevolent, caring, and trustworthy organizations. They hoped that this positive image would enhance the second part of their community relations strategy, communicating with the public on economic and political issues. These communication efforts overlapped with those emanating from the national business organizations like the NAM and the Chamber of Commerce. With the encouragement of these organizations, companies attempted to teach the public about the economic principles of the free enterprise system, its superiority, and the necessity for its preservation. They also sought to sell the company itself to the public. Employers tried to familiarize the public with the products, policies, and objectives of the firm, while also emphasizing the company's economic support of the community through payrolls, taxes, and contributions. Companies believed that the payoff from greater public understanding of business would result in increased product sales, improved work force recruitment, and favorable treatment from local governments on issues like taxes or zoning. Finally, companies hoped they could rely on community support in times of labor struggle.

Companies used all sorts of media to send their messages into the community. Institutional advertising surged in the years immediately after World War II as companies made a concerted effort to sell themselves and their values to their neighbors.[57] In the late 1940s, many ads dealt with the specter of spreading communism and the threats Truman's policies posed to individual freedom. General Electric advertisements, for instance, explained "the facts about *hidden taxes*" and how "the profit motive is the driving power of our free society." They also made clear that their opposition to "compulsory unionism" was related to what GE decried as the way "Communists seek to get and keep control of labor unions." During 1950, Locke Incorporated of Baltimore sponsored a series of ads warning readers that the "cradle-to-grave security" and the "free medical service" promised by the government meant "socialism—the end of your individual freedom."[58] The International Nickel Company's Huntington, West Virginia, campaign avoided broader political issues in favor of ads reminding the public that "your Inco friends and neighbors help in many ways to make Huntington a good place to live in." Companies tended to step up advertising just before elections and either before or during strikes, as they went to the public with their side of the issues.[59]

Other advertisements targeted special audiences. Pittsburgh steel companies, for example, wooed friends from the black community with ads in the black press. During 1954, U.S. Steel bought space in the *Pittsburgh Courier* for the picture of a black supervisor consulting with an assistant superintendent. Below was the statement: "On the production line, in our mills, or in offices, or in transportation, quality people, for a quality product, are our first consideration. Numbered among these people are more than 32,000 Negroes willing and able to perform vital functions as members of a great team dedicated to the service of the nation." Earlier that year, Republic Steel praised "Negro Progress" in an ad stating "Greater Safety and better working conditions mean increased security for Republic's sixty-eight thousand employees, thousands of whom are Negroes." The company then pledged its "continued support in helping you continue to progress."[60]

Increasingly, radio, and later television, carried the business message to the community. Local business associations used radio to showcase industry. In Wisconsin, during the late forties, "The Cavalcade of Racine Industry" radio program dramatized "the history and romantic growth" of local industry, while the Oshkosh Associated Industries, "Wings of Industry," brought "industry right into the home." Each program focused on a member firm, beginning with a description of the company, the investment required for each employee, and details of plant growth and sales volume. An interview with workers taped "right on the job" created a first-hand view of the part played by industry in community life. According to one employer, the show demonstrated that "what is good for business is good for everybody."[61]

Individual firms found radio an effective community relations tool. Some, like the Gerity-Michigan Corporation, simply used radio spot commercials to sell free enterprise. Others associated the company with popular community activities. Armco Steel and the Gardner Board and Carton Company broadcast high school football and basketball games, using the commercial time to explain what the problems, accomplishments, and contributions of industry meant to community welfare.[62] Firms also inaugurated weekly or even daily radio programs in a variety of formats to help integrate the company into the community. The programs of Youngstown Sheet and Tube Company, Keystone Steel & Wire Company, and the Mooresville Mills interspersed the sounds, voices, and news of the plant with public announcements of forthcoming community activities. Youngstown Sheet and Tube Company's daily program, begun in mid-1948, included editorials that regularly pointed out the importance of profits in the "American Free Enterprise System," and warned of threats to our "American Way of Life" from those who sought "to undermine the freedom of the individual" by setting up a "Welfare State." Watch out, the company advised, for government handouts, which were the first step toward socialism. Armstrong Cork's radio program, also launched in 1948, soon reached three of every four listeners in the Lancaster, Pennsylvania, region. It mixed company reports with musical entertainment, featuring company employees as well as professionals. In the mid-fifties, Caterpillar company moved into television with a weekly half-hour Sunday night news, weather and sports program that carried messages about the firm instead of product commercials. Timken-Roller Bearing was probably the most ambitious company in the media field, blanketing Ohio with five radio programs.[63]

Some forms of company communication were similar to mechanisms used in the in-plant human relations programs. Two Nebraska firms, the Kelly Ryan Equipment Company and the Formfit Company, used stunts, like paying employees in smaller cities and towns with silver dollars. These dollars then circulated among local businesses dramatizing the economic impact of company payrolls.[64] Companies also used plant tours and open houses to educate the community and humanize the factory. Even before World War II, some companies had a tradition of opening their doors and displaying their products to the public. After the war, the number of firms offering tours skyrocketed. Opinion Research Corporation reported that among the companies it surveyed, the number sponsoring tours increased from 26 percent to 70 percent between 1948 and 1950. Companies widely advertised their open houses and attracted the public with promises of child care, refreshments, and souvenirs. Attendance at some of these events testified to their popularity. In a single day, the Youngstown, Ohio, plants of the Carnegie-Illinois Steel Corporation and the Lynn General Electric plant each attracted thirty thousand visitors. A three-day open house conducted by the S. D. Warren Company, employing twenty-eight hundred workers manufacturing paper, brought fourteen thousand visitors to Westbrook, Maine, a town of twelve thousand.[65]

Unlike prewar tours that concentrated primarily on technology, postwar open houses stressed ideas. A. D. LeMonte, of the Mullins Manufacturing Corporation, advised a 1949 conference of public relations executives that "the modern open house . . . actively, not passively, attempts to create opinions or develop action that eventually will profit the company that's paying the bill." S. C. Allyn of National Cash Register was more blunt about corporate objectives. The goal was to "indoctrinate citizens with the capitalist story." He asserted that "experience shows that people are eager to go through factories; that when they are taken through and given an indoctrination in the sociology of the industrial system, they are able to play back the story with remarkable fidelity."[66] These new "interpretive" public tours overlapped with those targeted at employee audiences, teaching the same kinds of lessons. The goal was to show plants as working models of capitalism and to point out benefits flowing to people from the free market system.[67]

Like the business associations, individual companies appreciated the role that community leaders or "opinion molders" played in shaping ideas. They sent copies of plant papers or special newsletters to business, education, club and church leaders. Caterpillar's mailing list included over six thousand names. Noting that "barber shops were the idea crossroads of America," in 1950 Caterpillar began inviting Peoria barbers to special plant tours, lunches, and discussions to ensure that they could "talk factually about the company and its policies." Other firms sponsored special open houses for teachers, clergy, and doctors.[68] General Electric, Johnson and Johnson, and Republic Steel established speakers bureaus that addressed the gatherings of these professionals as well as other groups. Over a three-year period Republic Steel representatives made three thousand talks to an audience of more than one-quarter of a million people.[69]

The occasions that brought together all aspects of corporate community relations were the ceremonies attendant to the opening of new plants or company anniversaries. These events symbolized the mutuality of factory and community. In 1950, Wichita, Kansas, designated a "Coleman Week" with activities honoring Coleman Company's fiftieth anniversary and the founder's eightieth birthday. Bigelow-Sanford Carpet Company's 125th anniversary began with a special "Influence Group" dinner for 140 leading citizens. An open house attended by 12,000 visitors capped off the celebration which, according to the company, demonstrated "the high degree of friendship between the company and the town" and "emphasized the interdependence of the two for maintaining prosperity in the community."[70]

Typical of a communitywide celebration of a new plant was the dedication in 1952 of the Parker Pen Company plant in Janesville, Wisconsin. A Citizens' Planning Committee, representing business, labor, youth, and women's groups sponsored the event, while school children participated in a contest naming the factory. On opening day "factory whistles tooted" and "church bells rang." Finally, Allegheny Ludlum Steel Corporation's 1949 celebration brought together the entire community in the towns of Dunkirk, New York, and West Leechburg, Pennsylvania: schools declared holidays; merchants, who had installed street decoration and window exhibits, closed shops to permit employees to attend the event; volunteer firemen and members of local civic clubs served as special traffic police; women's clubs set up free babysitting in churches to care for children; high school students and other organizations presented the company with flowers; and newspapers printed special editions in which merchants placed congratulatory advertisements.[71] Events such as these epitomized the intricate connections between business and the community, particularly in smaller cities and towns.

The business campaign to enmesh itself into local communities attracted the attention of liberals and labor activists. As early as 1946, the sociologist Robert S. Lynd cautioned trade unionists about business infiltration at the grass-roots level. Lynd observed that the NAM had "suddenly become vastly solicitous about local people." He contended that its concern was part of a long-range strategy to systematically capture grass-roots public opinion. Sympathetic local communities, Lynd believed, could be manipulated to provide political support for the people and issues business favored. Business leaders sought to establish in everybody's mind "that 'freedom of initiative' is what America is all about," and "to put labor in the doghouse in public disesteem up and down the Main Streets of the United States— and to keep it there." Of the entire spectrum of the business community's attempt to reshape political culture, Lynd believed that most dangerous of all was this movement "to capture—body and breeches, mind and soul—the local community."[72]

Trade unionists responded strongly to the NAM's early community relations campaign. In 1946, Irvine Kerrison of the Detroit Teachers' union, charged that "high-powered NAM speakers" were appearing in the high schools "expounding subtle but effective antilabor and pro-NAM propaganda." Particularly after 1946, when the NAM took the advice of public relations experts and played down its sponsorship of the local campaign, labor found business propaganda even more insidious. Labor worried that probusiness ideology might be more persuasive if local people thought it originated in the community. Thus, the CIO charged that ads carrying the names of local business firms actually were prepared by the NAM. The *Guild Reporter* published an exposé, which was reprinted by a number of other labor papers, of the NAM's attempt to "hoodwink" club women with propaganda. Through program kits distributed to over 36,000 women's club program directors, the NAM planted antilabor speeches, "ostensibly prepared by women who have standing in the community as the studied opinion of the speakers." The kits, the *Guild Reporter* derisively noted, even suggested planting people in the audience to ask specific questions for which the kit provided the answers.[73]

The Harrisburg Central Labor Union issued broader warnings about NAM underground work. It cautioned: "So watch out for the new look on big business propaganda. Look out also for phony committees which will rise in the community. Pretend to be interested in public welfare and get a lot of publicity in the daily press. . . . We must not be fooled by the new line. It must not happen here."[74]

Throughout the fifties, trade unionists worried about industry's "unending efforts to get people to accept its ideas as their own." Unions warned members about the "propaganda" that poured forth from newspapers in the form of institutional advertising and editorials. The *Connecticut CIO Vanguard*, for instance, attacked a series of ads sponsored by an organization of manufacturers called Industries of Naugatuck Valley, which charged that the stockholder got too little because workers got too much. The UAW reacted as strongly to company community economic education as it did to the in-plant education efforts. In 1955, it warned autoworkers of the ways companies used the mass media. They used radio and television, often "to sell the corporation's ideas more than its products." The UAW charged that many huge corporations, which sold only to other companies and not to the public, "now sponsor lengthy, expensive programs as well as those featuring news analyses or commentaries." It was not surprising, then, that "the corporation's economic, labor and political ideas turned up on these broadcasts in the form of "comments" or commercials.[75]

\* \* \*

Industry's community relations clearly irritated labor, but what tangible benefits did business attain through its increased attentiveness to community? As with the campaign to reshape workers' attitudes within the shop through building company consciousness, employers often had difficulty pointing to specific achievements. Early on, however, some saw an impact in both the political and economic realms. In 1950, the Associated Industries of Alabama reported to the NAM convention on the aftermath of its free enterprise communications program. It claimed that since the inception of the campaign, which stressed the "tremendous federal tax burden corporations are carrying," there had been no additional taxes levied on industry by the state legislature. Ohio business leaders could also link campaigns like Forward Hamilton to the surprising reelection of Robert Taft in 1950, despite heavy labor opposition. The business community was also convinced that its efforts within the community were critical to the election of Eisenhower.[76]

Especially in the area of labor relations, business expressed satisfaction with its community relations programs. Within a few years after developing the most ambitious and wide-ranging corporate community relations program, General Electric believed that it had created a much better understanding among its neighbors of the company's aims, policies, and objectives. Proof, according to GE spokespersons, was the community response to union strife in 1950, 1951, and 1952. It asserted that community leaders urged workers to refrain from striking and, in the few places where plants struck, General Electric claimed "we found public sentiment in our favor." Unlike 1946 "there were no clergymen in the picket lines. Merchants did not go against us. Newspapers did not run stories and editorials against us. Most of them knew about our offer and urged the union to accept it." This, General Electric proclaimed, was "the real payoff."[77]

## Notes

1. *Christian Science Monitor,* Dec. 19, 1950.
2. S. C. Allyn, "Industry as a Good Neighbor" (Address before the 53rd

Annual Congress of American Industries, Dec. 1, 1948), Accession 1411, NAM, Series I, Box 1 (hereafter Acc. 1411, NAM I/1).

3. John Cameron Aspley and Eugene Whitmore, *The Handbook of Industrial Relations*, (Chicago: Dartnell, 1952), p. 1104; "Your Community: Labor's New Frontier," *NB*, Oct. 1954, pp. 29–31, 84–85.

4. In early 1950, Seth Russell, Dean of Sociology at Penn State University observed that "four or five years ago labor leaders began urging the workers to participate in chests, drives, and all sorts of community welfare. The war was over, collective bargaining was legal—now to consolidate the gains in community acceptance. As this idea caught on with members of organized labor, an interesting thing happened. Management began a conscious and diligent effort in the same direction. If you have a good thing, the competition will get in on it." Russell, "What Can Unions Do to Make a Better Community?" *Unions in the Community*, 1950, pamphlet, Baker Library, Harvard University, Boston, Mass.; C. C. Carr, "Public Relations at the Local Level," *PRJ* 2 (Feb. 1946): 3; James W. Irwin, "Public Relations Responsibilities in the Crucial Period Ahead," *PRJ* 2 (Jan. 1946): 3.

5. On GM's views on the connections between industrial and community relations see L. L. L. Golden, *Only by Public Consent: American Corporations Search for Favorable Opinion* (New York: Hawthorn Books, 1968), pp. 107–9; Clark W. King, "Information in the Stream of Human Relations" (Address before the Ninth Ohio Personnel Institute, Ohio State University, May 12, 1948), Box 4, AOF IV, LMDC; John W. Welcker, "The Community Relations Problems of Industrial Companies," *HBR* 27 (Nov. 1949): 771–73.

6. "Merchandising the Business Story to Opinion Moulders in Education and the Churches," 1945, Acc. 1411, NAM I/27; Associated Industries of Cleveland, *Speak Up, Cleveland!: A Plan of Action in Industrial Public Relations*, 1949, pamphlet in Box 16, AOF I, LMDC.

7. Peter H. Irons, "American Business and the Origins of McCarthyism: The Cold War Crusade of the United States Chamber of Commerce," in *The Specter: Original Essays on the Cold War and the Origins of McCarthyism*, ed. Robert Griffith and Athan Theoharis (New York: New Viewpoints, 1974), pp. 72–89; District Chairman, Americanism Department to Club President, c. 1953, Acc. 1411, NAM I/223.

8. On the link between anticommunism and patriotism, see David Caute, *The Great Fear* (New York: Simon and Schuster, 1978), pp. 21, 26–28, 350–51; Elmira Freedom Committee, news release, c. Sept. 1951, Acc. 1411, NAM I/2. Communities also reaffirmed their commitment to freedom through participation in the nationwide "Crusade for Freedom" campaign conducted by the American Heritage Foundation to raise money for Radio Free Europe. Abbott Washburn, "Mobilizing Public Opinion for Freedom," *PRJ* (Sept. 1950): 5–6, 10, *NYT*, July 28, 1950.

9. "Proceedings," the General Federation of Women's Clubs Seminar on Economic Policy for Freedom," Mount Union College, Alliance, Ohio, June 13–14, 1951, Acc. 1411, NAM I/223.

10. On the NAM's wartime community relations program see the correspondence and reports in Acc. 1411, NAM III/8, *NAM News*, Dec. 4, 1948.

11. "Industry Leaders Program," c. 1949, Acc. 1411, NAM I/80. See issues of *Exchange* (NAM newsletter), Acc. 1411, NAM I/122; *NAM News*, Dec. 4, 1948.

12. *NAM News*, Nov. 15, 1947.

13. "Industry Leaders Manual," Acc. 1411, NAM I/66.

14. *NAM News*, Jan. 15, 1947, Aug. 7, 1948.

15. Ibid., May 22, Aug. 9, Oct. 4, 1947, Jan. 10, 1948; *PRN*, Feb. 28, 1948, Jan. 9, 1950.

16. *NAM News*, Oct. 30, Nov. 15, 1947, Nov. 14, 1948; Ray Booth to Industry Leaders Meetings Participants, Jan. 15, 1948, J. V. Thompson to Members of the Tri-State Industrial Association, Inc., Feb. 3, 1949, R. C. Oberdahn to W. Stewart Clark, et al., Feb. 12, 1948, Acc. 1411, NAM I/60.

17. *NAM News*, May 24, Nov. 15, 1947, Jan. 17, Apr. 10, May 15, 1948.

18. *NAM News*, Mar. 22, Sept. 27, 1947.

19. Ibid., Dec. 4, 1948; "Merchandising the Business Story to Opinion Moulders in Education and the Churches"; *NAM News*, Nov. 22, 1947, Feb. 14, June 12, 1948.

20. *NAM News*, May 24, June 5, Oct. 16, 30, 1948; *Birmingham News*, Nov. 17, 1948.

21. Bannan quoted in "An Analysis of the Operation of the National Association of Manufacturers and Recommendations," Aug. 20, 1953, Box 69, William Grede Papers, SHSW.

22. *PRN*, Nov. 8, 15, Dec. 20, 1948, Feb. 7, July 4, 1949; Henry C. Link and Albert D. Freibers, "What Went Wrong with the Opinion Poll: And How This Should Stimulate PR Programs," *PRJ* 4 (Dec. 1948): 1–3, 21.

23. "An Analysis of the Operation of the National Association of Manufacturers"; "Proceedings," Committee on Cooperation with Community Leaders of the National Association of Manufacturers, May 17, 1950, Acc. 1411, NAM I/109.

24. "Committee on Cooperation with Community Leaders," report, c. 1950, Acc. 1411, NAM I/270; "An Analysis of the Operation of the National Association of Manufacturers"; *NAM News*, Nov. 12, Dec. 3, 24, 31, 1949, Nov. 18, 1950, Nov. 3, 1951, National Association of Manufacturers Committee on Cooperation with Community Leaders, "Community Public Relations, 1949–1950," c. 1950, Acc. 1411, NAM I/109.

25. *NAM News*, Nov. 12, 1949; "Industry Leaders Follow-Up Meeting," c. Oct. 1951, Acc. 1411, NAM I/80.

26. *NAM News*, Apr. 15, 1950; "Schedule for A Co-ordinated Community Relations Plan," c. 1950, Acc. 1411, NAM I/80; Barbara Griffith, *The Crisis of American Labor: Operation Dixie and the Defeat of the CIO* (Philadelphia: Temple University Press, 1988).

27. The Roanoke American Way of Life Committee, "The 1950 Program under 'The Roanoke Plan' for Publicizing the Value of Freedom and the American Way of Life," Appendix to Fall Report to Committee on Cooperation

with Community Leaders, 1950, Acc. 1411, NAM I/109; *NAM News,* Apr. 15, 1950.

28. "Proceedings," Committee on Cooperation with Community Leaders of the National Association of Manufacturers.

29. Walter Petravage, "The Chamber of Commerce Does Something about It," *PRJ* 16 (Nov. 1960): 6–8, 18; Chamber of Commerce of the United States, *Annual Report,* 1954, p. 15; "Economic Discussion," *Stet,* Nov. 1957, pp. 1–3; *Explaining Your Business News-Bulletin,* Oct. 1960.

30. *CIO News,* July 18, 1948; *PLN,* July 4, 1948.

31. Elmer W. Earl, "Syracuse Citizens Tackle Employee Education," *MRec* 10 (Sept. 1948): 451–52; "Proceedings," Committee on Cooperation with Community Leaders of the National Association of Manufacturers, May 17, 1950.

32. "Weed Killing in the Grassroot Area," *M&F* 43 (July 1948): 117–19; Earl, "Syracuse Citizens Tackle Employee Education," pp. 451–52.

33. "Big Business Organizes a Successful Political Action Committee in Hamilton," *Ammunition,* Feb. 1950, pp. 12–14; *UAW,* Packard Local 190 Edition, Jan. 1950; *Delco Sparks,* UAW Delco-Remy Local 662, Dec. 22, 1949; *UAW,* Dec. 1949; Claude Anderson, *Sit Down in Anderson: UAW Local 663, Anderson, Indiana* (Detroit: Wayne State University, 1968), pp. 99–100.

34. PRN survey cited in "Public Relations Expenditures," *MRev* 37 (Apr. 1948): 180.

35. Don E. Lewis, "One Company's Community Program" (Address before the Seventh National Conference of Business Public Relations Executives, May 5, 1950, New York City), Acc. 1411, NAM I/1; Clark King, "American System Re-Sold to Workers and Public," *FMM* 105 (Nov. 1947): 236–38.

36. "Let Business Tell Its Story—NOW," *PRJ* 9 (Mar. 1953): 2; John J. Pike, "Industry Joins the Community," *AB,* Aug. 1955, pp. 20–21; "Management's Self-Conscious Spokesmen," *Fortune,* Nov. 1955, p. 108; "Who's Got the Pipeline," *FMM* 114 (Oct. 1956): 329.

37. Morrell Heald, *The Social Responsibilities of Business: Company and Community, 1900–1960* (Cleveland: Press of Case Western Reserve University, 1970), p. 221.

38. John L. McCaffery, "First Live Right—and Then Tell About It," *FMM* 107 (Mar. 1949): 90; Frank W. Abrams, "The Businessman's View," in Committee for Economic Development, *How Can a Better Understanding of Our Economic System be Fostered?* (New York: 1950), pp. 10–11.

39. Metropolitan Life Insurance Company, *Community Relations: Getting Acquainted with the Community,* (New York, 1950), p. 8; *PRN,* Apr. 30, 1956; Heald, *The Social Responsibilities of Business,* pp. 221–28; Henry M. Gallagher Jr., "Building New Good Will Licks Old Problems," *AB,* July 1949, pp. 22–24, 46; General Foods, "Public Relations Present Activities and a Look Ahead Thru 1952," 1952, Baker Library, Harvard University. On GE's community relations see General Electric, *The GE Plant Community Relations Program,* (New York, 1952), pamphlet, Baker Library.

40. John L. McCaffrey to D. Chimenti, Sept. 9, 1948, Box 23, William Grede Papers, SHSW.

41. J. Handly Wright and Byron H. Christian, *Public Relations in Management* (New York: McGraw-Hill, 1949), pp. 110–11; General Foods, "Public Relations Present Activities and a Look Ahead Thru 1952," n.p.; the Bureau of National Affairs, Inc., *Community Relations*, Personnel Policies Forum Survey No. 18 (Aug. 1953): 3–4; Heald, *The Social Responsibilities of Business*, pp. 221–27.

42. "Current Trends in Industrial Decentralization," *MRev* 37 (Nov. 1948): 546–47; "Is Industry Seeking Smaller Communities?," *FMM* 104 (Nov. 1946): 89; "Industry Goes West, South—and to Smaller Cities," *MRev* 37 (Apr. 1948): 175.

43. Metropolitan Life Insurance Company, *Community Relations: Being A Good Neighbor* (New York, 1949): 7–9; *Christian Science Monitor*, Dec. 17, 1953; "Employee Relations Important Factor in Planning American Paper Goods Plant," *AB*, Nov. 1946, p. 64.

44. Hugh C. Higley, "Tested Community Relations," *PRJ* 7 (Apr. 1951): 9; Fred R. Jolly, "Public Relations in Our Own Back Yard," *PRJ* 3 (Aug. 1947): 22–27, 32; Louis B. Lundborg, "Public Relations in the Local Community: Helping Local Causes and Civic Institutions," *PRJ* 6 (Feb. 1950): 3–5, 24–26.

45. George Weinstein, "Athletes in Overalls," *Coronet* 29 (Apr. 1951): 58; Guy L. Sharp, "Tying Employee Recreation into the Community," *FMM* 104 (June 1946): 149–51; William J. Duchaine, "Industrial Recreation Here Embraces the Entire City," *ISJ* 13 (Aug. 15, 1952): 27–28, 31; Sal Prezioso, "Cooperation of Industrial and Community Recreation," *Recreation* 44 (Nov. 1951): 342–44.

46. "How Does Your Community Like Your Company," *FMM* 104 (Aug. 1946): 129.

47. "Industry Expands 'Small Fry' Activity," *ISJ* 13 (Nov. 15, 1952): 12–13; "Company Recreation Programs for Children," *MRec* 22 (Mar. 1960): 5–6; "Get the Kids into the Act," *ISJ* 15 (Feb. 1954): 12–16.

48. "New Community Relations Techniques," *FMM* 108 (Oct. 1950): 124.

49. Quentin J. O'Sullivan, "Student Post-Prom Parties," *PRJ* 8 (October 1952): 13–14; "Company Recreation Programs for Children," p. 7.

50. "Raybestos Recreation Includes Children," *ISJ* 13 (Dec. 15, 1952): 13.

51. New York State School of Industrial and Labor Relations, Third Annual Seminar in Community Relations for Business and Industry, July 18–23, 1955, pp. 18–20, 36, 55; William H. Form and Delbert C. Miller, *Industry Labor and Community* (New York: Harper & Bros., 1960), pp. 60–61, 80; Gallagher, "Building New Good Will Licks Old Problems," p. 24.

52. American Iron and Steel Institute, *Civic Activity for Better Community Relations*, pamphlet, unpaged.

53. On business and the Community Chest movement see Heald, *The Social Responsibilities of Business*, chaps. 4–8; Harold L. Wilensky and Charles N. Lebeaux, *Industrial Society and Social Welfare: The Impact of Industrialization on the Supply and Organization of Social Welfare Services in the United States* (New York: Free Press, 1965), pp. 269–82.

54. Heald, *The Social Responsibilities of Business*, 259–69; W. J. Held, "Cor-

porate Giving Sensitive Tool of PR," *PRJ* 10 (Nov. 1954): 8–9; David Finn, *The Corporate Oligarch* (New York: Simon and Schuster, 1969), pp. 223–26.

55. Heald, *The Social Responsibilities of Business*, pp. 202–6, 258–61; Vaughn Davis Bornet, *Welfare in America* (Norman: University of Oklahoma Press, 1960), pp. 117–38, 166–67; Wayne Hodges, *Company and Community*, pp. 75–91.

56. Wilensky and Lebeaux, *Industrial Society and Social Welfare*, p. 276; Bornet, *Welfare in America*, pp. 124–59.

57. S. Prakash Sethi, *Advocacy Advertising and Large Corporations: Social Conflict, Big Business Image, the News Media, and Public Policy* (Lexington, Mass.: D. C. Heath, 1977), pp. 14–15.

58. Raymond H. Ganly, "Handling Employee Relations as a *Sales* Challenge," *Printers' Ink*, Apr. 16, 1948, pp. 37, 82; "Locke, Inc.," *Trends*, Apr. 1950, p. 6; "Plant Gives Company Facts in Local Ads," *FMM* 105 (June 1947): 100–101.

59. G. W. Freeman, "How We Do It," *PRJ* 10 (Aug. 1954): 14; James De-Camp Wise, "Positive Management Action in Human Relations," AMA Personnel Series 124 (1949): 27.

60. Dennis C. Dickerson, *Out of the Crucible: Black Steelworkers in Western Pennsylvania, 1875–1980* (Albany: State University of New York Press, 1986), p. 185.

61. *PRN*, Dec. 22, 1947; *Exchange* (NAM newsletter), Feb. 1949, Acc. 1411, NAM I/122.

62. *Exchange*, Feb. 1949, Acc. 1411, NAM I/122; E. T. Gardner, "Clarity Is the Keynote of Our Communications," *AM* 16 (Nov. 1951): 8.

63. F. C. Minaker, "Novel Idea in Community Relations," *AB*, June 1953, p. 24; "Putting More Life into Small-Town Community Relations," *MI* 25 (Apr. 15, 1953): 93–98; "Low-Cost Local Radio Program Builds Community Relations," *FMM* 107 (Sept. 1949): 98–99; Youngstown Sheet and Tube Company Radio Editorials, transcripts, Box 5, Youngstown Sheet and Tube Company Records, OHS; Robert Newcomb and Marge Sammons, *Employee Communications in Action* (New York: Harper and Bros., 1961), p. 107.

64. "Silver Dollars Spread Message," *FMM* (June 1959): 144; *PRN*, Oct. 10, 1949.

65. *POII* 8 (1950): 15; Geneva Seybold, "Industry Holds Open House," *MRec* 10 (Apr. 1948): 216–22; *Dun's Review and Modern Industry*, Aug. 1954, p. 29; *PRN*, Oct. 24, 1949, July 5, 1949; Chamber of Commerce of the United States, *How to Tell Your Business Story with Plant Tours*, pamphlet, c. 1949.

66. A. D. LeMonte, "The Community Open House" (Address before the Sixth National Conference of Business Public Relations Executives, New York, Feb. 4, 1949), Acc. 1411, NAM I/1; Allyn, "Industry as a Good Neighbor."

67. Jean Gordon, "Walter Baker Plant Tour: A Case History," *PRJ* 4 (Nov. 1948): 28–29, 32; "Plant Tours—A New Pattern," *MRev* 37 (Nov. 1948): 547–49.

68. Fred R. Jolly, "How We Did It," *PRJ* 6 (Oct. 1950): 11–12; Don Layne, "Firm with Home Town Pride," *NB*, Mar. 1946, p. 47; *PRN*, June 2, 1947, July 10, 1950.

69. "Republic Steel Cultivates the Art of Public Speaking," *American Metal Market*, Feb. 5, 1953; Lawrence S. Hamaker, "The Impact of Communications," *MRec* 20 (Apr. 1958): 132; H. W. Hopwood, "Speakers Bureau—Republic Steel Corporation" (Address before the American Iron and Steel Institute's Communication Conference, Jan. 1963), Acc. 1631, Box C8, AISI.

70. *PRN*, Nov. 13, June 12, 1950.

71. *PRN*, Jan. 24, 1949, May 26, June 9, Nov. 10, 1952, Jan. 12, 1953, Mar. 8, Dec. 13, 1954, Sept. 19, 1955, Jan. 23, 1956; "How to Get a Brass-Band Welcome for Your New Plant," *FMM* 112 (Nov. 1954): 98–101.

72. Robert S. Lynd, "Labor and the Grass-Roots Community," *L&N*, Apr.–May 1946, pp. 20–22; Robert S. Lynd, "Labor-Management Cooperation: How Far, to What End?" *L&N*, Jan.–Feb. 1948, pp. 37–38; *Ammunition*, Feb. 1949, p. 35.

73. *PLN*, July 19, Sept. 6, 1946, Feb. 20, 1948; *CIO News*, Feb. 23, Sept. 27, 1948; *Guild Reporter*, Sept. 24, 1948.

74. *PLN*, Aug. 20, 1948.

75. "The Secret Struggle to Change Your Ideas," *Ammunition*, Sept. 1955, pp. 6–7; *Connecticut CIO Vanguard*, Oct. 1949; "Political Advertisement," *Ohio CIO Council Newsletter*, Apr. 4, 1952, Box 54, AUF, LMDC; *Ithaca Union Labor Review* (Ithaca, New York, Central Labor Union), Apr., 1954, June 1955, Box 30, AUF LMDC; "Two Billion for Your Thoughts," *Ammunition*, July 1953, pp. 4–5.

76. *NAM News*, Dec. 6, 1950; Herschel C. Atkinson, "Unions and Political Action—The Ohio Story" (Address before State Chamber Labor Relations clinic, Forty-Fourth Annual Meeting of the Chamber of Commerce of the United States, Washington, D.C., Apr. 30, 1956), Box 63, George Meany Papers, GMA.

77. General Electric Company, *The GE Plant Community Relations Program*, pp. 39–40. For a description of GE community relations program in action during the 1952 strike at its Lockland, Ohio, plant, see Paul Burton, *Corporate Public Relations* (New York: Reinhold Publishing, 1966), pp. 113–22.

# PART 4 | Institutions

# 7 | *Educating for Capitalism: Business and the Schools*

In its quest to win public support, the business community reached into virtually every facet of American society. Education was a constant target. Employers had long recognized schools as important institutions for imparting skills and values, and business contributed heavily to the education system. In return, the schools in many communities loyally served the interests of local companies. During the Depression, however, business's close relationship with the schools fractured over budgets and ideological struggles. Employers feared that their influence had drastically diminished.

Beginning in the early forties, but with increasing fervor and sophistication after World War II, corporate leaders attempted to restore their influence over education as part of their broader campaign to create an economic and political climate favorable to business. First, business needed to reestablish trust. Then, building upon that trust, employers could promote among teachers and students a particular understanding of the economic system. Standard Oil executive Frank Abrams observed in a CED meeting in 1950 that "without trust, our economics will not be believed, no matter how right it may be. With trust our economics may be believed even by people who do not fully understand it."[1] In seeking trust, the business community became solicitous of the needs of educators, offering increased financial support while courting administrators and teachers whom they perceived to be instrumental in shaping young minds. Not surprisingly, organized labor, particularly unionized teachers, objected to the heightened business presence within the schools.

\* \* \*

The business community's interest in education can be traced back to the origins of the public school system in the early nineteenth century. Faced with the tensions resulting from industrialization, urbanization, and immigration, business and professional classes supported the common school movement as a means of socializing workers for the factory, and as a way of promoting social and political stability. But, by the turn of the century, inculcating the general business values of hard work, industriousness, and punctuality was not enough. Progressive-era reforms, such as at-large school elections, shifted control over education from local politicians with allegiances to their working-class constituencies to elites, almost guaranteeing "that school boards would represent the views and values of the financial, business, and professional communities." Business leaders encouraged schools to adopt a corporate model of organization and called for the education system to more explicitly prepare workers for the labor market through testing, vocational guidance, and vocational education. To achieve these goals, employers formed alliances with a new professionally trained corps of school administrators who shared in the business community's vision of scientifically managed, efficient, and cost effective schools.[2]

Business dominance of the education system met many challenges, however. Unionized teachers in a few localities joined with organized labor to contest corporate control of the schools, specifically targeting administrative and curricular reforms. Unions called for a broad liberal education as opposed to vocationalism, which they charged reflected employers' desires to produce docile workers. Nevertheless, until the 1930s, business proved to have the strongest influence over education, and business values permeated the school system.[3]

The relationship between the business community and educators changed dramatically with the onset of the Depression. Throughout the thirties, conflict over funding and ideology created suspicion on both sides. The economic crisis precipitated a struggle over resources that weakened the traditional alliance between business leaders and school administrators. Tied to the local economy, school income fell as factories and businesses shut their doors. The business community met the school's economic needs with indifference if not hostility. Hardpressed employers and business organizations like the Chamber of Commerce, which had previously supported education generously, led a campaign to reduce school taxes and slash school budgets. The Chamber's demands for reduced teacher salaries and the elimination of "fads and frills" alienated administrators and teachers alike.[4]

Many leading educators adopted a radical critique of the American economy, which contributed to the deteriorating relationship between schools and the business community. As the Depression deepened and conditions for teachers worsened, educators openly criticized business and began questioning the dominant values of society, particularly those associated with the free enterprise system. Progressive educator George Counts, for instance, argued that the economic collapse proved that the age of rugged individualism and competition was over and called for schools to assume leadership in building a new social order based upon collectivism. Many social studies textbooks of the 1930s, especially those developed by Harold Rugg, incorporated this critique of American society, and thousands of schools adopted them.[5]

This new educational philosophy helped create the image "that radicals were taking over the schools." In the late thirties, this impression touched off a series of attacks on schools by such ultrapatriotic organizations as the American Legion. Ever since the red scare following World War I, conservative Americans feared communist infiltration of the schools; in the twenties some states had enacted loyalty oaths. The new social studies textbooks confirmed these fears and provided a ready target. Leaders of the National Association of Manufacturers and the Chamber of Commerce joined the Legion in charging that collectivists were indoctrinating students through the textbooks and reducing the younger generation's trust in the free enterprise system. NAM President H. W. Prentis warned that "our free institutions and the heroes of the American republic have been derided and debunked by a host of puny iconoclasts, who destroy since they cannot build."[6]

The NAM encouraged employers to investigate their local schools. In late 1940, the NAM commissioned a review of social studies textbooks to evaluate their attitudes toward America's political and economic institutions. The study unleashed a storm of controversy as educators condemned the NAM's study as an exercise in censorship and redbaiting. Alexander J. Stoddard, superintendent of the Philadelphia school system, asserted that "by innuendo and endless repetition, which cover up the lack of real evidence, the American people are being asked to suspect that their schools, their teachers, their youth, and their textbooks are disloyal and subversive." Aghast at this response, the newly elected NAM president, Walter D. Fuller, protested in a letter to almost fifty thousand educators that the textbook review was intended as an "inherently constructive undertaking." Nevertheless, the textbook controversy epitomized the chasm that existed between the business community and educators on the eve of World War II.[7]

During the forties and fifties, many business leaders were unhappy with the state of American education, but were divided over how best to change the system. A small but vocal segment of the business community, representing the most conservative employers, continued to attack the schools, arguing that socialists and communists had taken over education.[8] At the national level, this wing of the business community supported such organizations as America's Future, the Committee for Constitutional Government, the Constitutional Educational League, the National Council for Education, and a host of others that attacked schools, teachers, and textbooks. The National Economic Council, for instance, distributed a million pamphlets titled "Treason in the Textbooks." One of its cartoons depicted a teacher putting black glasses over two children reading a booklet called "The American Way of Life." The cover of the Employers' Association of Chicago's nationally distributed pamphlet "How Red Is the Little Red Schoolhouse?" showed a "brutish soldier, bayonet over one shoulder, cartridge belt over the other, sickle and hammer on helmet, sinister expression on face" injecting a hypodermic of bright red fluid into a red schoolhouse as children, oblivious to the danger, were happily at play. During the late forties and fifties, as the cold war intensified at home and abroad, these organizations' charges of subversion found a more receptive audience. At the local level, where many of the struggles to fire teachers or ban textbooks were played out, the ideological attacks against the schools meshed with business-backed 'citizens' councils' demands for economy in education and a return to fundamentals.[9]

A much larger segment of the business community viewed the majority of educators as misguided rather than subversive. Less concerned about overt communist infiltration, these business leaders worried that a lack of understanding of the American economic system and a Depression-fostered distrust of business led teachers, like many factory workers, to lean toward the liberal ideas associated with the New Deal. They believed students absorbed their teachers' skepticism of business and its goals. Opinion polls provided evidence for their fears. In October 1947, Ford executive William T. Gossett pointed to surveys that showed that educators supported government control of prices more emphatically than any other group. Additionally, teachers favored government ownership of utilities, the railroads, and the oil companies more strongly than the public at large. When asked to rate who had done more to improve living standards in the United States, high school social science teachers favored organized labor over business two to one. Similarly, a 1951 Opinion Research Corporation study of high school seniors found that only 39 percent believed that keeping the profit incentive alive was essential to the survival of the American business system, while 66 percent believed that stiff progressive taxation, although hard on the individual, was good for the country as a whole.[10]

To change these attitudes, the mainstream of the business community concluded that employers needed to create an educational climate more favorable to business and the capitalist system. Practical conservatives of the NAM, as well the more moderate business leaders associated with the CED, agreed that support rather than criticism was the best way to achieve this goal. From the early forties on, the business community utilized a wide array of strategies to bring business and education closer together, ranging from providing direct financial support to building personal ties to educators.

* * *

The business community's campaign to promote private higher education exemplifies its attempt to shape political attitudes within education. After World War II, higher education underwent a dramatic change as many of America's colleges and universities became transformed from elite to mass institutions. Touching off this expansion was the GI Bill of Rights, which offered millions of service men and women a subsidy to continue their education. In 1946, over a million veterans flooded college campuses, nearly doubling the student population. Classes became overcrowded, teachers were in short supply, and college officials projected ever higher enrollments as the baby boom moved through the education system. Public higher education institutions grew disproportionately, especially to meet American society's growing demands for teachers and other professionals. In the fifties, students in state colleges and universities began to outnumber those in private schools.[11]

Private higher education institutions felt beleaguered. Educators at private colleges and universities complained that higher costs due to inflation and dwindling incomes from investments were making their schools less competitive. Indeed, by 1951 half of the country's nine-hundred privately endowed schools were in the red. In the late forties, private colleges and universities began soliciting corporate America to bail them out of their chronic financial predicament.[12]

A powerful segment of the business community proposed a "marriage of business and education" based on the financial rescue of independent education. In 1952, a group of leading industrialists that included Alfred P. Sloan of General Motors, Frank W. Abrams of Standard Oil Company of New Jersey, Henry Ford II of Ford Motor Company, John L. McCaffrey of International Harvester Company, Irving S. Olds of United States Steel Corporation, Henning W. Prentis of Armstrong Cork Company, and Laird Bell of Weyerhauser Timber formed the Council for Financial Aid to Education. With the assistance of the Council, corporate contributions grew dramatically in the fifties, especially after a 1953 New Jersey court decision sanctioned the right of corporations to contribute funds to educational institutions within reasonable limits. That court ruling spurred the growth of a number of company-sponsored foundations to facilitate company giving. Business gifts, independent of grants for industrial research, rose from $24 million in 1948 to $136 million in 1958. By 1965 corporate donations had reached $280 million a year.[13]

The nature of corporate contributions changed as well. Formerly, companies like General Motors, Du Pont, and General Electric had provided scholarships for employees and their families or supported technical or science programs. While business expanded these efforts, corporations also began to provide greater support for the liberal arts and social sciences, often in unrestricted grants that allowed the college or university to decide how to allocate funds. Gilbert F. White, president of Haverford College, observed that "for the first time in their history, American liberal arts colleges are systematically seeking financial support from industrial corporations; for the first time they are receiving such support."[14]

General Foods' giving to higher education was typical. In the forties, it had provided only small and irregular grants to Harvard and Princeton for their business and industrial relations programs despite growing requests for corporate aid to education. Following the New Jersey Court decision, General Foods set up a charitable foundation called General Foods Funds, Incorporated. In its first year of operation, General Foods directed $85,000 or 19 percent of its charitable contributions into the educational aid program. By 1958, the company gave $380,000 to education, 54 percent of its total contributions. The principal feature of the program was the annual gift of $25,000 made to independent, privately supported, liberal arts colleges.[15]

Business had concrete purposes for its rescue of private higher education. Beginning with World War II, companies became increasingly dependent on higher education for scientific and engineering research and development as well as for the training of future managers. Business leaders wanted to ensure the growth and vitality of this relationship. Moreover, corporations wanted to ensure that a core of America's colleges and universities involved in this activity remained independent of the state.[16]

Business leaders saw the dramatic growth of public higher education as another example of the growing influence of the government in society. They argued that tax-supported public institutions answered to government, while the private schools maintained the tradition of independent scholarship. Academic independence was the "counterpart of economic freedom." By supporting private higher education, the business community saw itself defending individual freedom. Indeed, Irving Olds suggested that capitalism and free enterprise "owed their survival to no small degree to the existence of our private, independent universities." Likewise, *Factory* warned that without greater support America's private system of higher education, "a potentially crucial bulwark for freedom of enterprise" would be undermined.[17]

Advocates of business aid to education contended that companies gave without strings but suggested that government funding implied outside control. In 1953, the *Nation,* a voice of liberalism, contended that "to make such a distinction was unrealistic." Candid employers admitted as much. At a 1958 National Industrial Conference Board meeting, John A. Pollard, vice president of the Council for Financial Aid to Education confessed that there was a "certain quid pro quo" in corporate giving. Companies wanted research and training, but many also hoped to shape the political climate on campus. William J. Grede, a Wisconsin industrialist, for instance, directed aid at small liberal arts colleges where the Board of Trustees and administration were "completely in the free enterprise camp." Irving Olds advised educators "to preserve those fundamental principles of freedom upon which American Freedom itself depends." Employers hoped that their gifts to higher education would help create among educators feelings of obligation and indebtedness to business, or at the very least it would heighten their sense of trust in the business system. According to General Electric, the ultimate payoff for this educational investment was improving the "economic, social, and political climate necessary for the continued existence and progress of competitive free enterprise."[18]

Corporate leaders used more than dollars to shape the economic and political climate on campuses. Increasingly alarmed about the "widespread misunderstanding" of the economic system among educators and students, the Foundation for Economic Education and a host of leading firms established exchange programs, summer conferences, and seminars that brought faculty from public and private higher education institutions into personal contact with the business community. The political intent of these programs was evident in the choice of educators in the humanities and the social sciences, particularly economics and political science.[19] Between 1947 and 1950, Goodyear, Du Pont, International Harvester, Chrysler, Standard Oil, and Swift, began educators' conferences. Small groups of senior faculty from across the country spent from ten days to three weeks at corporate headquarters. They participated in a series of seminars, plant tours, and discussion groups, during which top executives explained the operations and philosophy of the firm.[20]

At the 1955 Du Pont Educators Conference, participants learned about the firm's products, manufacturing process, industrial relations program, and pension and welfare benefits. Participants then debated the issue of corporate bigness and monopoly. Highly placed executives argued vigorously against government intervention in business and complained that government welfare programs destroyed individual "initiative and responsibility." Gatherings at meals, cocktail parties, and "golfing foursomes" allowed for informal social contact between faculty and corporate officials. The involvement of top executives, such as Chairman of the Board Walter Carpenter and President Crawford Greenewalt, showed the company's commitment to this effort, and participant Howard Horsford admitted that he felt flattered. He observed that "when a $3,800-a-year instructor has the chance over the dinner table for an hour and a half sociably to dispute the views of a $600,000 executive, on everything from the tariff to financing education, the gain in understanding—if not agreement—is for the instructor at least commensurate."[21]

The Foundation for Economic Education's College-Business Exchange Fellowship program, which began in 1948, targeted young faculty members, hoping to catch them "when they are open minded." By 1954, 112 major firms, including Allis-Chalmers, Alcoa, Bristol-Myers, Caterpillar, Du Pont, Firestone Tire and Rubber, Ford, Gulf Oil, Nabisco, Sears, United States Steel, and Westinghouse sponsored one or more fellows, providing transportation and stipends. The publicly stated objective was to give the faculty member a comprehensive picture of the operations of a business firm. Privately, some executives admitted that their underlying goal was to inculcate "the professors" in the "philosophical basis of free enterprise." For a period of six weeks, faculty members worked in close proximity with supervisors and top executives, where they learned about pricing, production, incentive systems, finance, and industrial and public relations.[22]

What impact did these programs have on faculty? Sponsors found immediate evidence of their effectiveness. Foundation official W. M. Curtiss reported that one of Du Pont's first Fellows in the College-

Business Exchange program came "there frankly skeptical of big business . . . but after his six-weeks, he was certain that du Pont was O.K." Curtiss concluded that "such an experience cannot help but have a profound influence on his future academic work."[23] A 1953 survey of participants conducted by the Opinion Research Corporation as well as letters of thanks to participating firms from faculty members suggested that many did absorb the corporate message, coming away with a favorable impression of business. One participant remarked that the "program removed some false conceptions I had about big business." Another observed that the experience "altered and broadened my viewpoints regarding the solutions, particularly, of complex economic problems, and made me rather proud of the U.S. free enterprise system." Following the 1954 Du Pont Conference, Grover A. J. Noetzel, dean of Business Administration at the University of Miami, wrote that informal "bull sessions" were of "extraordinary value" in increasing "the realistic appraisal of the American business scene on the part of the academic people who are going to teach your children and grandchildren and also mine."[24]

Business-sponsored college speakers bureaus complemented programs focusing on specially targeted faculty. The New Jersey State Chamber of Commerce established a bureau in 1949 that enlisted colleges to host monthly meetings. In a typical program, a business leader spoke to the entire faculty and student body about "his own and his company's struggles and successes." During the 1950–51, school year nineteen Chamber representatives spoke to forty-eight thousand New Jersey students.[25] The NAM's College Program began in 1948 with similar goals. It sought to place the "economic facts of life" before students, whom the NAM claimed were "too often exposed to leftist philosophies." In a typical speech during his 1948 tour of thirty-five college campuses, Earl Bunting, NAM managing director, attacked the "collectivist" proponents of planning and argued that the only way to bring about improvements in workers' standard of living was increased productivity. By the mid-fifties, NAM speakers were making over seventeen hundred similar talks each year to almost two hundred thousand students and faculty.[26]

\* \* \*

Business viewed higher education as just one part of its educational strategy to shape the political climate of the country. The business community's principal effort, however, involved primary and secondary education, another area where corporate leaders feared their influence had declined greatly in the thirties. As in higher education, the public schools' continuing fiscal problems provided business leaders an opportunity to restore friendly relations and create feelings of trust in the business community.

In the forties and fifties, acute shortages of teachers and classrooms at all levels of education contributed to a sense of crisis. Underfunded during the Depression, World War II had placed new pressures on public school systems. Wartime priorities meant that school repair and building programs, on hold through the thirties, continued to be postponed. Moreover, poorly paid teachers fled the classroom for more lucrative wartime positions. Few returned after the war and low salaries failed to attract enough replacements. Skyrocketing enrollments, as the children of the baby boom reached school age in the late forties and fifties, exacerbated these problems.[27]

As class sizes rose and teacher morale sank, educators sought more financial support. Believing that the local and state funds that traditionally supported education had been exhausted, educators focused primarily on the federal government to help pay teacher salaries, build schools, and to address the inequities between the richest and poorest classrooms. Both the AFL and the CIO provided staunch support for federal aid. Until the late fifties, however, federal aid to public schools foundered on religious and racial disputes as well as conservative opposition to federal involvement in education.[28]

Key organizations in the business community, meanwhile, began mobilizing on behalf of the public schools. Beginning in the early forties, the National Association of Manufacturers and the Chamber of Commerce, both of which had been unsympathetic to schools during the Depression, began urging their members to promote adequate support for the schools, particularly to raise teacher salaries.[29] To enlist employer support for higher state and local taxes, the NAM and Chamber warned of the potential appeal of unionism to underpaid teachers. Moreover, they asserted the economic value of education, contending that money invested in education was akin to capital invested in a business enterprise. Education, they argued, repaid higher taxes with a high standard of living, economic growth, and prosperity. In 1948, Frank W. Abrams of Standard Oil and the Committee for Economic Development added the special postwar emphasis on the links between education and greater productivity and increased consumption. If, he charged, "our hope of an advancing American economy involves reducing costs, increasing individual productivity, and devising better ways of doing things, we must consider that we have a major interest in helping American education."[30]

For business, however, aid needed to come from private or local resources. Although they risked alienating educators, much of the business community opposed federal aid to the public schools, arguing that it would lead to federal control of education and destroy local initiative. Conservative business groups like the NAM and the Chamber of Commerce even predicted that federal aid would open the door to the socialization of the American economy. By taking the initiative in the campaign for better schools, the business community hoped to undercut the drive for federal aid. According to NAM executive Earl Bunting, "the ever present pressure for federal aid to education, which could only mean federal control of education, can be successfully counteracted only by the determination of businessmen to provide adequate funds for educational purposes." Business support for education, then, always emphasized community initiative and local or state level funding.[31]

Confident in the power of advertising, business leaders suggested selling the notion of a crisis in education to arouse public interest. In the fall of 1947, the Advertising Council convinced 250 corporate leaders to launch a campaign to awaken the American public to the "urgency in the crisis in education." U.S. businesses gave millions of dollars of advertising to support the campaign. Newspaper and radio advertisements; thousands of outdoor posters; cards in buses, trolleys, and subways described the plight of public schools and urged citizen action. In 1949, the Advertising Council joined forces with the newly formed National Citizens Commission for the Public Schools, headed by former Du Pont executive Henry Toy, and funded by a grant from the Carnegie Corporation. Posters bearing the words, "Our Schools Are What We Make Them—Good Citizens Everywhere Are Helping," directed the public to write to the commission, which encouraged the establishment of independent community groups to work toward improving local public schools.[32]

Addressing the schools' fiscal plight was but one way for business to increase its influence over education. Corporations also stepped up their direct contact with teachers and students, emphasizing two overlapping goals. First, business involvement in career and guidance activities and its support for improving science and math instruction was designed primarily to enhance industry's recruitment of workers and to assure the availability of enough technically trained personnel. Equally important to industrialists was inculcating teachers and students in the values of business. This message was implicit even in the supposedly nonideologically driven activities supporting vocational and technical education. United States Steel's widely distributed teaching aid, *Science in Steelmaking,* for example, emphasized new developments in steel research and technology without overt political or economic messages. But U.S. Steel candidly admitted that by showing that technological strides "made for human betterment by American industry," it hoped that students would learn "for themselves the social values of the free enterprise system." In 1943, Henning W. Prentis ominously warned of the 30 million public school children who would be voting by 1955: "Unless they are thoroughly grounded in knowledge of, faith in, and practice of the principles on which the American republic rests, they will be easy prey for the demagogue."[33]

To sell these principles, business relied on a variety of mechanisms, some of which replicated and overlapped with their opinion-molding programs in the community. Initially this involved the NAM's effort to bring school administrators together with business leaders. The NAM had earlier promoted free enterprise in the schools, mostly by disseminating literature, but it had no formal relationship with education. In late 1941, worried about the hostility created by the Robey Report, the NAM proposed to the National Education Association a series of joint conferences to increase cooperation between business and education. Through personal contact, the NAM hoped to convince educators of "the sincerity of the American businessman." The National Education Association, primarily an organization of school administrators, responded readily in the hope that closer ties to business would pay off in greater business financial support for the public schools. Between 1942 and 1945, 45 regional meetings and over 250 community discussion groups involved thousands of business leaders and educators throughout the country.[34]

The NAM used its contact with school administrators to its advantage. Aware of the NEA's support of federal aid, the NAM worked to keep that subject off conference agendas. Instead, employers explained to educators what business wanted from the public schools. They asked that students be well-prepared to enter the job market, but they also wanted schools to instill students with the correct attitudes. In March 1945, at a Portland, Oregon, conference, businessman J. C. Yeomans urged that schools "indoctrinate students with the American way of life" and teach that "the American system of free enterprise has done more for human comforts than any other system." In the postwar years, the NAM expanded efforts to establish a more cooperative relationship with school administrators at the national level by setting up an Educational Advisory Committee. Although, the committee had no formal relationship with the

NEA, it recruited many NEA members, including a past president of the organization.[35]

While business leaders recognized prominent administrators as an important audience, they believed that building relationships with educators at the local level was equally important. This was part of the broader corporate community relations campaign to integrate business and industry into community life. To accomplish this, Chamber of Commerce affiliates began establishing committees on education. Their number grew from two hundred in 1944 to thirteen hundred in 1949. Similarly, between 1948 and 1953, local employer groups and even individual companies developed close working relationships with their respective school systems. These organizations sponsored vocational guidance programs and provided teaching materials exploring local industry's "contribution to the nation" and "to better living," as well as introducing some of the "basic facts" about the economic system.[36]

The classroom teacher was the principal target of much of the business community's attention. Employers worried about teachers' alleged economic illiteracy and their suspicion of business, fearing that they might consciously or unconsciously transmit their prejudices to schoolchildren. Some also worried that hostility toward business combined with low salaries were driving teachers into organized labor's camp. The NAM advised that "union membership naturally breeds sympathy which goes beyond immediate interest." Unionized teachers, it contended, promoted labor's agenda in the classroom, adding force to organized labor's drive for power.[37]

Beginning in the late forties, employer organizations across the country began sponsoring Business-Industry-Education days to correct "misconceptions" about business. Employers persuaded local school officials to close schools for a day to enable teachers to tour local firms where they learned "the story of the enterprise system first hand." The NAM and the Chamber of Commerce provided detailed instructions to local affiliates on staging the event. Divided into small groups, teachers went down into coal mines at Taylorville, Illinois, inspected Birmingham, Alabama, steel mills from chairs on moving railroad flat cars, studied the operations of breweries in St. Louis or watched amateur actors from a Lancaster, Pennsylvania, firm put on a dramatic presentation of "The Role of Profits." On a typical BIE day, lunch with company officials followed the tour. As the Lansing, Michigan, Chamber of Commerce observed, lunch afforded an opportunity "for the host firm representatives and the teaching staff to really get acquainted and somewhat chummy in a social way." Company officials then usually spent the balance of the afternoon discussing with teachers the firm's history, policies, and employment practices, emphasizing industry's benefits to the community and "basic economics of the American system." In some communities, educators reciprocated by inviting employers to visit the schools and learn of their problems and contributions to the community.[38]

Closer contact with employers gave some teachers a new enthusiasm for business and the free enterprise system. "The hospitality of everyone was overwhelming" remarked one of the teachers after the 1950 Hartford BIE day. "Never in my life did I ever see any group made to feel so welcome as we were." A Chicopee teacher, Sophie Chumura, left the Spaulding Company tour with "further insight into how important it was to teach the interdependence and dependence of man and our local industry." Carrie L. Clements, an East Point, Georgia, high school teacher, concluded that the tours helped teachers "understand how the free enterprise system has given America the highest standard of living in the world." Similarly, Floyd A. Denicola, a Hillside, New Jersey, high school teacher reported that he had a "better understanding of capitalism at work."[39]

Chamber of Commerce records demonstrate the extent of the movement. By early 1955, 693 chambers had sponsored 1,489 BIE Days involving over thirty-six thousand businesses and three hundred thousand teachers. NAM affiliates picked up the tactic, sponsoring a host of others. By the end of the fifties, teachers in seven hundred localities, ranging in size from small towns to cities as large as Hartford, Connecticut, and St. Paul, Minnesota, annually participated in factory tours. In 1952, *Public Relations Journal* observed that for many years employers labored to "find new and effective ways to explain and defend American business enterprise." BIE day, it concluded, "does that for the choicest kind of an audience."[40]

Not content to rely solely on teachers to shape young minds, the business community reached out directly to students. In 1953, over 2 million school children read B. F. Goodrich Company's cartoon-type booklet "Johnson Makes the Team," in which Tommy Johnson, a son of a Goodrich tire dealer, learns about the American free enterprise system through teamwork in football. Hundreds of thousands of others watched the NAM's film, "The Price of Freedom," which explored the hidden danger of security achieved through the growth of the government. It told the story of Fred Vollmer, a young newspaper man who joins the staff of his father's paper. He visits Germany and learns that public complacency to the expanding powers of the state fostered Nazism. Returning home, he sees the same threats to America's democratic institutions and resolves to expose them in a series of "stirring editorials." Initially, for some unexplained reason, his father refuses to print his son's editorials. But later, influenced by Fred's arguments, he finally runs the series and thereby joins in the fight for freedom.[41]

Corporations brought students, like their teachers, to their plants to learn the business story. The children's experience was shorter and less intensive but nonetheless visually powerful. In 1947, for instance, Detroit students read a series of Ford Motor company booklets and then eighty thousand of them saw steel poured and cars assembled at the River Rouge Plant. That same year, St. Louis employers, rocked by the postwar strike wave, contributed $40,000 for an essay contest that impressed upon students the need for labor harmony. The essay topics were "Worker and Employer, Partners in Business," "What Do Strikes Cost the Worker?" and "What Free Enterprise Means to My Future." Three years later some two thousand Worcester, Massachusetts, children wrote about "More Taxes or Less Government" and "Freedom Is Everybody's Job." In Junior Achievement, students recruited through the high schools and advised by local business firms, formed minicorporations that over the course of the school year produced and sold products. Junior Achievement Incorporated, founded in 1919, promised that the program taught youngsters to "appreciate the profit system," thereby helping to "strengthen our American way of life."[42]

Pamphlets, tours, and Junior Achievement were not new to the postwar years. Business had used some of these mechanisms in earlier efforts to shape public opinion through the schools. The National Electric Light Association, for instance, distributed millions of pamphlets during the twenties to block regulation of electric companies and the NAM sent a steady stream of literature into the schools in the thirties. Teachers welcomed some of these aids, like General Electric's traveling science exhibit, "House of Magic," but many educators were antagonized by propaganda-ridden material.[43]

But after World War II, business brought a new intensity and sophistication to the task of influencing children. It was in the late forties, for instance, that Junior Achievement began to expand nationally to help combat "the shift towards collectivist thinking" among students. Participation in Junior Achievement grew steadily from under five hundred companies in 1946 to three thousand a decade later. Business-sponsored teaching aids—booklets, filmstrips, teaching kits, and movies—also came of age in the years after the Second World War. Business associations and individual firms, such as General Mills, U.S. Steel, General Electric, American Cyanamid, Standard Oil, General Motors, and many others, sent more of this material than ever before into the schools. In 1950, the NAM alone distributed almost four and a half million pamphlets to students, representing a 600 percent increase over 1947. It also doubled school usage of its films between 1947 and 1949; by 1954 over 3.5 million students watched about sixty thousand showings of NAM films. That year, school superintendents estimated that the investment in free material at $50 million, about half the amount public schools spent annually on regular textbooks. At the end of the decade, one in five corporations reported supplying teaching aids.[44]

Some corporations established education departments or hired consultants to help allay teacher suspicion of sponsored materials. One effective technique was enlisting teachers in their production. In 1951, the NAM set up an advisory council of educators to review its publications. Similarly, General Mills turned to University of Minnesota faculty and school administrators or teachers in Austin and Duluth, Minnesota, to help prepare lessons in economics. In January 1951, executives from thirty of America's leading companies met in Des Moines to hear the story of how General Mills and educators cooperated to produce the teaching unit "Freedom of Choice" that explored what happened "when we fail to keep and exercise individual freedom of choice." Other firms ran summer workshops for teachers on the use of industry resource materials in the classroom. By the late fifties, the National Science Teachers Association conceded that "teachers and administrators have greater confidence in industry and in the motives behind industry's offerings to schools."[45]

* * *

The most systematic effort to shape ideology in the realm of education was the campaign to promote the teaching of economics. Business leaders were united about the importance of addressing "economic illiteracy" but divided over the content and control of economic education. In the schools, the strident free enterprise ideology that characterized the NAM competed with the more corporatist-oriented philosophy of the Committee for Economic Development. Both confronted the hostility of organized labor. Charting these conflicts highlights the difficulties business leaders faced in their efforts to selectively address the economic illiteracy of American students.

In the early fifties, the American Economic Foundation and the NAM began offering systematic instruction in economics to public schools. They utilized economic education programs originally created for factory workers. The AEF's "How We Live in America" was an offshoot of its factory program, "In These Hands," while the NAM adapted "How Our Business System Operates" for use in high schools.[46] The message changed little from the factory to the classroom. Both programs presented an explanation of the workings of the American economy, stressing praise for the accomplishments of the "American Business System." HOBSO, for instance, emphasized the centrality of competition and individual freedom to business success and warned of the dangers inherent in an economy controlled by the government. It advised that "freedoms are indivisible." Economic freedom was inseparable from political freedom and "when we interfere arbitrarily with one, we endanger the other." HOBSO instructed teachers and students that the safest path to personal security was through individual achievement rather than collective dependence on the government.[47]

To promote their programs, business leaders drew upon newly developed ties with the education community. NAM and AEF representatives attended education conferences and staged demonstrations for individual principals and superintendents. Manufacturers' associations also invited educators to special education-industry meetings that featured HOBSO. In late 1953, NAM staffers reported that at one such conference in Trenton, New Jersey, their revelations about the degree to which students supported government ownership of banking, the railroads, and the steel industry made Trenton Central High School authorities immediately "anxious" to implement HOBSO. Companies further encouraged adoption of the programs by buying the HOBSO kits and audio visual materials associated with "How We Live in America" for local schools.[48]

Although neither the NAM nor the AEF included educators in developing their economic curriculum, both required schools to adopt their program without modification. To maintain control over the content and method of instruction the NAM and the AEF required that teachers attend week-long workshops to develop familiarity with the material and an "understanding of basic economic principles." By 1956, NAM reported having trained two thousand teachers to present HOBSO in their classes. The following year, the AEF boasted that "How We Live in America" had been adopted in high school systems embracing more than twelve percent of all secondary schools.[49]

One of the primary impediments preventing the NAM and the AEF from dominating economic education was a competing framework backed by the more moderate wing of the business community. In 1949, the Committee for Economic Development helped form the Joint Council on Economic Education. Through the Joint Council, the CED hoped to bring about greater public understanding of the importance of increasing employment, productivity, and living standards, while maintaining economic stability. Although the CED shared with the NAM the belief that individual freedom was "the cornerstone of our economic system," it also asserted that economic stability depended upon an expanded role for the government in the economy. It viewed the Joint Council as a key institution for generating public support for its program.[50]

The Joint Council's official mission was to assist school systems in improving the quality of economic education through curriculum research, workshops and the publication of materials for teachers and students. The CED provided seed money and helped the Council obtain support from the Ford Foundation. Through the fifties, CED trustees remained prominent in the Joint Council's inner circles and played a major role in shaping the organization's policies. Not surprisingly, the Joint Council's policies reflected CED ideology. The Joint Council, for instance, refused to promote the special interest of any group and stressed objectivity, expertise, and nonpartisanship. This closely resembled the CED's philosophy that there existed a "general interest" independent of class interests that "could be ascertained through the application of expert knowledge to the problems of modern life."[51]

Arguing that management-run programs were "too rabid, too extreme, and aroused too much suspicion," the Joint Council sought to be objective in the treatment of competing economic ideology. The emphasis on balance and expertise was reflected in the Joint Council's organization and program. Professional educators led the Council and were advised by a board of trustees including representatives of business, labor, and agriculture. Regional and state councils, affiliated with the national organization, were also governed by boards representing the major interest groups.[52]

Organized labor's involvement gave the Joint Council an aura of legitimacy designed to undercut opposition. Impressed with the Joint Council's commitment to labor representation and its professed objectivity, trade unionists participated in its activities and prominent union leaders served as officers in the national and regional councils. Solomon Barkin of the Textile Workers Union, who served as an officer of the Council, recalled that although his participation gave a "stamp of legitimacy" to the Joint Council, he stayed in the belief that he could help "ensure the balance."[53]

Business-Industry-Education Days were designed to improve teachers' understanding of the American business system. Reprinted from *American Business*, Sept. 1951.

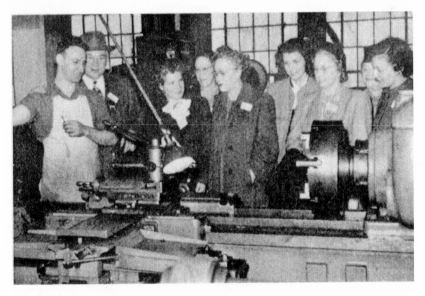

The superintendent of the mechanical division conducts a group of teachers through the machine shop of the Wester Cartridge Company during the East Alton, Illinois, 1950 Education Day. Reprinted from *American Business*, Sept. 1950.

This widely distributed NAM comic book advised students to be skeptical of union promises of "cradle to grave" security; courtesy of State Historical Society of Wisconsin.

# Is the Trouble With My Work - - *me?*

● *Let's face it. Maybe the trouble with my work isn't the boss, or the folks I work with, or the way the stuff is coming through . . . Maybe it's me!*

And maybe the trouble with *you* started about the time you decided to skip church for some extra sleep, for fishing, or just fooling around the house.

For nothing can take the place of church in your life — in anyone's life. It fills a deep-seated human hunger for peace of mind and all the satisfactions that spring from it.

New thousands every day are finding this is so. By going to church, by reaffirming their faith, they're gathering new strength, new hope, new courage.

Families, finding themselves through faith, are being brought closer . . . becoming *real* families, strong against the world, happier, more tolerant among themselves.

Men and women everywhere are gaining a new sense of "the balance of things" . . . the *inner* security that brings success to work as well as to life . . . by finding themselves through faith.

Can you honestly say that things have been better for *you,* going it alone? Or wouldn't you rather join your neighbors . . . and find a happier, more successful life — through faith?

### *Find Yourself Through Faith . . . . . . Come To Church This Week!*

Companies used employee magazines to urge workers to attend church. *Vernon Alcoan,* Apr.–May 1950; courtesy of the Archives of Labor and Urban Affairs, Wayne State University.

After World War II, conservative religious organizations charged the Federal Council of Churches with advocating communism. Reprinted with permission of Laymen's Commission of the American Council of Christian Churches; courtesy of the State Historical Society of Wisconsin.

Dr. William Holmes Borders speaking at a religion-labor luncheon in Atlanta, Georgia, about 1945. John Ramsey is seated at Borders's right. John Ramsay Papers; courtesy of the Southern Labor Archives, Georgia State University.

Bringing labor and the religious community together was a central focus of the CIO's community relations program in the 1950s. John Ramsay is at right. John Ramsay Papers; courtesy of the Southern Labor Archives, Georgia State University.

J. Howard Pew, chairman of the Laymen's Committee of the National Council of Churches; courtesy of Grove City College.

# MONOPOLY
## IS
## *ALWAYS WRONG!*

No thinking American approves of a monopoly, regardless of what form it may take. For many years, it has been specifically against the law for business firms to merge or to enter into agreements that result in a monopoly or even a near-monopoly of the available market.

These antitrust regulations are well-known to most of the public. But surprisingly few of us realize that labor unions are specifically *exempt* from such laws.

This *double-standard* is directly contrary to the concept of equal justice under law.

The basic trouble with monopoly lies in the fact that it enables a company or a union to impose its will on the public. It has been demonstrated that the public always *benefits* whenever monopoly is eliminated or controlled.

We, as a nation, must be consistent. Every instance of monopoly, *whatever its source*, must be stopped in its undemocratic tracks!

A SERVICE OF THE NATIONAL ASSOCIATION OF MANUFACTURERS

NAM flyers charged that the newly merged AFL-CIO was a powerful labor monopoly that trampled on workers' individual rights. National Association of Manufacturers Records; courtesy of the Hagley Museum and Library.

AFL-CIO lithograph, 1957; courtesy of the George Meany Memorial Archives.

# 'We are convinced

ARCHBISHOP ALTER — ARCHBISHOP HOBAN — BISHOP WALSH

# that right-to-work laws would not

BISHOP REHRING — BISHOP MUSSIO — BISHOP ISSENMANN

# solve our problems'

During the 1958 election, six Catholic bishops issued a statement opposing the proposed right-to-work amendment. John Ramsay Papers; courtesy of the Southern Labor Archives, Georgia State University.

Flier distributed by the United Organized Labor of Ohio during the 1958
right-to-work campaign. Sam Pollock Papers; courtesy of the Archives of
Urban and Labor Affairs, Wayne State University.

This more balanced structure carried over into the Joint Council's activities. One of the Council's important early programs was sponsoring university-based summer workshops for teachers. Over the first three years of the program, thirty-five hundred high school teachers participated in forty-eight workshops that sought to increase teachers' understanding of economics and to produce resource units and study guides. The workshops were deliberately designed to present teachers with differing points of view. Over the course of three weeks, teachers listened to professional economists as well as representatives from business, labor, and the government present competing analyses of the structure, operation, and problems of the American economic system.[54]

These workshops posed a sharp contrast to those run by the NAM and AEF, which excluded organized labor and limited discourse, offering only one legitimate way to think about economic problems. Indeed, by 1957, the NAM was so disturbed with the Joint Council's workshops it resolved to "step up" its activities to counteract what it considered "unsound" economic education. George Fern of the NAM Education Department charged that NAM speakers and materials were excluded from workshops. Moreover, during the sessions, the staff of the Joint Council was "extremely effective in creating economic impressions in the minds of teachers . . . more akin to the philosophy of labor union economists and advocates of bigger and bigger government than to the beliefs of NAM." To neutralize the influence of "liberals," the NAM increased its participation in Joint Council workshops. Moreover, the NAM placed pressure on the Joint Council by informing industrialists who contributed support to Council efforts "of the economic philosophy their money is helping to spread."[55]

Organized labor could not match business's resources in promoting its interpretation of economics, but its vocal opposition posed another impediment to conservative business dominance of the schools. Beginning in the late forties, unions began protesting corporate efforts to tie industry and education together. Labor papers published articles exposing the campaign to "influence the mind of the youth," criticizing such mechanisms as corporate-sponsored teaching aids and Junior Achievement. Particularly galling for labor were Business-Industry-Education days, which unions felt were merely a medium for spreading anti-Labor propaganda to captive audiences. During the 1950s, the AFL regularly passed resolutions condemning "the use of propaganda" and the "in-roads that industrial groups have made in shaping school curricula." In 1954, the AFL Executive

Council warned that "there was a movement well planned by certain industrial leaders to indoctrinate teachers and pupils with a belief that our nation's future rests upon the acceptance of the status quo," and upon the repeal of "most social legislation which has been adopted for the common good."[56]

While both the AFL and the CIO evinced concern about the heightened business presence in the schools, the Federation gave the issue greater attention, mostly because its ranks included the American Federation of Teachers. The AFT constantly rallied Federation opposition to business propaganda in the public schools. The teachers' union questioned the sincerity of the business community's concern about the financial problems of public education, arguing that corporate leaders simply sought to subvert federal aid. Moreover, the AFT accused business of joining with administrators in the National Education Association to stem the growth of unionism among teachers.[57]

AFL objections frequently fell on deaf ears, however. In 1950, the Peoria Trades and Labor Assembly complained to the superintendent of schools about the circulation of NAM comic books among the city's students. Local unionists particularly disliked "Watch Out for the Big Talk." In the comic, a union organizer promises a crowd "cradle to grave" security. A skeptic in the audience challenges his promises, recalling that America's heroes like Benjamin Franklin, Daniel Boone, and George Washington Carver achieved success through individual initiative. "Folks," the skeptic urged, "Don't ever believe this 'Big Plan' malarkey—this something—for nothing idea— it's the oldest confidence game in the world." Promises of security, he reminds, led to Hitler, Mussolini, and Stalin. The comic concludes with the audience rejecting the labor organizer and vowing "None of those 'planned economy' pipe-dreams for us." Despite labor protests, the Peoria schools continued to distribute the NAM literature. In Akron, Ohio, unionists unsuccessfully fought the introduction into the schools of a history text that was written and published by the Chamber of Commerce. This text ignored unions and devoted fifty-four pages to the rubber companies and a whole chapter to the Quaker Oats Company.[58]

Organized labor also fought BIE days. In 1950, 25 percent of Minneapolis teachers registered opposition to the city's first BIE day by refusing to participate. Detroit trade unionists formed a committee to investigate a program of "Trips to Industry" sponsored by the Institute for Economic Education. The Detroit Teachers Federation reported that the Institute used funds, contributed by sixty Detroit firms, to "wine and dine teachers, and to tour school children through the plants," where they were "given the anti-union company point of view." The teachers union distributed flyers to Detroit workers asking, "Do you want your children to be educated—or hypnotized" into "Docile—Anti-Union, Anti-Fair Deal Company Stooges."[59]

The record of unions in stopping BIE days was mixed, but perhaps the most fierce struggle occurred in Pennsylvania. In 1949, an organization called the Americans for the Competitive Enterprise System (ACES) began sponsoring BIE days and other programs designed to demonstrate the superiority of the free enterprise system over all forms of collectivism, including unions and the welfare state. The Pennsylvania CIO Council and the state Federation of Labor denounced the program, but ACES succeeded in establishing programs in school systems throughout the state. In 1953, however, when ACES set up shop in Reading, a city with strong socialist and trade union traditions, its effort to "mold the pliable mind of school children," sputtered. The labor and socialist press blasted ACES, and the Central Labor Union lodged a strong protest with the superintendent of schools and the school board, which included members sympathetic to organized labor. Labor's influence in the community was powerful enough that the ACES program was halted in Reading. However, it continued in outlying school districts, which unions charged were controlled by representatives of big business. In these communities, a few unionists and socialists refused to permit their children to participate.[60]

A small segment of the labor movement critiqued the rapprochement of educators and businessmen. Unions complained that while business was glorified in the classroom, workers and their organizations were either neglected or maligned. Schools, they contended, had an obligation to teach students of workers' contributions and why unions were socially necessary institutions. Instead, according to AFT President John M. Eklund, "the rights and privileges of monopoly, of Big Business, of the A.M.A. are rarely challenged; the rights of labor to organize for collective action are constantly attacked."[61] Such attitudes, unionists cautioned, threatened labor's "long and impressive record" as the "most powerful, loyal and true friend of the public schools and of teachers." Moreover, the AFL and the CIO reminded educators that unions were among the strongest proponents of federal aid to education.[62]

A few unions, including the AFT, the ILGWU, and the UAW, more vigorously competed with business in shaping students' and teachers' attitudes toward labor. In 1948, the United Electrical Workers Union, seeking to counteract the NAM's influence in the schools, began offering a "teachers kit," including publications and films. It included the comic book "Chug-Chug: A Children's Story for the Whole Family," which recounted how only after their father's factory organized could Donnie and Susan buy a much coveted toy train. Similarly, concerned that too many students left high schools "with hostile and erroneous views about trade unions," AFL and CIO central bodies convinced the Newark, New Jersey, school superintendent to allow labor representatives a week to meet with the senior American history classes. The event was so unusual that it was widely reported in the press. The UAW in Michigan and the ILGWU in New York City also reached out to students as part of their commitment to strengthening relations with the community. The UAW encouraged the development of labor curricula and ran one-day institutes for teachers, while the ILGWU hosted student visits at its New York City headquarters and regularly sent speakers into the schools.[63]

Ultimately, labor had neither the resources nor the commitment to match business in the schools. Teachers who wished to balance material from business with literature from organized labor found unions unable to comply with their requests. The AFL's Committee on Education admitted that labor "could not possibly hope to compete with the N.A.M. in this propaganda by sheer force of money resources." Although the labor press routinely railed against "attempts to alienate their sons and daughters from the trade union movement," union resistance was mostly paltry. Even in the Joint Council of Economic Education, where labor's voice was welcomed, few unionists took seriously the opportunity to challenge business. In 1952, Solomon Barkin, one of the few labor people active in economic education, commented on labor's weakness in the Joint Council, observing that unions could "leave a mark on these institutions if we were more adequately manned." Their failure "must be charged to our own account rather than to the other party."[64]

\* \* \*

On the whole, competitors to the business community were faintly heard in the schools. Most unions tended to focus on the more immediate conflict in the political and economic realms, conceding to business the longer range ideological struggle carried out through education. As a result, labor would continue to complain that the "atmosphere in our schools, as a whole, is anti-union." Through the fifties, without a strong competitor, business was often the sole outside voice in shaping the educational climate in the schools. Conservative and moderate business leaders might struggle over the details of the business message but agreed on certain fundamental principles, particularly the need to emphasize individualism and freedom. While evidence concerning the reception of this message is fragmentary, some educators were well aware of the implications of the business campaign to recapture the schools. In early 1957, educator Lloyd P. Williams wrote of the overwhelming corporate influence over education, arguing that business leaders sought to purify school and university faculties, screen campus speakers, censor textbooks, and control curriculum. The business presence was so pervasive that "business philosophy has become orthodox and, hence delimits the concept of truth." By 1963, economics professor Daniel R. Fusfeld could also testify to the impact on students of the business community's free hand in the schools. He found that many students were "captives of the ideology of the right," having been successfully "indoctrinated" with an economic interpretation that taught that the American economy was "free, competitive and individualistic" and must be retained without change.[65]

## Notes

1. Frank Abrams, "The Businessman's View," in Committee for Economic Development Board of Trustees minutes, May 18–19, 1950, Box 78, Lou E. Holland Papers, HST.

2. Joel Spring, *The American School, 1642–1985* (New York and London: Longman, 1986), chaps. 4–8, esp. p. 228.

3. Julia Wrigley, *Class Politics and Public Schools: Chicago, 1900–1950* (New Brunswick, N.J.: Rutgers University Press, 1982); Spring, *The American School,* pp. 156–58, 259–66.

4. Spring, *The American School,* pp. 269–73; Marjorie Murphy, *Blackboard Unions: The AFT & the NEA, 1900–1980* (Ithaca: Cornell University Press, 1990), pp. 133–37; S. Alexander Rippa, "Retrenchment in a Period of Defensive Opposition to the New Deal: The Business Community and the Public Schools, 1932–1934," *History of Education Quarterly* 2 (June 1962): 76–81.

5. Gerald L. Gutek, *Education in the United States: An Historical Perspective* (Englewood Cliffs, N.J.: Prentice Hall, 1986), pp. 226–27, 247–51; Diane Ravitch, *The Troubled Crusade: American Education, 1945–1980* (New York: Basic Books, 1983), pp. 85–89.

6. Spring, *The American School,* p. 270; Prentis quoted in S. Alexander Rippa, *Education in a Free Society: An American History* (New York: David McKay, 1971), p. 271.

7. Stodard Rippa, *Education in a Free Society,* pp. 258–76, quoted on p. 275;

Colleen A. Moore, "The National Association of Manufacturers: The Voice of Industry and the Free Enterprise Campaign in the Schools, 1929–1949" (Ph.D. diss., University of Akron, 1985), pp. 533–58.

8. Robert L. Lund to Jasper E. Crane, Dec. 15, 1952, Box 2, Jasper E. Crane Papers, HML.

9. Morris Mitchell, "The Battle for Free Schools: Fever Spots in American Education," *Nation*, Oct. 27, 1951, pp. 344–47.

10. William T. Gossett, Speech at the University of Michigan, Oct. 2, 1947, Ford New Bureau release, Box 54, AOF I, LMDC; Frank G. Schultz, "Horse Sense and Buggy Economics," *School and Society* 77 (June 3, 1953): 373.

11. Ravitch, *The Troubled Crusade*, pp. 12–14, 183–84; Gutek, *Education in the United States*, pp. 282–87.

12. Morrell Heald, *The Social Responsibilities of Business: Company and Community, 1900–1960* (Cleveland: Press of Case Western Reserve University, 1970), pp. 211–12; "Should Business Support the College?" *Fortune*, Dec. 1951, p. 74.

13. Frederick DeW. Bolman, Jr., "A Romance Between Colleges and Industry," *Educational Record* 36 (Apr. 1955): 150; "The Corporate Citizen," *Overview for All Educational Executives* 1 (Sept. 1960): 48–49; "Trends in Corporate Aid to Education, *MRev* 44 (June 1955): 389–90.

14. Frank W. Abrams, "Growth of Corporate Giving to Education," *School and Society* 86 (Jan. 18, 1958): 28–30; A H. Raskin, "The Corporation and the Campus"; "The Tuition Plan's Forum on 'Education and Industry,'" *School and Society* 77 (Feb. 21, 1953): 120.

15. "How to Support Higher Education," *MRec* 21 (May 1959): 173–74.

16. On the growing research ties between business and higher education see David F. Noble, *Forces of Production: A Social History of Industrial Automation* (New York: Oxford University Press, 1986); Harry A. Bullis, "Should Business Support Higher Education?," *Education Digest* 20 (Feb. 1955): 17.

17. Heald, *The Social Responsibilities of Business*, pp. 212–17; Olds quoted in "Should Business Support the College," p. 74; "Business Aid for Our Colleges—Voluntary or Involuntary?" *FMM* 113 (Feb. 1955): 145–46.

18. "Business Is Just That Practical," *Nation*, Feb. 21, 1953, p. 159; Pollard quoted in "How to Support Higher Education," p. 178; F. Gano Chance to William Grede, Feb. 27, 1957, Grede to Chance, Mar. 6, 1957, Box 4, William Grede Papers, SHSW; "Should Business Support the College?" p. 74; General Electric, "One Viewpoint on Corporate Aid to Education," *Harpers*, Dec. 1957, reprint in Box 11, Mark Starr Papers, ALUA.

19. "Professors: Learn from Industry," *Iron Age*, Nov. 4, 1954, p. 71; *Community Relations Bulletin*, Sept. 1953, Box C8, Acc. 1631, AISI.

20. "Industrial Relations Forum Meets Again at Goodyear," *AB*, Aug. 1950, pp. 54–55; "Industry Achieves Better Understanding Through Company-Educator Seminars," *POII*, Nov. 1953, pp. 10–31.

21. Howard Horsford, "A Du Pont Precept," *Princeton Alumni Weekly*, Oct. 28, 1955, pp. 8–11; Public Relations Department to Executive Committee, Dec. 30, 1955, Box 846, Series II, Walter S. Carpenter, Jr. Papers, Du Pont Records, HML.

22. Jasper E. Crane to Gordon O. Andrews, Apr. 22, 1947, Box 1, Crane Papers; "Professors and Scholars Intern in Corporations," *AB*, Feb. 1953, p. 34; Richard H. Leach, "Attacks on the Ivory Tower," *Journal of Higher Education* 25 (Nov. 1954): 435; Minutes of the Special Meeting of the Board of Trustees of the Foundation for Economic Education, Nov. 4, 1953, Box 37, Crane Papers.

23. W. M. Curtis to Jasper E. Crane, Aug. 26, 1948, Box 846, Series II, Carpenter Papers; H. R. Arthur to J. Howard Pew, Box 19, J. Howard Pew Papers, HML.

24. "Industry Achieves Better Understanding through Company-Educator Seminars," p. A-2; Grover A. J. Noetzel to Walter S. Carpenter Jr., July 16, 1954, Box 846, Series II, Carpenter Papers.

25. *PRN*, June 25, 1951.

26. Moore, "The National Association of Manufacturers," p. 711; *NAM News*, Nov. 1948, June 11, 1949; Jan. 21, July 8, 1950; "Educational Activities," Dec. 1954, Accession 1411, NAM, Series I, Box 51 (hereafter Acc. 1411, NAM I/51); F. Kenneth Brasted to NAM Educational Advisory Committee, May 31, 1955; Acc. 1411, NAM I/63.

27. Murphy, *Blackboard Unions*, pp. 180–81; Ravitch, *The Troubled Crusade*, pp. 3–15.

28. Ravitch, *The Troubled Crusade*, pp. 26–42; "Improve Educational Opportunity thru Federal Aid," *Economic Outlook* (CIO, Department of Education and Research), May 1949, Box 4, Greater Buffalo Industrial Union Council Records, LMDC; "School Days," *American Federationist*, Oct. 1955, p. 18.

29. Moore, "The National Association of Manufacturers," pp. 688–94; Herbert B. Mulford, "Big Business Wishes to Expand Educational Opportunities," *American School Board Journal* 110 (Jan. 1945): 75–78.

30. Frank W. Abrams, "The Stake of Business in American Education, *Madison Quarterly* 8 (Mar. 1948): 42–47, esp. 45; Harry A. Bullis, "Should Business Support Higher Education?" *Education Digest* 20 (Feb. 1955): 17–19; Moore, "The National Association of Manufacturers," pp. 685–88.

31. Ravitch, *The Troubled Crusade*, pp. 27–28; B. P. Brodinsky, "Better Schools?, Yes!, Federal Aid, No!" *Nation's Schools* 43 (May 1949): 26; Bunting quoted in "NAM and NEA Iron Out Their Wrinkled Relations," *School and Society* 75 (Mar. 29, 1952): 204.

32. Charles Eugene Litz, "The Growth of American Business Interest in Educational Reform, 1945–1968" (Ph.D. diss., University of Michigan, 1970); *PRN*, Sept. 22, 1947; "Brief Account of Meeting of National Citizens Commission for Public Schools," New York City, Jan. 16–17, 1950, Box 9, Victor Reuther Files, UAW Department of Education Records, ALUA; Advertising Council, *Business Steps Up Its Candle Power: The Fifth Year of The Advertising Council, March 1, 1946–March 1, 1947*, Box 17, Charles W. Jackson Files, Harry S. Truman Papers, HST.

33. On the growth of business involvement in the teaching of science see Robert Bruce Sund, "The Activities of Business and Industry to Improve Science Education" (Ph.D. diss., Stanford University, 1959); Prentis quoted in Sol Alexander Rippa, "Organized Business and Public Education: The Educa-

tional Policies and Activities of the Chamber of Commerce and the National Association of Manufacturers, 1933–1936" (Ph.D. diss., Harvard University, 1958); *PRN,* Apr. 23, 1951.

34. "Minutes," National Industrial Council Breakfast, Dec. 3, 1942, Acc. 1411, NAM III/844; Rippa, "Organized Business," pp. 97–112; "NEA-NAM Conferences," *NEA Journal* 32 (Jan. 1943): 22; *Trends* Nov. 1944, pp. 1–3. Joel Spring, *Images of American Life: A History of Ideological Mangagement in Schools, Movie, Radio, and Television* (Albany, N.Y.: State University of New York Press, 1992), pp. 148–51.

35. Henry E. Abt to Walter Weisenburger, May 24, 1943, Acc. 1411, NAM III/843; Yeomans quoted in Rippa, "Organized Business," p. 103; F. Kenneth Brasted to Earl Bunting, Mar. 23, 1951, Acc. 1411, NAM III/852.3; *American Teacher,* Feb. 1952, p. 4; "Education Department Program, History, Present Program and Recommendations for the Future," Sept. 19, 1956, Box 70, Grede Papers.

36. B. P. Brodinsky, "Little and Big Business," *Nation's Schools* 43 (May 1949): 25; *PRN,* Nov. 22, 1948; J. Fred Essig, "An Adventure in Community Co-operation," *Ohio Schools* 28 (Sept. 1950): 262–3.

37. Community Relations Department, National Association of Manufacturers, "Influencing the 'Balance of Power' Groups through Opinion-Makers," July 1, 1946, Acc. 1411, NAM I/109; National Association of Manufacturers, *This We Believe About Education* (New York: National Association of Manufacturers, 1954); 38–39; Eugene Whitmore, "Why Invite School Teachers to Visit Your Plant?" *AB,* Sept. 1951, p. 19.

38. Dawley, "B-I-E Day," pp. 384–86; "Teachers Learn about Industry During Factory Tours"; *AB,* Sept. 1950, p. 54; PR Opportunities of B-E Day," *PRJ,* May 1955, pp. 12–13; "Outline of Business-Industry-Education Day, Lansing Michigan, Mar. 9, 1948," Acc. 1411, NAM I/15.

39. *Hartford Courant,* Apr. 13, 1950; Interview with Sophie Chumura, Feb. 23, 1988, Chicopee, Mass.; Carrie L. Clements, "Business-Education Day: A Must for Business Teachers," *Balance Sheet* 36 (Sept. 1954): 13; Floyd A. Denicola, "Teacher-Industry Day: A Once-A-Year Partnership," *Business Education World* (May 1958): 19.

40. "PR Opportunities of B-E Day," *PRJ,* May 1955, p. 12; *NAM News,* Oct. 14, 1950; *PRJ,* Mar. 1952, p. 12.

41. *PRN,* Apr. 13, 1953; B. F. Goodrich Company, *A Case History in the Story of Competitive Enterprise in America* (teachers' manual for *Johnson Makes the Team*), n.p., c. 1953, Box 58, AOF IV, LMDC; J. Austin Burkhart, "The Battle for Free Schools: Big Business and the Schools," *Nation,* Nov. 10, 1951, pp. 401.

42. *PRN,* Apr. 7, 1947; "St. Louis Businessmen Plan Program to Improve Labor-Management Relations," *AB,* June 1947, p. 57; "Juniors Learn the Business," *MRec* 13 (July 1951): 247–49, 269; Blake Clark, "Getting the Facts of Business Life," *AB,* Aug. 1955, pp. 12–14, 34–35; *Labor's Daily,* Dec. 15, 1956.

43. Moore, "The National Association of Manufacturers," pp. 213–16; G. A. Rietz, "Industry Lends a Hand," *Bulletin of the National Association of Second-*

*ary School Principals* 43 (May 1959): 182; Alan C. Kerchhoff, "Big Business and the Public Schools," *Journal of General Education* 9 (Jan. 1956): 73–81.

44. *PRN*, May 26, 1947; "Junior Balances the Books," *Steelways*, Apr. 1957, pp. 14–15; "Juniors Learn the Business," p. 247; *NAM News*, Feb. 17, 1951; Mary June Burton, "Sponsored School Materials are 'Coming of Age,'" *PRJ* 13 (Apr. 1957): 8; *NYT*, Jan. 4, 1959.

45. N. D. McCombs and George W. Hohl, "Business Can Help Teach Economics," *School Executive* 72 (Feb. 1953): 80–82; John Burger, "Steps toward Economic Understanding," *AM* 19 (Apr. 1954): 24–26; *PRN*, July 14, 1952; Burton "Sponsored School Materials," p. 8.

46. Fred G. Clark to J. Howard Pew, Aug. 20, Dec. 11 1952, Box 213, Pew Papers, HML.

47. Rippa, "Organized Business and Public Education," pp. 166–71; NAM, "A Resource Unit for How Our Business System Operates," pamphlet, n.d., Acc. 1411, NAM I/65.

48. American Economic Foundation, "Annual Report to Contributors, Members and Friends," Nov. 15, 1957, Box 2, Crane Papers; NAM Education Department, "Report of HOBSO Activities, Jan. 1, 1956 through Dec. 31, 1956," Acc. 1411, NAM I/65; Stanley L. Phraner to Ransum P. Rathbun, Dec. 11, 1953, "Report on St. Louis Program for Implementing 'HOBSO' in Schools," c. 1953, Acc. 1411, NAM I/70.

49. American Economic Foundation, "Annual Report to Contributors, Members and Friends," Nov 15, 1957, Box 2, Crane Papers; Rippa, "Organized Business and Public Education," pp. 163–64.

50. Haig Babian, "Economic Education: How It Began and Why," *Challenge* 7 (Mar. 1964): 3–4; Alfred C. Neal, "Economic Education: The Businessman's Interest," *Challenge* 7 (Mar. 1964): 30; Edward Christopher Phren, "The Influence of the Economic Education Movement on the Public Schools of New York City, 1946–1966" (Ed. D. diss. Teachers College, Columbia University, 1968).

51. On CED philosophy see Robert M. Collins, *The Business Response to Keynes, 1929–1964* (New York: Columbia University Press, 1981), pp. 83–87, 204–9; Haig Babian, "Economic Education: How it Began and Why," pp. 3–4; Phren, "The Economic Education Movement," pp. 41–49; *Summary Report of the Joint Council on Economic Education, 1948–1951* (New York, 1951), pp. 6–8.

52. Interview with Solomon Barkin, Apr. 7, 1988, Amherst, Mass.; Edward J. Allen, "Program of the Joint Council on Economic Education," *Journal of Higher Education* 30 (Feb. 1959): 96.

53. Interview with Solomon Barkin, Apr. 7, 1988. Other unionists, however, remained suspicious of the Joint Council and refused to cooperate. For a revealing debate over labor's position, see "Minutes," American Federation of Labor, Workers Education Bureau Fall Conference, 1953, Chicago, Ill., Dec. 3–4, 1953, Box 439, United Textile Workers of America Papers, SLA.

54. Prehn, "The Economic Education Movement," pp. 41–44, 51–54; Marion B. Folson to Eugene Meyer, Jan. 19, 1953, Box 103, Eugene Meyer Papers, LC.

55. "Memo," enclosed in George H. Fern to Kenneth H. Miller, Sept. 4, 1957, Ellsworth Chunn to George Fern, Aug. 19, 1957, Fred A. Miller to Don F. Mallerry, July 19, 1957, Acc. 1411, NAM I/65.

56. Unionists at a CIO Regional Conference in Atlanta, Ga., complained that employers regularly gave "all sorts of talks against organized labor" in the high schools and that "hundreds of thousands of dollars are being spent every year by the Chamber of Commerce, National Manufacturers Association and other anti-Labor organizations for preparing and sending out propaganda material to all the High School teachers and students." Their goal was to "create in the minds of the teachers and pupils an attitude that is reactionary and hostile to the labor movement." "Minutes," CIO Regional Conference, Jan. 22–23, 1954, Box 1556, John Ramsay Papers, SLA; *PLN,* July 19, Sept. 6, 1946, Feb. 8, 1948, July 21, Nov. 17, 1950, *FF,* Feb. 28, 1948, *Guild Reporter,* May 12, 1950; *Ithaca Labor Union Review,* Jan. 1955; *Labor's Daily,* Dec. 15, 1955; Mark Starr, "The Struggle for the Schools," *American Teacher,* Mar. 1954, pp. 11–12. Among the attacks on BIE days in the labor press see for example: *Reading New Era,* Sept. 22, 1955, *719 News,* June, July 1950. See also, AFL, *Proceedings,* 1953, pp. 321, 542–44; AFL, *Proceedings,* 1950, p. 43; AFL, *Proceedings,* 1954, p. 321.

57. *California Teacher,* Nov. 1953; *Detroit Teacher,* May 13, Sept. 23, 1953; Irvin R. Kuenzli to George Meany, Apr. 29, 1953, Box 28, George Meany Papers, GMA.

58. O. Harold Wade to John D. Connors, Nov. 20, 1950, "Memo: Inre BIG TALK ('comic' book), Nov. 22, 1950," National Association of Manufacturers, *Watch Out for the Big Talk* (New York, c. 1950); Joseph Mire, "Recent Trends in Labor Education" (Paper presented to the Conference on Labor's Public Responsibility, Nov. 17–20, 1959, Madison, Wis.), Box 99, David J. McDonald Papers, HCLA.

59. "Transcript of the Three Hundred Thirty-Fifth Meeting of the Conference Board, Nov. 20, 1952," Box 42, National Industrial Conference Board Records, HML. Through the fifties, Minneapolis union teachers continued to resist BIE days, *American Teacher Magazine,* Sept. 1955, p. 5, Dec. 1959, p. 20; "The Corporations Are Undermining the School System!" and "Where Do You Stand," flyers, Box 2, UAW Department of Education Records, 1948–1955, ALUA; *AFL News Reporter,* Dec. 26, 1951. Also on Detroit labor investigation of the Institute for Economic Education see Economic Club of Detroit folder, Box 5, Series I, Wayne County AFL-CIO Papers, ALUA.

60. *Teachers Union News* (Philadelphia AFT), June 1954; Benjamin Barkas to Derwood Baker, Mar. 15, 1954, Box 2, Benjamin Barkas Papers, UA; Harry Boyer to All Affiliates, Aug. 3, 1950, Box 54, AUF, LMDC; *Reading New Era,* Mar. 6, 15, Apr. 24, May 1, 8, Nov 12, 1953, Jan 21, 1954; Aug. 3, 10, 1957.

61. Mark Starr, "Do Schools Teach the Facts of Union Life?" *Industrial Bulletin* (New York State Department of Labor), Jan. 1959, reprint in Box 11, Starr Papers; *Detroit Teacher,* Mar. 19, 1956; John M. Eklund, "The School Problem Is Still With Us," *American Teacher Magazine,* Apr. 1950, p. 13; *Ithaca Union Labor Review,* Jan. 1955.

62. "The Record of the AFL in Support of Education," *American Teacher Magazine*, May 1943, p. 2; CIO, *Labor and Education* (Washington, D.C., n.d.)

63. United Electrical, Radio and Machine Workers of America, *Chug-Chug: A Children's Story for the Whole Family* (New York, 1947) Box 24, Mark Starr to John D. Connors, Nov. 5, 1956, Box 11, Mark Starr to William D. Boutwell, Mar. 3, 1950, Box 12, all in Starr Papers; David E. Weingast, "A New Way in Newark," *Education*, Apr. 1952, pp. 526–29; R. Lyle Stone to Edward Coffey, Feb. 20, 1952, Box 3, Ernest Oppman to Brendan Sexton, Dec. 14, 1951, Mar. 18, 1952, Box 2, Ed Coffey Papers, UAW Department of Education Records; *Ammunition*, Apr. 1949, pp. 52–55; *Michigan CIO News*, June 2, 16, 1955.

64. George T. Guernsey to Dear Sir and Brother, Apr. 10, 1950, Box 4, Greater Buffalo Industrial Union Council Records; Matthew Woll to William Green, Mar. 17, 1952, Box 8, Series 8, AFL Papers; *New Jersey Labor Herald*, Apr. 1951; Solomon Barkin to George T. Guernsey, Nov. 13, 1952, Box 6, Series A, Textile Workers Union of America Records, SHSW.

65. Lloyd P. Williams, "The Educational Consequences of Laissez Faire," *School and Society* 85 (Feb. 2, 1957): 38; Daniel R. Fusfeld, "Economic Education—Or Indoctrination?" *Challenge*, Dec. 1963, pp. 15–17.

# 8 | Walking "Hand in Hand": Business, Labor, and Religion

During the fall of 1950, Sun Oil executive J. Howard Pew, a well-known conservative, recruited fellow business leaders to serve as lay sponsors for a new ecumenical body, the National Council of Churches. This new council would incorporate the older Federal Council of Churches (FCC), which since 1908 had been the voice of liberal Protestantism. Pew's invitation surprised many in the business community since Pew had been a prominent critic of the FCC, charging that it promoted socialism and collectivism. Indeed, just two years earlier, Pew had agreed to finance a book exposing "the subversive activities of the Federal Council." But, by 1950, he had decided that rather than fight the Council from outside, more could be "accomplished from within." The need of the National Council of Churches for new sources of funds provided Pew and his conservative supporters with the opportunity to infiltrate a historically liberal organization that was perhaps the most important institution of mainline Protestantism.[1]

Business leaders believed that the clergy, like educators, played an important role in the creation of public opinion. Surging church membership in the forties and fifties reinforced the importance of reaching the clergy with the message of free-enterprise capitalism. But elements of organized labor, particularly unions associated with the CIO, contested the business agenda. They too sought to walk "hand in hand" with the clergy, asserting that goals of religion were "identical with the aspirations of organized labor."[2] Equally significant, conservative business leaders confronted opposition from their more moderate counterparts in their attempts to shape the policies of national church organizations. Finally, the clergy had its own objectives, which did not mirror completely those of any other group. In this complex mix, the story of the Lay Committee serves as perhaps one of the most dramatic examples of the business community's campaign to shape American ideology in the decade after World War II.

* * *

Business criticism of church organizations in the 1940s was a phase in a constantly changing twentieth-century relationship. Through the late nineteenth century, entrepreneurs had enjoyed close ties to churches, especially Protestant denominations. The churches' emphasis on evangelism, personal salvation, and religious individualism meshed closely with traditional business values. The Social Gospel emerging at the turn of the century, however, questioned many business practices and called for the church to help reform society. Liberal and conservative Protestants began struggling over the role of the Christian church in a secular world. Those committed to the Social Gospel called for church involvement in economic, political and cultural struggles, while evangelical Protestants and much of the business community rejected religion's entanglement with such concerns, stressing the church's primary goals of piety, personal salvation, and individual morality. Those opposed to the Social Gospel triumphed temporarily during the twenties. In many churches, the emphasis on social reform gave way to the task of the moral regeneration of individuals in the business-dominated cultural climate of that decade.[3]

Depression-era economic crisis, however, revived the Social Gospel, driving a wedge between business and the churches. The 1920s celebration of business methods and values disappeared, replaced by sharp criticism of the business community and capitalism itself. In 1932, as unemployment and suffering spiraled, several Protestant churches called for the replacement of America's unplanned, competitive, profit-seeking economy with a planned industrial system aiming to provide economic security for all. The Federal Council of Churches provided enthusiastic support for the New Deal, noting that it "embodied many of the social ideals of the churches." Its revised "Social Creed" advocated social planning, the rights of workers to organize collectively, social control of credit, and economic relief for farmers through price controls.[4]

During World War II, despite wartime pressures to support the status quo, liberal Protestant leaders, such as G. Bromley Oxnam and John Bennett, continued to worry about the unbridled power of capitalism. A 1942 conference of the Federal Council of Churches' Commission on the Bases of a Just and Durable Peace advocated a postwar "experimentation with various forms of ownership and control, private, cooperative and public."[5] Business leaders bristled at the continued "socialistic trends" within the Federal Council and at reports that members of the FCC staff were actively aiding CIO organizing.

The widely publicized pronouncement at the 1948 meeting of the World Council of Churches that "Christian churches should reject the ideologies of both Communism and laissez-faire capitalism" created even more consternation among business leaders. *Fortune* magazine noted the importance of these ideas, but asked, "how much do the churchmen really know about economics?"[6]

In contrast to Protestantism's fluctuating relationship with capitalism, the Catholic church had fewer ties to big business. Informed by the 1891 papal encyclical, *Rerum Novarum*, the Catholic church generally took a more progressive stance than Protestants on industrial issues in part because its members were more heavily working class. Beginning in the late nineteenth century, parish priests often encouraged their working-class flocks to join labor unions. After World War I, American cardinals expressed disenchantment with capitalism, and many major Catholic periodicals repudiated the free enterprise system. Inspired by another papal encyclical, *Quadragesimo Anno* (1931), Catholic priests and lay organizations, including the Association of Catholic Trade Unionists, developed a close alliance with organized labor, especially the CIO. Catholic priests formed labor schools, acted as union chaplains, joined picket lines, and even became full-time union organizers, using their moral prestige to persuade the Catholic working class to join the new industrial unions. Still, not all Catholic organizations or clergy advocated industrial planning or supported organized labor; as among the Protestants, many conservatives disapproved of liberal tendencies within the church.[7]

The fact that liberalism was but one tendency within American religion provided little comfort to business leaders. In the 1940s, the NAM formed a Committee on Cooperation with Churches to change "misconceptions," which nourished among some clergy "doctrines inimical to the American system of freedom." The NAM worried that the church's "inherent sympathies" with the weak had led the clergy to support the growth of state-oriented collectivism and "of movements to win greater social protection and advantage for labor." Du Pont executive Jasper Crane, who served as a chairman of the NAM Committee, asserted that churches of all faiths and business should be united in a common concern with "the rising tide of collectivism," a system, "in which man's dignity and independence is lost to him, and he becomes a slave to the state."[8] Crane's Committee hoped to remind the clergy of business and religion's mutual interests in the sanctity of individuals and each individual's political, religious, and economic freedom. Infringement upon any one of "our constitutional freedoms," the NAM warned, could mean "the loss of all freedom" including the freedom of worship.[9]

To drive home this message, the NAM sponsored a series of local and regional conferences in the early 1940s, similar to those held with educators. The Jackson, Mississippi, Chamber of Commerce recruited participants to its January 1943 conference with the promise that closer cooperation between business and the clergy would aid in halting the "subversive forces that would destroy that (our) Way of Life and at the same time blow out Christianity and American Business." By the end of that year, twenty-six hundred business and clerical leaders had participated in these meetings. Conferences held in 1944 and 1945 emphasized creating a consensus around the question of postwar reconstruction. Business speakers stressed to the clergy the postwar corporate catechism, that improved standards of living and maximum employment could best be achieved through "one basic method—*greater production*."[10]

The NAM encouraged local business executives to form groups to meet regularly with the clergy. A Philadelphia committee, formed in 1944, included such eminent local business leaders as William Disston, vice president of Henry Disston & Sons; Larry E. Gubb, chairman of the Board of the Philco Corporation; Charles S. Redding, president of Leeds & Northrup Company; George L. Russell, president of John B. Stetson Company; and Charles R. Shipley, president of John Wanamaker. Similarly, the Detroit Conference, organized in 1945 and still meeting regularly during the 1950s, was supported by key automobile industry executives. In West Virginia, businessman F. Steele Ernshaw created the "Moundsville Church Plan." Asserting that he had heard too many sermons that "were on the left-hand side," he invited the community's nine ministers to lunch. That lunch, he recalled "changed the complexion of the whole situation." He suggested becoming better acquainted so that "maybe I can do something for you six days a week" to make "your job easier and maybe on Sunday you can do something for me." By 1950, Ernshaw's "Moundsville Church Plan" included the employers from the other three plants in town for monthly meetings with the Ministerial Association, after which he proudly reported that he had proved to the Moundsville ministers that both "church steeples and smokestacks are necessary to the welfare of our community."[12]

The opinions of many ministers, however, were less pliable than those in Moundsville. At a conference in Cleveland, in 1940, fifteen ministers met with fifteen local business leaders and several NAM officers. One minister reported that J. Howard Pew, then a NAM vice president, raised the specter of "industrial totalitarianism" in a speech that was "in effect a plug for free enterprise and an indictment of government control." As the meeting adjourned for lunch, several of the clergy "slipped quietly out . . . seeking to overcome the feeling of disgust and dissent that the morning session had evoked." At other conferences, clergy proposed that labor be represented. A 1943 Brooklyn Church and Industry meeting degenerated badly for local businessmen. Dominated by the clergy, the participants called for the state "to curb the excesses of the profit motive" and to control competition. They also endorsed industrial democracy, advocated full employment, and observed that clerical participants shared "a unanimity of opinion for the labor movement and its goals."[13]

Following World War II, the NAM expanded its Clergy-Industry Program. Noel Sargent, NAM secretary, assumed responsibility for maintaining contact with national church bodies, such as the Federal Council of Churches, the National Catholic Welfare Conference, and the Synagogue Council of America. An active Episcopalian layman, Sargent became a member of the Board of the National Council of Churches at its founding in 1950. Other NAM staff members developed contacts with theological seminaries, arranging for addresses to students, conferences with faculty members, and the distribution of NAM educational materials. Special attention was given to those seminaries where faculty members' initial reception was "cold or even hostile." As part of its mission, the NAM ensured that business was well represented at the increasing number of church-sponsored industrial conferences being held in the postwar period. Meanwhile, it increased the circulation of special publications to the clergy and even courted editors of church publications to encourage the use of NAM-supplied articles on economics and social topics.[14]

The NAM, as well as the Chamber of Commerce, also helped local business leaders cement personal ties with their community's clergy. These efforts were an extension of business's broader postwar community relations programs. Firms like General Electric, Allis-Chalmers, Caterpillar, Crouse-Hinds, Eli Lilly, and Bristol-Myers distributed company publications to local clergy and invited them to plant tours and luncheons. In December 1949, for instance, over five hundred Indianapolis ministers, priests, and rabbis toured the Eli Lilly company plant just a month after Indianapolis teachers had participated in a Business-Industry-Education Day. Both groups learned about Lilly's employee welfare plans and its contributions to the community.[15]

More important, corporations provided support to private organizations that were dedicated to defending individualism and freedom by teaching free enterprise economics to the clergy. One such group, Spiritual Mobilization, was founded by Reverend James W. Fifield during the thirties in response to religious support for the New Deal. It struggled without significant support until 1948 when J. Howard Pew began bankrolling the operation. With a new board of directors composed of leading businessmen and with financial support of many of the country's largest corporations including General Motors, American Cyanamid, IBM, Inland Steel, Johns-Manville, and United States Steel, Spiritual Mobilization significantly expanded its program. By the mid-fifties, it sponsored a weekly dramatic program for 400 radio stations, a monthly magazine distributed to twenty-two thousand clergy, editorial columns published in 350 newspapers, and summer conferences for clergymen, educators, students, and business leaders. In all these formats, it taught that "the free market economy, informed with the moral and spiritual self disciplines of stewardship, was the only known economic system consistent with Christian principles."[16]

Another group, the Christian Freedom Foundation, shared Spiritual Mobilization's goals. Founded in 1950 by conservative clergymen Norman Vincent Peale and Howard E. Kershner, it was originally financed entirely by Pew, albeit anonymously. Like Spiritual Mobilization, it cosponsored seminars with business groups during which Kershner warned clergy that "creeping socialism, state socialism, government controlled agriculture, government subsidies for schools, price and wage fixing" were all "steps toward collectivism." It also published *Christian Economics*, which was sent to over 175,000 Protestant ministers. It called for the church to speak up for capitalism and kept up a steady drumbeat of warnings that the survival of religion depended upon the survival of capitalism.[17]

Corporate interest in religion meshed with a religious upsurge that characterized the postwar era. In the years after World War II, church membership grew at a faster rate than the population, books on religion led the bestseller lists, and evangelical rallies drew thousands. In a world threatened by atomic extermination and by the specter of communism, religion gained a new place in public life. Prayer breakfasts in Washington, D.C., attracted the highest public officials; the phrase "under God" was added to the formerly secular Pledge of Allegiance; Presidents Truman and Eisenhower repeatedly reaffirmed their own religious faith. Eisenhower went so far as to contend that "without God there could be no American form of government, nor an American way of life."[18]

Driven by a variety of motives, the business community actively promoted this surge of piety. Corporate leaders recognized that religion could act as a conservative force in society. Accordingly, religion was integrated into the campaign to preserve the American way of life and the free enterprise system from internal and external threats. In 1949, the Advertising Council launched the first of annual nationwide advertising campaigns emphasizing the importance of religion and church attendance in family and community life.[19]

Employers not only believed that God could be enlisted to help fight communism, but also that he was "a good partner to have in the firm." In many ways reminiscent of the welfare capitalist programs of the Progressive Era and twenties, postwar employers began bringing religion directly into the plant in an effort to "inject religious faith into industry." During the spring of 1950, General Electric inaugurated special Holy Week services for employees of its Schenectady, New York, works. Two years later, US Steel spent $150,000 to purchase subscriptions for its 125,000 employees to *Guideposts,* an inspirational monthly edited by Norman Vincent Peale. By the mid-fifties, over eight hundred other companies were distributing religious literature to employees. *Nation's Business* observed that "not since the Victorian era . . . has there been anything like the spate of religious printed matter which employees receive today."[20]

At the turn of the century, company-supported YMCAs held noontime bible study meetings in factories; postwar America saw the return of this kind of activity. In 1954, John C. Harmon, Director of the Church-Industry Relations Southern Division of the NAM, reported that employees at Solar Aircraft Company in San Diego, California, and Lone Star Steel Company in Dallas, Texas, worshipped daily at work in company-built chapels. Moreover, during the fifties, employees who gathered for regular devotional services at the Severance Tool Industries in Saginaw, Michigan, or at Ford's River Rouge Plant joined workers in at least a thousand other companies across the nation in making prayer an integral part of their work day.[21] Taking these measures a step further, some companies brought religion into the workplace by hiring ordained ministers as industrial chaplains to conduct religious services and counsel employees on personal problems. During World War II, R. G. LeTourneau, Incorporated was one of the first firms to hire a full-time industrial chaplain at its Peoria, Illinois, plant. Within a decade, approximately forty other firms would follow suit, and many others employed local ministers part-time.[22]

For some employers promotion of religion was simply an expression of their own personal religiosity and reflected no ulterior motives. Business leaders, like many other Americans, were participants in as much as promoters of the postwar revival. They sought to apply Christian principles to industrial and community problems and to share their spiritual values with their workers. In cities across the country, laymen's groups made up of employers earnestly discussed how to reach these goals. Likewise, religion did not need to be foisted on workers; while some workplace religious activities were begun by management, others grew out of employee initiatives.[23]

For many employers, however, religion in the plant was a useful complement to harmonious production. Industrialists hoped that religious workers would be more cooperative, sober, and industrious employees. One company acknowledged that "while we would say emphatically that the purpose of our chaplain program is not just to get more production . . . it is our belief that these are by products of our program." Similarly, in early 1952, the management of the Plymouth, Indiana, plant of Gerber Enterprises reported that since the initiation of daily religious services, church membership among employees had increased, profanity had disappeared from the workplace, and grievances had declined. According to company officials "the workers are content and have found that they can talk out any problem with management."[24]

* * *

The corporate religious campaign confronted a determined foe in organized labor, particularly unions associated with the CIO. In 1953, John Ramsay, head of the CIO Community Relations Department, warned that "the National Association of Manufacturers is making great inroads into the control of religious institutions on the national and local levels and of all religious faiths. Clergymen who stand out for social justice need our support."[25] He urged the CIO to intensify and to expand its informal church-labor program, one that was begun in the early forties in part to counter the NAM's religious activities.

Since the late nineteenth century, unions had reached out to organized religion to provide justification and legitimacy for their social, political, and economic goals. Labor's efforts had met with varying degrees of success. The Catholic church, whose congregations were more working class in makeup, viewed cooperation with organized labor, particularly its more conservative elements, as a means of reaching Catholics who had strayed from the church. As noted earlier, the Catholic church readily clasped hands first with the AFL in the early twentieth century and then the CIO in the thirties, particularly its anticommunist elements. CIO leaders, many of whom were Catholics, quickly developed close ties with the Catholic church hierarchy as well as with labor priests.[26]

Labor's relations with Protestantism were more problematic. During the Progressive Era, when the Social Gospel was most influential, some AFL unions developed institutional connections with liberal Protestants sympathetic to labor's efforts to reform society and to improve the plight of the working class. Clergy, for instance, served as fraternal delegates to central labor bodies. Following World War I, however, as labor was tarred with the brush of Bolshevism, most Protestant clergy distanced themselves from unions. During the depths of the Depression, national denominational bodies reaffirmed their support for unions as active players in the Christian struggle for the rights of the downtrodden. At the local level, however, ministers who relied on donations from congregations made up of business leaders as well as workers remained suspicious of organized labor. Some unionists carried bitter memories of ministerial opposition to CIO organizing drives in the 1930s.[27]

In the forties, CIO unions began making tentative steps toward bringing labor and the Protestant religious community together. To offset business's close relationship with Protestant faiths that stressed individualism, organized labor spoke of mutualistic commitments to equity, social justice, and the rights of all men and women. In 1947, speaking from the pulpit of Boston's St. Paul's Episcopal Cathedral, the CIO's Van A. Bittner asserted that organized labor had just one aim, "the achievement of the brotherhood of man through the limitation of the competitive and the development of the cooperative."[28] Similarly, Steelworkers Secretary-Treasurer David J. McDonald pointed out that the "teachings of God have laid a lasting foundation for a civilization based on justice and religious law." "We in the CIO," he continued "are devoted to enforcing that justice and righteousness by protecting and improving the economic life of the millions of working men and women who are the backbone of organized religion."[29]

Some unionists viewed religion simply as a tool, for building a broader base of support for organized labor. Walter Reuther, for instance, had little formal commitment to religion but used religious imagery when appealing for the clergy's support for labor. Others, such as John Gates Ramsay, turned to religion as part of a genuine desire to infuse Christianity into the labor movement. Throughout most of the 1940s and 1950s, Ramsay devoted his full powers to representing labor to religious leaders. A steelworker and devout Presbyterian, Ramsay joined the Steelworkers Organizing Committee in 1936 and became its public relations representative. An active layman within the church, he mixed evangelical Protestantism with the social vision of industrial unionism. "To me," Ramsay declared, "the forerunner of social progress is evangelism. Without new lives we will not have changed conditions that will prove enduring."[30]

Ramsay's first experience as a liaison between the CIO and the church occurred in the spring of 1941 during the steelworkers organizing drive at the Bethlehem Steel plant in Buffalo, New York. The NAM, as part of its church campaign, had entertained the city's clergy at a dinner that Ramsay recalled "resulted in some clergymen preaching against our union." Called in by the steelworkers to combat the clergy's opposition to labor, Ramsay borrowed the NAM's technique and invited Buffalo clergy to meet with union workers; if the "National Association of Manufacturers could entertain at dinner, we could afford to entertain at luncheon." At the end of the first lunch between workers and clergy, Bishop Austin Pardue of the Episcopal church said "Gentlemen, it seems to the union that some of us are preaching against is doing what we preach about." After several more interracial, interdenominational luncheons, the clergy passed a resolution in support of the organizing campaign.[31]

In 1943, impressed by these results, Philip Murray assigned Ramsay to devote full time to "bridge the gap of separation between religion and labor." In this task, Ramsay was assisted by a small group of Protestant lay persons and ordained ministers who doubled as union leaders and who shared his vision of a Christian labor movement. They included Lucy Randolph Mason, a Southern reformer and labor organizer; Orville C. Jones, a Congregational minister who became education director of the Ohio CIO; Charles Webber, a Methodist minister who in the thirties became an organizer for the Amalgamated Clothing Workers and later served as president of the Virginia state CIO council; and David Burgess, a Congregational minister turned labor organizer in the forties and executive-secretary of the Georgia CIO council in the fifties.[32]

Ramsay and his associates relied on a variety of tactics to reach the clergy with labor's message. Pamphlets, articles in the religious press, and radio broadcasts publicized statements from national denominational bodies and prominent clergy endorsing labor's right to organize. One pamphlet acknowledged that American workers had often been apathetic toward religion, but chided clergy for failing to actively support labor. It also quoted Jesus, who claimed that "He has anointed me to preach the gospel to the poor, He has sent me . . . to set at liberty they that are oppressed." Sadly, according to this CIO publication, "from those who profess to walk in the footsteps of the Carpenter of Nazareth, workers have sought bread and often received a stone."[33]

Personal contacts with individual ministers, speeches at clerical gatherings, and the formation of fellowship groups also opened up the channels of communication between labor and religion. The fellowship groups grew out of Ramsay's experience in Buffalo. With Ramsay as guiding spirit, labor leaders in cities across the nation established monthly luncheon meetings of clergy and unionists to discuss the aims of labor and religion and correct misunderstandings between the two groups. Ramsay attracted clergy to the fellowships by promising to help win alienated workers back to the church. One of the earliest fellowships was formed in 1942 in Columbus, Ohio. Still meeting in the late fifties, it provided a forum for labor and religious leaders to exchange ideas on such issues as housing, race relations, and collective bargaining. According to *Steel Labor,* the core of the fellowship meetings was a "simple but effective belief: that no minister can in good conscience oppose the union once he is given the opportunity to know its people and its aims."[34]

In 1946, when the Southern organizing drive, Operation Dixie, began, Ramsay worked closely with Lucy Randolph Mason. Appointing Ramsay director of Community Relations of the CIO Organizing Committee, the CIO hoped he could help overcome church hostility to labor, a formidable barrier to organizing in the South. His primary focus was winning over hostile evangelical mill-village ministers who viewed the CIO as an "un-Christian," "un-American," "communistic organization." With biblical quotations, they condemned strikers and warned their flocks that the CIO was the "mark of the beast" and the "work of the devil," and that C.I.O. stood for "Christ Is Out." Over the next seven years, through radio broadcasts, pamphlets, and meetings, Ramsay, Mason, Burgess, Webber, and other CIO organizers tried to win respectability and legitimacy for labor by demonstrating the CIO's commitment to anti-Communism and its devotion to the principles of Christianity.[35]

At the same time they appealed directly to religiously-oriented Southern workers using the language of the Bible. In a 1949 Textile Workers Union–sponsored radio broadcast in Gallatin, Tennessee, for example, Ramsay asked "every Christian worker" to "realize his own personal, moral responsibility to become a member of the labor movement which has done so much to benefit humanity." Ramsay cited the first verse of the 133d Psalm—"Behold, how good and pleasant it is for brethren to dwell together in unity"—and in Galatians—"Bear ye one another's burdens, and so fulfill the law of Christ"—as Biblical justification for collective action. The CIO's full-color comic book, "The Bible and the Working Man" aimed at the religious rank and file who had a "distorted picture" of the labor movement's aims. It featured a minister assuring an autoworker fresh from the countryside that "unions were Christian," for "unions want justice and justice is Christian."[36]

The CIO's campaign for support from the Southern church, however, failed to achieve significant union gains. Although there were nineteen fellowships meeting in Southern cities, labor made few inroads among most of the Southern clergy. In November 1951, Ramsay admitted that most religious leaders in the South were "still skeptical of the labor movement, if not opposed to it." The historian of Operation Dixie concludes that the weak labor-religious coalition forged by the CIO could not overcome the "totality of the cultural opposition" it encountered during the organizing drive.[37]

Despite the rather discouraging results in the South, interest in expanding labor's ties to religion grew within the CIO. In early 1953, for instance, the UAW formed the "Religion-Labor Conference of Metropolitan Detroit." Seeking a "more effective channel of communication between the church and labor," the conference brought Catholic, Protestant, and Jewish clergy together with unionists on a monthly basis to learn more about labor's thinking on such questions as the guaranteed annual wage, pension agreements, and collective bargaining.[38] Meanwhile, the United Gas, Coke and Chemical Workers, led by George Crago, urged the 1953 CIO convention to establish a CIO National Committee for Church Liaison. The union was "painfully aware of the power and influence of the church" as a negative force during Operation Dixie. Crago wanted the CIO to cultivate the "wholesome influence the church can exert when it cares to do so."[39]

First considered as a program in 1944, CIO leaders Crago, Ramsay, Al Whitehouse of the Steelworkers, Ellis Van Riper of the Textile Workers, and Tilford Dudley of the CIO central office finally got the CIO to formalize its church program in December 1954. It established a Committee on Religion and Labor that was headed by Victor Reuther, with Ramsay as secretary. Charles Webber joined Ramsay as a second full-time labor liaison to the religious community. In 1955, the newly merged AFL-CIO continued the CIO's program with the Office for Religious Relations, which interpreted the ideals, aims, and achievements of the labor movement to the clergy, while at the same time encouraging trade unionists to join and participate in a religious organization. Ramsay and Webber, often in direct competition with their NAM counterparts, traveled throughout the country, representing labor at national religious meeting, participating in church-sponsored social action conferences, addressing seminary students and ministerial associations, and continuing to promote religion and labor fellowships.[40]

Like business, the CIO cooperated with independent religious groups sympathetic to their aims. In the mid-fifties, the CIO took virtual control of the National Religion and Labor Foundation, an organization founded in 1931 by a small group of liberal Protestant theologians to enlist church support for the hardpressed labor movement. It taught classes about unions to seminary students and organized conferences and local fellowships that brought labor and religious leaders face to face. Although unable to elicit much interest from AFL craft unionists, it quickly attracted labor leaders from the ranks of the CIO. Over the years, members of the Foundation's Executive Board included such CIO leaders as Van Bittner, James B. Carey, Walter Reuther, Joseph Beirne, and David McDonald. But labor did not have a controlling influence until 1954, when the CIO became anxious to achieve a higher profile in the religious community. The CIO Committee on Religion decided to "work with and through the NRLF," strengthening its existing facilities through grants and staff assistance. A tiny, financially strapped organization, the Foundation was willing to trade some independence for the CIO's "whole-hearted support." The CIO cemented this relationship with an initial $25,000 grant and steady support, which continued after the merger. The increasing conservative tenor of the country during the fifties seemed to make this alliance all the more imperative.[41]

*       *       *

There was perhaps no greater prize in the struggle between labor and capital over religion than the National Council of Churches. The product of a 1950 merger of the Federal Council of Churches and eleven smaller Protestant ecumenical bodies, the National Council quickly emerged as the most important voice of religious authority in a predominantly Protestant society. At its formation, businessman Jasper Crane predicted that it "will almost certainly be one of the most influential organizations in American life."[42] The Council's endorsement of either business's or labor's values promised to confer upon these values an aura of legitimacy.

The creation of the National Council occurred while business was seeking to increase its influence over the preeminent voice of Protestantism. But business leaders' efforts were fraught with difficulty. Indeed, they approached the Federal Council and later the National Council with a distinct disadvantage. First, divided between moderates and conservatives, business leaders clashed among themselves over their objectives. Second, business leaders faced the tough job of shifting the Council from its identification with liberalism. From its inception in 1908, the Federal Council had stood as a friend of labor and liberalism. Finally, business's task was complicated by the fact that the church was not a pliable institution to be controlled by the most strong-willed outsider. Clerical leaders in the Council had their own agenda independent of either labor or business. Despite these impediments, closer investigation of the business community's involvement with Protestant ecumenicalism demonstrates its ability to shape pronouncements more in tune with business's political agenda.

By the mid-1940s, there were forces already encouraging the Federal Council of Churches to move from its commitment to liberal social change. During the twenties and thirties, the Federal Council's identification with religious and political liberalism had cost it the support of a sizable group of Protestants.[43] Among the Federal Council's most virulent critics were religious evangelicals and political conservatives. In the early forties, their dissatisfaction with the Federal Council culminated in the formation of two competing ecumenical bodies, the American Council of Christian Churches headed by fundamentalist Carl McIntire, one of the FCC's most extreme critics, and the National Association of Evangelicals, a broader coalition of conservatives, seeking to create a unified voice for Protestant evangelicalism.[44]

Attacks on the Federal Council intensified after World War II. The American Council of Christian Laymen, the Committee for Constitutional Government, and Spiritual Mobilization, among other conservative organizations, largely financed by business, joined McIntire in charging the Council's leadership with apostasy and with advocating communism. The American Council's widely distributed pamphlet, *How Red Is the Federal Council of Churches,* depicted Federal Council leaders enmeshed in an ominous spider's web of "Communist, Communist-front and Socialist organizations." These accusations gained more weight in light of the growing fear of communism in postwar America.[45]

Anxious about these attacks and its waning prestige, the Federal Council sought to disarm its critics. Building upon earlier efforts of a small group of evangelicals in its ranks, the FCC sought to work more closely with the conservative, evangelically oriented, interdenominational bodies of Protestantism. This cooperation culminated in 1950 with the formation of the National Council of Churches. The Federal Council also confronted the issue of communism, asserting in 1946 that, contrary to recent allegations, the FCC sought to reform society while working within the system of private and public ownership. It issued a statement making "perfectly clear the irreconcilable conflict between Christianity and the Communistic philosophy as set forth by the Russian state."[46]

The Federal Council hoped to restore its influence by reasserting "the relevance of a Christian perspective on world affairs." During the war, the Council regained credibility by helping to shape a consensus around America's international role in the postwar world. It led the struggle within religion against isolationism, mobilizing public support for the United Nations. The Federal Council wanted to play an equally significant role in domestic affairs, but its postwar economic vision met ridicule for questioning aspects of capitalism. Consequently, Protestant leaders turned to more subtle messages in an effort to win over significant sectors of American public opinion.[47]

One way the FCC sought to expand its appeal was to associate more closely with the economic philosophy and business leaders of the Committee for Economic Development. In December 1946, the election of Charles P. Taft, a lawyer, as the first lay president of the Federal Council of Churches reflected the Council's search for an economic approach that would appeal to a wider audience. Unlike his brother, Republican Senator Robert A. Taft, Charles Taft was a CED trustee and business moderate who served under Roosevelt and supported some of the New Deal programs. According to a *Time* reporter, "knowing delegates" saw his election as "presaging a new era of lay leadership and political activity" for Protestantism. Taft's more conservative colleagues in the business community looked forward to his driving out "the socialists, pinks and reds that have worked their way into the various levels of policy and positions of power in the organization."[48]

Taft, however, was less concerned about "socialists, pinks and reds" and more interested in helping the Federal Council adopt the CED's more moderate economic positions. He repeatedly argued that "a substantial majority of church people" were "clearly on the conservative side," and that when the Council charged ahead on progressive social and economic issues they left "the constituency 'way in the rear." On the issue of labor, as Taft saw it, the Federal Council need no longer treat unions as "the underdog." He observed that the "twelve-hour day in steel is long since gone, most large companies arbitrate their discharges and labor for some years has been top dog."[49]

Concurrent with Taft's election, the appeal of the CED's economic philosophy was apparent in seven position papers the Council published during 1946. These papers were part of an educational project which culminated in February 1947 in the FCC's first National Study Conference of Church and Economic Life. They analyzed the economic situation Christians faced in the postwar period often in language that mirrored the CED's. Study number five spoke of a middle way between absolute economic freedom and social or governmental control, calling for increasing the influence of moderate organizations representing various economic interests. Sharing the CED's corporatist ethos, Council writers envisioned society as an "equilibrium of numerous functional groups where each group endeavors to adjust its interest to the common interest." Praising the CED as "one of the most constructive recent efforts of progressive business leaders," the FCC suggested creating a corporatist type device called the Congress for Economic Development, representing business, labor, agriculture, and consumer groups. Like the CED, it would rely on impartial studies by experts and explore "the possibilities of voluntary organization" in the private sector to orchestrate reform.[50]

While CED-thinking influenced, it certainly did not yet dominate the Council's understanding of economy. Other sections of the studies that spoke of the worker concern for security praised the revolutionary potential of organized labor and the cooperative movement and analyzed the necessity of promoting purchasing power as well as addressing the maldistribution of income hearkened back to earlier FCC traditions.[51] These issues were anathema to business leaders of both conservative and moderate stripes. Retired Du Pont executive Jasper Crane called the studies "terrible tripe" worth ignoring, but he worried about the impact of these "poisonous pronouncements" on Protestant ministers.[52]

The convening of a three-day conference by the Federal Council in mid-February 1947 to discuss the economic issues raised by the studies provided an arena for both business and labor to contest future FCC pronouncements. Indeed, this conference was unique for its degree of lay participation; two-thirds of the delegates in Pittsburgh were laymen.[53] Sensing an opportunity, the NAM's Noel Sargent mobilized a strong conservative business representation and strategy for the conference. Charles Taft was just as determined to see to it that there would be no "one-sided" pronouncements passed. He recruited an impressive array of CED-types to attend.[54] Outnumbered by the business representatives but extremely articulate were the representatives from the labor movement. The CIO's core of religious activists with assistance from a few AFL representatives joined in alliance with a group of liberal clergy headed by Methodist Bishop G. Bromley Oxnam, who had just stepped down from the Federal Council's presidency. They came to the conference in the expectation that the gathering would come out strongly for greater government control over the economy and an enhanced welfare state. This faction pushed for the adoption of resolutions endorsing full employment, cooperatives, and a guaranteed annual wage and condemning private "concentration of ownership and control."[55]

The liberals quickly ran into opposition from business leaders and the proceedings bogged down. Outraged by labor's proposals and wary of Oxnam's influence, the NAM caucus met with Taft and threatened to issue a minority report or to withdraw. As the conference stood on the verge of disintegrating, business moderates led by Taft took the initiative and developed a compromise. Economic issues raised by labor or the NAM faction would be incorporated in the final report in the form of questions, preventing either interest group from using the FCC to promote their agenda. The conference concluded by recommending that the church take a more active role in the economic sphere. Having saved the conference, business moderates emerged with increased prestige within the Council.[56]

To meet its new mandate, the Federal Council changed its Industrial Relations Division to the Department of Church and Economic Life, charged with providing the clergy and the laity with religious guidance on economic issues. The Industrial Relations Division, from which most of the Federal Council's pronouncements on economics originated, had long been a source of irritation to the business community. Its professional staff was identified closely with organized labor and liberalism. The division, for instance, endorsed Operation Dixie, and division secretary, Cameron P. Hall, told Southern employers that it was their Christian duty to encourage their workers to join the CIO. To many business leaders this division represented the worst socialistic tendencies within the FCC.[57]

Taft hoped that a reorganized Industrial Relations Division could serve as a sophisticated vehicle for promoting the economic agenda of the moderate wing of the business community. He had a low opinion of most of business's educational activities on behalf of capitalism. The NAM's campaigns either sounded "phony" or came off as "a hysterical anti-Communist witch hunt." Taft envisioned the new department teaching the clergy how "the United States built up the highest standard of living and the least misery and poverty of any nation in history."[58]

The Federal Council's professional staff contested the new direction. Cameron Hall, a Presbyterian minister with a long background in social action, headed the new department and Hall enlisted such prominent trade unionists and liberal clergy as Walter Reuther, A. Phillip Randolph, Van A. Bittner, Bishop Bromley Oxnam, and Reinhold Niebuhr. Taft, however, recruited business moderates, many with close connections with the CED, who had supported him during the Pittsburgh conference.[59] They helped Taft get the resources to expand the department's activities. With Rockefeller Foundation funding obtained in 1949, Taft borrowed the CED staff economists to conduct a series of studies on the role of ethics in economic activity. These reports reflected the CED's outlook, suggesting the importance of increasing productivity and stabilizing the economy as well as warning of the increased coercive power of organized labor.[60] But, throughout this period, Taft struggled with only partial success to limit the input of Hall and his staff who retained their commitment to liberalism and organized labor.[61]

Conservative elements of the business community found the moderates' involvement in the Federal Council no more appealing than labor's. The moderates' willingness to accept a role for the government in regulating the economy, however small, was as damaging as labor's advocacy of the welfare state. Conservatives, however, were divided over what approach to take to counter their opponents influence on the FCC. The most conservative, evangelical business leaders denounced both the Council and religion's involvement in any secular affairs. In contrast, the leaders of the NAM's Committee on Cooperation with Churches argued that this was "neither a realistic nor effective position for businessmen to take." Standard Oil President Robert E. Wilson argued that whether business liked it or not the church was going to continue to take positions on economic and political issues. He warned that if businessmen boycotted the Federal Council "when others are trying to use it for left-wing purposes, we shall have to expect a lot of left-wing pronouncements." Consequently, in 1947, NAM secretary Noel Sargent joined the Department of Church and Economic Life, hoping to temper both the influence of moderate business leaders as well as organized labor.[62]

The Federal Council's second National Study Conference on Church and Economic Life, however, jolted all elements of the business community. The February 1950 Detroit conference, was a replica of the Pittsburgh conference, bringing labor and business factions together in fierce competition for the clergy's allegiance. Walter Reuther, head of the labor delegation, gave the keynote address, which "took the place by storm." Bromley Oxnam recorded in his diary that Reuther's speech was "grounded in such an understanding of human beings" that it became "emotionally powerful. For a time it seemed we were listening to one of the Hebrew prophets." Noel Sargent, in turn, defended the "advocates of free enterprise as the true liberals of the 20th century." His performance failed to measure up to that of the more dynamic Reuther, however. Taft tried to make the conference's final report a moderate, well-balanced document that "fully recognizes the basic importance of enterprise system," but instead it had strong prolabor undertones, reflecting the attitudes of the liberals.[63] The conference, which received wide publicity, convinced a powerful group of business leaders who had been standing aloof to reverse course. They decided that the best way to stop the Federal Council's "subversive activities" was to join the organization and to work from within to correct it.[64]

The formation of the National Council of Churches provided these conservatives with just such an opportunity. Planning for a new ecumenical organization that incorporated the FCC and eleven other Protestant bodies had begun during World War II. The planning committee included critics of the Federal Council from more evangelically oriented bodies, who emphasized that the progressive leaders of the FCC had lost touch with local churches. The more evangelical clergy hoped to push the new organization in a more conservative direction by bringing a large number of laymen into the new organization and by using these laymen as a major source of financial support for the new Council's ambitious program of operations.[65]

In early 1950, planners formed a Laymen's Committee to seek the "vital participation" of lay members in the National Council's work. For chairman they wanted a man of nationwide reputation with demonstrated executive ability, "preferably with experience in financing of eleemosynary institutions." After trying unsuccessfully to recruit several moderate business leaders, in July 1950, the planning committee approached J. Howard Pew, chairman of the board and recently retired president of Sun Oil Corporation.[66] On the surface, Pew was an unusual choice. A self-proclaimed fundamentalist, he was a supporter of organizations that attacked the Federal Council and had even commissioned his own exposé of its "subversive" activities. In December 1948, he declared that he was adamant in his determination to never give financial assistance to the Federal Council of Churches or any organization linked to it. An active member of the Liberty League in the 1930s, to the American public his name was "virtually a symbol for ultra-conservative positions" on political, economic, and social issues. But, the planning committee was prepared to overlook this past. It had learned that Pew was among the conservative business leaders who had decided that backing the FCC's opponents was a mistake. Equally important, Pew was also a man of substantial means with connections to some of the wealthiest people and corporations in the country.[67]

Pew's service had a price. He demanded assurance that lay leaders would have the opportunity to discuss major questions of policy, especially in the area of economics, on an "equal footing" with clerical leaders. He privately confided that he did "not propose to be put into a position that businessmen will provide the organization with the money with which to implement a campaign of Socialization." He argued that only if business leaders and the clergy worked as equals could they correct ministers' misunderstanding of "the relationship of freedom in economics, education, and politics to the basic principles of the Christian religion." Eager for his participation and his money, the planning committee acceded to his demands and were "just walking on air" when they learned that "Mr. Pew is with us." Pew immediately pumped $60,000 into the planning committee's budget.[68]

The National Council of Churches gave Pew a free hand in selecting the members of the Lay Committee, which he began assembling immediately. He searched for a group of individuals who shared his commitment to freedom, individualism, and Christianity, which, like many conservative fundamentalists, he wove together. If, Pew asserted, "we want to be free to continue in business, the leadership of the people of our country must believe in the fundamentals of Christianity." Pew's recruitment pitch stated: "We never can hope to stop this Country's plunge toward totalitarism until we have gotten the ministers' thinking straight." Pew promised potential members that, unlike the Federal Council, the new organization would avoid "political involvements and controversies." He repeatedly argued that "conservative control is possible." To ensure this, the Lay Committee, which grew to almost two hundred members, would "maintain close contact and surveillance" over all the NCC's activities. With these powers, Pew boasted that "we have a very real opportunity to get the National Council of Churches established on a firm foundation."[69]

Joining Pew's Lay Committee were manufacturers, educators, bankers, lawyers, doctors, scientists, and public officials. The most active members of the lay committee were the business leaders. Among them were an array of major corporate executives, including Harry A. Bullis of General Mills, Harvey S. Firestone of Firestone Tire and Rubber Company, Charles R. Hook of Armco Steel Corporation, B. E. Hutchinson of Chrysler Corporation, H. W. Prentis of Armstrong Cork, Colby M. Chester of General Foods Corporation, Robert E. Wilson of Standard Oil, Charles E. Wilson of General Electric, and Jasper Crane, recently retired from Du Pont, who shared Pew's dedication to remolding the basic values of the American public. All of them were involved in a similar campaign in their companies' factories, local schools, and communities.[70]

Under pressure from the Council to create a representative committee, Pew also searched for the right kind of labor leaders. Dismissing CIO unionists as "Socialists," he induced a small group of "trustworthy" labor leaders from AFL affiliates to join. Pew's associate, Lois Hunter, named several "free enterprisers" who had earlier rejected serving on the "too radical" Department of Church and Economic Life. Included were: George MacGregor Harrison and Glen B. Goble, president and vice-president of the Railway Steamship Clerks; Earl W. Jimerson, president of the Amalgamated Meat Cutters; and J. Scott Milne, secretary-treasurer of the International Brotherhood of Electrical Workers. Pew subsequently recruited them to the Lay Committee.[71]

In late November 1950, at the first convention of the National Council of Churches, Pew's presentation of the Lay Committee and its intention to play a significant policy-making role shocked most of the delegates, few of whom had even heard of its existence. Immediately, debate ensued over the Lay Committee's status. Was it, as Pew envisioned, a permanent overarching committee attached directly to the General Board with sweeping powers of participation and review, or was it a temporary advisory body designed to help integrate the laity into the National Council's structure and to raise funds?[72] Worried about censorship, liberal Bishop G. Bromley Oxnam led the opposition to the creation of an autonomous Lay Committee that met separately from the clergy. They "seem to think that they have everything settled and that anyone who disagrees with their dogma is a revolutionist," he argued, adding that we "dare not set a precedent which in any way gives to a group of men not in the organization and not chosen by the churches the right to review, directly or indirectly, the pronouncements of a great church." Impressed by Oxnam's argument, the General Board held off approval of the Lay Committee and appointed a committee to study the issue.[73]

As the Council's committee weighed the Lay Committee's future, a number of prominent liberal clergy, including Oxnam, John Bennett and Reinhold Neibuhr, remained alarmed at the prospect of a group of conservative laity overseeing the NCC's activities. Oxnam suspected that "big business has decided that the proper way to handle what it has regarded as too progressive announcements on the part of the church is to get on the inside and to control it." While

Oxnam worried about selling "our soul for a mess of pottage," other clergy within the Council's leadership, however, were still impressed with Pew's potential to attract great wealth to the organization. Moreover, the more evangelical members recently incorporated into the National Council shared many of Pew's religious and political views. Still others, such as National Council Secretary Samuel Cavert, believed Pew posed little threat. Cavert dismissed Pew as "an old man today," yearning for "the recognition he once had when he was directing a great enterprise." Cavert even anticipated that the liberal clergy could give men like Pew a greater appreciation of the "social meaning of Christianity."[74]

Finally, in April 1951, the General Board reached a compromise on the Lay Committee's status. The Lay Committee was invited to continue in a planning capacity with a role more limited than Pew had desired. As a concession, however, ten members of Pew's committee were appointed to the General Board. These Lay Committee representatives, like other Board members, now had the opportunity to review all proposed pronouncements before they came up for approval by the General Board. Members of the Lay Committee moved rapidly into the Council's structure; Jasper Crane, for example, was elected vice president of the National Council and served on eighteen different committees.[75]

Pew viewed the purse strings as the key to business influence. The National Council turned over to the Lay Committee the task of raising money for the organization's first year of operations, and business leaders wielded their clout. Charles R. Hook, chairman of the board of Armco Steel and a former NAM president, headed the fundraising activities. Pew worked closely with Hook, personally pledging $100,000 towards meeting the first year's budget deficit. Between 1951 and 1952, Pew sent out over twenty-five hundred letters to business leaders, increasing corporate donations by almost 60 percent. In these letters to donors, Pew emphasized that the National Council was in a formative stage with a more pragmatic leadership than the old FCC but that fund-raising was critical to the Lay Committee's success in "influencing the Council to declare for sound principles." He advised Donaldson Brown, former head of General Motors, that "if our Committee, working with the Finance Committee, will raise this money, take an interest in the work of the Council and develop their budgets," then "the clerics will think twice before they would allow to go out any such pronouncements as formerly were released by the Federal Council." Pew deflected criticism of corporate fund-raising, arguing that private property was in jeopardy unless they succeeded in teaching "economically illiterate ministers" what is good for our country.[76]

Pew followed through with his promise to use money as a weapon. When disagreements arose over policy, he regularly threatened to withdraw his personal donations. Similarly, Hook threatened loss of corporate donations if the NCC failed to follow business leadership.[77] With money as its bludgeon, between 1951 and 1955 the Lay Committee worked to prevent the National Council from making pronouncements that it considered subversive. The increasingly conservative political atmosphere created by the rising tide of McCarthyism made it more difficult for the liberals to contest business's efforts. In this atmosphere, anything not "decidedly in favor of capitalism" was potentially suspect and could be defined as a brand of communism.[78]

Asserting that the church's primary role was evangelical, the Lay Committee successfully blocked passage of pronouncements dealing with political and international issues, race relations, and the economy. As a result of the Lay Committee's pressure, even the policy of issuing pronouncements, formerly considered one of the main tasks of an ecumenical body, came under scrutiny. In March 1952, attempting to placate Pew, the General Board voted to reduce the number of pronouncements passed and limit them to matters in which there was "an unmistakable ethical or religious concern," greatly reducing their number. Moreover, the General Board created a "screening committee" to ensure that department studies contained a balance of viewpoints. In June 1952, pleased with the Lay Committee's impact, Pew boasted that since his committee's organization "there hasn't been a single subversive pronouncement that has come out of the National Council."[79]

Pew focused most of his attention on controlling the source of most of the pronouncements on social and economic issues, the Department of Church and Economic Life. The National Council had incorporated the department intact, with Taft continuing as chairman and Hall as secretary. In early 1952, the *Christian Century* noted that of all parts of the NCC it was "most suspect by the more conservative denominations and by the conservative lay group newly interested in cooperative endeavors." Pew considered the department a hotbed of radical activity. While no friend of Taft, it was Hall and his supporters that Pew held responsible for propagating the "philosophy of the Welfare State" against what he felt were the wishes of most Americans. In particular, Pew rejected the department's perception that it should use the power of the church to get laws "to force taxpayers to alleviate social ills through governmental agencies."[80]

Pew's program to limit the department's influence had several strategies. First, through the Lay Committee's ability to review and edit proposals, Pew blocked or impeded the NCC's endorsement of a series of studies financed by the grant from the Rockefeller Foundation. These studies suggested that at times the profit motive might be incompatible with Christian ethics.[81] A second strategy was to undermine the department's relationship with organized labor. In early 1953, under pressure from Pew, NCC Secretary Samuel Cavert censured Cameron Hall for soliciting funds using union endorsement. When the Philip Murray Memorial Foundation offered to donate $200,000, Pew threatened that it would "open the Council to severe criticism and definitely close the door to all gifts from business and industrial sources." This enraged Oxnam, however, who vowed, "We are not going to take money from big business and turn it down from labor." Eventually the Council accepted the gift but with promises to Pew that it came with no strings attached.[82]

Finally, the Lay Committee forced the rewriting of the department's statement on the application of Christian principles to economic life. Originally drafted in 1948 by liberal theologian John Bennett, it was revised during 1952 and sent to the General Board for approval in early 1953. Based on the Social Gospel, it read like a liberal manifesto, consistently challenging the rhetoric of free enterprise. Revising the statement monopolized Pew and his supporters for months. Representatives of the Lay Committee met with moderate members of the department, including Taft and Wesley F. Rennie, executive director of the CED.[83] Supported by the business moderates, Taft incorporated many of the Lay Committee's suggestions but balked at the most extreme statements, such as Pew's contention that any criticism, even "intelligent criticism" of capitalism could be equated to promoting communism. After a year of revision, the Lay Committee was still unhappy with the revised document, but Jasper Crane admitted that as a result of their objections and suggestions "it had been very considerably altered and toned down." The document carefully skirted the government's involvement in the economy, eliminated the earlier version's interpretation of organized labor as a "great movement of protest," and observed that "uncritical recourse to the state to remedy every evil creates its own evils."[84]

The Lay Committee's growing influence on the National Council alarmed the liberal community. As early as 1952, liberal theologian John C. Bennett warned of the danger of appeasing "powerful individuals who are known to be aggressively conservative on economic issues and who represent a spirit that is opposed to the prophetic tradition of the Federal Council." Bennett ominously predicted that if these men succeeded in controlling NCC policy it would be "a catastrophe for American Christianity." Reverend Emerson G. Hangen of the First Congregational Church of Long Beach agreed with Bennett and linked Pew's involvement in the Council to "part of the wave of reaction which has been afflicting laymen across the country." Labor leaders with an interest in the Church were also concerned. By late 1951, David Burgess of the Georgia Industrial Union Council and John Ramsay were worried that Pew's financial clout was buying him undue influence over the Council. Burgess advised Cameron Hall that he was "greatly alarmed by the trend toward the right in the organization which supposively [sic] will speak for the Protestant churches of America." A year later, it was clear to George Crago of the Chemical Workers that the National Council was "under the thumb of Big Business to a considerable extent."[85]

Suspicious from the start, Oxnam fought back against the "very dangerous" existence of an autonomous group within the Council's ranks. Supported by liberal clergy, he led several unsuccessful efforts to eliminate the Lay Committee, but was rebuffed by moderate clergy who decided that the Lay Committee represented "too great a present and potential resource to risk alienating."[86] Failing to rid the NCC of Pew's committee, Oxnam and the Council's liberal staff simply chose to ignore the General Board where the business influence was most apparent. The Lay Committee had blocked several "highly controversial" pronouncements, one on inflation and another placing the Church in opposition to the Bricker Amendment, which would have restricted the president's authority to make treaties. But, in both cases, liberals in National Council departments circulated and publicized their positions in other forms, much to the Lay Committee's dismay.[87] Later, in 1953, Oxnam, Episcopal Bishop Henry Knox Sherrill, and Charles Taft ignored General Board procedures giving the Lay Committee time to review pronouncements and issued a statement urging Congress to stop the House Committee on Un-American Activities' procedural abuses. In particular, the NCC protested the Committee's "vicious" practices and the "forcing of citizens, under pretext of investigation of subversive activities, to testify concerning their personal economic and political beliefs." Furious at these actions, Lay Committee supporter columnist David Lawrence blasted the National Council's lax attitude toward Communism and asked what gave the NCC the right to use "the dignity and spiritual power of the church" to meddle in politics.[88]

The following year was even worse for the Lay Committee. The Board failed to halt an increasingly large number of pronouncements that supported "Federal Government intervention in the work and life of the American people in ways not countenanced by the Constitution nor by the American principles of freedom." The NCC also began asking Congress to support federal aid to education and public housing. Lay Committee members began complaining of their impotence in Council affairs. According to Crane, "lay people are hardly being called upon for service except in financial and business matters." Pew became convinced that a "hard core of Socialists who really dominate the policy of the National Council" were out to "destroy" the Lay Committee.[89]

The Lay Committee attempted to wield its financial stick. Threatening mass resignation to enforce its view, it demanded that the NCC stick to spiritual issues and refrain altogether from speaking out on any controversial political, economic or sociological questions. A coalition of liberal clergy and moderate business leaders united in opposition to the threat. Even several Lay Committee members, including Noel Sargent and Edwin Lindsay, refused to follow Pew's lead. They endorsed Taft's argument that "what we laymen really want is not to muzzle our Churches so that they cannot speak on economic and political issues which often do involve moral and spiritual values," but rather we want to "try to have the Churches speak on the right side of issues." At the September 1954 General Board meeting, Oxnam warned that the Lay Committee's threat was "an attempt to silence the Church at the very moment when the Church ought to be vocal." In the end, the liberals rallied even the evangelically oriented clergy against limiting the National Council's freedom of action.[90]

Ever hopeful of the power of forgiveness, NCC officers initiated a flurry of meetings with the Lay Committee in a final futile effort to bring about a rapprochement. The two groups resolved nothing, and in June 1955 the committee quietly went out of existence. With little tolerance for rejection, Pew refused the Council's invitation to join another committee or department in the organization. He concluded that he had not only failed in redirecting the NCC but that even putting together the Lay Committee was the "most unfortunate decision of my life." Pew's close associate, Jasper Crane, however, dismissed his histrionics. Crane noted that "some bad practices have been stopped, some most undesirable pronouncements have not been made, and protest has been entered against some things which we have not been able to prevent." Undaunted, Pew turned his attention to combatting liberalism within his own church and increased his support to conservative groups like Spiritual Mobilization, the Christian Freedom Foundation, and the Foundation for Economic Education.[91]

While many Lay members followed Pew out of the National Council, others, including Robert E. Wilson, Charles E. Wilson, Harvey S. Firestone, and Charles Hook, decided to maintain a presence within its ranks. Chrysler executive B. E. Hutchinson, one of the most active of the Lay members, was unconvinced that the struggle was over. He stayed on the NCC's General Board to at least "'keep our seats warm.'" L. J. Fletcher, vice president of Caterpillar Tractor Company, asserted that "we who know the ideals and practices of American business, and have also spent our lives in the Church," must not "abandon this field to those who sincerely—or otherwise—would misbrand the actions and idealism of American business."[92]

In the years to come, the presence of these business conservatives as well as the continuing important role played by moderates would have an affect on how the NCC responded to issues of importance to business. With the disbandment of the Lay Committee in 1955, business leaders may have lost the battle, but in many respects they won the war. Despite the hopes of the clerical liberals, the end of the Lay Committee failed to immediately change the Council's cautious social policy. For the balance of the decade, it remained hesitant to become entangled in controversial issues. In 1960, it elected businessman J. Irwin Miller, who promised fewer pronouncements on "hot subjects" to its leadership.[93]

While the attention of many business leaders remained focused on the National Council, others were equally concerned with the implications of Catholic social action. In the late forties, like their Protestant counterparts, business conservatives began attacking the National Catholic Welfare Conference's Social Action Department, the equivalent of the Department of Church and Economic Life, for supporting organized labor. In 1953, they founded the Council of Business and Professional Men of the Catholic Faith, which became the "center of the ideological right in the Church." Although at a disadvantage because they opposed much of the Church's traditional social teaching, they found allies among some of the more conservative bishops. Although this movement has yet to be closely studied, historian Steve Rosswurm observes that these business leaders helped narrow "the ideological limits of Catholic social theory and practice in the 1950s."[94]

* * *

Admittedly, conservative business leaders failed to turn the churches into advocates of free enterprise ideology. But the broad impact of the business community—both its moderate and conservative wings—on religion during the years after World War II cannot be easily dismissed. Within Catholicism, business leaders played an important role in making the Catholic church's traditional commitment to organized labor a much more contentious issue. The business community's impact on Protestantism was perhaps even more significant. Business leaders could easily find tangible evidence of their achievement. By middle of the fifties, NAM Secretary Noel Sargent reported with satisfaction "a substantial change in the utterances and philosophy of church pronouncements" since the end of the war. He pointed as an example to the "distinct change in the entire philosophy of the economics statements" between the first and second meetings of the World Council of Churches. Where the 1948 Amsterdam meeting criticized the "prevailing (capitalist) economic system," the 1954 assembly in Evanston, Illinois refused to condemn capitalism, while praising private property and criticizing centralized government control of economic activities.[95]

Similarly, in sharp contrast to the mid-forties when the Federal Council "was passing bristling resolutions and going far out on hazardous limbs" in an effort to promote a more equitable distribution of the fruits of society, the 1956 Department of Church and Economic Life's study conference had little of the "old fire and flash of Christian economic debate." Emphasizing a consensus created by an economy of abundance, caution was the password as statements "even mildly critical of corporations or capital . . . were challenged with vigor." Although, the conference report did speak of the church's traditional concern for redressing issues like racial discrimination and economic injustice, business's moderating influence was apparent as even these issues were treated in a "careful, cautionary" manner.[96] All this suggests that in the years after World War II, aided by increasing affluence and a cold war atmosphere that made advocacy of collective solutions to social problems suspect, business leaders played an important role in helping to silence an important segment of the religious community and to prod the institutions of the church in more moderate directions.

## Notes

1. Two accounts provide a basic summary of the history of the Lay Committee. Henry J. Pratt, *The Liberalization of American Protestantism: A Case Study in Complex Organizations* (Detroit: Wayne State University Press, 1972), pp. 84–104, relies heavily on J. Howard Pew's *The Chairman's Final Report to the*

*National Lay Committee,* 1955. Eckard Vance Toy, Jr., "The National Lay Committee and the National Council of Churches: A Case Study of Protestants in Conflict," *American Quarterly* 21 (Summer 1969): 190–209, uses the papers of James W. Clise, a conservative West Coast businessman and member of the Lay Committee. Both accounts place the Lay Committee in the context of the ideological struggle within the Protestant church between evangelicalism and the Social Gospel; J. Howard Pew to H. P. Eells, Aug. 16, 1950, Box 168, J. Howard Pew Papers, HML.

2. John Ramsay to Mrs. Alex Kerchman, July 8, 1946, Box 1, John Ramsay Papers, OHS.

3. George M. Marsden, *Religion and American Culture* (San Diego: Harcourt Brace Jovanovich, 1990), pp. 106–30; Rolf Luden, *Business and Religion in the American 1920s* (New York: Greenwood Press, 1988), passim.

4. Luden, *Business and Religion,* pp. 181–83; Robert Moats Miller, *American Protestantism and Social Issues, 1919–1939* (Chapel Hill: University of North Carolina Press, 1958), pp. 66, 89; Paul A. Carter, *The Decline and Revival of the Social Gospel: Social and Political Liberalism in American Protestant Churches, 1920–1940* (Hamden, Conn.: Archon Books, 1971), p. 175.

5. William McGuire King, "The Reform Establishment and the Ambiguities of Influence," in *Between the Times: The Travail of the Protestant Establishment in America, 1900–1960,* ed. William R. Hutchinson (Cambridge: Cambridge University Press, 1989), pp. 123–27, esp. 126.

6. George W. Robnett to Charles P. Taft, Mar. 31, 1947, Box 88, Charles P. Taft Papers, LC; David Lawrence, "Mixing Religion and Politics," *United States News,* Mar. 28, 1947, pp. 26–27; "The Churches Speak to Business," *Fortune,* Dec. 1948, pp. 122–23.

7. Aaron I. Abell, *American Catholicism and Social Action: A Search for Social Justice, 1865–1950* (Garden City, N.Y.: Hanover House, 1960); Neil Betten, *Catholic Activism and the Industrial Worker* (Gainesville: University Press of Florida, 1976).

8. "Merchandising the Business Story to Opinion Moulders in Education and the Churches," 1945, Accession 1411, NAM, Series I, Box 270, (hereafter Acc. 1411, NAM I/270); "Influencing the 'Balance of Power' Groups through Opinion-Makers," July 1, 1946, Acc. 1411, NAM I/109; *Understanding: A Quarterly Devoted to Cooperation Between Clergymen and Business,* Sept. 1946, p. 1.

9. "Merchandising the Business Story to Opinion Moulders;" NAM, *Report and Recommendations to Industry of the N.A.M. Committee on Cooperation on Churches,* 1943, Acc. 1411, NAM I/246.

10. Folder entitled "Material and Information on Churchman's Businessman's Conference, Robert E. Lee Hotel, Jackson, Tuesday, Jan. 19, 1943," Acc. 1411, NAM I/246; *Report and Recommendations to Industry of the N.A.M. Committee on Cooperation on Churches,* NAM, Series I, Boxes, 163, 246, 270, and Series III, Box 843 contain transcripts of various Church and Industry Conferences.

11. List of "Expected Attendance, Organization Dinner, Philadelphia Businessmen's Committee on Cooperation with Churches, Nov. 27, 1944, Acc.

1411, NAM I/270; "Survey of Church and Industry Activity," c. 1952, Acc. 1411, NAM III/852.1.

12. Committee on Cooperation with Community Leaders of the National Association of Manufacturers, "Proceedings," transcripts, May 17, 1950, Chicago, Ill., Acc. 1411, NAM I/109.

13. Edwin McNeill Poteat to Samuel McCrea Cavert, Nov. 11, 1940, Box 18, RG18, NCC; J. J. Blackwelder to George T. Mascott, Nov. 30, 1944, "Brooklyn Church and Industry Conference Summation Session," transcripts of proceedings, Jan. 14, 1943, Brooklyn, New York, both in Acc. 1411, NAM I/246.

14. Noel Sargent and Chris Gilson to All Division and Regional Managers and Church and Industry Relations Directors, Mar. 19, 1954, Noel Sargent to Church and Industry Directors, Jan. 17, 1955, Warren J. Taussig to Ransom P. Rathbun, May 3, 31, 1955, Jan. 23, 1956; NAM Public Relations Division, "Review of NAM's Clergy-Industry Program and Suggestions for Strengthening the Association's Activities in This Area," June 1, 1956, all in Acc. 1411, NAM I/163.

15. William Eugene Carroll, "The Clergy in Our Plant Communities," *MRev* 41 (Mar. 1952): 145–47; *PRN*, Nov. 14, 1949, Jan. 23, 1950, Dec. 29, 1952, Jan. 3, 1955; "Eli Lilly," *Trends*, Dec. 1949, pp. 4–5.

16. For history of Spiritual Mobilization, see Eckard Vance Toy, "Ideology and Conflict in American Ultra Conservatism, 1945–1960" (Ph.D. diss, University of Oregon, 1965), esp. 157; Spiritual Mobilization Contributors List, enclosed in James W. Fifield to J. Howard Pew, May 18, 1948, J. Howard Pew to Ira Mosher, June 21, 1948, Box 19, Pew Papers; "Forming the Shape of Things to Come," Memorandum to Corporate Contributors from Spiritual Mobilization, June 15, 1956, Box 51, Pew Papers.

17. Robert McAffe Brown, "Is It 'Christian Economics'?" *Christianity and Crisis*, Nov. 27, 1950, pp. 155–58; Clipping entitled "Kiwanis Club Fetes Pastors," n.d., Box 30, Pew Papers; "Report on the Organization Meeting of the Christian Freedom Foundation," Apr. 17, 1950, Box 180, Pew Papers.

18. Eisenhower quoted in Robert Wuthnow, *The Restructuring of American Religion*, (Princeton: Princeton University Press, 1988), pp. 66–67; Samuel McCrea Cavert, *The American Churches in the Ecumenical Movement, 1900–1968* (New York: Association Press, 1968), pp. 189–90.

19. Advertising Council, *How Business Helps Solve Public Problems: A Report on the Eighth Year of the Advertising Council, March 1949–March 1950*, 1950; *10th Annual Report of the Advertising Council*, 1951–52, the Harry S. Truman Library Book Collection, HST; "Ad Council Gives Good Advice," *CC* 75 (Nov. 12, 1958): 1294–95.

20. On religion and business in the early twentieth century, see Ken Fones-Wolf, *Trade Union Gospel: Christianity and Labor in Industrial Philadelphia, 1865–1915* (Philadelphia: Temple University Press, 1989); Duncan Norton-Taylor, "Businessmen on Their Knees," *Fortune*, Oct. 1953, p. 254; "Plant Religious Program," *Trends*, Sept. 1950, pp. 4–5; Clarence Woodbury, "Religion in Industry: 'Not Only to Make a Living'. . . but a Life," *NB*, June 1954, p. 30.

21. John C. Harmon, "Industrial People Explore New Pathways to God,"

Nov. 23, 1954, Acc. 1411, NAM III/852.1; "Religion in Industry," *FMM* 110 (Jan. 1952): 127.

22. Woodbury, "Religion in Industry," pp. 30–31, 74–75; Rev. Edgar M. Wahlberg, "The Industrial Chaplaincy," Feb. 1, 1954, Box 1, Edward Coffey Files, UAW Education Department Records, ALUA.

23. Norton-Taylor, "Businessmen on Their Knees," pp. 140–41.

24. Clair M. Cook, "The Industrial Chaplains," *CC*, Aug. 31, 1955, p. 993; "Employee Profanity Cut by In-Plant Worship," *AB*, Feb. 1952, p. 57; Woodbury, "Religion in Industry," p. 74.

25. John G. Ramsay to David J. McDonald, May 26, 1953, Box 132, David McDonald Papers, HCLA.

26. Among the literature on labor and Catholicism, see Michael Harrington, "Catholics in the Labor Movement: A Case History," *Labor History* 1 (Fall 1960): 231–63; Piehl, *Breaking Bread;* Ronald W. Schatz, "American Labor and the Catholic Church, 1919–1950," *International Labor and Working-Class History* 20 (Fall 1981): 46–53.

27. Mildred Jeffrey to Leonard Woodcock, attached memo on church and unions, Apr. 6, 1956, Box 35, Mildred Jeffrey Papers, ALUA; John G. Ramsay to George E. Sweazey, Feb. 13, 1948, Box 1566; Untitled Report by James A. Crain, Executive Secretary, Department of Social Welfare, The United Christian Missionary Society, c. 1946, Box 1561, John G. Ramsay Papers, SLA.

28. *CIO News*, Oct. 27, 1947.

29. "Labor Executives Speak on 'What Religion Means to Me,'" *Economic Justice*, Jan. 1948, pp. 4, 6.

30. Brian Abrams, "John Ramsay and the Evolution of Church Labor Relations in the CIO" (M.A. thesis, Georgia State University, 1985), pp. 28–29. Abrams' fine thesis focuses on the CIO's efforts to woo Southern clergy during Operation Dixie.

31. John G. Ramsay to Cornelius A. Wood, May 12, 1947, Box 1561, Ramsay Papers; John G. Ramsay, "The Reconciliation of Religion and Labor," in *Labor's Relation to Church and Community*, ed. Liston Pope (reprint; Freeport, N.Y.: Books for Libraries Press, 1972), pp. 107–11, esp. 109; John Ramsay, Oral History Transcript, p. 13, HCLA.

32. "From C.E. to Organized Labor: The Story of John G. Ramsay," *Christian Endeavor World*, July 1945, p. 5; John A. Salmond, *Miss Lucy of the CIO: The Life and Times of Lucy Randolph Mason, 1882–1959* (Athens: University of Georgia Press, 1988); David Burgess to John Ramsay, Feb. 11, 1947, Box 1579, Ramsay Papers.

33. Among Ramsay's many articles in religious press, see John G. Ramsay, "How Can the Church Win the Laboring Man," *Michigan Christian Advocate*, Feb. 28, 1946, pp. 16–17; John Ramsay, "The Methodist Church and Labor Unions," *Christian Advocate*, Sept. 3, 1953, pp. 6–7, 29.

34. On Ramsay's early efforts to establish fellowships, see correspondence in Box 1558 such as John G. Ramsay to Vin Sweeney, Oct. 23, 1944, Mar. 19, Apr. 11, 1945, John Ramsay to Reverend Celestin J. Steiner, Oct. 30, 1944, Box 1, John G. Ramsay Papers, OHS; *Steel Labor* (Southern Edition), Feb. 1950.

35. On religion and Operation Dixie, see Abrams, "John Ramsay and the Evolution of Church Labor Relations"; Barbara Griffith, *The Crisis of American Labor: Operation Dixie and the Defeat of the CIO* (Philadelphia: Temple University Press, 1988), pp. 106–22; David S. Burgess, "The Captured Churches of Milltown," *Economic Justice*, Sept. 1953, p. 3; Script of Textile Workers Union of America, CIO Organizing Committee, Station WDOD, Chattanooga, Tennessee, Oct. 30, 1950, Box 1560, Ramsay Papers.

36. Script of Textile Workers Union of America, CIO Organizing Committee, Station WHIN, Gallatin, Tennessee, Oct. 2, 1949, Box 1568, Ramsay Papers; "The Bible and the Workingman," n.d. c. 1946, Box 163, Michigan AFL-CIO Records, ALUA.

37. Abrams, "John Ramsay and the Evolution of Church Labor Relations in the CIO," pp. 95–109; *Steel Labor* (Southern Edition), Feb. 1950; Griffith, *The Crisis of American Labor*, p. 118.

38. Walter Reuther to August Scholle, Apr. 3, June 4, 1953, Box 54, Michigan AFL-CIO Records, "Report of the Continuations Committee," adopted at a Meeting of The Religion-Labor Conference, June 11, 1953, Box 5, Coffey Files.

39. Executive Board, United Gas, Coke and Chemical Workers, United CIO Convention Proposal, typescript, Oct. 23, 1953, Box 1556; George A. Crago to John G. Ramsay, Feb. 25, 1953, Box 1577, Ramsay Papers.

40. "Resolution," enclosed in George De Nucci, acting secretary-treasurer, Ohio CIO Council to Philip Murray, Nov. 16, 1944, Box 1, John Ramsay Papers, OHS; "Minutes of Meeting," CIO Standing Committee on Religion and Labor, Mar. 4, 1955, Box 1556, Ramsay Papers; John G. Ramsay to James B. Carey, Sept. 29, 1954, Box 1909, Ramsay Papers; Charles C. Webber to George Meany and William F. Schnitzler, Dec. 1956, Mar. 2–Apr. 3, 1959, Box 38, George Meany Papers, GMA.

41. Miller, *American Protestantism and Social Issues, 1919–1939*, pp. 247–48; Clair M. Cook, "Religion and Labor Working Together," *AFL-CIO American Federationist*, Aug. 1959, p. 9; Willard Uphaus to David J. McDonald, Apr. 4, 1949, Box 100, David McDonald Papers, HCLA; Witherspoon Dodge to Victor Reuther, July 31, 1954, Box 49, CIO Washington Office Files, CIO Records, ALUA; "Board to Expand Program," *Economic Justice*, May 1955, p. 1.

42. Jasper Crane to Warren J. Taussig, Sept 6, 1950, Crane Papers.

43. Robert A. Schneider, "Voice of Many Waters: Church Federation in the Twentieth Century," in *Between the Times*, ed. Hutchinson, pp. 104–12; Pratt, *The Liberalization of American Protestantism*, pp. 48–49.

44. Robert Wuthnow, *The Restructuring of American Religion*, pp. 173–79; Schneider, "Voice of Many Waters," pp. 111–12.

45. American Council of Christian Laymen, *How Red Is the Federal Council of Churches* (pamphlet), 1949, Box 1592, Ramsay Papers, Verne P. Kalb (American Council of Christian Laymen), *The Federal Council of Churches Takes Its Stand With Enemies of America* (pamphlet), c. 1940, Pamphlet Collection, SHSW.

46. Schneider, "Voice of Many Waters," p. 110; Pratt, *The Liberalization of*

*American Protestantism*, pp. 24–30; Charles P. Taft to R. C. Robbins, Apr. 25, 1947, Box 88, Taft Papers.

47. William McGuire King, "The Reform Establishment and the Ambiguities of Influence," in *Between the Times*, ed. Hutchinson, pp. 123–25.

48. "Politics for Protestantism," *Time*, Dec. 16, 1946, p. 61; J. P. Seiberling to Charles P. Taft, Jan. 3, 1947, Box 85, Taft Papers.

49. Charles P. Taft to Cameron P. Hall, Apr. 2, 1947, Box 85, Charles P. Taft to Samuel M. Cavert, Mar. 2, 1948, Box 89, Taft Papers.

50. Department of Research and Education of the Federal Council of Churches of Christ in America, "Christianity and the Economic Order, Study No. 5, Freedom and Social Control in the Economic Order," *Information Service*, Dec. 21, 1946, pp. 7–8.

51. Department of Research and Education of the Federal Council of Churches of Christ in America, "Christianity and the Economic Order, Study No. 1, The Economic Situation and the Christian Conscience," *Information Service*, Feb. 23, 1946, "Christianity and the Economic Order, Study No. 2, Labor-Management Relations," June 29, 1946.

52. David Lawrence, "Sniping at Profit-and-Loss System," *United States News*, Dec. 27, 1946, pp. 24–25; Jasper E. Crane to Fred G. Clark, Dec. 10, 1946, Box 1, Crane Papers.

53. "Protestants and the Profit System," *Newsweek*, p. 72.

54. Warren J. Taussig to Jasper Crane, Feb. 26, 1947, Box 89, Crane Papers, Warren J. Taussig to Holcombe Parkes, Feb. 27, 1949; Charles P. Taft to Charles E. Wilson, Jan. 21, 1947, Box 85, Taft Papers.

55. Noel Sargent to Mr. Weisenburger, Feb. 25, 1947, Box 31, Crane Papers; *CIO News*, Mar. 3, 1947; *NAM News*, Mar. 1, 1947; Francis W. McPeek, "The Church and Economic Life: Pittsburgh Conference Impressions," *Social Action*, June 15, 1947, pp. 4–25.

56. Howard M. Mills, "The Department of Church and Economic Life of the National Council of Churches, 1947–1966: A Critical Analysis" (Th.D. diss., Union Theological Seminary, 1970), pp. 134–39; Taussig to Parks, Feb. 27, 1947, Noel Sargent to Weisenburger, Feb. 25, 1947, Alfred P. Haake to Jasper E. Crane, Mar. 3, 1947, Box 31, Crane Papers; "Churches Study Our Economy," *CC*, Mar. 5, 1947, pp. 293–94.

57. "Minutes," Industrial Relations Division, Federal Council of Churches of Christ in America, Apr. 26, 1946, Box 1582, Ramsay Papers; Jasper E. Crane to Dr. Stanley High, Oct. 13, 1949, Box 31, Crane Papers.

58. Paul G. Hoffman to Charles P. Taft, May 29, 1947, Charles P. Taft to Frank W. Pierce, May 27, 1947, Box 85, Taft Papers.

59. Charles P. Taft to Dr. Cameron P. Hall, Apr. 2, 1947, Cameron Hall to Charles P. Taft, Apr. 21, 1947, Charles P. Taft to Frank W. Pierce, May 27, 1947, Box 85, Taft Papers; Samuel McCrea Cavert, *Church Cooperation and Unity in America: A Historical Review* (New York: Association Press, 1970), pp. 133.

60. Cavert, *Church Cooperation and Unity*, pp. 133–34; Charles P. Taft to C. M. Chester, June 15, 1948, Box 89, Charles P. Taft to Cameron Hall, Mar. 13, 1950, Box 86, Charles P. Taft to John A Stephens, Mar. 19, 1951, Box 99, Taft Papers.

61. Cameron P. Hall to department member and enclosure titled "Possible Subjects for Policy or Other Statements by the Department," Dec. 31, 1948, Box 85; Charles P. Taft to Cameron P. Hall, Nov. 7, 1950, Box 86, Taft Papers; Charles P. Taft to Samuel M. Cavert, May 17, 1947, Box 18, RG 18, FCC.

62. Warren J. Taussig to Jasper E. Crane, Sept. 24, Oct. 25, 1946, Mar. 26, 1947, Box 58, Crane Papers; H. P. Eells to William J. Grede, May 9, July 24, 1950, Box 6, William G. Grede Papers, SHSW; Robert Wilson to H. P. Eells, Jr., May 19, 1950, Noel Sargent to H. P. Eells, May 19, 1950, Box 23, Grede Papers; Robert Wilson, "Business's Duty to the Church," *Trends*, Sept. 1950, p. 8.

63. G. Bromley Oxnam Diaries, Feb. 16, 1950, G. Bromley Oxnam Papers, LC; Charles P. Taft to Rev. James R. Smith, May 31, 1950, Box 86, Taft Papers, Howard M. Mills, "The Department of the Church and Economic Life," pp. 151–56; H. P. Eells to Wm. J. Grede, July 24, 1950, Box 6, Grede Papers.

64. Thomas M. Bloch to H. P. Eells, May 19, 1950, John L. Lovett to Arthur S. Fleming, Feb. 21, 1950, Cola G. Parker to H. P. Eells, n.d., Box 23, Grede Papers; J. Howard Pew to H. P. Eells, May 24, 1950, Box 168, Pew Papers.

65. Pratt, *The Liberalization of American Protestantism*, pp. 30–41, 84–88; William M. King, "The Reform Establishment," p. 137; "Suggested Plans for Financial Undergirding in Proposed National Council of Churches," Jan. 13, 1950 and additional correspondence and reports in Box 3, RG 1, NCC.

66. The planners first attempted to recruit John D. Rockefeller, Jr., Thomas J. Watson, and Cleveland E. Dodge. "Memorandum Concerning Plans for the Lay Advisory Committee," c. June 27, 1950, Box 3, RG 1, "Suggested Plans for Financial Undergirding in Proposed National Council of Churches," Samuel McCrea Cavert to Bishop William G. Martin, Jan. 2, 1953, Box 3, RG 4, NCC.

67. J. Howard Pew to A. A. Zoll, Dec. 21, 1949, Box 15, J. Howard Pew to H. P. Eells, Aug. 16, 1950, Box 168, J. Howard Pew to Allan M. Frew, Dec. 31, 1948, Box 16, Pew Papers; "What Laity Are to Be Represented," *CC*, Dec. 13, 1950, pp. 1475–76; Pratt, *The Liberalization of American Protestantism*, pp. 85–86, Cavert to Martin, Jan. 2, 1953.

68. J. Howard Pew to Harold E. Stassen, July 7, 1950, J. Howard Pew to Lois Black Hunter, July 8, 1950, Lois Hunter to J. Howard Pew, July 18, 29, Sept. 20, 1950; Box 162, Pew Papers; "Summary of Convictions Expressed by Mr. Pew Regarding Basic Relationships of Economics and Religion," enclosed in Roy G. Ross to Luther A. Weigle, et al., Aug. 28, 1950, Box 3, RG 1, NCC.

69. J. Howard Pew to Donald J. Cowling, Oct. 2, 1950, J. Howard Pew to John L. Lovett, Oct. 20, 1950, Box 168; James W. Fifield to B. E. Hutchinson, Oct. 26, 1950, Box 162; J. Howard Pew to Jacob France, Nov 9, 1951, Box 152; J. Howard Pew to L. E. Faulkner, June 30, 1952, Box 148;, Verne P. Kaub to J. Howard Pew, Mar. 5, 1951, Box 30, Pew Papers.

70. "Acceptances, Lay Committee of the New National Council of the Churches of Christ, as of October 23, 1950," Box 59, Crane Papers; Jasper E. Crane to Wesley F. Rennie, Sept. 28, 1953, Box 146, Pew Papers.

71. Lois B. Hunter to J. Howard Pew, Sept. 29, 1952, Box 168, Pew Papers.

72. "What Laity Are to Be Represented?" CC, Dec. 13, 1950, pp. 1475–76; Frank E. Holman to J. Howard Pew, Dec. 1, 1950; Luther Wesley Smith to Samuel McCrea Cavert and Roy G. Ross, Dec. 27, 1950, Box 4, RG 5, NCC.

73. Oxnam Diaries, Dec. 2, 1950, Jan. 3, 1951; Frank E. Holman to J. Howard Pew, Dec. 1, 1950, Jasper E. Crane to Frank E. Holman, Dec. 14, 1950, Box 59, Crane Papers; Pratt, *The Liberalization of American Protestantism*, p. 89.

74. Oxnam Diaries, Jan. 3, Sept. 19, Dec. 26, 1951, Jan. 25, 1952; Samuel McCrea Cavert to Dr. Emerson G. Hangen, June 10, 1952, RG 4, Box 3; Roy G. Ross to Fred Goodsell, June 5, 1952, Box 18, RG 5, NCC.

75. Jasper Crane to Herbert C. Cornuelle, Apr. 12, 1951; Jasper E. Crane to Wesley Rennie, Sept. 28, 1953, Box 146, Pew Papers.

76. Jasper E. Crane to Henry R. Luce, Aug. 23, 1951, Box 59, Crane Papers; "Review of Fund Raising Operations in 1951 and Recommendations for a Future Program," Presented to the Executive Committee of the Committee on Business and Finance, Jan. 24, 1952, Box 161; J. Howard Pew to Robert E. Wilson, Nov. 13, 1951, Box 152; J. Howard Pew to Donaldson Brown, Aug. 6, 1951, Box 152; J. Howard Pew to B. E. Hutchinson, Sept. 13, 1951, Box 168, Pew Papers.

77. Oxnam Diaries, Mar. 10, 1954; Charles R. Hook to Rev. Henry Knox Sherrill, Feb. 25, 1955, Box 165, Pew Papers; Charles R. Hook to Roswell P. Barnes, Jan. 15, 1954, Box 7, RG 4, NCC.

78. Wuthnow, *The Restructuring of American Religion*, p. 143.

79. J. Howard Pew to Members of the National Lay Committee of the National Council of Churches, Apr. 10, 1953, Box 3, RG 4, NCC; J. Howard Pew to L. E. Faulkner, June 30, 1952; J. Howard Pew to Charter Members of the National Laymen's Committee, June 24, 1952, Box 59, Crane Papers; Mills, "The Department of Church and Economic Life," pp. 86–90.

80. "Just Who Can Say What," CC, Jan. 23, 1952, p. 92; J. Howard Pew to Dr. Derwood Fleming, July 21, 1952, Box 148, J. Howard Pew to Bishop William C. Martin, June 26, 1953, Box 147, Pew Papers.

81. J. Howard Pew to Henry K. Sherrill, Oct. 6, 1952, Box 3, RG 4, NCC; A. Dudley Ward to Charles P. Taft, Nov. 13, 1952, Box 102, Taft Papers; Department of Church and Economic Life, Division of Christian Life and Work, National Council of Churches of Christ in the U.S.A., Meeting of the General Committee, Minutes, Oct. 19–20, 1951, Box 39, RG 6, NCC; "National Council Problems," CC, Jan. 2, 1952, p. 8.

82. Samuel McCrea Cavert to Cameron P. Hall, Mar. 20, 1953, Box 2, RG 4; Jasper E. Crane to J. Howard Pew, July 1, 1954, Box 60, Crane Papers; Committee on Policy and Strategy, Minutes, Aug. 1954, Box 8, RG 4, NCC; Oxnam Diaries, June 18, 1954.

83. Mills, "The Department of Church and Economic Life," pp. 222–64; Hutchinson, *The Liberalization of American Protestantism*, pp. 93–94; Roy G. Ross to Edwin B. Lindsay, Sept. 9, 1954, Box 7, RG 4, NCC; Pew to Bishop W. C. Martin, Apr. 14, 1953, Box 147. See Box 7, RG 4, NCC, Box 98, Taft Papers, Box 59, Crane Papers and Box 146, Pew Papers for correspondence dealing with revision of the statement.

84. "Remarks of Charles P. Taft at the General Board, National Council of Churches," Jan. 20, 1954, Box 60; Charles P. Taft to L. B. Odell, June 1, 1954, Box 99; Jasper E. Crane to Paul E. Wise, Aug. 29, 1955, Box 107; William Adams Brown to Charles P. Taft, Jan. 15, 1954, Box 98, Taft Papers; Mills, "The Department of Church and Economic Life," pp. 265–93; "Christianity and Economic Life," *Social Action: A Magazine of Christian Concern,* Jan. 1955, pp. 6–15.

85. John C. Bennett, "Whither the National Council," *Christianity and Crisis,* Jan. 7, 1952, pp. 177–78; Emerson G. Hangen to Executive Committee, National Council of Churches, June 5, 1952, RG 4, Box 3, NCC; David Burgess to Cameron Hall, Oct. 10, 1951, Box 41, RG 6, NCC; George A. Crago to John Ramsay, Feb. 25, 1953, Box 1577, Ramsay Papers.

86. See Oxnam diaries for his continuing concern about the Lay Committee and his efforts to undercut its influence; J. Howard Pew to B. E. Hutchinson, Oct. 27, 1953, Dr. H. N. Morse to Dr. Roy G. Ross, Mar. 15, 1954, Box 60, Crane Papers.

87. Pew to Samuel McCrea Cavert, Jan. 29, 1953, Box 4, RG 4, NCC; "Laymen and Clergy at Odds on Role of Church in Politics," *U.S. News & World Report,* Feb. 3, 1956, p. 44; J. Howard Pew, *The Chairman's Final Report to the Members of the National Lay Committee of the National Council of Churches of Christ in the USA,* Dec. 15, 1955, pp. 33–35, Presbyterian Historical Society.

88. *NYT,* Mar. 12, 1953; David Lawrence, "Keep the Churches Out of Politics," *U.S. News & World Report,* Apr. 2, 1954, p. 132.

89. Jasper E. Crane to Bishop William C. Martin, May 14, 1954, Box 60; Jasper E. Crane to Dr. Eugene C. Blake, Oct. 18, 1954, Jasper E. Crane to Bishop G. Bromley Oxnam, Oct. 8, 1953, J. Howard Pew to B. E. Hutchinson, Oct. 27, 1953, Box 60, Crane Papers.

90. "National Lay Committee Report," May 9, 1954, Jasper E. Crane to Bishop William C. Martin, May 14, 1954, B. E. Hutchinson to Jasper E. Crane, July 13, 1954, Box 60, Crane Papers; Edwin B. Lindsay to J. Howard Pew, June 9, 29, 1954, Box 104, Taft Papers; Charles P. Taft to J. Howard Pew, July 2, 1954, Box 61, Crane Papers; Oxnam Diaries, Sept. 14, 1954, Jan. 5, 1955.

91. "Meeting of National Council Officers with Subcommittee of the National Lay Committee," transcript, Oct. 29, 1954, Box 165, Pew Papers; Eugene Carson Blake to J. Howard Pew, Jan. 19, 1955, Box 9, RG 3, NCC; J. Howard Pew to Jasper E. Crane, June 10, 1955, Box 165, Pew Papers; Jasper E. Crane to J. Howard Pew, July 14, 1954, Box 60, Crane Papers; Toy, "The National Lay Committee," p. 203.

92. B. E. Hutchinson to J. Howard Pew, May 24, 1955, Box 41, Charles R. Hook to H. Howard Pew, Aug. 4, 1954, Box 61, Crane Papers; L. J. Fletcher to J. Howard Pew, Mar. 29, 1955, Robert E. Wilson to J. Howard Pew, Feb. 17, 1955, Box 165, Pew Papers.

93. Businessmen like Charles E. Wilson, Robert E. Wilson, Charles R. Hook, B. E. Hutchinson, and even Charles P. Taft continued to put pressure on the Council to limit the number of statements on controversial issues. See, for instance, Charles E. Wilson to Roy Ross, Sept. 25, 1956, Box 13, RG 11, Roy

Ross to Charles E. Wilson, Oct. 3, 1956; Charles R. Hook to Dr. Eugene Carson Blake, Feb. 14, 1955, Box 165, Pew Papers; Pratt, *The Liberalization of American Protestantism*, pp. 103–4.

94. Steven Rosswurm, "A Betrayal of Isaiah's Promise: Labor Priests, Labor Schools, the ACTU and the Expelled Unions," paper presented to Chicago Area Labor History Group, Newberry Library, Sept. 15, 1989.

95. Businessman Frank W. Pierce argued that "lay participation is making the Protestant denominations and the National Council more acceptable to the average American. The change in attitude toward private enterprise and the profit motive is the result of more lay people in contact with church leaders." Frank W. Pierce to Louis Hunter, Sept. 17, 1954, Box 61, Crane Papers; Noel Sargent to Dr. William Harllee Bordeaux, Jan 18, 1955, Acc. 1411, NAM I/163; Noel Sargent to H. C. McClellan, Aug. 28, 1954, Acc. 1411, NAM I/164.

96. "No Smoke in Pittsburgh," *CC*, May 2, 1956, pp. 541–43.

**PART 5** | **After the Merger**

# 9 | A Matter of Individual Rights

By 1956, despite a decade of campaigns designed to capture the hearts and minds of workers and their communities, despite the expenditure of millions of dollars on "economic education" and other public relations, despite a veritable flood of words and images extolling the benefits of American capitalism, some business leaders, particularly from the most conservative wing of the business community, remained uncertain of the loyalty of the workers. To be sure, a Republican sat in the White House, and the nation's political atmosphere seemed more conservative. Moreover, the passage of Taft-Hartley and the defeat of Operation Dixie had helped stem the labor movement's growth. But, union membership remained high and some employers still feared that the public had yet to view industry as "the symbol of progress and hope for the majority of people."[1]

What particularly raised new concerns among these business conservatives was the merger of the AFL and the CIO. Many saw in the merger the specter of a labor juggernaut. In January 1956, Kenneth R. Miller of the NAM proclaimed that "one of the gravest threats to management's right to manage is the vastly increased size and power of organized labor." Unions, he continued, "possess a private power of unprecedented scope and influence. The potentials of this power are in themselves crucial and confront industry as well as the country, with problems of far reaching significance."[2] It was against this background that conservative business leaders launched yet another major campaign to capture public opinion and redraw the laws governing labor relations at both the state and federal levels. This campaign, and labor's response, marked the decade's final effort by both sides to shape the nation's understanding of the postwar social order. As such it reveals both the character and limits of America's postwar consensus.

\* \* \*

There were opposing interpretations of the AFL and CIO merger's long-term implications. In December 1955 as the two organizations officially united, *The Iron Age* observed that "labor unity opens a chapter in the American labor movement which will frighten some industrialists and encourage others." More moderate business leaders, who believed that unions had a legitimate and important role in society, predicted the merger would result in more responsible unionism, in a decline in jurisdictional strikes, and in better informed and more creative collective bargaining. They felt that George Meany, the new head of the AFL-CIO, was much more conservative than the CIO's Walter Reuther. Meany, they hoped, would use methods "other than strike and bombast to make gains for labor." All this would promote the moderates' primary industrial relations goal—stabilizing labor-management affairs.[3]

While business moderates applauded the merger of the AFL-CIO as a step toward "responsible unionism," a much larger group of business conservatives viewed the merger as a threat demanding renewed mobilization by the business community. Labor unity, they felt, meant increased union strength and militancy. No longer could employers play the AFL against the CIO. Conservatives foresaw a major organizing drive, the emergence of labor as the most powerful political force in the country, and greater leverage in collective bargaining. Employers' ever present fear of union power over the economy and politics was seemingly on the verge of becoming reality. In December 1955, NAM Chairman Charles Sligh wondered if the AFL-CIO might not "become a ghost government, in which a handful of people not elected, not authorized by the American people would pull strings behind the scenes to direct the destinies of the nation."[4]

Much of the popular press reinforced this interpretation, emphasizing the danger to the public posed by "big labor." *U.S. News & World Report,* for instance, predicted that the repercussions of a more powerful and richer labor movement would reverberate in a negative way throughout society. Housewives would feel the effects in increased living costs. Taxpayers would "get the impact as the increasing political power of organized labor is translated into Government policies and tax rates." Finally, the nation's youth, would experience greater economic uncertainty as their work "more and more" conformed to restrictive "union rules and practices."[5]

As the nation debated the implications of the merger, the conservative wing of the business community took action. The NAM embarked upon a public relations campaign to expose "the abuses and evils of organized labor" with the ultimate goal of arousing the public to demand legislation to curb labor. Employers wanted to weaken labor through state "right to work" laws designed to destroy the union shop, and a national labor act that toughened Taft-Hartley on the issue of union monopoly. The NAM's program focused on publicizing five areas of "abusive" labor practices—compulsory union membership; coercion of employees and employers through violence, racketeering, and other "illegal, unethical, and undemocratic activities"; "monopolistic dictation" of labor relations through pattern bargaining, and restrictive practices; and the "misuse" of union organizations and funds for political purposes. In outlining its new program, the NAM observed that only an aroused public opinion could assure protection against the continuation and expansion of these "evils." A public sympathetic to management would help strengthen politicians' resistance to labor coercion, assist management in dealing with "giant unions," and "oppose illegal and immoral political action of any labor group or leader."[6]

"Semantics" were an important part of the business community's new public relations campaign. Despite the publicity associated with the merger, the NAM believed that the public still tended to view labor as "the underdog." Employers thus needed to tread carefully for fear of inadvertently arousing sympathy for their opponents. To address this difficulty, the NAM clothed its assault on unions in a disclaimer that it was not antiunion and did not seek to destroy organized labor. Instead, the NAM claimed that employers simply sought to protect the values associated with the "American Way of Life."[7]

Indeed, the business community's attack on labor consciously drew upon traditional themes embedded in American political culture, such as the danger of monopoly and the concept of individual rights. This was not a new strategy. From the origins of the labor movement, employers had attacked unions as monopolies. In fact, that had been the core of the NAM's first open shop drive during the early twentieth century. So again, the NAM emphasized that unions had become a "labor monopoly" that evinced no concern for the public interest. It charged that the vast "uncontrolled" economic and political power of labor, which made unions capable of "paralyzing a single plant, an entire industry, or the country as a whole," was evidence of this monopoly.[8] "Today," declared NAM President Ernest G. Swigert in 1957, "the greatest concentrations of political and economic power in the United States of America are found not in the over-regulated, over-criticized, over-investigated, and over-taxed business corporation." Nor were they present in "their hag-ridden, brow-beaten, publicity-fearful managers." Instead, monopoly power was to be "found in the under-regulated, under-criticized, under-investigated, tax-exempt and specially privileged labor organizations," and in "their belligerent, aggressive, and far-too-often lawless and corrupt managers."[9]

Second, employers characterized their drive against labor as a crusade to protect the freedom and the rights of the individual, which they characterized as the "bulwark and foundation of the whole American system." According to business leaders, unions invariably ignored individuals. Experience had shown, claimed the NAM, "that as a labor organization and its officials increase in size and power, the freedom of individuals is correspondingly diminished." Employers thus argued that their main concern was protecting the rank and file against exploitation by union leaders, an emphasis that flowed naturally from employers' use of personalized human relations in the factory.[10]

In its campaign to create an antilabor atmosphere, business leaders sought to activate the community leaders they had been targeting for almost a decade. NAM departments drafted new literature on "the existing evils and potential threat of Big Labor," and sent it to employers, to leaders of women's organizations, farmers and farm groups, educators, politicians, and opinion leaders. One such flyer entitled "Monopoly Is Always Wrong!" showed two tiny workers and an even smaller employer facing a giant AFL-CIO. It observed that laws prevented business monopoly but exempted unions. This double standard was "directly contrary to the concept of equal justice under the law." Monopolies enabled a company or union to impose its will on the public and the flyer concluded: "We, as a nation, must be consistent. Every instance of monopoly, *whatever its source,* must be stopped in its undemocratic tracks!" The NAM also provided pattern speeches for employers to use at meetings and on radio or television and supplied material to news and broadcast journalists to ensure that the general public was "properly informed, alerted and active against the real and potential threat to the national welfare."[11]

The NAM believed that one of the best ways to alarm the public about the "abuses of monopoly power by labor unions" was to throw the "cold light" of publicity on actual cases. It searched the press for material and also called upon employers to help provide a steady flow of reliable "human interest stories." By 1955, the Employers' Association of Chicago was already collecting "documented" case histories and publishing them in a series of folders headed "MR AND MRS CITI-

ZEN: IS THIS AMERICA?" for distribution to employees and opinion leaders. "The Heroic Story of Mrs. Esther Quigley" told of one family's experience in a strike called by "a handful of union biggies" to force "the company to knuckle." Mrs. Quigley, determined not to let "a handful of local union bosses lead 450 people around by the nose," organized a successful back-to-work movement. She reported that the experience taught her that "we working people have a job to do in ridding ourselves of bad union bosses" and getting "real responsible leaders."[12]

Into 1956, the NAM worried that there was not yet enough public understanding of the implications of union "monopolistic abuses" to successfully implement a drive for national legislation.[13] But, the business community did feel that it had enough support to proceed at the state level on the issue of "compulsory unionism." Indeed, employers had enough confidence in the tenuousness of labor's hold on public opinion that they targeted union strongholds. Hence, the mid-1950s witnessed an aggressive business campaign to spread "right-to-work" legislation in heretofore union states.

\* \* \*

Right-to-work laws prohibited contract provisions compelling union membership. Although the first two right-to-work laws were passed in 1944, it was really Section 14b of the Taft-Hartley Act that ceded to states jurisdiction over union security restrictions. Thus, as antiunion sentiment was on the upswing, states could prohibit the closed shop, the union shop, and maintenance of membership agreements. By 1947, fourteen states, mostly in the South and West, passed right-to-work laws. Between 1948 and 1954, six more states followed, but state labor movements helped repeal several of these statutes, including ones passed in the northern states of Delaware and New Hampshire. Unions opposed right-to-work because they believed that these laws were designed primarily to weaken the labor movement. Trade unionists argued that union security provisions provided a "sound basis for a collective-bargaining relationship that benefits both workers and employers." Moreover, they asserted, nonclosed shop relations bred suspicion and created constant conflict between the union and the employer and union members and nonunionists. Such conditions made it difficult for organized labor to grow and prosper.[14]

Before 1954, most of the activity surrounding right-to-work took place at the local level in states with weak labor movements; there was little national debate over the issue. However, interest increased in 1954 as local employer organizations helped enact legislation in three states. In 1955, impressed with their success but fearing a labor counterattack, the NAM, the Chamber of Commerce, and the newly formed National Right to Work Committee began coordinated national educational campaigns to assist local employers in promoting or defending right-to-work. In 1956, when Louisiana and Washington unionists succeeded in "repealing and repelling union security provisions," these national organizations redoubled their efforts.[15]

Conservative national business organizations sought to shape the debate over right-to-work. Business leaders asserted that their primary concern was protecting the public interest and the moral right of the individual to choose. It was "an American tradition" asserted a Chamber of Commerce spokesman, "that no person should be forced to support opinions and policies with which he disagrees." In 1957, NAM Vice President Charles R. Sligh put it even more bluntly: "compulsory unionism is a blight on the spirit of American justice; a skeleton in freedom's closet."[16] Not only did union security clauses attack individual rights; but also "compulsory unionism" directly contributed to the concentration of undemocratic power in the hands of union officials. Labor's "bigness" increased the chance of corruption since the membership was a captive audience. The NAM believed that emphasizing corruption and the union boss's "domination over the individual member," would turn the American public against labor.[17]

While the National Association of Manufacturers, the Chamber of Commerce, and the National Right to Work Committee did not directly participate in state legislative battles, they provided financial support, advice, and educational materials to the companies and state affiliates involved in campaigns. As a way of providing more generalized assistance, the NAM encouraged national organizations like the Bar Association, the American Legion, and the Daughters of the American Revolution to take a public stand on right-to-work. It also attempted to interest national magazines and newspaper chains in exploring the impact of the issue. Regional offices of the NAM encouraged company communications to employees and the association sent right-to-work kits to schools throughout the country.[18]

Seeking support for their attacks on union security, employers focused especially on the religious community. The clergy had assumed a particularly prominent role in the debate over right-to-work. The 1954 struggles on the issue touched off a discussion that continued for some years thereafter in the religious press. Numerous religious leaders from all three major faiths came out against the statutes, fewer in support. Stung by their stand, the NAM cited the "recent interest taken by the clergy" as an important reason for national business organizations to give "full-scale attention" to the right-to-work drive.[19]

Of the three major faiths, Catholic clergymen were loudest and most persistent in their opposition to laws banning union security. The church itself did not adopt an official position with regard to right-to-work legislation, but since the 1920s the Catholic church had forged strong ties to the labor movement.[20] Monsignor George C. Higgins and Father John F. Cronin, directors of the Social Action Department of the NCWC made clear their personal opposition to right-to-work on the grounds that such laws were contrary to the Christian principle of social justice. The "net effect of these laws would be very bad for the cause of peaceful and orderly industrial relations in the United States," they argued.[21]

A host of other priests joined in denouncing right-to-work. Archbishop Henry J. O'Brien of Hartford, Connecticut, flatly rejected the claim "that a fundamental right of the individual is invaded if he must join a union." He argued that "it is neither immoral nor unethical to require union membership for the greater common good of the group." According to Father William J. Smith in his *La Crosse Register* column, those advocating right-to-work only pretended to be concerned with protecting individual workers; their real aim was "to destroy unions, or at least to weaken them to a point tantamount to destruction." He and most other Catholic writers saw right-to-work as introducing chaos into "what should be an ordered economy" by creating strife and suspicion among workers and between labor and management.[22]

The support of many Catholic clergy as well as other religious leaders gave union opposition to right-to-work a higher authority. In 1955, when Maryland was considering open-shop legislation, the International Association of Machinists sent each legislator a booklet containing moral studies of right-to-work laws by Father William J. Kelley, Rabbi Israel Goldstein, and the Reverend Dr. Walter G. Muelder. The Baltimore Federation of Labor also sponsored a rally featuring Father William J. Kelley and distributed recordings of his speech throughout the state. Unions paid close attention to the discussion in the religious press and sought to quietly bolster their supporters. The Steelworkers, for instance, provided Father Jerome Toner, with information for his anti-right-to-work study, *The Closed Shop*, and later convinced Monsignor Higgins to engage a "competent theologian with a thorough social and economic background" for a debate to be published in *The Homiletic and Pastoral Review*.[23]

The National Association of Manufacturers countered labor's influence with the clergy on the question of right-to-work. It distributed a pamphlet entitled "Ethics, Economics, and the Church," which
quoted an 1891 encyclical of Pope Leo XIII, but it brought a sharp
rebuke from some it was supposed to influence. Monsignor Francis
J. Lally, editor of the *Pilot,* a Boston Catholic weekly, called it "a totally absurd piece of propaganda." He went on to say, "it is almost
unbelievable that serious business men can pay to have this kind of
stuff peddled around the country." The pamphlet, he concluded, was
a "dreadful insult to [the clergy's] intelligence."[24]

Undaunted, the NAM and other business groups searched for clergy, particularly Catholic priests, who opposed the union shop. The
NAM found an article in the *Tablet,* a Brooklyn Catholic paper, by
Catholic layman Joseph A. Byrd, which NAM official Nathaniel Hicks
characterized as one of the "most favorable and best documented
pieces in support of right-to-work laws which has come to our notice so far from the religious press." The NAM then distributed the
piece to Catholic publications, religious editors of the daily press,
prominent Catholic churchgoers, and Catholic seminaries throughout the country.[25]

The NAM soon discovered other Catholic allies. In September 1956,
Father Ferdinand Falque of Staple, Minnesota, appeared on the NAM's
radio program "It's YOUR Business," where he defended right-to-work
statutes on the basis of protecting "our American freedom and our
traditions of democracy" from the domination of labor unions. Like
other advocates, he cited the current pope, Pius XII, and the AFL's
own Samuel Gompers as proponents of voluntarism. Father Edward
A. Keller of Notre Dame University was perhaps the most well known
representative of the Catholic clergy to defend right-to-work. In the
summer of 1956, the Heritage Foundation of Chicago published
Keller's *The Case for Right-to-Work Laws—A Defense of Voluntary Unionism,* which sought "to correct the impression that American Catholics are unanimously opposed" to such legislation on moral grounds.
Before publication, NAM manager Noel Sargent had met with Keller
at Notre Dame to review "various economic questions in which industry is interested, especially the Guaranteed Annual Wage and Right
to Work."[26]

Protestants tended to be somewhat more tentative than Catholics
on right-to-work. Indeed, the liberal Protestant journal, *Christian Century,* repeatedly chided the National Council of Churches for failing
to take a stand. Of course, this coincided with a period when conservative business leaders carried more weight with Protestant orga-

nizations.[27] However, aware of the intense interest in right-to-work, the National Council's Department of Church and Economic Life undertook a study of the issue in 1957. Standard Oil's Board Chairman Robert E. Wilson and the NAM's Noel Sargent tried to block a statement opposing right-to-work in language similar to that of an earlier FCC statement. Wilson asserted that "instead of reaffirming the church's traditional position of protecting the rights of the individual against coercion whether by employer or union, and backing the state in affording such protection, the proposed statement says *such protective laws are not in the public interest!*" Labor representatives protested the delay of a statement that affected "so directly the basic welfare of the whole labor movement," arguing that Protestant churches were "missing a very important and crucial opportunity to demonstrate their understanding of the real heart and soul of the labor movement."[29]

Sympathetic to labor, the Department of Church and Economic Life eventually voted to forward the draft statement on "Union Membership as a Condition of Employment" to the General Board of the NCC for adoption as official policy. Conservatives and liberals confronted each other at the June 5, 1956, meeting of the General Board. An impassioned five-hour debate ensued, the longest ever conducted on any single subject. B. E. Hutchinson, a retired Detroit industrialist and former Pew ally, led the fight against the statement, while Tilford Dudley of the AFL-CIO gave a "fiery speech" denying that the object of right-to-work was to protect the "little man." Moderate businessmen, like Irwin Miller and Charles Taft, also spoke on behalf of the statement. The debate eventually ended inconclusively when the General Board refused either to adopt or reject the statement disapproving the right-to-work laws of eighteen states.[30]

While disappointed that the statement was not entirely squashed, conservative business leaders were generally pleased with the Board's decision. They worked hard to ensure that distribution of the division's right-to-work statement was limited and that the National Council promptly corrected "misleading" articles, such as one published in the *AFL-CIO News*, implying that the NCC had taken an official stand against right-to-work. Noel Sargent reported to J. Howard Pew that the "Labor Union people who are on the General Board were very bitter about the failure to approve the report." To Sargent, it was clear that the "strong actions" taken by Pew and the National Lay Committee before its disbanding were responsible for the "substantial improvement" in the General Board's decisions in economic and social matters.[31]

One of the most dramatic expressions of the changing attitudes toward unions was the results of the 1957 legislative campaigns for right-to-work. While right-to-workers lost in Louisiana and failed by just a small margin in Idaho, they won a referendum ballot in Kansas for the 1958 elections and passed a statute in Indiana. The victory in Indiana was of special significance, for it was the first highly industrialized, strong union state to enact legislation restricting union security. In 1956, a coalition of employer organizations that included the Indiana Chamber of Commerce, the Associated Employers of Indiana, and the Indiana Manufacturers Association formed the Indiana Right to Work Committee (IRWC), a state level counterpart to the National Right to Work Committee. The IRWC asserted that it was not an employers' organization but a nonpartisan independent citizens committee.[32]

Several factors contributed to the IRWC success. The IRWC stimulated local business activity by holding legislative clinics in twenty-one Indiana communities, attended by twenty-five hundred employers. Throughout 1956, right-to-work proponents conducted meetings, published pamphlets, purchased newspaper space and radio time, met with workers on the job, and spoke before civic groups. Lobbyists cultivated legislators with a series of breakfast meetings and gained the public support of the Lieutenant Governor and Speaker of the House. Right-to-work advocates also played upon what Stephen C. Noland, president of the NRTW claimed was "a wave of revulsion" against union-inspired violence associated with the long 1955 Perfect Circle strike over the closed shop. Meanwhile, labor was divided; the state bodies of the AFL and CIO had yet to merge and personal animosities and differing political perspectives hobbled the union defense. All this contributed to the employer victory, but state Chamber of Commerce leader William Book pointed specifically to the long corporate effort to reshape the political atmosphere. He observed that "business organizations here have worked long and hard to spread the gospel of conservatism. Our new right-to-work law could not have become a reality without such seed-planting."[33]

* * *

One of the reasons the IRWC's seeds fell onto such fertile ground was the growing public concern over corruption in organized labor. Unions had come under increasing scrutiny during the early fifties. In 1951, the New York State Crime Commission began hearings on the New York waterfront, uncovering evidence of money stolen from union locals, unsolved murders, bribes, kickbacks, shakedowns, and job selling. Other investigations and hearings followed. Eisenhower's attorney general, Herbert Brownell, made racketeering a primary focus of his department, beginning fifteen hundred investigations in his first two years in office. In 1953 and 1954, House and Senate committees held public hearings on corruption on the waterfronts and in the building trades. Also in 1954, a Senate subcommittee began a two-year investigation of union mismanagement of welfare and pension funds.[34]

All this contributed to a growing public consciousness of union corruption, piqued by the 1954 release of the highly popular motion picture "On the Waterfront" and the acid-throwing assault in 1956 on a syndicated labor columnist shortly after he had broadcast details of shady dealings in a construction union. But, it was the sensational televised hearings of the Senate's Select Committee on Improper Activities in the Labor Management Fields, popularly known as the McClellan Committee, that splattered the labor movement's dirty laundry across the front pages of the country's newspapers. The committee held hearings for two-and-one-half years, examining both legal and illegal practices. It discovered evidence of theft, embezzlement and misuse of funds, undemocratic procedures, infiltration by gangsters and racketeers, violence and threats against employers and recalcitrant union members, and labor-management collusion. At the behest of business, it also peered into union political practices, secondary boycotts, and organizing tactics. Employer antiunion devices, however, received considerably less attention from the press than the labor abuses.[35]

The business community exploited the revelations of the McClellan Committee in its campaign against labor. Here, at last, was proof of the impact of big labor. NAM Chairman Cola G. Parker charged that "monopoly power and compulsion are being used to maintain crooks, racketeers, gangsters and hoodlums . . . in the top positions in many unions." "With one hand," he continued, "they keep a tight grip on the working man's throat, so that he can neither move nor cry out in protest; with the other they reach into his pay envelope and into his welfare fund in order to enrich themselves." While privately cheering the Committee, however, the NAM took care not to become closely associated with the Senate investigation. It quietly encouraged employers to provide evidence to the committee, but adroitly decided to "stay on the side-lines" to avoid the danger of tainting the hearings with the charge of being under the business community's control.[36]

The hearings provided the NAM with ammunition to promote the second part of its legislative campaign, the drive for a national labor reform act. In October 1957, NAM officials concluded that the time was right "to crystallize" the "public reaction against labor abuses into specific reform legislation."[37] To do this, employers had to reach the individual in the community, stimulate his identification of labor problems with his own economic well-being, "promote his idea to action individually in an attempt to correct these abuses by writing to his own congressman and senator, and through that procedure spark determination in Congress for corrective legislation" at the national level.[38]

This self-consciously political effort meshed with the NAM's more generalized antilabor public relations program. The employers' association marshalled its supporters, publicizing, among other items, the National Council of Churches's resolution calling for legislation to correct the abuses revealed by the McClellan committee.[39]

To arouse women, "who would have a lot to do with the kind of legislation that is passed," the NAM designed a new women's club program titled "Are You the Victim?" With the shape of a frightened woman splattered on the cover, the kit evoked the powerful image of rape. During 1958, five thousand clubs across the country used the kit, which exposed the "uncontrolled power, wealth and political influence of unions and union bosses" and explained how the activities of unions directly impinged on each individual. For instance, the NAM's kit charged that union monopoly power, used "to restrain trade, to restrict production and to fix prices" was behind the resurgence of inflation in the late fifties. The clubwoman leading the program called upon her audience to mobilize to "make our club's strength felt in the fight for clean, democratic unions," by writing to Washington and by carrying the message of the meeting home to husbands, friends, and relatives.[40]

The NAM also produced a new film titled "Trouble, U.S.A.," which was widely distributed to professional groups, educators and fraternal organizations. Like the club package, the film and accompanying discussion material drew on the McClellan committee evidence. NAM advised viewers that "this is not a pretty picture," but "a true one" depicting events that were "vitally affecting your own community." The documentary, it continued, "was disturbing, might provoke indignation, but it should encourage local constructive action to restore law and order in your own community and in the nation."[41]

The right-to-work campaigns, the series of union corruption hearings, and the NAM's activities fed a growing public criticism of organized labor's role in society. The adoption of right-to-work as the debate topic for the nation's colleges and universities during the 1957–58 academic year reflected the issue's growing significance, a significance that seeped into popular culture as well. In the comic strip, *Orphan Annie*, for instance, there was the suggestion of tyrannical behavior on the part of a union boss.[42]

Public opinion polls conducted in late 1957 provided tentative evidence that organized labor had lost many friends in the American populace. An American Institute of Public Opinion survey showed a twelve-point drop in "pro-union" sentiment across the country, the greatest defection occurring in the highly industrialized East. Reflecting on the results of this poll, labor official Mark Starr observed that the public's former identification with the "little guy and the underdog" had produced a "certain amount of sympathy for unions." Now, he worried that "all this goodwill was in danger of being alienated by the allegations about union monopoly and about the unethical behavior of the union bosses."[43]

The passage of the Indiana Right-to-Work Law and the McClellan investigation goaded the AFL-CIO into addressing the "new and intensive anti-union campaign" of "reactionary forces and vested interest groups." In mid-1957, the AFL-CIO adopted a code of ethical practices for unions and then expelled three of the worst offenders— the bakers, the laundry workers, and the teamsters. Having publicly cleaned house, the AFL-CIO argued against the need for federal legislation. The Federation argued that the McClellan hearings were "one-sided and overdramatized," and that the committee ignored management corruption. It also contended that the press was using the committee's findings "to do a hatchet job on the trade union movement." Union leaders called for organized labor "to offset the efforts of its enemies." According to Steelworkers President David McDonald, unions had to reach a "badly misinformed" general public that had no "real understanding of what labor is actually seeking to achieve not only for its rank and file, but also for the betterment of the entire nation."[44]

Despite dire business predictions of the impact of the AFL-CIO merger, the new federation had spent less, not more on public and media relations during 1955 and 1956. Indeed, national labor organizations provided little support to the state central bodies fighting right-to-work. When Robert Lenaghen, president of the Idaho State Federation of Labor, sought AFL-CIO assistance, he was "frankly appalled at the lack of a coordinated program to counter-balance the serious attack which we were facing across the nation."[45] The scene changed in 1957, however. When the National Right to Work Committee's campaign reached the UAW's home state of Michigan, the AFL-CIO embarked upon a program to "arouse and unify" the labor movement. The executive council set up a high level right-to-work subcommittee instructed to "monitor state right-to-work agitation, coordinate defense efforts, and aid repeal drives." The AFL-CIO began to bring "the true facts of this 'Right-to-Work Question'" to the public's attention through a series of canned radio and television spots, a fifteen-minute documentary, a series of popular leaflets, and a handbook and speaker's manual, summarizing the principal arguments. Sensing the need to expand its base, the Federation also initiated and funded an anti-right-to-work citizens group called the National Council on Industrial Peace. Led by such well known liberals as Eleanor Roosevelt and New York Senator Herbert Lehman, the NCIP included employers, clergy, and professionals. To raise money for all this activity the AFL-CIO created a special fund "to combat the millions of dollars being poured" into right-to-work campaigns by employer groups.[46]

During 1958, the AFL-CIO's anti-right-to-work drive meshed with a more broadly gauged public relations campaign. Upping its public relations budget by 58 percent to $1.2 million a year, the Federation's revamped program looked a lot like that of its arch-rival's, the NAM. The goal was to create a new image for labor that stressed unions' "day-by-day contributions to the whole of society." Commercials on the AFL-CIO's news programs, for instance, emphasized labor's community services, using "words of positive emotional value," like "freedom," "America," "democracy," and "neighbors." Similarly the AFL-CIO's new television program, "America at Work," portrayed workers' contribution to "America's industrial might." This fifteen-minute program, carried on sixty-seven stations, mirrored the NAM's "Industry on Parade." Indeed, its initial title was "Labor on Parade."[47]

To gain positive publicity from the press, in June 1958, the Federation began issuing one or two television news releases each week to a hundred stations throughout the country. The stories publicized a range of AFL-CIO political issues, including legislation for an increased minimum wage, school construction, and housing, as well as stressing labor's constructive community activities, such as blood bank drives, Christmas parties, and the community services program. Like employers, the AFL-CIO also reached out to opinion leaders. It initiated a direct mail campaign aimed at influential minority spokesmen, religious leaders, and intellectuals, and established a Speakers' Bureau that provided union officials to speak before religious, civic, fraternal, and school groups.[48]

* * *

The 1958 election served as the first test of labor's new program. The election took place within the context of sharpening labor-management conflict. Beginning in mid-1957, the economy dropped into a recession even as inflation surged. Segments of American industry, like steel, experienced their first serious wave of foreign competition. Many employers met this weakening economic climate with a determination to reduce labor costs. Without totally abandoning human relations, managers shifted from the more subtle antiunionism of the earlier fifties to an outright attack on organized labor. The doubling of unfair labor practice cases in the late fifties reflected this new strategy. In addition, companies adopted a more aggressive position at the bargaining table, seeking to restore wage flexibility and to speed up production by abolishing restrictive work rules. To the AFL-CIO it was clear that employers were adopting "class war methods on the bargaining front."[49]

The struggle between business conservatives and labor became one of the principal themes of the 1958 election. Before the election, business stepped up its political activity and set up workshops promoting employer political participation. In addition, Republican politicians began an "experimental" program to teach "practical politics" to junior executives from scores of companies in three dozen targeted congressional districts.[50] The conservative business community's primary goals were to promote right-to-work and to elect a Congress sympathetic to the enactment of a strict labor reform act, hoping to undercut labor's political power. According to Gulf Oil Senior Vice President Archie D. Gray, "If we are to survive, labor's political power must be opposed by a matching force—among the corporations that make up American business." In a number of localities, industrialists financed dissemination of a "notorious" pamphlet smearing Walter Reuther, who employers tagged as the "phantom candidate" for a variety of offices in more than twenty states.[51]

The Republican party, which was the chief beneficiary of corporate political activity, joined in the attack on labor. The Republican Policy Committee issued a monograph entitled, *The Labor Bosses: America's Third Party*, which asserted that the Democrats were "dominated by certain politico-labor bosses and left-wing extremists." The choice, it warned, was between the Republican party or going down "the left lane which leads to socialism." Vice President Richard Nixon played up this theme in speeches across the country.[52]

Some of the most intense battles between business and labor took place in those states voting on right-to-work. Right-to-work advocates had turned to the referendum as a means of placing the question on the ballot in California, Idaho, Washington, Colorado, Ohio, and Kansas. Business support for the campaigns was crucial. In Washington, for instance, Boeing Aircraft revived a lagging drive for signatures for the ballot referendum. Three weeks before the deadline for filing petitions, Boeing Aircraft sent a letter to all supervisors enclosing copies of the petition and instructing them to get additional names. Some twenty other industries followed Boeing's lead. Washington business leaders also formed an organization of "minute men" and built a war chest of $500,000. The General Electric Company at the Hanford Atomic Works in Washington aided the campaign by sending a letter to their nine thousand employees urging them to support the initiative. Similarly, in California, GE sponsored a newspaper advertising campaign, becoming the first major corporation in the state to endorse the right-to-work proposal.[53]

Perhaps the most telling battle over right-to-work took place in Ohio. In early 1958, buoyed by the previous year's right-to-work victory in Indiana, the Ohio Chamber of Commerce formed the Ohioans for Right-to-Work (ORW). The group began collecting signatures to place an amendment to the state constitution on the ballot in November. The Ohio Manufacturers' Association, some city chambers, and several companies backed the ORW, feeling that right-to-work laws in both Ohio and Indiana could start a major trend. Among the firms active in the drive were several that had been leaders in the business community's campaign to reshape the climate of opinion, including General Electric, Timken Roller Bearing, and Armco Steel. Timken blanketed their plant cities with the story of right-to-work, and all of their advertising carried the slogan, "The Right-to-Work Shall Not Be Abridged or Made Impotent." The company also spearheaded the movement to get signatures on the petitions, circulating the first four hundred petitions issued. Business support for right-to-work, however, was not unanimous. Many large firms steered clear of the issue, and a few moderate business leaders like Charles P. Taft came out strongly against right-to-work.[54]

Organized labor met the challenge by forming the United Organized Labor of Ohio (UOLO) in late March 1958. The UOLO argued that the real issue behind right-to-work was not the union shop or individual rights but whether unions had a right to exist. To defend against the antiunion drive, Ohio trade unionists followed a two-pronged strategy. First, they mounted a major effort to register union members and their families to ensure a high working-class turnout on election day. Second, labor looked to the community for defenders. Blacks, for instance, rallied to the side of unions; the Ohio State Association of Colored Women's Clubs and the NAACP condemned right-to-work and aided the union drive to mobilize the minority vote. City councils, fraternal orders, and civic organizations, among other organizations, also passed resolutions condemning the amendment.[55]

Much of the religious community came out on labor's behalf. Catholic support was strongest. In March 1958, the six Catholic Bishops of Ohio issued a statement asserting that the proposed amendment "would not solve our problems but might lead to more intensified struggle." Catholic clergymen were active in the fight against right-to-work, often denouncing it from the pulpit. The Ohio Council of Churches also opposed the right-to-work proposal, but the UOLO felt that its story was not getting to the Protestant ministers. In a bid for their support, trade unionists contacted their own pastors and the UOLO distributed the Ohio Council's statement to clergy throughout the state. Others took more direct action; on Sundays after services, UAW Local 12 members in Toledo passed out the Bishops' statement in front of Catholic churches and the Ohio Council's statement at Protestant churches.[56]

Both sides conducted intense public relations campaigns. The ORW and the UOLO deployed speakers throughout the state, distributed millions of pieces of literature, and ran ads in newspapers and on the radio and television. By late summer, however, the right-to-work proponents seemed to be prevailing. In August 1958, they filed the petitions to place the right-to-work issue on the ballot, having collected a hundred thousand more signatures than required. In forty-nine counties, they had twice as many signatures as needed. Feeling that victory was assured, the ORW slackened its public relations drive and placed more emphasis on recruiting political allies. Business leader Charles Hook of Armco, for one, worked hard to get the support of prominent Republican politicians and praised Republican gubernatorial candidate William O'Neill for endorsing the ORW and conducting "a marvelous campaign in face of opposition of the labor bosses."[57]

In contrast, the labor movement redoubled its public relations efforts. The UOLO kicked off the "home-stretch drive" with a mass rally on September 7 in Columbus and the formation of a prolabor citizens committee, subsidized by the AFL-CIO national office. Campaign literature emphasized the dire economic consequences of right-to-work. Aware that forty percent of the electorate were "housewives," unions aimed a special appeal to them, holding "Kaffee Klatches" and distributing pamphlets like "Mrs. Ohio Homemaker: Beware the Quirk in 'Right-to-Work,'" which emphasized that right-to-work undermined unions. Once that happened, wages invariably fell, weakening family security. The Women's Activities Division of the state AFL-CIO did much of the volunteer work necessary in bringing labor's message to women and the rest of the public.

In late October, the right-to-work proponents made a tactical error. They shifted from arguing for the issue on the basis of protecting individual freedom to a strident attack against unionism. In doing so, the ORW inadvertently provided proof of the labor movement's contention that the business community's primary goal was the destruction of trade unionism.[58]

On election day 1958, the Republican party and the conservative business community suffered a major defeat. Voters rejected right-to-work referendums in five of the six states where it was on the ballot. Only in Kansas, where business faced a small labor movement, did right-to-work prevail. Nationwide, Republican losses were massive, with Democrats achieving their largest gains in congressional elections since 1936. The continuing economic slump certainly contributed to Republican losses. Crucial, too, was the attack on the labor movement. The labor movement at least temporarily became more united and politically active than it had been in years. It also created broad-based liberal coalitions, including community groups, minorities, and the clergy, all of which proved significant. One analysis of the vote, for instance, found that the opposition of the Catholic bishops to right-to-work had a major impact on the way Catholics voted.[59]

The election taught the business community that while there was certainly outrage over the abuses uncovered by the investigations, the public still accepted the legitimacy of unions and was uncomfortable with a blatant attack on organized labor as an institution. Future efforts to limit the power of labor needed to differentiate between unions as institutions and the abuses of labor leaders. Moreover, business leaders needed to cleave more closely to the idea that they sought not only to contain the "monopoly" power of unions but also desired to protect the democratic rights of individual workers.

*   *   *

In spite of the victories won by labor and the Democrats in the 1958 elections, business leaders renewed their campaign for restrictive new labor legislation in the Eighty-sixth Congress. For the business community, the election was merely a temporary setback. They immediately applied the lessons learned from the 1958 right-to-work campaigns to the drive for national labor reform. One advantage for business was the much broader base of support within the country for labor reform than right-to-work. The McClellan hearings had convinced even the friends of labor that greater regulation of unions was necessary. The major question was what form such regulation would take. There was general agreement that reform should make the labor movement more democratic in its internal affairs. By early 1958, even the AFL-CIO had come around to accepting the need for legislation, but only a law aimed solely at the correction of the most flagrant abuses revealed by the McClellan investigation. Employers and their conservative allies in Congress wanted more. They hoped to move beyond internal regulation of unions to further restricting the powers of labor in collective bargaining. The NAM wanted to make all secondary boycotts and organizational picketing illegal.

During 1958, Congress first considered labor reform, and the Senate passed a mild measure, the Kennedy-Ives Bill, that was acceptable to labor. This bill required publication of detailed financial reports by unions and regulated union trusteeships and elections. It faced stiff opposition. Arguing that the proposal, which did not address secondary boycotts and organizational picketing, was too weak, the NAM and the Chamber of Commerce lobbied vigorously against it. At the same time, the Teamsters and Mine Workers fought the bill on the grounds that there was no need for any regulation. This unusual coalition helped defeat the measure in the House of Representatives.[60]

In early 1959, labor reform was back on the nation's agenda. Although it had issued an interim report in March 1958, the McClellan Committee continued its hearing through 1959, keeping the issue of union corruption before the public's eyes. At the same time, the NAM, the Chamber of Commerce, and other business organizations continued to do their part in raising public consciousness about labor abuses. It became clear that there was little chance of unions avoiding a labor reform law, as a commitment to doing something about labor-management problems became a litmus test of political responsibility. Nevertheless, the business community faced a tough political assignment. Republican party losses in the 1958 election had resulted in the seating of a Congress with seemingly liberal, prolabor inclinations. As a result, the AFL-CIO approached the political battle confident that there was little chance of Congress passing a punitive law.[61]

During the spring and summer of 1959, several labor reform bills were introduced and debated in the House and Senate. The labor movement became divided over the issue and the unity that it had forged in the struggle against right to work quickly dissipated. The AFL-CIO supported "soft" legislation, while other segments of the labor movement pursued entirely different agendas. The Mine Workers continued to fight all legislation, while other individual unions within the Federation lobbied for their own interests. Almost to the end, the AFL-CIO believed that it had enough congressional support to render unnecessary a massive drive to mobilize the public in labor's defense. Unions relied instead on high level consultation between congressional and labor leadership and on lobbying to influence individual legislators. Throughout the struggle, however, labor tended to be disorganized, rigid, and so zealous in lobbying that it antagonized rather than won support. At one point, the teamsters had four hundred lobbyists on Capitol Hill lecturing and threatening the legislators.[62]

The forces advocating a strict labor reform bill that incorporated the demands of employers were much more united than labor. The Eisenhower administration provided vigorous and effective legislative leadership, while maintaining close liaison with business groups. On cue from the administration, employer organizations mobilized their members to place steady but more subtle influence on legislators. Management lobbyists stayed in the background and relied on somewhat less intimidating forms of communication—mail and telephone contacts. They emphasized repeatedly that "the people" wanted a strong law. At a crucial moment, when the House began debate on labor legislation, President Eisenhower delivered a televised address in which he endorsed the promanagement Landrum-Griffin Bill and urged the public to demand "strong" labor reform legislation. In perhaps one of Eisenhower's most political speeches, he presented his appeal as a "non-partisan" one. As a lame duck president, he could easily claim to have "no political motivations" and to speak for the people. Eisenhower's request brought a tremendous volume of mail and gave "legitimacy to the fight for the Landrum-Griffin bill," making "it hard for its opponents to resist."[63]

The White House also helped coordinate the public relations drive for labor reform. Outnumbered in Congress, the Republicans realized that they needed widespread public support to achieve their goals. The Eisenhower administration found friends in the press. Most newspapers editorially supported tough labor reform legislation and the press continued to provide extensive coverage of labor corruption. The employer associations, however, were the foot soldiers in this campaign to arouse public opinion to demand a strict labor bill. The entire business community mobilized "to an unprecedented extent." Its goal was to flood Congress with mail demanding a tough bill. Trade associations sponsored newspaper advertising and provided legislative kits to members that included posters, pamphlets, prepared speeches, advertisements and letters for distribution to employees. In one critical congressional district, a corporation sent its foremen out "to ring neighbor's doorbells." The company claimed that this tactic resulted in three thousand letters in one week, urging a stiff bill.[64]

Radio and television were also important. In April, as Congress began consideration of labor reform legislation, Armstrong Cork Company's Circle Theatre ran an hour-long drama about labor racketeering entitled "The Sound of Violence." It concluded with an appeal from Senator John L. McClellan to "do something about the evils shown." The program was rerun in July, and employer associations ran advertisements and sent out over 4 million letters urging the public to watch and write to their legislators. Beginning in August, spot ads featuring Congressmen Landrum and Griffin and Senator McClellan ran frequently in thirty-five crucial congressional districts. McClellan had played a key role in the shift in Congress from a mild to a much stronger bill when he presented in an "impassioned speech" a "bill of rights" for the laboring man. It was this theme that business promoted. One administration spokesman recalled, "We wanted this to look like the people against the labor bosses and not Big Labor against Big Business." Thus, conservatives did not again make the mistake of an outright attack on unions but emphasized defending the rights of the individual.[65]

The public responded with a tremendous deluge of mail. Congressmen reported receiving more mail on labor reform than on any other previous issue. During one week in August 1959, 1 million letters inundated the Capitol. Most of the letters advocated a tough labor law. Alarmed, the AFL-CIO began distributing a leaflet entitled "Get Crooks—Not Unions" and urged union members to write to their legislators. Still, there was little prolabor mail. In early September 1959, Congress passed the Landrum-Griffin Act.

Substantially reflecting the interests of business, it was the "worst defeat for organized labor" since the passage of Taft-Hartley twelve years earlier. It prohibited all secondary boycotts, severely restricted organizational picketing, and "imposed stiff requirements of disclosure and standards of conduct that tightened the web of legalistic complexity already choking the labor movement."[66]

To Mark Starr of the ILGWU, the adoption of the Landrum-Griffin Act showed how the image of labor had been successfully smeared in the public mind. He believed that as a result of the business campaign in the schools, churches, and communities a "large segment of the general public" accepted the fallacy that "labor unions were a monopoly run by union bosses" and that "labor bosses not only had too much power but were also corrupt." The AFL-CIO's Committee on Political Action also concluded that unions had "sat passively in the galleries while the structure was set up to give labor a public smearing." Labor then came into the struggle "unprepared and unorganized and was out-smarted and out-maneuvered by Business and Industry who operated in a more skillful manner, with greater resources, better teamwork, and better support and cooperation from Members of the House and Senate."[67]

The business community agreed that the passage of the Landrum-Griffin Act was the political payoff of their efforts to forge a more favorable climate of public opinion. According to NAM Vice President Charles R. Sligh, "a wave of overwhelming public opinion," combined with a determined president and an effective conservative coalition of Republicans and Democrats "forced Congress to take labor reform seriously."[68]

The struggles over right-to-work and labor reform demonstrated how far business had come in the years since the strike wave of 1946. Business had achieved solid results from its last campaign of the fifties to limit the power of labor. While most of the 1958 right-to-work initiatives were defeated, the fact that business was able to generate enough support to place the question on the ballot in northern, industrialized states reflected a considerable shift in attitudes about organized labor. Landrum-Griffin further proved, at least to business leaders, that they had decisively shaped public opinion. Public opinion had played a central role in the passage of legislation that placed further limitations on the power of labor. Although unions had won significant electoral victories in 1958, they found little political support in the halls of Congress. Indeed, labor fought a rearguard battle against the erosion of its status and power; its voice in public debate was weak and its ability to offer a compelling alternate vision was apparently absent. The business community had contained the threat a united labor movement posed to its agenda for the nation's political and economic future.

## Notes

1. Edward Maher, "NAM Public Relations—Policies and Objectives," Feb. 1957, pamphlet, Neilson Library, Smith College, Northampton, Mass.

2. Kenneth Miller to Staff Operating Executives, Jan. 16, 1956, Accession 1411, NAM, Series I, Box 248, HML (hereafter Acc. 1411, NAM I/248).

3. "How Labor Unity Affects You" (reprint of *Iron Age* article), *MRev* 45 (Jan. 1956): 32–33; "AFL-CIO is Born," *America*, Dec. 17, 1955, p. 325; Sidney Lens, "Will Merged Labor Set New Goals?," *HBR*, 37 (Mar.–Apr. 1956): 57–63.

4. "Charles Sligh Discusses Labor Issues," May 21, 1957, radio transcript, Box 63, George Meany Papers, GMA; "Super Union: Something Else for You to Worry About," *FMM* 113 (Mar. 1955): 84–89; "A New Era & Added Punch," *BW*, Dec. 19, 1955, p. 26.

5. "What the AFL-CIO Merger Means," *U.S. News & World Report*, Dec. 16, 1955, pp. 23–30; "Big Labor: The Aim Is to Make It Bigger," *Newsweek*, Feb. 21, 1955, pp. 71–72; "Is Big Labor Good or Bad?" *Life*, Dec. 1955, p. 28.

6. "1956 Public Relations Program for NAM—Campaign against Labor Monopoly Abuses," Feb. 1956, Acc. 1411, NAM, III/ 851.1.

7. Sybyl S. Patterson to Coordinating Committee, Jan. 5, 1956, Sybyl S. Patterson to Field Staff, Jan. 3, 1956, Box 19, both in Acc. 1412, Industrial Relations Department Papers, NAM.

8. Sarah Lyons Watts, *Order against Chaos: Business Culture and Labor Ideology in America, 1880–1915* (New York: Greenwood Press, 1991); "1956 Public Relations Program for NAM—Campaign against Labor Monopoly Abuses."

9. Ernest G. Swigert, "What Shall We Do about the Growing Shadow of Organized Labor" (Address before the Economic Club of Detroit, Detroit, Michigan, Sept. 30, 1957), Acc. 1412, NAM, Box 19.

10. "1956 Public Relations Program for NAM—Campaign against Labor Monopoly Abuses"; Paterson to Field Staff, Jan. 3, 1956; "It's Your Business," script, Jan. 28, 1956, Box 63, Meany Papers.

11. "1956 Public Relations Program for NAM—Campaign against Labor Monopoly Abuses"; "Monopoly is Always Wrong!" flyer, Acc. 1412, NAM, Box 19.

12. D. L. Mewhinney to National Industrial Council (Dramatizing Abuses of Union Power), Feb. 3, 1956, Acc. 1411, NAM I/248; "MR AND MRS. CITIZEN," "IS THIS AMERICA?" pamphlets, Box 51, AOF I, LMDC.

13. "Outline of a Public Relations Program on Major Labor Issues for 1955," Feb. 28, 1955, Acc. 1411, NAM I/13.

14. Gilbert J. Gall, *The Politics of Right to Work: The Labor Federations as Special Interests, 1943–1979* (New York: Greenwood Press, 1988), chaps. 2 and 3; Michael Goldfield discusses the vast literature on the impact of right-to-work on union growth in *The Decline of Organized Labor in the United States* (Chicago: University of Chicago Press, 1987), pp. 184–87.

15. Gall, *The Politics of Right to Work*, chap. 3, esp. p. 81; *National Industrial Council Supplement* (NAM newsletter), June 29, 1956, National Right to Work Committee news release, Jan. 28, 1955, both in Acc. 1411, NAM I/13; *WSJ*, July 25, 1956.

16. "Outline of a Public Relations Program on Major Labor Issues for 1955"; Arthur Erwin, "The Case for Right-to-Work Laws," *PJ* 36 (Oct. 1957): 167; Charles R. Sligh, "Will the McClellan Hearing End Abuses of Union Power?" (Address before the Associated Industries of the Quad-Cities, Rock Island, Ill., Oct. 10, 1957), Acc. 1412, NAM, Box 19.

17. "1956 Public Relations Program for NAM—Campaign against Labor Monopoly Abuses"; Erwin, "The Case for Right-to-Work Laws," pp. 168–69; "Outline of a Public Relations Program on Major Labor Issues for 1955."

18. "Outline of a Public Relations Program on Major Labor Issues for 1955"; "Some Suggested Activities for NAM's Labor Program—1958," n.d., Acc. 1412, NAM, Box 14.

19. Eleanor G. Astor, "Skids under Labor: The Right-to-Work Laws," *Nation* 180 (Apr. 2, 1955): 285; "Outline of a Public Relations Program on Major Labor Issues for 1955."

20. *Round Table* (St. Peter's College Institute of Industrial Relations, Jersey City, N.J., newsletter), Feb. 7, 1955; Benjamin L. Masse, "What's Happening to Right-to-Work Laws? *America*, May 7, 1955, p. 150; Neil Betten, *Catholic Activism and the Industrial Worker* (Gainesville: University Presses of Florida, 1976).

21. "Father George," *Fortune*, Apr. 1955, p. 30; Msgr. George G. Higgins to Reverend Leo F. Dworschak, Feb. 1, 1955, George G. Higgins Papers, Department of Archives and Manuscripts, The Catholic University of America, Washington, D.C.; John F. Cronin, "'Right-To-Work' Laws," news release, Feb. 18, 1955, Social Action Department, National Catholic Welfare Conference, Box 6, General Files of the Legislative Office, USA/A.

22. O'Brien quoted in Masse, "What's Happening to Right-to-Work Laws?"; *La Crosse Register*, Jan. 27, 1955; "Sideglances," *The Liguorian*, Sept. 1955, pp. 561–63; Benjamin L. Masse, "Court Upholds the Union Shop," *America*, June 16, 1956, pp. 283–84.

23. Harry Cohen and J. C. Turner, "We Beat 'Right to Work,'" *American Federationist*, May 1955, p. 18; "Union Security: The 'Right-to-Work' Controversy," *Labor's Economic Review* (AFL-CIO Department of Research), p. 3; Steve Levitsky to Frank Hoffmann, Mar. 9, 1955, Frank N. Hoffman to Charley Hogan, Sept. 6, 1957, Box 5, General Files of the Legislative Office, USA/A.

24. Lally quoted in *Round Table*, Feb. 7, 1955; Clair M. Cook, "Those 'Right-to-Work' Laws," *CC*, May 4, 1955, p. 530.

25. D. L. Mewhinney to National Industrial Council, July 18, 1955, Nathaniel Hicks to Division and Regional Managers, Apr. 21, 1955, Acc. 1411, NAM I/13; John A. Stuart to Members of the Coordinating Committee, Apr. 22, 1955, Acc. 1411, NAM I/163. In its right-to-work information packet, the Chamber of Commerce also distributed the statements of clergy, United States Chamber of Commerce Information Packet, Box 5, General Files of the Legislative Office, USA/A.

26. "It's YOUR Business," transcript, Sept. 22, 1956, Acc. 1411, NAM I/13; *Michigan Catholic*, Aug. 1957; Noel Sargent to Mr. Harvey Frye et al., Mar. 16, 1955, Acc. 1411, NAM I/163.

27. "Those 'Right-to-Work' Laws—and the Churches," p. 4; "Union Shop Issue Is Widely Contested," *CC*, Mar. 20, 1957, p. 74; "Labor Security an Election Issue," *CC*, Nov. 5, 1958, p. 1260.

28. Howard M. Mills, "The Department of Church and Economic Life of the National Council of Churches, 1947–1966: A Critical Analysis" (Th.D.

diss., Union Theological Seminary, New York, 1970), see chap. 8 above for Lay Committee and NCC.

29. "Historical Development of the National Council of Churches Policy Position on Union Membership as a Condition of Employment," c. 1960, Department of the Church and Economic Life, Proposed Statement on Union Membership as a Condition of Employment, Explanatory Memorandum, n.d., Box 103, Charles P. Taft Papers, LC; Robert E. Wilson to Members of Executive Board of the Division of Christian Life and Work, May 18, 1956, Cameron P. Hall to Mr. Olsen, Apr. 27, 1956, all in Box 3, RG 6, NCC.

30. "NCC Board Fails to Pass Judgment on 'Right to Work' Laws," *Living Church*, clipping, June 24, 1956, Box 152, J. Howard Pew Papers, HML, Jasper E. Crane to Henning W. Prentis, Aug. 16, 1956, Box 61, Jasper E. Crane Papers, HML.

31. Noel Sargent to J. Howard Pew, July 9, 1956, Box 167, Pew Papers; Robert E. Wilson to Charles P. Taft, July 19, 1956, Box 103, Taft Papers; Cameron P. Hall to Glenn W. Moore, May 1, 1957, Box 3, RG 6, NCC; Eugene Carson Blake to Saul Miller, July 17, 1956, Box 61, Crane Papers.

32. Gall, *The Politics of Right to Work*, pp. 93–97; "Here's Way to Sound Laws," *NB*, June 1957, 42–44; Fred Witney, "The Indiana Right-to-Work Law," *ILRR* 11 (July 1957): 506–17.

33. Witney, "The Indiana Right to Work Law," pp. 506–17; Gall, *The Politics of Right to Work*, pp. 93–97; Melvin A. Kahn, *The Politics of American Labor: The Indiana Microcosm* (Carbondale: Southern Illinois University Labor Institute, 1970), pp. 233–38; "Here's Way to Sound Laws," p. 42–44, esp. 42.

34. H. W. Benson, *Democratic Rights for Union Members: A Guide to Internal Union Democracy* (New York: Association for Union Democracy, 1979), pp. 178–86; *Congress and the Nation, 1945–1964: A Review of Government and Politics in the Postwar Years* (Washington, D.C.: Congressional Quarterly Services, 1965), pp. 1716–17, 1729–30, 1734, 1745–47; "Labor Racketeering," *Fortune*, July 1955, pp. 50–52.

35. Sar A. Levitan and J. Joseph Loewenberg, "The Politics and Provisions of the Landrum-Griffin Act," in *Regulating Union Government*, ed. Marten S. Estey, Philip Taft, and Martin Wagner (New York: Harper & Row, 1964), pp. 31–37; Samuel C. Patterson, *Labor Lobbying and Labor Reform: The Passage of the Landrum-Griffin Act*, Inter-University Case Program, Inc. #99 (Indianapolis: Bobbs-Merrill, 1966), p. 1; *Congress and the Nation*, pp. 1745–47.

36. Parker quoted in *NAM News*, Apr. 12, 1957; Sybyl S. Patterson to Charles R. Sligh, Sept. 12, 1957, Acc. 1412, NAM, Box 14.

37. John A. Stuart to Sybyl Patterson, Oct. 15, 1957, Acc. 1412, NAM, Box 14.

38. Sybyl S. Patterson Inter-Office Memo, Oct. 30, 1957, Sybyl S. Patterson, Acc. 1412, NAM, Box 14; "Promotional Ideas on Labor-Management Problems," Oct. 4, 1957.

39. Patterson, "Promotional Ideas on Labor-Management Problems," "Resolution on the Moral Crisis in the Labor Union Movement and in Labor-Management Practices," adopted by the Triennial General Assembly, the Na-

tional Council of Churches of Christ in the U.S.A., Dec. 5, 1957, Box 103, Taft Papers.

40. *NAM News*, Apr. 4, 1958; "Prospectus—Industrial Relations Division," Jan. 1959, Acc. 1412, NAM, Box 14; "The Ladies Quiz Industry on—The Power of Labor Unions," n.d., "Are You the Victim: A Complete Program Guide for Clubs," n.d., Box 19, Acc. 1412, NAM; *Program Notes*, Apr. 1958, Acc. 1411, NAM I/223.

41. "Trouble USA: A Documentary Film," pamphlet, Box 14, Acc. 1412, NAM.

42. *NAM News*, Aug. 23, 1957; D. L. Mewhinney to Industrial Relations Group, Oct. 29, 1957, Acc. 1411, NAM I/13; "Meeting of Staff," Oct. 3, 1957, USA Washington Office, Box 6, General Files of the Legislative Office, USA/ A; Mark Starr, "Business, Labor and Education," (Paper presented to International Association of Machinists Fall Conference, Sept. 28–29, 1957), Box 11, Mark Starr Papers, ALUA.

43. *New York Herald Tribune*, Sept. 23, 1957; Starr, "Business, Labor and Education."

44. John W. Livingston, "The Smear Drive Is On," *AFL-CIO American Federationist*, Sept. 1958, p. 6; *Textile Labor*, Oct. 1957; H. W. Benson, *Democratic Rights for Union Members*, pp. 186–87; Henry C. Fleisher, "The Council Takes Action," *AFL-CIO American Federationist*, July 1957, pp. 10–11.

45. Robert Leneghen to George Meany, Nov. 6, 1958, Box 38, Meany Papers; "AFL-CIO: Influencing People," *BW*, Jan. 7, 1956, p. 66; Mrs. P. M. Anselone to George Meany, Nov. 21, 1957, Box 37, Meany Papers; J. to Andy Biemiller, Dec. 18, 1957, all in Box 55, AFL-CIO Department of Legislation Files, GMA.

46. Gall, *The Politics of Right to Work*, chap. 4; Report of the Sub-Committee of the Executive Council dealing with Right-to-Work Laws, Apr. 16, 1958, Report of Staff Committee on Restrictive Legislation, Aug. 14, 1958, National Council for Industrial Peace, Outline Plan of Operations, 1958, all in Box 2, William Schnitzler Papers, GMA; George Meany to Presidents of National and International Unions, Mar. 5, 1958, Box 38, Meany Papers.

47. Henry C. Fleisher to Members of Committee on Public Relations, c. Nov. 1957, Report of Sub-Committee on Public Relations, Apr. 29, 1958, all in Box 320, Walter Reuther Papers, ALUA; "Report of Committee on Public Relations to the Executive Council," Apr. 30, 1958, Box 2, Schnitzler Papers; Gerald Pomper, "The Public Relations of Organized Labor," *Public Opinion Quarterly* 12 (Winter 1959–60): 486–94; Sara U. Douglas, *Labor's New Voice: Unions and the Mass Media* (Norwood, N.J.: Ablex Publishing, 1985), pp. 31–58.

48. Zack to Schnitzler, Aug. 14, 1959; Report of Committee on Public Relations to the Executive Council, Apr. 30, 1958, Albert J. Zack to Secretary-Treasurer Schnitzler, Feb. 12, 1959, all in Box 2, Schnitzler Papers; *WSJ*, Apr. 11, 1958; Pomper, "The Public Relations Of Organized Labor," p. 487.

49. Mike Davis, *Prisoners of the American Dream: Politics and Economy in the History of the US Working Class* (London: Verso, 1986), pp. 121–24; Michael Goldfield, *The Decline of Organized Labor in the United States*, pp. 189–97.

50. Horace E. Sheldon, "Businessmen Must Get Into Politics," *HBR* 37 (Mar.–Apr. 1959): 37–41; *WSJ*, Oct. 14, 1958; "Business Gets the Political Urge," *BW*, Oct. 11, 1958, p. 125; L. R. Boulware, "Politics: The Businessman's Biggest Job in 1958" (Address before the Annual Meeting of Phoenix Chamber of Commerce, May 21, 1958), Acc. 1411, NAM I/5.

51. "Labor Goes on Political Defensive," *BW*, Oct. 18, 1958, p. 149; Benjamin L. Masse, "Industrial Relations Re-examined," *America*, Jan. 3, 1959, pp. 394–95; R. Alton Lee, *Eisenhower & Landrum-Griffin: A Study in Labor-Management Politics* (Lexington: University Press of Kentucky, 1990), p. 93; *John Herling's Labor Letter*, Oct. 4, 1959.

52. More moderate Republicans tended to be leery of attacking labor and of being too closely identified with right-to-work; David W. Reinhard, *The Republican Right Since 1945* (Lexington: University Press of Kentucky, 1983), pp. 142–48; Masse, "Industrial Relations Re-examined"; Lee, *Eisenhower & Landrum-Griffin*, p. 93.

53. Gall, *The Politics of Right to Work*, pp. 97–120; "Report of Staff Committee on Restrictive Legislation," Aug. 14, 1958, Box 2, Schnitzler Papers; "Drive against 'Work' Proposals Moves into High Gear," Sept. 24, 1958, news release AFL-CIO News Service, Box 2, John Ramsey Papers, OHS.

54. For more extensive accounts of right-to-work in Ohio, see Glenn W. Miller and Stephen B. Ware, "Organized Labor in the Political Process: A Case Study of the Right-to-Work Campaign in Ohio," *Labor History* 4 (Winter 1963): 51–67; John H. Fenton, "The Right-to-Work Vote in Ohio," *Midwest Journal of Political Science* 3 (Aug. 1959): 241–53; Gall, *The Politics of Right to Work*, pp. 93–121; USA Executive Board Minutes, Aug. 12, 1958, USA; Minutes of the Meeting of Advisory Committee United Organized Labor of Ohio, June 20, 1958, Box 8, USA District 33 Records, USA/A; Right-to-Work excerpt from the speech of Charles P. Taft to the American Baptist Convention, Cincinnati, June 17, 1958, Box 313, Taft Papers.

55. Miller and Ware, "Organized Labor in the Political Process," pp. 56–59; Elmer Cope to John Johns, Aug. 18, 1958, Box 14, USA District 27 Records, USA/A; *Home Front* (UOLO newsletter), June 12, July 1, 1958, Box 8, USA District 33 Records, USA/A; *Fact Book on Proposed Ohio 'Right-to-Work' Amendment* (Columbus, Ohio: National Committee for Industrial Peace, 1958), p. 5, in Box 2, Ramsey Papers, OHS.

56. Fenton, "Right-to-Work Vote," pp. 250–53; Michael J. Lyden, "Ohio Labor Fights Back," *AFL-CIO American Federationist*, July 1958, pp. 6–7, 28; *Home Front*, June 11, 1958, Box 8, USA District 33 Records, USA/A; *Local 833 Reporter* (UAW), Apr. 4, May 2, 1958; Walt Davis to Members of the Advisory Committee, Oct. 2, 1958, John J. McGinty and Jesse Gallagher to Sir, Sept 19, 1958, all in Box 2, Ramsey Papers, OHS.

57. Minutes of the Meeting of Advisory Committee United Organized Labor of Ohio, June 20, 1958; *Home Front*, Aug. 11, 1958, Box 8, USA District 33 Records, USA/A; Hook quoted in Gall, *The Politics of Right to Work*, pp. 115, also 107–21.

58. Miller and Ware, "Organized Labor in the Political Process," pp. 65–

68; *Home Front,* Sept. 10, Oct. 14, 1958, Box 8, USA District 33 Records; "Mrs. Ohio Homemaker: Beware the Quirk in 'Right-to-Work,'" pamphlet, c. 1958, Box 458, AUF, LMDC.

59. The *New York Times* in analyzing the failure of right-to-work said "A labor-church independent coalition was generally credited in Ohio for the smashing defeat of the right-to-work amendment," Nov. 9, 1958. On the important role of religion, see also Fenton, "The Right-to-Work Vote in Ohio," pp. 241–53; "Churchmen Help Beat Right to Work Laws," *America,* Nov. 26, 1958, p. 1357.

60. For detailed legislative histories of labor reform see Alan K. McAdams, *Power and Politics in Labor Legislation* (New York: Columbia University Press, 1964) and Lee, *Eisenhower & Landrum-Griffin.*

61. McAdams, *Power and Politics in Labor Legislation,* pp. 1–16, 50; Lee, *Eisenhower & Landrum-Griffin,* pp. 72–73, 94–99.

62. McAdams, *Power and Politics in Labor Legislation,* pp. 66–68, 115–19, 193–201, 210–11; Lee, *Eisenhower & Landrum-Griffin,* pp. 118–19, 142–44; Sar A. Levitan and J. Joseph Loewenberg, "The Politics and Provisions of the Landrum-Griffin Act," in *Regulating Union Government,* ed. Estey, Taft, and Wagner, pp. 44–56; Sar A. Levitan, "Union Lobbyists' Contributions to Tough Labor Legislation," *Labor Law Journal* 10 (Oct. 1959): 675–82.

63. McAdams, *Power and Politics in Labor Legislation,* pp. 74, 80–81, 193–98, 211–15, 272–73; Lee, *Eisenhower & Landrum-Griffin,* chaps. 4–7; Robert Griffith, "Dwight D. Eisenhower and the Corporate Commonwealth," *American Historical Review* 87 (Feb. 1982): 108.

64. McAdams, *Power and Politics in Labor Legislation,* p. 212; Samuel G. Patterson, *Labor Lobbying and Labor Reform,* pp. 21–23.

65. McAdams, *Power and Politics in Labor Legislation,* pp. 158–59, 176–77; Patterson, *Labor Lobbying and Labor Reform,* pp. 23–24.

66. "The Debate Boils to a Climax," *BW,* Aug. 15, 1959, p. 120; *Get Crooks—Not Unions!* pamphlet, Box 54, AUF, LMDC; Levitan, "Union Lobbyists," p. 675; Patterson, *Labor Lobbying and Labor Reform,* pp. 18–22; Robert H. Zieger, *American Workers, American Unions: 1920–1985* (Baltimore: Johns Hopkins University Press, 1986), p. 187.

67. Mark Starr, "How Business Invades the Schools," *American Teacher Magazine,* Feb. 1960, p. 9; "COPE Planning Committee Report to James L. McDevitt, National Director," c. Nov. 30, 1960, Box 2, General Files, USA Legislative Office, USA/A.

68. Charles R. Sligh, Jr., "Public Affairs and the Association Executive" (Address before the National Industrial Council Industrial Relations Group, Dearborn, Michigan, Aug. 25, 1959), Acc. 1411, NAM I/48.

# Conclusion

In 1959, labor journalist Bert Cochran observed that "the business-man's intellectual reconquest of America" after World War II was "a more remarkable achievement than was his reassertion of long exercised power after World War I."[1] In 1945, business faced an aggressive labor movement that sought to reassert New Deal liberalism. Unions called for full employment, social planning, and the expansion of the welfare state, essentially a reorientation of American society orchestrated through the continued growth of labor and state power.

The business community had a different agenda. It sought not only to recast the political economy of postwar America but also to reshape the ideas, images, and attitudes through which Americans understood their world. Employers hoped to restore the public's allegiance to an individualistic ethos that had been shaken by the travails of the Depression. They asserted that economic decisions should be made in corporate board rooms not in legislative committee chambers. Prosperity, they argued, would be achieved best through reliance on individual initiative and the natural harmony of workers and managers that business saw as inherent in the free enterprise system. According to many industrialists, a socially responsible capitalism, relying on increases in productivity and economic growth rather than on the redistribution of income, would solve society's problems and bring the good life to all.

These ideas made up a part of the conservative ideology often associated with the 1950s. This work contends that this conservatism was politically constructed and was in large part the result of the business community's "intellectual reconquest" of America. It had its origins in a variety of campaigns conducted by American business (and consistently in opposition to labor) to shape the public's political, social, and economic ideas; and particularly, to again associate the American way with the ethic of competitive individualism. The business community had two primary goals. First, it hoped to destroy or discredit the ideological underpinnings of New Deal liberalism. Second, it wanted to undermine the legitimacy and power of organized labor. Unions posed a significant challenge not only in the shop but in the political realm as the backbone of the Democratic party coalition. Industrialists would accomplish these goals through campaigns to sell Americans on the virtues of individualism as opposed to collectivism, freedom as opposed to state control, and on the centrality of the free enterprise system to the American way of life.

The most obvious efforts to shape ideology and to create a more conservative political climate took place at the national level. National business organizations, like the Advertising Council and the National Association of Manufacturers, orchestrated multimillion dollar public relations campaigns that relied on newspapers, magazines, radio, and later television to sell business and capitalism. Yet, even as they conducted these national mass media campaigns, business leaders recognized the limitations of relying on this strategy alone. They believed that employers needed an even more direct connection with the public. The most logical place to begin was within the plant with their own workers serving as a captive audience. Even employers who recognized unions believed that organized labor fundamentally challenged their ability to shape worker attitudes and provide political leadership. Thus, moderate, as well as conservative, business leaders sought to increase worker productivity and undermine union power by creating a separate company identity or company consciousness among their employees. To win workers' allegiance, managers in a wide range of firms reshaped their personnel policies by blending the insights of human relations with the techniques of welfare capitalism. Economic education campaigns sought to build worker allegiance to the firm and to the American economic system while welfarism provided tangible evidence of employer concern for workers. Thus, expanding the community of interests beyond the immediate confines of the factory to encompass the worker's leisure and home life.

Fearing for lost authority beyond their factory gates, employers also instituted sophisticated community relations programs that both promoted the free enterprise system and built goodwill for individual firms. In January 1960, National Industrial Conference Board President John S. Sinclair concluded that as a result of these efforts business had probably "never enjoyed a more favorable climate of public opinion." In part, he admitted, this mellowing of public attitudes toward business was the result of continuing prosperity. Equally important in "the gradual recession of distrust" was industry's willingness to help alleviate social problems, particularly in the fields of health and education and its "efforts to assume the role of a good neighbor in the communities in which it operates."[2]

Organized labor also sought to shape worker consciousness, attempting to compete for worker loyalty and public sympathy both within the factory and in the community. During the Depression and World War II, unions had become an increasingly potent force not only in the plant and in national politics but also in local communities, establishing connections that grew in the postwar era with such important institutions as the Community Chests. Attempting to resist the business community's ideological onslaught, organized labor promoted the notion that worker success and security as well as America's future depended on the collective power of organized labor and on the continued ability of the state to regulate business. Unions sought to associate the American way with the cause of social justice and economic equality rather than individualism.

The labor movement could never match the resources available to the leaders of American business. As a result, the political and cultural landscape of the postwar era was increasingly dominated by the images and ideas produced by a mobilized business leadership. This indeed marked "the businessman's intellectual reconquest of America." How far this reconquest went, how deeply rooted it was, remains unclear. We know what business leaders wanted workers and other Americans to believe. Moreover, we know that the images and ideas of business were pervasive, filling much of America's cultural space with a series of selectively distorted symbols that made it difficult, if not impossible, for Americans to discover and articulate competing visions of the American polity. To this degree, at least, the "businessman's intellectual reconquest of America" succeeded.

Admittedly, we know much less about what the public actually believed, for even the most sophisticated polls do not begin to plumb the private reservoirs of dissent and disengagement that characterized American popular culture. Nevertheless, the polls do suggest a shift during the fifties from the more "collectivist values" of the thirties to the older value system of individualism. The sociologist Seymour Lipset suggests that this drift back to an individualistic ethos, which labeled unions as suspect because of their collective character, served as an important element in the gradual decline of organized labor.[3]

Beyond the capital-labor struggle, how does this work help us better understand the post–World War II period. This study suggests that the common characterization of the fifties as an age of consensus needs to be rethought. Many historians depict this consensus as emerging in an almost sweeping, determistic process from broad historical forces, including the "exhaustion of ideology" in the wake of two decades of depression and war, the impact of the cold war and McCarthyism, and the spread of consumerism and mass culture. All of this supposedly left a complacent, quiescent society with those on the left and right drifting toward the "broad political center."[4] This study argues that this apparent consensus was neither as simple nor as complete as these accounts suggest. The forces of conservatism were not drawn into this "broad political center" but maintained their opposition to the changes unleashed by the New Deal. Beneath an apparent calm surface, powerful conservative opposition to New Deal liberalism never really disappeared, for even in its attenuated state conservatives still found liberalism threatening. It was the continuing attraction of liberalism and organized labor that was behind the ideological assault described in this book. This assault contributed to the containment of liberalism, the spread of domestic anticommunism, and the checks on the growth of the welfare state in the 1950s.

How has business's reconquest of America fared since the fifties? Obviously, the business community has continued to recognize the powerful role of ideology in shaping America's political economy. It would turn to ideology again when it found its power threatened. During the late sixties and early seventies, the probusiness environment constructed during the fifties came under siege. Social movements, including civil rights, women's rights, environmentalism, and consumer and worker protection, arose—all of which threatened to place powerful constraints on business. Legislation growing out of these movements created new regulations that cut into profit margins and corporate control over the workplace at a time when business faced growing foreign competition.[5]

Beginning in the mid-seventies, threatened by shrinking profits and worried about the loss of public confidence, the business community remobilized in a fashion not seen since the fifties. Again business sought to shape public opinion by reaching out to employees and the public. Economic education programs aimed at workers, teachers, and students proliferated as did institutional advertising. W. R. Grace Company's television ads, for instance, emphasized the principles of freedom and small government, and Mobil Oil began an advocacy advertising program that continues to the present time.

In 1976, the Advertising Council launched the biggest economic education project in its history, the "American Economic System" campaign, which like the Council's campaign of the late forties, sought to address public "misunderstanding" of the private enterprise system. Underpinning this wider public campaign was an effort to "lay the scholarly and theoretical groundwork for a major shift in public policy favoring business" by funding the work of "highly respected" but independent conservative scholars and conservative think tanks, like the American Enterprise Institute, the Hoover Institution, and the Heritage Foundation.

Finally, the business community increased its political effectiveness with the formation of the Business Roundtable in 1973 and with the revitalization of the Chamber of Commerce. The Roundtable, composed of the chief executive officers of the nation's largest firms, became the "political arm of big business." At the same time, the Chamber of Commerce, which had emerged from the sixties a large but stagnant organization, became a vehicle for politically mobilizing small business. Key business leaders revived the Chamber, which began serving as a base for grass roots lobbying, bringing the force of large numbers to supplement the Roundtable's more elitist forms of lobbying. As was the case in the fifties, corporations began expanding on that base through the politicization of employees and stockholders. A new tactic of the seventies, made possible by changes in campaign finance laws, was the formation of business political action committees which collected large sums of money from employees and funneled the funds to probusiness politicians.[6]

All this effort helped create a major political shift that would culminate in the election of Ronald Reagan, the subsequent tax cuts benefiting the wealthy, the elimination of regulation, and the severe cutbacks in social services. The business community laid the ideological and institutional foundations for the nation's movement toward a more individualistic ethos. Because the shift in the 1980s was so striking and sweeping, it has often been portrayed as something entirely novel. But in fact, few elements in the creation of the Reagan revolution were new. Indeed, perhaps Ronald Reagan best symbolizes the continuity. Beginning in 1954, the future president of the United States spent eight years in the employment of General Electric, hosting a television program and speaking to employee and local civic group audiences as part of the company's public relations and economic education program. During that time, Reagan finetuned a message that he would repeat in the late seventies, warning of the threat that labor and the state posed to our "free economy."[7]

Thus, put in the context of business's efforts in the immediate post-war years, Reaganism appears as the fruition of a half-century's campaign for the "intellectual reconquest of America."

## Notes

1. Bert Cochran, ed., *American Labor in Midpassage* (New York: Monthly Review Press, 1959), p. 2.

2. John S. Sinclair, "The Role of Business in Public Affairs," *Management Record* 22 (Jan. 1960): 7–8.

3. Seymour M. Lipset, "North American Labor Movements: A Comparative Perspective," in *Unions in Transition: Entering the Second Century*, ed. Lipset (San Francisco, California: Institute for Contemporary Studies, 1986), pp. 421–52; David Brody, "Barriers of Individualism in the Path of American Unions," *Dissent* 36 (Winter 1989): 71–77.

4. J. Ronald Oakley, *God's Country: America in the Fifties* (New York: Dembner Books, 1986), p. 315.

5. Thomas Byrne Edsall, *The New Politics of Inequality* (New York: W. W. Norton, 1984), pp. 112–14, 128–30, Dan Clawson and Mary Ann Clawson, "Reagan or Business?: Foundations of the New Conservatism," in *The Structure of Power in America: The Corporate Elite as a Ruling Class*, ed. Michael Schwartz (New York: Holmes and Meier, 1987), pp. 202–4; Samuel Bowles, David Gordon, and Thomas Weisskopf, *Beyond the Waste Land: A Democratic Alternative to Economic Decline* (Garden City, N.Y.: Doubleday, 1983), chap. 3; Thomas Ferguson and Joel Rogers, *Right Turn: The Decline of the Democrats and the Future of American Politics* (New York: Hill and Wang, 1986), pp. 78–83.

6. Clawson and Clawson, "Reagan or Business?" pp. 205–25; Edsall, *The New Politics of Inequality*, pp. 107–40; Ferguson and Rogers, *Right Turn*, pp. 83–92; Paul H. Weaver, "Corporations Are Defending Themselves with the Wrong Weapon." *Fortune*, June 1977, pp. 186–96; "Industry's Schoolhouse Clout," *BW*, Oct. 13, 1980, pp. 159–60; Rogene A. Buchholz, *Business Environment and Public Policy: Implications for Management and Strategy Formulation* (Englewood Cliffs, N.J., 1989), 513–27; Sar A. Levitan and Martha R. Cooper, *Business Lobbies: The Public Good and the Bottom Line* (Baltimore: Johns Hopkins University Press, 1982).

7. Ronald W. Schatz, *The Electrical Workers: A History of Labor at General Electric and Westinghouse, 1923–60* (Urbana: University of Illinois Press, 1983), p. 11.

# Primary Sources Consulted

## Archives and Libraries

Baker Library, Harvard University, Boston, Mass.
    Thompson Products Company Records
Bentley Library, University of Michigan, Ann Arbor, Mich.
    Charles Sligh Papers
Department of Archives and Manuscripts, The Catholic University of
America, Washington, D.C.
    CIO Papers
    George G. Higgins Papers
George Meany Memorial Archives, Silver Spring, Md.
    George Meany Papers
    William Schnitzler Papers
Hagley Museum and Library, Wilmington, Del.
    American Iron and Steel Institute Records
    Chamber of Commerce of the United States Papers
    Jasper E. Crane Papers
    J. Howard Pew Papers
    National Association of Manufacturers Records
    Walter S. Carpenter Jr. Papers, Du Pont Records
Harry S. Truman Library, Independence, Mo.
    Lou E. Holland Papers
    Paul G. Hoffman Papers
    Charles W. Jackson Files, Harry S. Truman Papers
Historical Collections and Labor Archives, Pennsylvania State
University, University Park, Pa.
    Howard R. Hague Papers
    David J. McDonald Papers
    United Steelworkers of America Archives
        General Files of the Legislative Office
        USA District 30 Records
        Department of Education Records
        USA Executive Board Minutes

Public Relations Department Records
Labor-Management Documentation Center, Cornell University, Ithaca, N.Y.
  AIF Files
  AOF Files
  AUF Files
  Amalgamated Clothing Workers of America Records
    Bessie Hillman Papers
  Greater Buffalo Industrial Union Council Records
  Geneva, N.Y. Federation of Labor Minutebook
  Inter-University Labor Education Committee Records
  UAW Local 686 Records, Buffalo, N.Y.
  ILGWU Papers
Library of Congress, Washington, D.C.
  Eugene Meyer Papers
  G. Bromley Oxnam Papers
  Charles P. Taft Papers
Manuscripts and Archives, University of Massachusetts, Amherst, Mass.
  Solomon Barkin Papers
  William Belanger Papers
Neilson Library, Smith College, Northampton, Mass.
Ohio Historical Society, Columbus, Ohio
  John Ramsay Papers
  Youngstown Sheet and Tube Company Records
Presbyterian Historical Society, Philadelphia, Pa.
  National Council of Churches Records
Southern Labor Archives, Georgia State University, Atlanta
  AFL-CIO Papers, Region 8
  John Ramsay Papers
  United Textile Workers of America Papers
Urban Archives Center, Temple University, Philadelphia, Pa.
  Benjamin Barkas Papers
  Philadelphia United War Chest/United Fund Records
Walter P. Reuther Library for Labor and Urban Affairs, Wayne State
University, Detroit, Mich
  CIO Executive Board Minutes
  CIO Office of the Secretary-Treasurer Papers
  CIO Washington Office Records
  Michigan AFL-CIO Records
  Mildred Jeffrey Papers
  Mark Starr Papers
  UAW Education Department Records
    Victor Reuther Files
    Edward Coffey Files
  UAW Executive Board Minutes
  UAW Local 248 Papers
  UAW Recreation Department Records

Walter P. Reuther Papers
Wayne County AFL-CIO Papers
Wisconsin Historical Society, Madison, Wis.
American Federation of Hosiery Workers Papers
American Federation of Labor Papers
Bruce Barton Papers
National Broadcasting Corporation Papers
Textile Workers Union of America Records
William Grede Papers
United Packinghouse Workers of America Records

## Newspapers and Periodicals

*A-C Views*
*Advanced Management*
*AFL News Reporter*
*AFL-CIO American Federationists*
*America*
*American Business*
*American Federationist*
*American Magazine*
*American School Board Journal*
*American Teacher Magazine*
*Ammunition, UAW*
*Antioch Review*
*Business Education World*
*Business Week*
*California Teacher*
*Challenge*
*Christianity and Crisis*
*Christian Century*
*Christian Science Monitor*
*CIO News*
*Connecticut CIO Vanguard*
*Detroit Teacher*
*Economic Justice*
*Economic Outlook*
*Education*
*Education Digest*
*Exchange*, NAM
*Explaining Your Business*
*Factory Management and Maintenance*
*Forbes*
*Ford Facts*, UAW Local 600
*Fortune*

*Guild Reporter*
*Harvard Business Review*
*Industrial and Labor Relations Review*
*Industrial Sports Journal*
*Iron Age*
*Ithaca Union Labor Review*
*John Herling's Labor Letter*
*Journal of General Education*
*Journal of Higher Education*
*Journal of Politics*
*Latrobe Bulletin*
*Labor*
*Labor and Nation*
*Labor's Daily*
*Machinists Monthly Journal*
*Management Record*
*Management Review*
*Michigan CIO News*
*Mill and Factory*
*Modern Industry*
*Monthly Labor Review*
*NAM News*
*Nation*
*Nation's Business*
*Nation's Schools*
*NEA Journal*
*New Republic*
*New York Herald Tribune*
*New York Times*
*Newsweek*
*Organizer*, UAW Local 248
*Packinghouse Worker*
*Personnel Journal*
*Pennsylvania Labor News*
*Public Opinion Index for Industry*
*Public Opinion Quarterly*
*Public Relations Journal*
*Public Relations News*
*Quincy Record*
*Quotes Ending*
*Reading Labor Advocate*
*Recreation*
*Saturday Evening Post*
*Saturday Review*
*School and Society*
*School Executive*

*719 News,* UAW Local 719
*Social Studies*
*Steel Labor*
*Steelworkers Sentinel,* USA Local 1533
*Stet: The House Magazine for House Magazine Editors*
*Textile Labor*
*Time*
*Trends in Education-Industry Cooperation*
*UE News*
*UE Shop News,* UE Local 450
*Unionaire,* UAW Local 842
*United Automobile Worker*
*UAW-CIO Assembler,* UAW Local 595
*U.S. News & World Report*
*Wall Street Journal*
*Wisconsin CIO News*

# Index

56–67, 137–52, 179–80; public opinion of, 16, 269; during thirties, 18–
19; during World War II, 19, 139–40;
defends OPA, 34–35; opposition to
business public relations, 44–46, 259–
60; weakness of public relations, 46–
48, 269–70; radio and television programs, 46–49, 118–19, 149–50; and
Taft-Hartley, 47–48; anticommunism,
53–54, 56; corruption and racketeering, 56, 266–69; attacks on company
consciousness, 108–13; efforts to
build union consciousness, 113–25;
and families, 122–23; and retirees,
123–24; suspicion of business community relations, 178–80; and
schools, 209–10; and religion, 218,
225–30, 233–35, 238, 241, 269–70;
and right-to-work, 263, 265–66, 271–
74; and labor reform, 275–78
Labor press, 117–18
Labor's League for Political Education, 48
Lally, Francis J., 264
Landrum, Phil, 277
Landrum-Griffin Act, 268, 271, 275–78
Lever Brothers, 91
Lewis, Fulton, Jr., 45, 47
Lionel Company, 96
Locke Incorporated, 175
Lockheed Corporation, 82
Lone Star Steel Company, 224
Lynd, Robert S., 16, 32, 42, 178

McCaffrey, John L., 8, 158, 170
McClellan, John L., 277
McClellan Committee, 267, 268, 269,
275
McCormick, Fowler, 74, 158
McDonald, David J., 144, 226, 269
McIntire, Carl, 231
Management: attitude toward organized
labor, 4, 22–24; attitudes toward
workers, 67, 69–72; control of shop
floor, 68–69; and human relations,
73–86; supervisory training, 75–76;
economic education, 83–86; welfare
capitalism, 86–96
—prerogatives: challenged by labor, 2–3,
15, 18, 19–20, 70, 257; defense of, 41,
54, 68

Managerial offensive, 3, 4, 41–43, 68
Maslow, Abraham H., 73–74
Mason, Lucy, 227, 228
Mayo, Elton, 73–74
Mazey, Emil 48, 116, 123
Meany, George, 258
Michigan CIO Council, 148, 149
Mills, C. Wright, 152
Mine, Mill and Manufacturing Corpora-
tion (3M), 77, 91, 93, 94
Mosher, Ira, 21, 46
Mueldet, Walter G., 263
Murray, Philip, 21, 227

NAM. *See* National Association of Manufacturers
Nash-Kelvinator Corporation, 27–28
National Association of Evangelicals, 231
National Association of Manufacturers
(NAM): and postwar mobilization of
business community, 5, 7; ideology,
7, 22; opposition to New Deal, 22,
25–27; opposition to Wagner Act, 23–
25; Soldiers of Production, 27; promotes productivity, 27–28, 264; and
women, 34, 260; radio programs, 41,
46, 52; films, 41, 202, 204; campaign
to amend Wagner Act, 42–43; moves
toward realism in industrial relations,
42–43; and Taft-Hartley, 43–44; liberals and labor attack, 44; Industry on
Parade, 52, 270; promotes human relations, 76–79; employee economic
education, 83–84; promotes welfare
capitalism, 90; and right-to-work,
261, 262, 264; and labor reform, 275–
78; mentioned, 6, 8, 9, 28, 51, 70, 71,
119, 148, 152
—community relations: Committee on
Cooperation with Community Leaders, 162, 165; industry leaders program, 162–63; town meetings, 164–65;
Roanoke Plan, 166–67; mentioned,
160
—public relations: postwar free enterprise campaign, 6, 39–41, 52; thirties
campaign, 25; World War II campaign, 27–28; price controls, 33–35,
39; against Full Employment Bill, 33,
39; financial support of, 39; late fift-